ON THE FREEDOM SIDE

ON THE FREEDOM SIDE

HOW FIVE DECADES OF YOUTH ACTIVISTS HAVE REMIXED AMERICAN HISTORY

Wesley C. Hogan

The University of North Carolina Press | Chapel Hill

© 2019 Wesley C. Hogan
All rights reserved

Designed by April Leidig
Set in Warnock Pro by Copperline Book Services, Inc.
Manufactured in the United States of America

The University of North Carolina Press has been a member
of the Green Press Initiative since 2003.

Cover illustration by Nathan W. Moehlmann, Goosepen Studio & Press.

Library of Congress Cataloging-in-Publication Data
Names: Hogan, Wesley C., author.
Title: On the freedom side : how five decades of youth activists
have remixed American history / Wesley C. Hogan.
Description: Chapel Hill : University of North Carolina Press, [2019] |
Includes bibliographical references and index.
Identifiers: LCCN 2019032093 | ISBN 9781469652474 (cloth) |
ISBN 9781469652481 (paperback , alk. paper) | ISBN 9781469652498 (ebook)
Subjects: LCSH: Youth—Political activity—United States. | Youth movements—
United States. | Civil rights movements—United States. | United States—Politics
and government—20th century. | United States—Politics and government—
21st century. | BISAC: HISTORY / African American
Classification: LCC HQ799.2.P6 H645 2019 | DDC 320.0835/0973—dc23
LC record available at https://lccn.loc.gov/2019032093

Lyrics to "Room in the Circle" by Bernice Johnson Reagon from the
1968 album *Give Your Hands to Struggle*. Used with permission.

*To Princess, Anki, Nikki, Reese, Afua, John,
Chantel, Jess, Kacey, Jeffrey, and David,
who taught me what was missing*

---

*To Briana and Danita,
who taught me how to put it back*

CONTENTS

INTRODUCTION

The Spark of Youth

1

ONE

Youth and Women Lead:
Ella Baker and SNCC

17

TWO

Southerners on New Ground:
Organizing at the Intersections

35

THREE

Recruiting the Justice League:
The Ella Baker Center Demystifies
Youth Organizing

65

FOUR

Make Room in the Circle:
Undocumented Youth Bridge Electoral
and Movement Politics

89

FIVE

The Intolerable Price of Self-Respect:
The Movement for Black Lives Organizes
Urban and Suburban America

121

SIX

Mní Wičoni—Water Is Alive:
Indigenous Youth Water Protectors Rekindle
Nonviolent Direct Action in Corporate America

157

CONCLUSION

Citizens of a World Not Yet Built

197

WHO'S THE EXPERT?

An Essay on Evidence and Authority

213

Acknowledgments 225

Notes 229

Bibliography 291

Index 337

FIGURES

1. SONG recruitment flyer, "The Economy and Lesbigaytrans Liberation," April 30, 1998 54

2. Call to SONG LBTQ retreat, 2001 60

3. Ella Baker Center, Facebook post, July 23, 2014 70

4. Ella Baker Center, Facebook post, June 30, 2015 78

5 & 6. Ella Baker Center, Facebook posts, October 2015 79

7. Infographic from the Ella Baker Center, 2016 87

8. Boy separated from parents at US-Mexico border, June 12, 2018 99

9. Freedom University tweet, February 2, 2016 119

10. Ferguson, Missouri, 2014 137

11. DeRay Mckesson tweet, December 14, 2014 138

12. Joe Walsh tweet, July 8, 2016 151

13. Movement for Black Lives platform, published August 1, 2016 152

14. Map showing the route of the Dakota Access pipeline 164

15 & 16. "Yes that's the blood of peaceful protestors on this dog's mouth" 168

17. Cannupa Hanska Luger's mirrored shields at Standing Rock 177

18 & 19. Posters by Joey Montoya and Tomahawk Grey Eyes 179

20. Morning prayers at Standing Rock 186

21. Excerpt from TigerSwan's "DAPL SitRep,"
February 27, 2017 190

22. White motorist threatens to run over civil rights
activists in Chapel Hill, NC, 1964 192

23. Car runs down protesters in Charlottesville, VA,
August 2017, killing Heather Heyer 192

24. Environmentalist Bill McKibben promotes work
of IIYC media coordinator Eryn Wise 195

25. Dream Defenders, Instagram post, June 22, 2018 199

26. "Organize!" poster 206

ON THE FREEDOM SIDE

INTRODUCTION

The Spark of Youth

Three basic truths inform this book: the future of democracy belongs to young people; today's generation of leaders in business and politics are in the process of leaving behind a mess of existential challenges; and more than anyone else, it is young people who are trying to find answers to the challenges of belonging, collaboration, and survival.[1]

The minute one leaves the chambers in which adult leaders conduct business (Congress, courtrooms, state assemblies, boardrooms, media centers, think tanks) and looks for regular people organizing at the base (in churches, classrooms, offices, dining rooms, fields), one finds young people at work. Some help out with efforts generated by elders, some try to modify and refine, some come up with their own organizing attempts. Some show up only once or twice; others make every attempt to see things through. In the aggregate, however, they show up by the thousands—day in and day out.

Yet young people, by and large, are not seen, their contributions overlooked as much as their insights ignored. The idea for this book emerged from the pain of not being seen and the tragedy of what results from not seeing. One could say it started with a kind of loneliness.

In 2007, three hundred students at Virginia State University (VSU) marched on campus in support of the Jena Six, the then-notorious case of Black high schoolers facing attempted second-degree murder charges in Louisiana for a schoolyard fight.[2] "Hardly anyone joined us," one of the VSU marchers told me afterward. "We were three hundred people on a campus of five thousand. We're just college students on an historically Black college campus. No one thinks we can do anything." Given the decisive role of students in American politics over the last century, this student's sense of isolation and despair spoke to a tragedy deep inside American culture.

Black students at historically Black colleges and universities started the Southern Negro Youth Congress in the 1930s, I thought. And during the sit-ins in the 1960s, they integrated southern lunch counters in damn near a semester. When a thousand Chicano high school students walked out of Abraham Lincoln High School in Los Angeles in 1968, those students forced the creation of Chicano studies programs and raised the intellectual content of social studies standards for teachers across the country. This reality sat on my shoulders like two buckets of bricks. *You've taught her this history—why does she have such an overwhelming sense of* not *counting?*

"The administrators didn't care," the VSU student continued. "Only three faculty showed up. No news media came. Just us, marching up and down College Avenue with our signs and chants. I know you think young people can make a difference, Professor Hogan. Or even that we are essential to any democracy—" She looked straight at me, kindness and sorrow in her eyes, and dropped her voice to a lower register. "But that might have just been back in the sixties. No one listens to young people now."

As I drove home, the student's words streamed through my mind. I marshaled counterpoint after counterpoint, thinking of young people who changed the course of US history. Abolitionist Sarah Parker Remond, who took to the stump against slavery at sixteen, eventually becoming a force in the international abolitionist movement. Twenty-one-year-old self-described "working girl" Clara Lemlich, who spoke against the intolerable conditions at the Triangle Shirtwaist Company in 1909. Carmelita Torres, the seventeen-year-old who refused the humiliating delousing procedure that US border agents demanded of day laborers and domestics living in Juárez but working in El Paso, shuttering this racist policy in 1917. The Black students who spearheaded the "New Negro" politics of the 1920s. The college students who risked expulsion during the anti-communist paranoia of the 1950s to throttle campus censorship in the Green Feather Movement. Sixteen-year-old Barbara Johns, who led high school walkouts in support of equal education in Virginia in the 1950s. College student Diane Nash, who stood toe to toe with the white mayor of Nashville in 1960 and compelled him to admit that he, too, believed it was wrong to allow Black people to shop at downtown department stores but bar them from eating at their lunch counters due to their skin color. Young people like Frances Fairbanks and Pat Bellanger, who built the American Indian Movement in the 1970s to ask how the US would account for the centuries of stolen lands and broken treaties. The Tinker siblings, who wore black armbands on their thin arms in protest against the Vietnam War and launched a lawsuit that required high schools across the nation to widen students' freedom of speech. Ten-year-old Kimberly, daughter of environmental justice pioneer Dollie Burwell, who insisted on accompanying her mother to march and be jailed in the fight against toxic waste in North Carolina in the 1980s. The students throughout the Midwest and South who formed gay-straight alliances in the 1990s and sculpted a remarkable shift in adult attitudes.[3]

I wondered: How much of this rich and ongoing history was part of the curriculum? Did young people ever learn about the many struggles of their own, aside from the occasional mention of the famous Greensboro sit-ins that started the 1960s civil rights movement?

With four younger kids in the Richmond, Virginia, public schools, I had plenty of textbooks in the house, from elementary to high school. That night, I began to comb through them. After weeks of searching, aside from the Greensboro Four, I couldn't find a single person under twenty-five. Not one.

Over multiple dinners during the months that followed, I continued to speculate on this with my husband down our noisy family table: "If young people at VSU can't see themselves having an impact historically, why would they feel a sense of power now? They did exactly what I'd hoped they would do—use their voice in a public square to shape the political agenda. How do I show them their voices can count?"

They could see little evidence in the images from cable TV in the years before America elected Obama: news photographs of torture at the Abu Ghraib POW camp. Black citizens in New Orleans shot by police for trying to flee Hurricane Katrina across a bridge into Metairie, a middle-class suburb that had backed former Ku Klux Klan Grand Wizard David Duke for governor of Louisiana in 1991. Film footage of other African Americans waving desperately from rooftops or suffering in the swelter of the Superdome in the aftermath of Katrina, often without water. President Bush sending 20,000 more soldiers to Iraq in a "surge," with the galling mendacity of his "Mission Accomplished" flight suit still fresh in our minds. Craven Democrats hunched down as cabinet members lied to the nation about Iraq's weapons of mass destruction, soon proved not to exist. Except for the much-heralded emergency personnel of 9/11, these Jena Six–era students did not come of age in a chapter from *Profiles in Courage*.

Later I remembered those dinner conversations in the early 2000s as an attempt to resist cynicism by sharing examples with my husband of young people changing the course of history, even as we smiled and busted our twelve-year-old for trying to text under the table and nudged our eight- and ten-year-olds to sit still. At one point my husband looked out at our hyperactive and inattentive offspring and muttered something about "youth energy" and "harnessing it for good." He gave a wry smile and turned his focus on his wife the historian: "Use the tools you have. Start documenting them. Write about them. Give others a sense—"

"Duh. Write a book about them, Mom," the eight-year-old interrupted, anticipating the windup toward a long old-folks speech. "That's what makes people know it's important."

I have a writer friend who says that if you have a deep, dark secret, one that would ruin you if people found out, publish it in a nonfiction book. But I think my eight-year-old is closer to the truth. And the truth of youth is my subject here. I've used the tools of the historian and the documentarian and then borrowed the format of a 1980s mixtape to present short tales from young movement innovators since 1960. I've especially zeroed in on aspects of freedom movements not commonly understood. How does a group of young people move from slogans like "Jim Crow must go" or "Water is life!" to strategies and tactics that actually get the job done? Which groups have illuminated the process of organizing everyday people to take political power? What are the best means of recruiting others? How do the best organizers work out internal conflict? How do they share their hard-won knowledge with newcomers to the movement? In what ways do grassroots activists, once they are older, pass on their insights so that coming generations don't have to reinvent the wheel? How do those younger generations build on earlier movements—sampling like a master DJ—and reinterpret those traditions to allow them to speak to new days yet unseen?

Early on, I observed a clear, perhaps predictable pattern in how the wider culture failed to notice important transformations happening right in its midst. Since 1960, the Davids gathering stones to take down Goliath are most often women of color. Those in the younger generations quickly come to see themselves struggling at the intersections of multiple identities and many-sided oppressions. To some degree, women and nonbinary organizers come to movement politics motivated by a "Rosa Parks" frame: that is, they enter movements the way Parks did, in order to defend or protect women and LGBTQ people from sexual or gender-based attacks, often literal assaults. This fundamental fault line of gendered and sexualized violence has recruited thousands of people into movements, as historian Danielle McGuire reveals in *At the Dark End of the Street*.[4] To some degree it has also driven people out when freedom movements could not figure out how to address sexual assault within the movement.

Not surprisingly, women of color play a prominent role in youth movements, for they are, in the words of Melissa Harris-Perry, the human version of canaries in the coal mine, providing "a democratic litmus test for the nation." How open and inclusive is our democracy? Who is seen, and who is brushed to the side? As southern activist Joan Garner responded in 2013 to a question about her primary "identity," "What do you mean am I first an African American or first a lesbian? I am an African American woman, lesbian—that's the total of me. I can't separate myself." She insisted that "we can no longer continue to separate ourselves"—all the issues connect.[5]

Quite likely, no one can see the limitations of, and no one can more fully raise the promise of, the country's vision of "liberty and justice for all" than young women of color. And yet, as the people in these pages show, movements for freedom are also, and importantly, intergenerational. Neither wisdom nor energy is the sole domain of particular age groups. Both young and old can be found among groups that have set out to live on the freedom side, as citizens of a world not yet built. This good news could be seen in the unlikely form of a math class in a high school gym in Petersburg, Virginia, in the early twenty-first century.

The gym was hot. At one end, the eighth graders lined up fifteen second and third graders and yelled out, "OK, five times four equals what?" Some sprinted off immediately, others thought for a second, eyes concentrated on their moving fingers. And then all flew down the wooden floor, running to the other end of the huge space. There, printed on brightly colored banners hung from ceiling to floor, were several big numbers: 8, 16, 20, 24. Marleen, an eighth-grade math literacy worker in the after-school program, hustled over to third-grader Jade and whispered, "You got the last three races right!" And when Jade's face lit up, she added, "You on your way to being a math star."

Even in the heat of the late southern summer, and though many children disliked math, the program got young people moving and kept them engaged. The idea was simple, the insight profound: fall behind in math, and you're likely to drop out. The college students said, "Let's create playful, creative ways to teach math, since math achievement is the best predictor of successful high school graduation and college attendance."

Failure to finish high school and enter college was endemic to the less affluent neighborhoods in Petersburg. Its public schools had the distinction of being among the worst-performing in the nation. A decade ago, only 11 percent of ninth graders were passing Algebra I. In practical terms, this meant that 89 percent of Petersburg's youth would be ineligible for college, locked out of the twenty-first-century information economy. This eighth-grade math literacy worker, Marleen, came to turn that equation around. She and her colleagues had been trained by high school students, who had in turn been taught by college students from Virginia State, just a few miles down the road.

This "each one teach one" system at first struck many people as improbable, if not downright dangerous. What parents would want a child only a few years older tutoring their children if they could learn from a certified, experienced teacher? Yet again and again, near-peer mentoring proved not just adequate but excellent at improving math skills and came with a host of other benefits. At each grade level, the younger kids saw examples of older kids who were both cool and good at math. One college student summed up the powerful secret: it sent a bolt of fresh confidence to see someone close to your age doing something formerly considered too challenging, someone whose life looked somewhat like your own. Their chant was, "If I can see it, I can be it!" And at each grade level, the older kids' math skills grew along with their leadership and teaching capacities. The program was called the Young People's Project. It was an outgrowth of the intergenerational Algebra Project, founded by 1960s civil rights activists Bob Moses and Dave Dennis, and run by young people.[6]

In Petersburg, like many other underperforming school districts, the Young People's Project took on a seemingly impossible challenge—create real opportunities for kids in environments that appeared to offer few. Over the years, many teachers, parents, and community advocates had become resigned to seemingly insurmountable challenges. Progress, it seemed, was simply not possible, the obstacles too numerous.

And then the Algebra Project moved in. In an effort that baffled even the most dedicated reform advocates and newly minted PhD "turn-around specialists," the percentage of all ninth graders passing Algebra I in Petersburg public schools rose, in just a few years, from 11 to 76 percent—*76 percent* who would now have access to the information economy and a door to a family-supporting income. Young people like Marleen had made the difference.

What is the connection between passing math and promoting democracy? Progress isn't inevitable. Not progress like that made in the Petersburg schools. And on a larger scale, Americans aren't guaranteed momentum toward an ever-more perfect union of "liberty and justice for all." Elected representatives of the people, for example, may plump up or starve school budgets. Even in low-income districts, elected representatives who serve themselves or their wealthy benefactors may well close the door on young people like Marleen. Hope seems to many an unaffordable luxury, and so they settle for arrangements that never begin to represent their deepest moral values.

This is hardly ill considered. A close look at human history indicates a sobering conclusion: people with power, people at the top of any society, never give it up without some form of struggle. Thus, progress toward democratization most frequently comes from the bottom up.

These bottom-up history makers make few appearances in history books. As mentioned, they almost never show up if they're young. As a young professor myself, I witnessed the math scene in the gym unfold in Petersburg in the early 2000s, exhilarated by the sense of possibility. Yet I searched in vain in textbooks, Hollywood films, popular novels, comics, cartoons, and television shows for stories of young people shaping history. Where were the Marleens of the 1870s? The 1930s? The 1960s? Despite their often-crucial contributions, young people as historical political actors are largely absent from the culture. A history of silence and omission helped no one but the already powerful, who often compounded the titanic pressures to forget. And as L. C. Dorsey, a civil rights activist from Mississippi, points out, "You can't do what you can't imagine."[7]

Joining the work of the young math literacy workers as an adult ally, I began to advocate for the program. "This won't work. It cannot be done," we heard. Principals, government officials, university leaders—all told us that we couldn't turn around the math achievement numbers in the Petersburg schools when we began working in 2004. By 2009 we had proved them wrong. Yet their reaction is not unique. This is the routine response of the voices of supposed maturity or reason when confronted with what are widely considered unreasonable hopes and dreams.

The voices of resignation reign as much in our heads as in our communities: they come through experts in business suits or via school principals and in the op-ed pages of major newspapers worldwide. They are anchored in corporate boardrooms, social media company C-suites, and Hollywood writers' rooms. Saturated by stories of crime, war, and celebrity, we paddle in the shallows of political discourse. We understand prior movements as a series of sound bites ("I have a dream!") and flashpoints represented by photographs of dogs biting children and horses on Selma's Edmund Pettis Bridge stomping dignified elders marching for "one person, one vote."

These sound bites and iconic images are false leads that mystify how to bring about justice in our own time. Caught up in the presumed realities of day-to-day life, we grow cynical, wary of others, doubtful of possibilities, resigned to angle for piecemeal progress and narrow political gain.

In every generation, young people learn about the aspirations embodied in the Declaration of Independence and the preamble to the Constitution and generate fresh ideas for how to live. The "hard realities" school of thought routinely suppresses these innovations in homes, classrooms, and workplaces. When a child comes home for dinner and asks across the table, "Can we vote on whether we can have hamburgers tomorrow night?," a parent might be too tired to engage questions about "why not?" In classrooms where teachers share the story of the founders creating a new Constitution, they rarely have time or training to respond when students ask, "If this is a democracy, can we write our own constitution for this semester on how we get graded?" And when young people are called to the boss's office for trying a new approach with customers, their innovations are not generally welcomed. Instead, the supervisor often responds with some version of "Shut up and do as you're told." And this is true despite the fact that the country is grounded in a radical idea: the foundation of all US law, the Constitution, roots its authority not in a king or in a god or in the military. All authority squarely rests in "we the people," the whole people, the common people.

The nation's founders wove this radical democratic impulse into the contradictions that many have pointed to since: the US Constitution at conception considered African Americans, Indigenous people, and white women outside the "we." There can be no doubt that some of the colonists who launched a revolution against Great Britain assumed that their revolution meant that it would be, as James Madison himself said at the Federal Convention, wrong "to admit in the Constitution the idea that there could be property in men."[8] But Madison, himself a slaveholder, remained entangled. The founders were settler colonists, the majority of them slaveholders, nearly all anti-Black to varying degrees. They created the wealth of their new republic, the foundation for America's future as a world power, on land stolen from Indigenous people and a system of racially hereditary enslavement of Africans taken in the enormous death machine of the Atlantic slave trade.

This contradictory truth at the country's point of origin produces multiple responses. Some say, "We are always going to fight for the vision that includes everyone in 'we the people.'" Others try this but retreat to cynicism or despair when only meager scraps result. And yet a third general tendency is to take one look at the long span of US history and say, "This was a setup from the beginning. No established leaders are interested in real democracy."[9] The range encompassed by these responses may help explain why, during twenty-five decades of practice since the creation of the United States, very few of Americans' enormous intellectual and cultural resources have focused on how to grow ordinary people into full citizenship. If we want young people to be able to use US history as a guide, we must do better in analyzing the past. This very much includes evaluating the key differences between (1) all those times when people have a lot of grievances, and perhaps even ideas about a better future, but very little happens (what we would consider "normal" times); and (2) those rare moments in history when people figure out how to act, and perhaps even start to act "as if" they were free to act, and in the process rearrange people's heads and lift cultures onto a different track. In short, most teachers and leaders at the local, state, and national levels don't prioritize how to act as a full citizen in a democracy, though the notion of democracy hovers like an ethereal mist over all of our public events and political speeches.

So where do young people find models? Ella Baker is one important guide to understanding how people move from simply inhabiting a place to living as an activated citizen. She was largely unheralded in her own time by formal leaders, yet she was among the foremost US experts in getting everyday people to the decision-making table in twentieth-century America. Baker particularly excelled in activating young people.

Born in 1903 in Norfolk, Virginia, she spent six decades as a tireless organizer for democracy. Baker's childhood among Reconstruction activists and a rich and varied lifetime of political experiences taught her that people in power were often overrated and that they nearly always failed to comprehend the centrality of grassroots leadership, or what she sometimes called "activity at the base." Even more importantly, time and again Baker experienced how those in power ignored the wisdom of the pinched toe and the empty belly. Too often, people at the top of schools, businesses, or governments rooted their decision-making on tradition, on wealth, on status, or on the presumed superiority of men over women, elders over youth, or white people over people of color.[10]

Baker confronted all of this hierarchical tradition with one basic idea, perhaps best expressed as "freedom politics."[11] This included encouraging people to learn by doing, to build networks of mutual help, to become active shapers of their own lives. What Ella Baker practiced for decades in multiple civil rights organizations could be described as the art of freedom politics—providing encouragement, facilitation, support, yet never telling anyone what to do.

Acting democratically is always messy and almost never efficient. It takes time and patience for people to work through discussions and conflicts. It takes time to figure out what they believe and how they want to act on those beliefs. Not unlike those legendary guides such as basketball coach Phil Jackson or bandleader Miles Davis, Baker worked to create the conditions for people to find their own voices rather than tell them what to express. Her underlying conviction was both simple and far-reaching: once people speak for themselves, they will be able to craft their own goals—the rest can be improvised within a commonly understood framework.[12]

Young people came first for Baker; as she said often, "They have the courage where we fail." From her earliest political experiences, including her work with the Young Negroes Cooperative League in the 1930s, she focused her impressive energies on supporting youth visions. As her colleague George Schuyler said when explaining why they kept membership in the league to people under age thirty-five, "We consider most of the oldsters hopelessly bourgeois and intent on emulating Rockefeller and Ford on a shoestring budget."[13]

While Baker herself defied this categorization, her work with young people reflected a larger historical truth: since the 1960s, students have taken the lead in pushing democratic reforms across the US and the world, particularly in China, Brazil, South Africa, and Iran. The groups in this book share a common trait: they have managed to climb onto the stage of history within what scholar Charles Payne termed "an organizing tradition" developed in North America and passed down through master teachers such as Ella Baker. And though the historical lineage was and is not always deliberate, or even conscious, it is unmistakable: they are Ella Baker's children.

Part of the invisibility of youth as effective political actors comes from what decision-makers choose to show on the nation's most powerful media platforms. On television, Americans see people at the top of society engaging in DC Beltway politics—pundits who rarely discuss the price of milk or gasoline or college. Major media organizations also don't show the young people I highlight in the pages that follow, unless the young are caught up in spectacles of violence or disruption. As newspaper editors still note, "If it bleeds, it leads." One might expand that cliché of youth to include apathetic millennials, or window-smashing, rampaging looters faced with clouds of tear gas, or kids holding up cell phones to film celebrities. In these flash-frozen images, young people often appear as immobile, shallow, or volatile agents of disorder. Black Lives Matter, for example, is visible but not seen as the serious political force it is, and is often wildly misinterpreted as violent or anti-white, among other misconceptions. When not invisible, therefore, youth are distorted so much they might as well be. What is almost entirely missing, in the media as much as in textbooks or academic scholarship,[14] is what one can find across time and place: young people as politically thoughtful and engaged decision-makers.

Strangely, it's not as if young people are missing from the collective radar screen. We see them in music, dance, technology, film, sports, and occasionally literature. Yet when it comes to youth activism and political innovation, adults from right to left turn blind. The reasons for this, no doubt, are numerous. But they all help to highlight a tragic irony: the most pressing challenges of today, from climate change to escalating inequality and war, are the result of mature, adult decision-making. Most innovations, from expanding human rights to protecting our environment or opposing war, have originated with young people. Whom should we rely on?

Getting out from under the enormous condescension of the received culture toward young people is a vital step—so we can see clearly the role that youth play in the nation's wider political life. "Freedom and justice do not come to us in hermetically sealed bags from Target and Costco," the civil rights scholar Charles McKinney riffed recently. "It is a freedom *struggle*."[15] Neither mainstream political pundits nor most media outlets have sufficient experience with what that struggle looks like—and certainly not what it looks like among young people working to update and reinvent tradition. Removing this set of blinders becomes an essential precondition for understanding the history and reality of US political cultures.

The book's first chapter examines youth in the 1960s involved in the Student Nonviolent Coordinating Committee (SNCC—pronounced "Snick"). A second chapter zeroes in on a 1990s grassroots organization of the NAFTA era, Southerners on New Ground (SONG). In chapter 3, we examine the pathbreaking work at the Ella Baker Center in Oakland, California, to train youth organizers to disrupt the school-to-prison pipeline and offer youth a brighter future. Chapter 4 focuses on those who initially called themselves "DREAMers," young people warning against twenty-first-century destruction of the American dream. Here, Latinx youth joined with African, Middle Eastern, and Asian immigrant youth to create fresh templates for citizenship. After Trayvon Martin's murder in 2012 and George Zimmerman's acquittal in 2013, the nation witnessed the early moments of the Movement for Black Lives, the subject of chapter 5. I finished a full book draft in the summer of 2016, just as the work of the International Indigenous Youth Council (IIYC) drew thousands to Standing Rock, North Dakota. Here, Indigenous youth led the fight to protect clean water for 10 million people against a multinational corporation seeking billions in oil profits. I hesitated, unsure how to navigate between the sharp and ancient shoals of either not writing a chapter on them (another colonist erasing Indigenous innovation) or risking writing about them in a way that deepened the rut of cultural appropriation. Yet given the titanic achievements the IIYC's nonviolent direct action embodied, this book could not go forward without a chapter on its work, the final chapter.

Like the mixtapes of the 1980s and 1990s, these essays stitch together connections between the ephemeral and the historical, between pop culture and world politics. My own mixtapes did not begin to capture that era but instead bounced between Prince and the Fugees, Whitney Houston's "I Wanna Dance with Somebody" and Nirvana's "Smells Like Teen Spirit." So, too, with these chapters. Their beats are strong, but they remain selective attempts to pull from contemporary evidence impressions of some of the crucial youthful innovations in American democracy since 1960.[16] Here we find more questions to investigate than easy answers for the future. These chapters are evocative and descriptive but also speculative and impressionistic. It is far too early for definitive histories, which are beyond my intent here in any case.

If my ambitions are modest, they are also vital. It is not only accurate but essential to spotlight bold youth as *instigators* in the nation's freedom struggle. Democracy is always aspirational. The promised land remains distant. This work lays out at ground level how movement participants have found the tools of freedom within themselves, which they then test out and improve and which on occasion have come to shape civil society and affect the lives of millions. This work explores specific ways that grassroots organizing traditions get passed on. Young people may find in these pages a past that provides both expected and unforeseen paths for reinventing, reclaiming, and remixing strategies to build on in their time— the mixtapes of their own generation. These stories resist a single line of influence and instead reach back to alternative genealogies whose historical dynamism often evades journalists and scholars. These chapters document some, but hardly all, of youth movements' most innovative riffs.

Young people have ignited original approaches, picking up the age-old rhythms of Latin, Appalachian, Indigenous, and African American cultures and political traditions and splicing them together anew, evidence yet again of the powerful strands of what one can call our remix culture.[17] Remix can be seen as a sign of stagnation and repetition of our collective imagination or as the source of vitality and regeneration—think jazz, hip-hop, film, or modern dance. The central point is to untangle these historic and contemporary movements. What makes them tick? How do they build on narratives and strategies we know from the 1960s and earlier and revise them to create new forms of political power emerging today?

Like any polyrhythm, recent movements draw on civil rights/Black Power exemplars for inspiration but also on 1970s Latin American popular education, Black feminist toolkits from the 1970s through the 1990s, the labor movement's innovations, and the last three centuries of Indigenous resistance movements. These multiple points of contact with the rhythms of different historical lineages of "organized people" produce a dynamic line of descent. Activists choose which intellectual heritages to call forth and remix when organizing people at the base.

Invoking "remix" highlights as well the ever-adaptable nature of freedom movements. Democracy—often misunderstood, frequently maligned, and sometimes hated—is too important and promising a concept to let suffocate in our dangerous and deepening social amnesia.[18] As one activist noted in 2011, "We're fighting for a society in which everyone is important." Here we can see democracy not as a fixed reality or port of arrival, not as a stodgy institution or a set of rules, but rather as a lived experiment, a constant process of exploration, struggle, invention, and reinvention, always guided by the vision of ordinary people wresting some power and authority away from the elite few.[19] In young people's creative redesign of how to live free, every generation builds its own set of remixes, producing original political possibilities.

Some of this youth innovation blossomed as movements developed internal processes for navigating disagreements or engineered political forms to hold the powerful accountable to the everyday people at the base. It also unfolded through the creation of music, film, art, and comedy. Television, poetry, music video, and digital platforms also reshaped public conversations, prodded by youth artists on the move. "The ingenuity of these modern day freedom fighters," notes Tory Russell, Missouri-based cofounder of Hands Up United, "is remixing sit-ins to die-ins, going from marches to parades, and substituting old gospel hymns for political chants with thirteen-year-old drummers putting our grievances to a hip hop beat."[20] SNCC activist Bernice Johnson Reagon once said that music "actually holds the analytical analysis of our people for our survival." One example of this could be seen as Janelle Monáe and her Afro-futuristic production company, Wondaland, created a new kind of protest song that built on ancient griotte rhythms and spirituals in "Hell You Talmbout," released in mid-August 2015, a year after the killing of Ferguson's Michael Brown Jr. Monáe posted on Instagram:

This song is a vessel. It carries the unbearable anguish of millions. We recorded it to channel the pain, fear, and trauma caused by the ongoing slaughter of our brothers and sisters. We recorded it to challenge the indifference, disregard, and negligence of all who remain quiet about this issue. Silence is our enemy. Sound is our weapon. They say a question lives forever until it gets the answer it deserves. . . . Won't you say their names?[21]

From Kunte Kinte through Muhammad Ali and #SayHerName, Monáe invoked the centuries-long freedom struggle's claim to personal and collective dignity. She didn't sing solo. She and her band chanted the names of those killed unjustly—from Emmett Till in 1955 and Amadou Diallo in 1999, to Sean Bell in 2006 and Tamir Rice in 2014, through Sandra Bland, Freddie Gray, and Walter Scott, all killed in 2015. Monáe's eclectic band took to the streets as well as the stage.

Monáe's group didn't release the song at a club. They didn't promote it through a commercial blitz on streaming platforms or satellite radio. Rather, they unfurled the song in the public square at a March for Black Lives through Philadelphia.[22] In the same way that the 1960s Freedom Singers sang "Which Side Are You On?" or Marvin Gaye's 1971 "What's Going On" laid out a series of images and asked Americans to consider where the country was headed, Monáe gathered people to reflect on the monstrous, grisly, multigenerational reality of white supremacy. The song's title was unapologetically Black: "Hell You Talmbout."

Parts of the youth remix are fashioned from tools sharpened in the long fight against slavery and its still mutating offspring. They also draw deeply on Indigenous traditions—from maroon communities to water ceremonies—as one can see in videos like #WeStand. Latin American *testimonios* and other tools fashioned in resistance to European colonialism have expanded young people's sense of their own insights and capacities. The young rebels in the pages that follow assembled these tools at the grassroots and set out to live as true citizens and "unacknowledged legislators" of an America where freedom and justice was experienced, not just mouthed during the Pledge of Allegiance in elementary schools and at the national anthem at ball games.[23]

Not long ago, writer Thomas King—Cherokee, German, Greek—noted that "the truth about stories is that that's all we are." He quotes the Nigerian storyteller Ben Okri: "In a fractured age, when cynicism is god, here is a possible heresy: we live by stories, we also live in them. One way or another, we are living the stories planted in us early or along the way, or we are also living the stories we planted—knowingly or unknowingly—in ourselves." Stories, Okri observes, can give our lives meaning. "If we change the stories we live by, quite possibly we change our lives."[24] The stories that follow offer an enduring record of what physicists call the potential energy to change the stories we live by.

ONE

Youth and Women Lead
Ella Baker and SNCC

The scene appeared bleak despite the beautiful spring weather. Birmingham, Alabama. May 1961. White supremacists had firebombed earlier buses carrying Black and white "Freedom Riders" from Washington, DC, to New Orleans. Now this ride had come to a sudden, seemingly permanent halt. Reverend Fred Shuttlesworth, a legend for his fearless pastoring of Bethel Baptist Church in Birmingham, did not see a way for the rides to continue. No one could question his personal courage: he and his wife, Ruby, were nearly killed by the Klan when they enrolled their young daughter in an all-white school. Shuttlesworth had survived multiple bomb attacks on his house and church.

Still, given the mounting dangers, he warned Fisk College activist Diane Nash not to come to Birmingham to pick up the Freedom Ride. "Young lady, do you know that the Freedom Riders were almost killed here?" he asked. Nash, part of the Student Nonviolent Coordinating Committee, replied, "That's exactly why the movement must not be stopped. If they stop us with violence, the movement is dead. We're coming. We just want to know if you can meet us."[1]

In the end, people like Nash routed an oppressive system that had existed for nearly a century. In just five years, between 1960 and 1965, young activists—most Black, some not—dismantled large parts of legalized segregation, a system widely known as Jim Crow. They did so in the very places in which it was most deeply rooted—Mississippi, Alabama, Tennessee, and Georgia. Despite ferocious violence from white supremacists—beatings, whippings, burnings, rapes, tortures, killings—they themselves acted nonviolently. Routinely, observers were stunned. Then impressed. And, often, won over. Here were young people who defied all odds, who attempted the seemingly impossible. They not only questioned terrible, yet deeply ingrained, assumptions but went out to challenge them.

SNCC workers began to act "as if" the world made sense. As if the nation's mission statement that "all men are created equal" should be reality, not just window dressing. As if, of course, everyone should have the right to ride the bus, visit the beach, buy a meal—and, most notably, vote. One SNCC worker, Jack Chatfield, recalled that they acted as if "we were an almost divinely appointed cadre of young people setting out to reconstruct [the] world that had existed for centuries."[2]

Many aspects of their story have been told before, and told well—by SNCC activists themselves and by outsiders.[3] How these young people managed to pull off the impossible is unfortunately not part of the treasure chest of tales the nation tells about itself. Similar to many other stories of "the people" finding ways to assert themselves, this account remains buried among the pomp and circumstance surrounding the nation's hallowed heroes—from the founding fathers to sanitized versions of civil rights leaders like Frederick Douglass and Martin Luther King Jr.[4]

This chapter aims not to retell the story of the actual people who made the civil rights movement move but to illuminate one specific, and very important, aspect. How did the young people in SNCC manage to transform ideas into action?

It is a story with layers and complications. Like any movement organization, they experienced not only astonishing success but also flops, and even catastrophes. They had to learn from failure. A central character is Ella Baker, a civil rights elder by the early 1960s, in her fifties. She arguably did more than anyone else to allow activists to find out about themselves and in the process learn how to act   act in ways that held the promise of translating their ideas into cultural and political reality. She is possibly the greatest champion of American democratic politics that no one outside of certain circles has ever heard about—and a lodestar for group-centered leadership. She resisted the typical mode of individual heroics. Her legacy not only pervades the story of SNCC but also becomes visible in many of the movements that followed the civil rights/Black Power era, in the 1990s and again in the 2010s.

ORIGINS

SNCC was formed in April 1960, when Ella Baker helped bring together young activists from across the South. The students had one thing in common: all had participated in the sit-ins—in Greensboro, in Nashville, in Richmond, and in dozens of other cities.

Today, if people have heard of SNCC at all, the sit-ins are usually the one and only defining action of the group. It is an important origin point. Why that is so requires a brief reference to the larger historical environment. In 1945, after the end of World War II, the callous and catastrophic ideas of fascism, in their German, Italian, and Japanese versions, seemed finally defeated. The USA looked to be stronger and more unified than ever. American horizons appeared unlimited, both abroad and at home. In numbers previously unheard of, all kinds of people experienced new and expanding opportunities. After a short readjustment, the American economy began to boom. For millions of mostly white veterans, college and home ownership became affordable with the help of the GI Bill. Small businesses opened with the assistance of federally subsidized loans. Consumerism took on unprecedented dimensions.

Indeed, it certainly looked like the dawn of the American century. Across the globe, people drank Coca-Cola, traded in US dollars, and danced to American music. Yet it was not just an economic boom or a moment of military glory. Perhaps most significantly, it was a short-lived era that allowed the US to portray itself as the global beacon of democracy. No country had ever been better, freer, allowing for more opportunities for everyone.

Reality on the ground looked different. Above all, opportunities and freedoms existed in highly unequal fashion. And sometimes they did not exist at all. Some later described it as a time "when affirmative action was white" or as "freedom with violence" or as part of a persistent pattern, the "two faces of American freedom."[5]

Young Black students had particularly painful experiences. African Americans had fought and labored as hard as anyone during the days of hardship, mobilization, and world war. They, too, had died in the fight against the racist ideologies harnessed by the Nazis and Axis powers. They, too, believed in the dawn of expanded opportunities, new freedoms, an America finally able to live up to its own promises.

When Black students in the South came to college during the first postwar decades, having overcome the many hurdles of inequality and discrimination at home, they anticipated a full range of opportunities. Instead, they often found themselves barred from public spaces, excluded from choices afforded others.

Most universities and colleges did not admit them. On the campuses of those that did, mostly historically Black colleges and universities, they could go to the library, the student center, and the gym. Yet when they stepped off campus and went into town, they could buy school supplies—but not eat at the five-and-dime. They could go to the movies but had to sit in decrepit, segregated balcony seats. They could purchase clothing but couldn't try items on.

They could catch a ride on the bus but had to sit in the back—and give up their seats when the bus filled with whites.

While it may not have been Nazi Germany, what Black students lived in was certainly not a country of all people "created equal." Hitler would have approved of postwar American racial policies. Black college students, in any case, could not help but experience, day in and day out, the painful chasm between the American promise and Jim Crow's barbed wire gates.[6]

When four college freshmen sat at the five-and-dime counter in February 1960 in Greensboro, North Carolina, dressed in their Sunday best, and asked to be served a meal, Black collegians throughout the region realized, "This is something I can do." And so, within the span of a single college semester, students began to replace lawyers and ministers at the center stage of the freedom struggle.

It was the quality of creative action by young people that first caught Ella Baker's attention. In the spring of 1960, students built a path to act to topple Jim Crow—not just talk about it. During Baker's entire life, spanning decades of sustained political activism—as field secretary of the NAACP or as interim director of the Southern Christian Leadership Conference—she had embodied directness. A critic of leader-centered organizations, she believed in empowering people—through building relationships and training and, above all, thoughtful action. Her goal was simple and profound: she wanted to live in a society that provided dignity by allowing people a voice. Some would later call this vision a "true democracy."[7] Her own work in communities throughout the South had given her the confidence that everyday people not only had the right but, more importantly, had the ability to have a say in the decisions that most deeply affected their lives.

Baker had engaged in the hard work of on-the-ground organizing since her early adulthood in the 1930s. Not talking about or pondering or writing alone—but doing. She worked for gender equity at her college. She pushed for wage fairness, voting rights, and equal access to legal justice while working for a host of organizations. Always stylishly dressed, often with elegant hat and gloves, she had, time and again, driven people to ask the central question: "What do we need to *do*?"[8] By the time she organized a meeting of the young people who had generated the sit-ins in the spring of 1960, she had done this work for over thirty years. Yet she had never seen so many people, young people, getting organized so quickly and so effectively. She did know a hard reality of political engagement: if there was no attempt to organize the young sit-in activists, the fledgling movement would likely die.

The arrests of hundreds of sit-in activists in the spring of 1960 embarrassed mayors, filled jails, and made international headlines. Soviet and Chinese national newspapers in particular seemed to relish the indisputably unjust images emerging at US lunch counters. Suddenly, the world's beacon for democracy seemed rather dim. After eight weeks, over a thousand students had been arrested in fifty-four cities across nine states.[9] Through phone calls, meetings, and word of mouth, the message spread. Finally, students had found something to do—something that brought into stark relief the blatant injustices of Jim Crow, something that just might make a difference.

People throughout the South began to get organized—in most cases led by Black students—and do what had been inconceivable mere days earlier. They forced business owners to open up lunch counters and put the heat on municipal governments to allow access to public pools. And they didn't stop there. They moved on to pool halls, beaches, parks, churches, and motels. Then they focused on the one thing Black people would need in order to gain political self-determination: the right to vote. Later they organized for political and economic justice. "SNCC never got political power," recalled veteran white racial justice activist Anne Braden. But within a short decade, the group "set the agenda for the country. It was a humane agenda that was for all. It broadened democracy for everybody."[10]

Historically, it was an astonishing feat. A group of unexpected actors—young people—figured out a way to move a simple and profound yet seemingly unachievable goal from idea to action: get rid of Jim Crow. Baker had seen the freedom movement sputter and stall after the Montgomery bus boycott (1955–56) and Little Rock school integration crisis (1957). What to do next? What, in a climate of white supremacy, to do that was reasonably safe to do or, at least, had some chance of success? There were ideas galore, but, when it came to determining what actually to do, no one in the civil rights movement could figure it out.

The sit-ins of 1960 promised a new approach. They were relatively easy to replicate and helped recruit new activists who did not have to go through lengthy training or instructions. Above all, they landed a blow where it mattered: the purses of power. Wherever students appeared, occupying the stools of lunch counters, the aisles of movie theatres, or the seats of city buses, profits collapsed. And owners began to pay rapid attention. Rarely were they convinced by the cause of student unrest. Yet they were certainly interested in getting profits back on track, and fast.

Watching all of this, Ella Baker went into high gear in February and March 1960. Once the sit-ins had passed their peak, she realized, this mobilization of thousands of young people would likely fizzle out—unless they found a way to come together and figure out what to do next. And so "Miss Baker," as most everyone called her, did what she did best—she invited people to come together.

On April 16, 1960, some 120 student sit-in activists from fifty-six colleges and twelve states gathered at Baker's alma mater, Shaw University, in Raleigh, North Carolina.[11] Under her quiet, dynamic but barely visible tutelage, student sit-in activists spent three days sharing experiences, debating possibilities, and discussing plans. One clear result was this: all wanted to keep fighting, and to do so together. They decided to form an organization, the Student Nonviolent Coordinating Committee.

Every step of the way, Baker stayed with the students—listening, mostly. Sometimes she offered the occasional piece of wisdom acquired from over three decades of organizing. Fiercely loyal and resolute, she wanted nothing more than to see their vital freedom movement thrive.

Isolation, Baker knew, was a danger. Political change required strength—thus, movements required people. Large numbers of people coming together, on any issue, was rare. And difficult. People needed to be recruited; they needed something to do; they needed to have some faith that what they were doing made sense. And the steeper the climb, the more activists needed help from the outside—people who could house them, open their wallets for them, put in a good word for them. Protect them.

If the students were going it alone, Baker had learned, the fledgling movement did not have much chance to achieve deep, sustained change. All her life she had cultivated a network, both wide and deep, among local and regional Black activists in the South. Yet it was largely a network of elders, of community leaders from churches and businesses and civic organizations—not usually the type of people who had much tolerance for the outlandish actions of young students, who seemed all too often unpredictable, uncontrollable, sometimes rash, and always dangerous.[12] Still, in Baker's mind, for either group to move forward, they had to come together and start supporting each other's work. Less clear was how exactly to bring that about.

In the fall of 1960, Baker made a life-altering decision: from then on, she would dedicate her work to young people, to their vision of change. It was an extraordinary act (and we'll come back to it). At this moment in time, it meant that she was available to the activists of SNCC—and not just for a conversation, or a day, or a weekend conference. She was there for the duration, and in every way she or they thought useful.

She sat in their meetings. She ate and worked with them. She helped students from different backgrounds hear and see each other. And when the movement grew and began to include not just Black southern students but students from across the country, she provided invaluable advice on how to act, how to be, when doing "recruiting work" in the Deep South. Students not only respected her but also took her advice. They trusted her council. "You had students from all over the country, some of whom came from the 'best' schools, who came into the deep rural South, and partnered with farmers and sharecroppers who had virtually no formal education," recalled SNCC activist Diane Nash. They learned to respect people in a democratic sense—not condescend or lead but hear and learn together. "We didn't come in saying, 'This is what you should do.'" Rather, they built partnerships, and "the result was that SNCC was able to do things that neither [youth nor local southern leaders] could have done alone."[13]

Baker modeled an organizing approach that emphasized listening and relationship building on both sides. She taught people how to initiate and sustain democratic conversations. She showed how to move these relationships into public actions.

After close to a century of segregation and three centuries of unyielding white supremacy, it took fewer than three years for the urban South to desegregate its lunch counters. It happened for no other reason than the nonviolent direct action of young people. Yet they were far from justice's finish line. For as Baker wistfully remarked, what good does it do to be able to order a hamburger if you can't afford it?[14]

The lunch counters provided a clear target for students. The sit-ins helped create a movement. Desegregation was an important, and necessary, step in the right direction. In many ways, it was a great and stunning triumph. By itself, however, it did not provide better jobs or access to opportunities or, for that matter, a foot in the door of political decision-making. It was obvious, in short, that SNCC's work was far from complete. How to get there was far less clear. Some waxed eloquently about "economic and political democracy for Black citizens." It was quite easy to conceptualize, but not so easy to put into practice.

Over the course of 1962–63, members of SNCC decided to focus on the very foundation of a free and democratic society—the ballot. Without the vote, Black citizens would never have a voice or find adequate representation. And in the Deep South, Blacks did not vote. Whites in power did not let them—recognizing full well, as did SNCC activists by then, that the free vote was one essential pillar of power in America. Without the vote, any hope for a measure of control over one's own life melted away like ice in the sweltering heat of a Mississippi Delta summer day.

GIVING BIRTH TO NEW DEMOCRATIC FORMS

Gaining the vote could be accomplished, at least in theory, in two ways: play within the rules of the existing system and get people registered, or create alternative political institutions and try to put political power behind them. SNCC tried both.

Fresh from the sit-ins and Freedom Rides, young SNCC workers fanned out across the Deep South, talking to people, listening, and building relationships. They ran classes on how to register to vote. They went door to door—thousands of doors—for dozens of months. At first, their goal was simply to prove that Black citizens wanted to vote.[15] At church and barn meetings, in bars and out in the fields, people gathered, and SNCC workers made their case. What would life look like if we voted? Through conversations, everyone quickly realized that a lot more than simply the act of voting was at stake. Participants from the community said things like, "I want to be able to take my child to the doctor." A neighbor might respond, "Let's hire one of our own as tax assessor and get the streets paved first so that we can get places." Then a small landowner chimed in, "We need to focus on keeping our land. Black farmers need to be on the Agricultural Stabilization Board. No more Blacks cheated out of their cotton." Through such small, informal meetings, people made demands of themselves and their neighbors. They could sense expanded possibilities by thinking "if only." Voting. Yes, it sure would make a difference. Yet it was dangerous. What would happen if they tried anyway, if they went out to demand the vote?

It was work that required hundreds of conversations. It involved learning and listening. It demanded the organizers build trust between older members, who had spent their entire lives in their communities, and young people, outsiders at first, who came because they wanted to make a difference. This intergenerational bridging was work Ella Baker had done all her life.

Judy Richardson was a teen when she met Baker in the early 1960s. Richardson had just finished her first year at Swarthmore as one of a handful of Black students. Originally from Tarrytown, New York, Richardson was drawn into the sit-in movement along Maryland's Eastern Shore, a two-hour drive from her college. She first encountered Baker working in SNCC's Atlanta office and remembers how impressed she was: "To get somebody seventeen, eighteen, nineteen to think not just about next week, but next year, three years from now, was an amazing feat." How did Baker do it? "Part of it was that she always reminded us of our responsibility to the local community." She told young activists that, in many ways, local adults "were at greater risk than we were." Baker was blunt. "Look," she would say, "All that could happen to us is that we could die, which at a young age, you don't think can happen to you anyway." Yet the local populations they were trying to organize had more at stake: they were putting "their lives and livelihoods of not just themselves but their entire community" on the line to participate.[16]

Joyce Ladner was also a teen in Mississippi when she first met Baker. She explained how Baker "very much taught us that we had to start with where the people are." They could not tell people, "You're to do this, and to do that." It would have been not only arrogant but also ignorant. One first had to get a good sense of the lay of the land, learn about people and their concerns, and then, and only then, "work with them to build a consensus." It was a process fundamentally different from how most people commonly conceptualize leadership: the point was not to lead but to build leadership in others. By encouraging people to talk about the things they would like to see change in their community, leadership emerged from within the community. "Your job, as a facilitator," explained Ladner, "was to bring about the local leadership that already existed."[17]

Baker worked both ends of this radical equation, bringing young people together with established local networks rooted in southern hamlets and cities. She not only had to teach young people how to listen but had to encourage older community leaders to work with the energetic young people from SNCC, to give them a chance. As local Mississippi leader Victoria Gray Adams recalled, she and Baker talked about how to affirm, embrace, and support young people while also finding ways to get older folks involved. "As a result," Adams noted, "I became a mediator in Hattiesburg between the young civil rights workers and the local community."[18] Through her many years of work as an NAACP field secretary, Baker had cultivated a network in cities and states across the South. She knew a great deal about what kinds of things local communities had tried to organize. She called it "spadework"—the largely invisible relationship building and groundwork that local leaders laid with people in their networks. (In the 2010s, urban organizers Cathy Cohen and Barbara Ransby would bring Baker's style of bridging work to urban and suburban settings with young Black activists; Madonna Thunder Hawk and LaDonna Allard did the same to connect Indigenous youth organizers to urban and rural Indigenous communities.) And Baker knew who was likely to welcome the students' intensity and energy and who was not.

Baker's connections to local southern Black leaders paved the way, and the disciplined energy of young SNCC activists got things moving. The voter registration project was a case in point. In many ways, it was the brainchild of a local Mississippi grandchild of enslaved people, Amzie Moore. Born in 1911, Moore, a largely self-educated man who had been denied entry into college, had experienced his share of racist discrimination and racial hatred. And he had never put up with it. Tirelessly, he had resisted, organized, and fought. In his experience, Blacks needed to be economically independent in order to stand a chance. He built several small businesses, among them a grocery store and a gas station. And he had helped many others get on their own feet. Together with Medgar Evers, Moore had created the Regional Council of Negro Leadership.[19] It was little wonder that Ella Baker had known him for a long time.

More than most, Amzie Moore was ready for additional energy to help organize his community. When a young mathematician from New York by the name of Bob Moses came down south, and well before Moses himself would become a key architect of SNCC's Mississippi organizing drive, Baker knew whom Moses should talk to. "It was Miss Baker that gave me that name and put me in touch with Amzie Moore in Cleveland, Mississippi," recalled Moses. When Moses arrived in Mississippi, Baker's recommendation was enough entrée for Moore. He took out his maps of the whole Delta and said to Moses, "Look, we don't have a lot of lunch counters out here that we want to sit in, but we do have a lot of people around here that we want to take down to register to vote." Moore's research, gathered over two decades, laid out a clear plan for who in the state was ready to move on the vote.[20]

Moses invited Moore to the next regional SNCC meeting, where Moore set out to sell that program to SNCC.[21] It was Baker's vision come true: young and old together, building on existing networks, learning from local needs and supporting local leadership. It was the blueprint Moses would use for the next five years, leading the single largest on-the-ground organizing effort to push forward the passage of what later became the Voting Rights Act of 1965.[22]

Describing this accomplishment seems easy enough: Ella Baker modeled for SNCC youth how to create mutually respectful relationships with local leaders across the South. She then fostered connections between the students and the key local leaders in Mississippi, Alabama, and Georgia that became the central engine of SNCC voter organizing projects across the region. Yet her experiential wisdom is neither widely known nor appreciated. Hers was the kind of patient, on-the-ground, long-term work of bringing people together, and done in a way that was respectful of everyone's input and experiences, that is not easy to replicate.

It is a harsh reality that Baker's work—and that of others who worked in a similar manner—has largely been invisible, and thus difficult for subsequent generations of "Ella Bakers" to emulate. Indeed, it explains why successful democratic organizing happens so rarely. It is not because people don't have problems or don't desire change. More often than not, they just don't know what to do or how to do it. Time and again, it became clear that the deep experiential knowledge of an Ella Baker goes far beyond conceptual learning or libraries full of books containing theories on democracy.

Of course, the movement's ability to "move" was not just about building networks and bringing people together. It was also about *keeping* them together. As movement participants around the world have long understood, keeping together always presented a formidable challenge. Long-time SNCC activist Charles Jones explained Baker's insistence on relationship building, trust, and consensus. Early on in the life of SNCC, he, Diane Nash, Marion Barry, and several others fought so hard against each other that it felt like the new organization might fall apart. There was no shortage of issues on which to disagree—chief among them was whether to pursue more direct action like the sit-ins or whether to start focusing on voter registration.

"Ella would sit back calmly, and hear each of us," Jones recalled, "but would not let us turn each other loose." Baker was not going to settle for a simple majority vote but waited until "all of us, Diane, and Charles [Sherrod], and Chuck McDew and Tim [Jenkins], felt a common community." It was different from anything the participants had ever experienced. They were familiar with debating and winning (or losing) an argument and with trying everything to get their way. They were *not* familiar with consensus building, with the patient reaching out that required time, openness, and the building of trust. Jones simply called it "unique." Yet it was far more than that: it included all the building blocks that activists later would refer to as "the beloved community."[23]

This challenge of keeping movement networks together played out in many places and situations. Yet the tenor of conflict was often the same. Joanne Grant, an adult supporter of SNCC, remembered a meeting at which "a serious dispute" broke out. A scuffle among SNCC members ensued. Upset, Grant burst into tears. Ella Baker, sitting next to her, "stood up, pulled me to my feet, and began to sing 'We Shall Overcome,' which she referred to as 'old soothing syrup.'"[24] Baker's presence worked again and again in hundreds of situations where tempers and patience frayed.

It worked because, as Diane Nash realized, "I could trust Ms. Baker to be honest and truthful. She was direct; there were no games and dancing around issues." For young people thrown into the cauldron of activism and its resulting danger, Baker's approach was refreshing and uplifting. Above all, it created a sense of community, of shared purpose. "I was meeting situations that I didn't understand," Nash further explained. "People . . . would act in ways that seemed illogical to me." And Baker would help the young people not only see the situation from different perspectives but do so with a clear eye toward building an underlying consensus. She would say things like, "Well, [that other group is] in an organization that is concerned about their fundraising. If you students are successful, people will tend to want to send their donations to you instead of to that organization."[25] As in all movements, there were a lot of competing agendas. Most, if not all, had some legitimacy. Not all could be met. Yet the goals behind most of them were similar enough to fashion a common agenda.

And activists did. Despite disagreements, frustration, and anger, SNCC people learned to work through serious disagreements. The debates in SNCC were legend for their sheer length—measured, at times, not by hours but by days. Yet when they were done, consensus was reached, and things once again began to move forward. Nash remembers that Baker accomplished the seemingly impossible: instead of feeling exhausted, "I would feel like she had picked me up and dusted me off emotionally, and I was ready to get back into the fray."[26]

Something else Baker brought to the movement was the deep sense that it was not just "the movement" or its goals and visions that mattered. Rather, it was the people who made up the movement who mattered. Like a cherished family member—albeit one with high expectations—she tried to connect with everyone and did so from day one. SNCC workers generally recall that "she was never a stranger, somebody I had to get to know," and that, in fact, "her influence on me has been lifelong and lasting beyond her death." SNCC activist and movement scholar Bernice Johnson Reagon vividly remembered, "In the middle of the most intense movement crisis, Miss Baker would always ask you about your person, your home, your children, your food, your thinking." Quite simply, a movement, in order to be worth anything, "had to take care of the people who made up the movement." And yet Baker's persistence in caring for others was not just an organizing method. Much more importantly, it helped provide a sense of the society they all fought for, one they wanted to live in. Demanding respect and dignity and a fair playing field was hollow if one was not willing to also provide it for others. Here again, living "as if" the future was possible in the here and now, SNCC people created social relations that could form the bedrock of a new kind of political life.[27]

A RADICALLY DIFFERENT KIND OF LEADERSHIP

Leadership is a concept that occupies a prominent role in American culture. Books on leadership fill whole aisles at chain bookstores and libraries. New methods of leadership are taught across the land in colleges and seminars and weekend workshops. In some cases, one is led to part with a small fortune for the promise of becoming "an effective leader." And though the ideas and methods have changed—and, in any case, are far too numerous for anyone to summarize—it is fair to say that Ella Baker's model of leadership significantly parted from anything one might pick up in, say, a prestigious business school.

Of course Baker would likely not have been very interested in all the theories about leadership. Her ideas about what leadership meant, at bottom, were informed by two things: realities on the ground and her vision of a free and democratic society. People who needed a leader in order to move would stop moving once the leader was gone. Worse, following a leader (and his or her agenda) inevitably robbed people of discovering or building upon their own ability to act. And what, in the end, was the meaning of freedom or democracy if it did not empower people to have a voice in their own affairs?

People outside of movements frequently ask, "How do you build a movement?" The most straightforward answer that Baker and those in SNCC offered is that one had to look for leadership in everyday people and help people grow. Give them opportunities and training to believe in themselves and develop their skills. Baker had the ability, as Joyce Ladner summarized, to "inspire people of every imaginable ilk." It was a genius that "flowed from her deep faith in people's capacity to do what is necessary to respond to their needs and to resolve the contradictions of their lives"—with information, social networks, support. Failure was not just an inevitable part of that journey; it was a good and necessary part. Nothing new and better ever happened unless the unknown was attempted, and such attempts necessarily involved failure—a lot of it. Baker "taught us that we had to be resilient. Just because you fall down doesn't mean you don't keep getting up."[28] Baker routinely—even doggedly—insisted "the salvation of a person and a people must come from within." For her, the key was that "the struggle must be engaged by the struggler."[29]

The centrality of this lesson is hard to overstate. So many compassionate people try to help others by doing *for* them. One need only look at the models that are dominant among twentieth- and twenty-first-century nonprofit organizations, social services, and foundations. Baker's blueprint fundamentally differed. Victoria Gray Adams defined what she learned from Baker this way:

"The struggle must be engaged by the struggler, in cooperation with significant others having the compassion and needed elements which they themselves do not possess." Baker herself noted, "We have rights only as long as we are willing to struggle for them."[30]

Baker not only possessed this central insight but also had the "training, experience, courage and compassion to offer and share the missing elements" where needed. In this way, she "assisted people in discovering their own gifts and talents" and encouraged them "to release these into the larger community." She modeled and lived this conviction in "giving of oneself to the development of the larger community." It was "her way of being, capital B-E-I-N-G," Adams realized. Living this way, day in and day out, Baker "inspired and created a broad body of leadership that spans the country and reaches into every segment" of the US. In this way, she "dedicated her life to the premise that a strong people have no need for strong leaders."[31]

Baker was concerned with the base—the people who populated society's bottom rail—as much as with the issues that made up the core of the problem. It is what made her embrace the word "radical," in its literal sense of "going to the root." As she shared with youth in SNCC, the key moments in her life happened when she gave herself permission to look for the root. "Radical" to her simply meant "you don't pick around the edges. You go to the root, and make a new world." Though raised Baptist, she did not talk much as an adult about her religious beliefs. Religious or not, she had one abiding faith—a faith that informed her entire existence. It was "that people, just plain people, should run the society they live in." It was a rare idea to come by—then and now. Yet as her longtime colleague Anne Braden noted, "She had a belief that it should happen, and it could happen."[32]

Wherever Baker was, she brought people together to begin that process. "She wasn't going to do it for them," Braden observed. Yet she had absolute faith that *they* could do it. That idea was "pretty damn radical," Braden recalled in 2000. "You have to start where you are. Whatever little town you are in. That's where you start."[33] Everyone can do it—not only was it an idea that Baker believed in, it was a belief she lived. Living it was almost contagious. People who operated in this kind of faith grew to meet its expectations. For psychologists it is not a new concept; only in the sophisticated circles of contemporary politics is it dismissed as naive. For Baker, it was grounded in the belief "that in every one of us there was something creative, tremendous, beautiful, and that could make a difference." The result was felt by all who worked with her. "Because she believed in us, we could believe in ourselves," said Victoria Adams.[34] It was "radical" because it radically departed from common political patterns, which were built on experts and hierarchical to the core. It was also essential for a movement that tried to break open some of those patterns, "because you can't build these movements without people who believe in themselves."[35] Later adherents would apply approaches that reflected this method to freedom struggles in urban settings, suburbs, and Indigenous homelands. It adapted profoundly well in each—and became the foundation for building power based on organizing people at the grass roots, rather than on hierarchical authority vested in a boss, bank account, or military might.

The hierarchies and restrictions that movement activists encountered on a daily basis in the 1960s, of course, were not limited to traditional politics, racism, and opportunities denied. Equal in their contributions, and often supreme in their courage, women saw themselves, time and again, relegated to positions of subservience and service—even within parts of the movement. Good enough to fix coffee and provide solace to anxiety-ridden men, women struggled to escape narrow gendered expectations. Sexism, it turned out, was alive and well in much of the freedom struggle.

No doubt, female activists experienced this environment in many different ways. But interviews suggest that most had something in common: they found in Baker a role model for freedom from gendered restrictions. SNCC organizer Jean Wiley recalled, "I wish to high heaven I had found, in my life before SNCC or in the years since, the freedom I as a woman found there." With Baker's guidance, many women began to take on prominent positions in the movement. "Fannie Lou Hamer was one of our most eloquent spokespersons," Wiley noted. "And Ruby Doris Robinson would soon become SNCC's executive secretary."[36] Legendary Alabama activist Annie Pearl Avery recalled that Baker had warned them against the male chauvinism she had seen in other civil rights organizations as well.[37] Baker maintained a simple principle: no one should be restricted on the basis of where they were from or their educational level. In this she stood within a sustained tradition of activists and thinkers, including people like Italian activist and philosopher Antonio Gramsci and Brazilian educator Paolo Freire.[38] She insisted no one should be limited based on gender, either. Good ideas and actions could come from anywhere.

TRANSLATING GOOD IDEAS TO ACTION

Before this chapter concludes, it is important to highlight a few more of the transformative qualities Ella Baker and SNCC brought forward within the long freedom struggle in particular and to those who want to move idea into action in general. These qualities are no easier to write about than they are to conceptualize. This is in part due to the fact that they implicitly question—tear down, really—a common cultural (mis)conception: the distinction between the personal and the political. Personal feelings, personal interactions—it's not the stuff of politics, we're told.

Over time, the distinction has left behind a seemingly endless history of senseless battles, discarded bodies, missed opportunities. The tales are common enough to be missed for their significance: the ferocious debates in which righteousness won over togetherness; a white activist trying to set the agenda for a group led by people of color; the activist sexually harassing or assaulting his female colleague; the speechifier who waxes eloquently about democratic social relations before cutting off his opponent by excluding him from the decision-making process. To say it is a pervasive phenomenon still misses its significance, for it is not just painful, and at times tragic. Above all, it provides a glimpse of possibility. Of alternative paths. Of what could have been if people had found a common ground, had supported rather than denigrated each other, had empowered each other rather than cut each other down.

Baker never formally reflected on this. Still, her entire presence was steadfast opposition to a competitive mode of being. She was living proof that an alternative, a truly cooperative reciprocity, was not only possible but clearly the superior path forward. Initially, people in her presence didn't understand it so much as they simply "felt it"—they felt heard, or acknowledged, or taken seriously, or encouraged. Without fail, they later began to reflect on it, attempted to parse it, to understand it. Yet probably there never was a single "it," so much as there was a multitude of ways in which Ella Baker's presence allowed others to partake in her faith—the faith that all human beings had in themselves the ability to live freely and democratically with each other.

Bob Moses talked about this quality in terms of Baker doing "the 'walk of the trees' for us." The phrase came from a 1976 *New York Times* article by novelist Toni Morrison. Morrison explored the way "healers and builders have always worked quietly among" African Americans. These were not "the heroes of old," those in prominent positions or famous or blindly followed. Nor were they "the Blacks who had accumulated wealth for its own sake, fame, medals or some public acknowledgment of success." No; they were the ones who made community happen, who did the labor of love. Morrison pointed to her grandmother Ardelia Willis as a case in point, someone who with an "exercise of the will," through steady and reliable presence, opened access to opportunity and education for her children. For Willis, "obstacles were just that and not fixed stars." Yet Morrison's grandmother merely represented a much larger presence, all those "whose work is real and pointed and clear in its application to the race," people who "refuse to imitate, to compromise, and who are indifferent to public accolade. Whose work is free or priceless." And, of course, they are all people who, day in and day out, "take huge risks economically and personally."[39]

Not always popular but always respected within their own communities, these healers and builders become the "unmistakable natural aristocrats of the race." Why? Because they are the ones who keep alive the promise of irrevocable and permanent change, who keep before people a vision of the impact they want to have in the world, without which all conflict becomes interpersonal conflict. They moved insistently, like "the slow walk of certain species of trees from the flatlands up into the mountains."[40]

Bob Moses learned the slow walk of the trees from Baker, who showed him three things. First, "It's a long, long walk. You have to learn it, but you can carve out a life in this country in struggle," he reflected in 2000. Second, "Your struggle should be radical, it should go to the root of the problem, and it should work with the people who are at the bottom." And third, "You don't sacrifice family on the walk, but you carve out, as you go, [to make] your family."[41]

Having learned Swahili as a teacher in Tanzania in the 1970s, Moses began to refer to Baker as "SNCC's *fundi*." It is a term with no English equivalent. More than an expert, a *fundi* is a person from the community "who masters a given craft" by learning within the community, by "coming up through the community" and being helped along by others who have mastered it. This person plies her craft, continuously learning and passing it along, without the role "ever being institutionalized" or given some kind of special prominence. Baker "mastered certain things as she grew up and became part of the movement," Moses pointed out. "She's taught us those things, and there is no institutionalization of those things." Yet it did not require institutions. Across the land, SNCC people who closely worked with Ella Baker carried on her work for decades, as teachers, community organizers, facilitators, trusted advisers. They worked in rural areas, as SNCC had, but also in Oakland, Jacksonville, Baltimore, and Chicago. They moved in and across the rapidly expanding suburbs in Atlanta, Los Angeles, and Minneapolis. In their own right, they have become *fundis*, doing the slow walk of the trees in their respective communities ever since.[42] Their presence has not gone unnoticed, and in the chapters that follow, we can see their vision kept alive by new human seedlings, ready to take the slow walk of the trees.

TWO

Southerners on New Ground
Organizing at the Intersections

Atlanta's Pride march began on a sweltering June day in 2000, at the city's downtown Piedmont Park. Despite its location at the heart of what was arguably the South's largest progressive city, the Atlanta Pride organizing committee had good reason to feel wary. Even at the beginning of the twenty-first century, it was common for participants of Gay Pride parades to be harassed—they were targets of urine-filled balloons or tripped and beaten by passersby. Sometimes, they were harassed and arrested by the police. They confronted taunts and shoves from the Klan, neo-Nazis, or other assorted white nationalists, occasionally having to stare down the barrel of a shotgun. Black marchers were primary targets, and in addition they had to contend with Atlanta's generations-long practice of police abuse of Black people.[1] Thus when late Sunday evening, white police approached Craig Washington and Termain Kyles, the two gay Black men's sense of danger perked up.

The two southern community organizers had been talking to Pepsi, a South African Black TV host visiting Atlanta to work with Kyles. The police officers walked past Washington and Kyles and pulled Pepsi aside. Washington and Kyles began to explain that Pepsi was their friend, he wasn't American, he'd been with them all day. Nothing to worry about. Additional police appeared and blocked Washington and Kyles from standing with Pepsi or from talking to the officers questioning him. Then, suddenly and without his consent, the police hustled Pepsi out of the park.

Washington and Kyles, getting desperate, kept inquiring why their friend was taken away. The officers threatened them with arrest. When Washington called out, "This is racist!," one officer retorted, "If you say one more thing about this being racial, I will arrest you right now." Turning to Pride officials for support, Washington spotted a white Pride worker with a security badge. He inquired whether the Pride worker might help resolve the situation. The Pride worker said he himself had called the police. When Washington asked why, the Pride worker replied that he had thought Pepsi was trying to sell incense in the park and had questioned him. Pepsi had presumably cursed at the Pride worker. "Nobody talks to me that way," the white Pride worker rejoined. He then turned away from Washington and spoke into his headset, "The police got the Black guy."[2]

Frustrated and upset, Washington and Kyles left the park feeling betrayed by the "disrespect and duplicity" of the Atlanta Gay and Lesbian Pride organization. They expected the "intimidation tactics of the Atlanta police department." Yet how could the Pride workers, who also stood for justice and equality, behave in such blatantly discriminatory ways themselves? Why didn't they address the conflict among themselves rather than call on the police, who in Atlanta had a deep history of oppressing both Black and lesbian, gay, bisexual, and transgender (LGBT) communities?

Reflecting on their experience, Washington and Kyles wrote an open letter to social justice groups in the Atlanta region. They demanded that the "black community as well as the LGBT community respond to this dehumanizing treatment of our American and South African brothers"—by both the police and the Pride organization. The latter was particularly painful: "This is a reflection of the white supremacist attitudes and behavior displayed by those who claim to work toward racial diversity in their organizing," they noted. "We cannot fight homophobia without addressing the racism that is equally pervasive throughout LGBT communities and society-at-large."[3]

It was a problem that freedom movements had faced for a long time—one could argue even for centuries, and certainly at least as early as the US Revolution and abolitionist movements. When organizing people at the base for freedom, whose freedom should be pushed forward as top priority? African Americans'? Workers'? Women's? Indigenous people's? LGBTQ citizens'? How did people who inherited and inhabited multiple identities fit in?[4] What to do with blatant forms of discrimination when they showed up *within* such movements? How to respond to civil rights activists who were sexist, or homophobic labor activists, or gay rights activists who were racist? How to confront opponents of the freedom movement who tried to exploit these divisions? Again and again, the lack of practical solutions to this basic challenge divided people, driving a stake into the heart of each respective freedom movement.[5]

This internal division contributed significantly to a simple truth visible throughout history: most attempts to organize people at the base fail. Industrial Areas Foundation (IAF) organizer Nicholas von Hoffman reflected a somber reality in 1963 that remains true today: most organizers arrive in communities, accomplish little, and then leave.[6] The wedge of "divide and conquer" remained throughout the twentieth century, but not for lack of trying to yank it from a firmly entrenched berth. Activists and organizers began to search for better answers. Indeed, more and more citizens openly acknowledged their struggles along multiple identities—working-class and female, or mixed-race and gay. By the 1990s, most activists also knew people or had friends who no longer thought about their struggles along clearly defined single identities; instead, multiple identities might look like a Muslim immigrant, now a proud American, but also a feminist with fluid gender identity and a desire to bring human rights and democracy to the Arab world. Or a white working man with a Puerto Rican partner who started a union effort while employed at Walmart.

Those fighting for freedom on multiple fronts included Craig Washington and Termain Kyles, the organizers highlighted at the top of the chapter. They were part of Southerners on New Ground (SONG). SONG was founded in 1993 by six LGBT activists, Black women Pat Hussain, Mandy Carter, and Joan Garner and white women Mab Segrest, Pam McMichael, and Suzanne Pharr. Washington and Kyles's challenge to Atlanta's LGBT community in 2000 came out of SONG's original framework. Headquartered in Durham, North Carolina, SONG's driving motivation was to "develop *transformative models of organizing* that connect race, class, gender and sexual orientation and to build lasting relationships among people and their organizations."[7]

By 2013, twenty years after its founding, SONG stood as a beacon of innovative organizing for queer youth in the South and across the US. How did such an unusual group get started? This chapter looks at its origins—how members created what Bob Moses called "crawl space" in the culture where one could experiment with a fresh organizing model. For many generations, at least since Sojourner Truth's 1851 "Ain't I a Woman" speech, ideas around intersectionality had been circulating in the culture. But no one had quite figured out how to organize using these ideas, with boots on the ground. Now, SONG had to figure out how to do this in the stronghold of the Moral Majority. If one could make change here, it offered hope across the country.

All six of SONG's founders had been part of or had collaborated with a range of different justice groups. In the 1990s, across the South, there seemed to be hundreds of these organizations—mostly small and almost exclusively focused on a single issue, such as labor rights, racial justice, gender equality, or gay and lesbian liberation. Many groups had tried for years to figure out how to move beyond "single-issue organizing."[8] Audre Lorde famously wrote in the early 1980s, "There is no such thing as a single-issue struggle because we do not live single-issue lives. Malcolm knew this. Martin Luther King, Jr. knew this."[9] Yet there was no simple path to common ground. In the abstract, SONG's founders realized that most everyone they talked with agreed—different justice groups needed to come together.

In reality, however, few walked the talk. So the story that follows is one of much trial and error. Yet it is also a story of patience and perseverance and crucial lessons that derived from failure. None of the particular components SONG experimented with were novel. In the end, however, SONG created a model for organizing: in the heart of Jesse Helms's reactionary white supremacist territory, members figured out how people on the ground in different issue groups could "intersect."

Their work drew on the work Black women had done over multiple generations—first in the abolitionist movement and later in SNCC, the Black Arts movement, the National Black Feminist Organization, and the creation of Black women's studies—and above all on the 1977 Combahee River Collective Statement. Mab Segrest noted that Combahee's term "simultaneous oppressions" had a deep impact on SONG. The term "intersectionality," coined by law professor Kimberlé Crenshaw in 1989, drew on and reflected this activist thinking among Black women, as did the work of Patricia Hill Collins.[10]

People "often mistakenly think intersectionality is only about multiple identities," Crenshaw reflected later. They understood it in terms of "'I've got three, you've got six,'" and in that way "the identity question goes on and on." For Crenshaw, "that's not at least my articulation of intersectionality." Instead she focused on "how structures make certain identities the consequence of and the vehicle for vulnerability."[11]

If someone wanted to know how many intersections mattered for a given person or institution, "you've got to look at the context," she explained. "What's happening? What kind of discrimination is going on? What are the policies, what are the institutional structures that play a role in contributing to the exclusion of some people and not others?"[12] Readers of Octavia Butler's *Kindred* might recognize this immediately: the time-traveling main character, Dana Franklin, experiences her Black middle-class heterosexual womanhood very differently in pre–Civil War Maryland than she does in 1970s Los Angeles. This is true for all identities, Crenshaw pointed out. The Combahee River Collective laid out an intellectual framework that drew from participants' own experience as organizers; Crenshaw clarified it. Now activists had to figure out how to put it in motion on the ground in organizing campaigns.

Women of color had long engaged in intersectional organizing—they had to.[13] As Combahee River Collective member Barbara Smith later recalled, if you "knew about SNCC, you at least had in the back of your mind that we're doing similar kinds of interventions around racial and gender politics and sexual identity politics." For her, intersectional thinking came from a desire to "organize across differences. How do we not erase each other's identities? How do we not be defensive when people raise issues that are not necessarily directly our own?" Combahee wanted to "create a real women's movement that is inclusive and for everybody."[14]

One of SONG's contributions was to make explicit that a lack of intersectional thinking was a practical problem for southern organizers. And while SONG organizers themselves were past their teens and twenties when they formed the group, they laid the essential foundation for SONG's youth organizers in the second decade of the twenty-first century, who worked in collaboration with youth immigrant rights activists and the Movement for Black Lives in particular. Intersectional organizing turned out to be a fresh and critical organizing tool in the 2010s—and it did not just fall out of the sky. SONG had tried, tested, failed, experimented some more, and, in the end, learned to identify and apply organizing tools that brought people from different movements together. Its origin story is thus central to understanding subsequent youth freedom movement innovations.

At its core, SONG's early focus was both political exploration and call for action. Quite simply, people had to show up for each other's causes. Otherwise they would remain part of the problem and, no less significantly, remain marginal. Other models such as union organizing or community organizing based on evolutions of the Saul Alinsky/IAF template had thrived in building people-power through industrial, religious, and community institutions, rooted in long-standing formal and informal social relationships. Yet people in union- and congregation-based organizing seemed more averse to conflict, and it was hard to know how to address cultural mores based in homophobia or racism with even the most expert facilitation. It was thus not clear to SONG organizers how to use a union or IAF model to merge single-issue campaigns to fight off the centuries-old tendency for opponents to use "divide and conquer" to keep freedom movements for women, African Americans, LGBT people, workers, and immigrants from banding together.[15]

In practical terms, SONG activists embraced every opportunity they could find to ask LGBT activists to show up for campaign-based work on racial justice, immigrants' rights, economic justice, and reproductive rights, or to ask racial justice activists to show up for LGBT rights and immigrants' rights, or to ask economic justice advocates to show up for racial justice and LGBT and immigrants' rights. And so on.

They all had their war stories. Mandy Carter was a lifelong economic justice organizer. She had participated as a teen in the Poor People's Campaign of 1968 with Martin Luther King Jr. A woman of regal bearing, great personal kindness, and high energy, she had worked in the peace movement, the women's movement, the LGBT movement, and the civil rights movement for decades and had built strong relationships in each. When she began to mobilize LGBT southerners in North Carolina to support immigrant farmworkers' labor rights in the 1980s, one lesbian activist told her, "Cucumbers? What's that got to do with my gay rights, Mandy? If you want to call me about something to do with gay rights, I'll come out. But I have no interest in pickles!" Some examples were almost legend. Major gay rights organizations did not add substantive racial equality demands to their platforms. Nor, for that matter, did organizations like the NAACP embrace equal rights for lesbians and gay men.[16]

In some cases, various activists began to compete for attention, highlighting their grievances by belittling, co-opting, or ignoring others. In one particularly challenging example of tone-deafness to the nation's history of white supremacy, the Gay and Lesbian Alliance Against Defamation (now known as GLAAD) announced in the early 1990s that "'Gay' is the new N-word." Worse still, when farmworker advocates showed up to support Pride marches, several LGBT advocates met them with "What are you doing here?" The simple truth staring into everyone's faces—that farmworkers could be gay or transgender, and that each group was "here for equality and justice"—seemed lost. Seeing this game play out time and again, the six colleagues who would soon create SONG felt astounded by the "volumes of cluelessness" they encountered among single-issue organizations.[17]

Something—anything—needed to happen to address this major dysfunction. Black activist Pat Hussain, with a knack for pithy explanations, said it this way: "I'm no longer going to choose between my ovaries, my skin, my lover Cherry, or my checkbook. Because they're all equally important to me. So I line those issues up one, one, one, one; rather than one, two, three, four." It was, no doubt, "a conscious break in the way we've been taught to think."[18]

Hussain was born and raised in Atlanta, and her drive for justice had early roots. As a precocious ten-year-old in the early 1960s, she walked to the corner of what was then Gordon Road and Lee Street in Atlanta's West End and entered a Krispy Kreme donut shop, where people were sitting-in against Jim Crow. When a grown white man came in, bought a coffee, and poured it down the back of a Black girl who was sitting-in, "everything went red," recalled Hussain. "I wanted to kick his ass. I was so angry I was shaking." Having already learned, at her young age, that rage could ruin a nonviolent protest, she pulled herself together. "I got up. I couldn't hear anything, everything went quiet, and I walked out, and I walked down the street, and I went home." She felt "so ashamed of myself for not being strong enough to be nonviolent." As for the brutish coffee-spiller, she wanted "to bite a hole in his throat. That was where I was." Yet she wanted to be part of it. So she "took about three giant steps backwards" and worked in "the back of the room in the civil rights movement"—stuffing envelopes, making phone calls, "anything that didn't put me out there." For several years, she watched the Freedom Riders, "those people putting their bodies on the line, and here was me—just too weak. The shame has lingered for that."[19]

Later, when she came out as gay, she felt ready to act. "The country has treated me like a second-class citizen because I have breasts and ovaries, because I have brown skin." To her, it was simply wrong. Above all, she was not going to be put down "because of who I love. I'm going to fight back." When organizers in Knoxville, Tennessee, asked her to come lead their first Pride march in 1990, she arrived only to find the Klan occupying downtown in anticipation of the march. After pacing all night, Hussain decided she had to go forward with the parade. And she did so in style. Driving a red convertible with the top down, Hussain passed Klansmen in full regalia. When a Ku Kluxer yelled, "There are those n—— f——ggots from Atlanta!," she coolly looked over: "You people must not have CNN! We are dykes. *Dykes!*" she called back. "We're lesbian."[20]

It was a moment of triumph. And now she felt ready for the challenges ahead. Her body surged with a bright, intense feeling, and the Klan "didn't touch me. They just went around me." She came away with newfound determination: "Well, maybe I can step up, maybe it's my turn at bat."[21]

Her chance arrived quickly. By 1993, the National Gay and Lesbian Task Force's (NGLTF) annual "Creating Change" conference had never been held in the South. Ivy Young, a Black lesbian working for the NGLTF, called Mandy Carter that year "and said they'd just lost the site for that year's conference and could they bring it to Durham." Carter enthusiastically agreed, "knowing what a good base of gay and lesbian activists we had in the area." Soon, however, the local conference organizers "started getting phone calls from people coming to the conference asking things like, 'Is there an airport down there?' and 'Why are we holding it in North Carolina? Isn't that where Jesse Helms is from?'" Carter replied succinctly: "We're holding it in North Carolina precisely *because* that's where Jesse Helms is from!" She found the anti-southern bias "unbelievable."²²

To address this bias in a straightforward way, Carter worked with Pat Hussain and southern white racial justice activists Suzanne Pharr and Mab Segrest to organize a pre-conference workshop "on what it means to be living and organizing in the South as gay people, as lesbians." North Carolina in the 1980s and early 1990s retained little of its post–World War II reputation among white liberals for civility in the wake of Joan Little's trial for first-degree murder against her jailer-rapist in 1975, an all-white jury's finding of "not guilty" for Ku Klux Klanners who murdered five people in the Greensboro Massacre in 1979, and the frequent media eruptions of its unreconstructed racist senator, Jesse Helms, inside and outside the Senate chamber in Washington. At the same time, a commitment to economic deregulation drew an increasing number of US-based multinational banks to Charlotte.²³ These twin buttresses of what some hoped was only part of the state's past—unvarnished racist institutions and economic deregulation—coexisted remarkably easily with one another but made organizing for racial and economic justice an enormous challenge.

Segrest, based in North Carolina, was a lively organizer and prolific writer with a wide smile and warm manner. She possessed an enormous breadth of vision generated during the 1980s and early 1990s as an organizer within a feminist lesbian writing collective, Feminary, and Southerners for Economic Justice, a powerful group of southern working-class and poor people. Segrest also worked for North Carolinians Against Racist and Religious Violence, a project of Southerners for Economic Justice, for which she had "traveled back roads that roiled beneath me like a riverflow on a journey into the ravages of racism." It was in this rich context where Segrest learned about the North American Free Trade Agreement (NAFTA). So, when the Creating Change conference organizers invited her to give the 1993 conference plenary speech, she chose the occasion to focus on the intersections between organizations— "why we as LGBT people have to care about NAFTA and other 'non-gay' issues"—and even more strongly addressed white supremacy and the need for white LGBT people to fight it as central to their own freedom.²⁴

The raucous reception to her plenary speech revealed significant divisions within the conference. Some activists were downright hostile. One man angrily requested to know "what the hell does this have to do with my gay freedom?" Yet the speech incited outbreaks of applause and a standing ovation by some at the end. The debates were heated and lasted well into the night. It stirred a conversation about class that was not just about identity (working-class, middle-class, and so on) but about capitalism and how it was working in the current moment to divide and conquer different groups of citizens.

Segrest asked what LGBT people had "invested in understanding and opposing a capitalism that worked with white supremacy and misogyny and homophobia." SONG members had been taught by the Combahee River Collective's combination of socialism, feminism, and anti-racism, so the speech set these issues within a materialist framework. The mixed reception added further fuel to SONG founders' realization of "how badly we needed to get people off single-identity politics," Suzanne Pharr recalled. There was a lot to be done, not only to "get LGBT people to take on race, class, and gender, in addition to LBGTQ identity," but also to "get the historic civil rights organizations to take on homophobia."[25]

Segrest felt undeterred. In the previous decade, she had organized against "a rampaging Far Right movement in North Carolina" through North Carolinians Against Racist and Religious Violence, and Southerners for Economic Justice had campaigned for worker justice in the era of "globalization of capitalism—kicked into higher gear by the collapse of the Soviet Union in 1989," Segrest recalled. Southerners for Economic Justice had been part of campaigns against NAFTA that would open up Canada, the US, and Mexico to what they saw as "increasingly exploitative capitalist arrangements."[26]

Segrest saw the connections intimately and immediately: the KKK sought "to restore the apartheid world of my Alabama childhood" and looked "toward a cataclysmic future, a globe in which only Aryans would survive their wars to purify the white race." Their extremism could survive in North Carolina "because they served the purposes of numb and greedy men and their systems built on dark-skinned people's bones and blood." The previous year, 1992, on the five-hundredth anniversary of Columbus's arrival to the Americas, Southerners for Economic Justice had organized a very broad-based conference, attended by people from Mexico and the Caribbean and translated into Spanish, Korean, and Chinese. "Several of us had been at the Quincentenary event," Segrest recalled, "and I had had a public dialogue with one of the Black guys, who had expressed some homophobia." She had run workshops on sexuality and queer issues, "presenting interesting issues of translation across the various communities involved." The work she and other SONG founders had been engaged in leading up to the 1993 Creating Change conference involved "bringing issues of sexuality and heterosexism into the radical analysis of Southern activists going back to SNCC."[27]

Thus the reactions of some members of the NGLTF against multi-issue organizing pushed the SONG founders further. Though many in the "queer left" had been working together within NGLTF much more comfortably than in other organizations like the Human Rights Campaign, and quite a few were from the South, there were some NGLTF members who resisted coming south for the Creating Change conference. Then, the spiky conversation linking LGBT rights to struggles for economic and racial justice revealed the scale of resistance to multi-issue organizing within Creating Change's community. Carter, Hussain, Segrest, and their allies said "Enough."

In frustration over these divisions, and out of hope for a better path forward, the women formed SONG. Their motivation was thus as clear as the focus of SONG's initial mission: "We were tired of choosing: 'I go to this meeting for this issue, and that meeting for another issue.'" The founders' own lived reality as people with complex identities rooted in the South was addressed nowhere; indeed, in no place that they knew of did people make sustained attempts to tie together the various strands of freedom movement organizing. The South's deeply ingrained traditions of hospitality and the centrality of the concept of "home" spoke deeply to each of them. It was a priority Ella Baker had held high as well—people needed a principal place where they felt they belonged. They shared a common desire: "There needed to be a place that was home."[28]

To create that home, it was by intent that the six founders consisted of three Black women and three white women. All had extensive experience in antiracist organizing. All understood racism to be part of the DNA of the United States, present at its very founding. Hussain put her finger on a basic reality: "If you're born white in America, you are racist. You are either in recovery from racism or you haven't found out that it's there yet." During her time in the US Marines, she developed a clarifying metaphor: white people who did not understand their white privilege were akin to people walking around with an invisible eight-foot-long two-by-four on their shoulders. Wherever they turned, they'd knock people down and then say with innocent astonishment, "Pat, stand up! What's the matter, girl? What's wrong?" Whites ignorant of their privilege, she said, were "dangerous to me." Yet it was not unalterable fate. "The white women of SONG, and the other anti-racist organizers I have encountered," Hussain noted, "have made me much more aware that [everyday people] didn't have to be like that."[29]

To the founders, organizing in the South was central for strategic reasons. Building on the rich braided threads of what scholar Charles Payne called the organizing tradition, they realized the truth in the old adage "When the South moves, the whole country shakes."[30] In the 1990s, the South was more populous than any other region of the country by a long shot. In 1990, three out of ten Americans resided in the South; by 2015, it was home to four out of ten Americans. In a "one person, one vote" democracy, that fact alone required it to be a central part of any political calculus for the nation. And history showed, time and again, the South had been the "fault line" for social movement success. If organizers could find a formula for victory in the South, the "middle of the iceberg" of oppression, as SNCC organizer Bob Moses once described it in reference to Mississippi, surely the rest of the country would follow.[31]

There was no shortage of challenges provided by developments in the broader society. SONG emerged at a time of economic hardship for many ordinary Americans. Throughout the 1990s, corporations flourished in the wake of the end of the Cold War, the NAFTA agreement, and massive privatization of markets in Eastern Europe, China, and Vietnam. Yet unlike the first few decades after World War II, US employers were laying off working people and shifting jobs overseas, and state and federal courts offered fewer protections for everyday people.

SONG cofounder Suzanne Pharr looked at the national political terrain and "saw a right wing building itself based on resentment" among white people getting the short stick.[32] It was a politically effective spin-off of Richard Nixon's 1960s strategy, invoking a "silent majority" to coalesce around all the predictable targets—mostly people who were seen to disturb or threaten the "traditional" American way of life. That tradition, of course, while rarely stated in explicit terms, was one of white male domination. Without naming them specifically, its targets were women, gays, immigrants, and farmworkers, as well as all those who fundamentally questioned the old status quo, such as environmentalists ("tree huggers") or progressives ("communists"). Nixon had targeted these groups in a classic divide-and-conquer strategy, pulling the attention of white working people away from the fact that his policies were making them less economically able to sustain themselves and instead focusing them on abortion, gay rights, and race quotas. Nixon's tactics effectively kept a significant number of white working people from directing their anger at those at the top of the economic hierarchy. SONG's founders realized one couldn't fight neoliberal austerity in separate issue groups—they needed to all band together to find power in numbers.[33]

Pharr had grown up in Georgia in the shadow of the Great Depression, one of eight children, where she had made her way to the segregated Women's College of Georgia. When she was "down to the last penny from my wages" in the late 1950s, it was her professors, mostly single white women, who put "anonymous envelopes containing $10 and $20 into my college post office box" and made it possible for her to graduate in 1961. Pharr, a woman of boundless energy, possessing a fierce intellect and passion for equality, had spent the years since then organizing for economic justice, writing extensively, and learning how those in power used racism to prevent ordinary people from demanding economic justice.[34]

Now she and the other women in SONG saw politicians in the 1990s deepening a well-worn groove carved out by Nixon. These white Republicans showed a special talent for the hate game, using "racial codes and innuendo" to tell poor and working-class whites that social and welfare programs favored people of color, created dependence, and endangered their jobs. Such tactics, if successful, served two mutually reinforcing purposes: they pitted working people against each other, and they often convinced whites from low-wealth communities to start arguing against the very programs that most supported them. The significant, and no doubt fully intended, consequence, of course, was that this strategy fatally undermined "the potential for solidarity among those who have the most to gain by uniting, and the most to lose by continuing to be divided," observed scholar Keeanga-Yamahtta Taylor. Elites in both politics and business generally understood the many benefits of "divide and conquer." It was, as the SONG activists realized, a "timelessly effective strategy to keep potential allies from joining together."[35]

As in previous eras, the early 1990s rightward surge in American politics found its footing in the South. And its opening battle was the US Senate race of 1990 in North Carolina. Here the moderate Democrat, Harvey Gantt, staged his first attempt to unseat one of the most unreconstructed standard bearers of Old Dixie, Jesse Helms.

Long before Republican political operative Kevin Phillips advised Richard Nixon to mobilize a Southern Strategy to create a white Republican majority based on racist resentment, Helms pioneered the tactic in North Carolina as a pundit on Raleigh's WRAL television station. Here he broadcast nearly three thousand shows between 1960 and 1972, stoking white fears of Black electoral domination.[36] He'd fought off former governor Jim Hunt in a neck-and-neck race in 1984 to retain his US Senate seat, where he had first used gay-baiting as an electoral strategy. Now in 1990, amid a recession and the sunset of both the Cold War and the Reagan era, the nation struggled to find its political bearings. Many were ready and open for new beginnings. For several months prior to the election, polls suggested that Gantt might accomplish the previously unthinkable—become the first Black senator since Reconstruction, and do so in Jesse Helms's very own state of North Carolina. Some national pundits suspected white North Carolinians had grown weary of Helms. He no longer appeared able to draw on the support he had long taken for granted. Helms himself seemed shaken, staying in Washington for nearly the entire campaign while Gantt logged over forty thousand miles in campaign travel around the state.[37]

Still, Helms proved far from willing to witness a new birth of the nation. On the contrary, he hit back like a brute, updating the country's large storehouse of retrograde racist smear tactics for the television generation. Trailing Gantt in the polls, Helms ran an infamous TV advertisement showing a white man's hand crumpling up a rejection notice for a job given to what the advertisement's anonymous narrator referred to as a "less-qualified minority." It was effective racist fearmongering. And, for Helms, it worked—not only by exacerbating already existing deep racial divides but also by employing the divide-and-conquer strategy to great effect by vilifying gays, immigrants, and "troublemakers" on college campuses. In a breathtakingly cynical move, his campaign even suggested that Helms was a longtime friend of the African American community and that, in fact, all these new groups—immigrants and LGBT advocates—were hijacking the civil rights movement.[38]

Having injected this level of fear and misinformation into the public debate, Helms's campaign not only regained traction but also threatened the very legacy of the freedom and civil rights movements of the post–World War II era. In the end, Helms won the 1990 race with 52 percent of the vote, consolidating the received political assumption that division and hatred could win elections.

Joan Garner had a unique view across the region. As head of the Fund for Southern Communities, she saw activists increasingly isolated and pushed against the wall. A graduate of the University of the District of Columbia and Howard University, she had come to Atlanta in 1978 and worked for its first African American mayor, Maynard Jackson. By the time of the Gantt-Helms race, she "realized how much unfinished business there was from the modern civil rights movement." For many of the veterans of the civil rights movement in general and the younger women who would soon form SONG in particular, it was a moment that required a decisive response to move public debate in an anti-racist direction. At the same time, "attacks on lesbigaytrans people threaten the entire peace and justice agenda."[39] Too many people had fought too hard for too long to succumb to fearmongers like Helms. They had seen this party trick played on generations of southerners too many times. No more.

ORGANIZING WORK

Initially, the six women envisioned SONG as a resource center for all LGBT southerners committed to democracy and justice. They set up and facilitated small group meetings and workshops across the region in areas they had experienced as "un-networked," where people were doing "their own little thing" and expressing "turfdom resistance" to coalition building.[40] Pat Hussain and Pam McMichael, as the organization's first codirectors, did "a lot of listening" through one-on-one meetings and held a range of small, intensive retreats. Because so many of the justice organizations had self-segregated membership, they worked with groups who were predominantly white to lead anti-racist workshops: at the women's music festival Rhythmfest, at the NGLTF's pre-conference intensive workshop, for the Fund for Southern Communities, and at the Center for Democratic Renewal's annual retreat. At the same time, they led LGBT awareness workshops for people of color, including at the National Women of Color in the Workplace conference.[41]

SONG's founders recognized there were many precursors to their work. Popular education methods had been spread across the region by the Highlander Folk School's work since the 1930s and by the citizenship schools led by Septima Clark in the civil rights movement since the 1950s and 1960s. A new infusion of energy into this tradition came from Paolo Freire's critical pedagogy in the 1970s and from the consciousness-raising groups of the women's movement of the 1960s, 1970s, and 1980s. SONG's founders also were familiar with the folk schools of Europe, Sylvia Ashton Warner's work with children in New Zealand since the 1960s, and John Gaventa's participatory research in Appalachia. Each used "facilitative and Socratic" methods rather than a lecture method, "working with people to bring out their own ideas." As Mab Segrest noted, "These are techniques that have been around for a long time." Sister organizations like Esperanza House in San Antonio and the Audre Lorde Project in New York were using such methods as well. Segrest wanted to see them even more widely used in the gay and lesbian community.[42]

SONG invigorated a vision carried forward in previous eras by Ella Baker, Highlander's Myles Horton, the Southern Christian Leadership Conference's Septima Clark, and the Southern Tenant Farmers Union's John Handcox. The group developed workshops not only for organizers but also for cultural workers—writers, musicians, artists. SONG integrated popular education, the arts, spirituality, and political activism. The founders insisted on bringing people together from divergent backgrounds and different identities and included those advocating disparate strategies, all for a common cause. Also echoing SNCC, SONG's founders centered their work on "how our cultural lives intertwine with our political lives."[43] If Ella Baker had once bridged a difficult conflict by standing up and boldly singing "We Shall Overcome," those in SONG drew explicitly on this heritage with the very name of their group.

People who grew up in the region, cofounder Suzanne Pharr recalled, "love the smells and sounds and tastes of the South"—why not build on this commonality? SONG thus set up workshops and retreats to include southern-infused cooking, storytelling and performance. In one example, workshop participants joined in singing Sweet Honey in the Rock's "I Remember, I Believe" while facilitators asked them to close their eyes and visualize the place they came from. Each person then said their name and described their homeplace. "The place we name is a sacred place for us. . . . We carry that place wherever we go." It was a way of grounding people in order to put them in greater touch with one another. SONG organizers paid attention to the visual aesthetics of retreat space. Music, spoken word, poetry, theater, dance, food, visual art—SONG committed to modeling all of these artistic forms "as a tool for social change and bringing people together across difference."[44]

Find common ground and build on it. It was a hard-earned insight of SONG organizers and Ella Baker before them. It was not, apparently, an inevitable lesson of organizing, perhaps because it warred against too many deeply ingrained cultural assumptions and daily habits, even among activists. Nonetheless, the evidence was clear and overwhelming: being right was not enough. Occupying the moral high ground was not enough, either. In fact, fighting a righteous battle for principles, or for ideological purity, tended to push people away. No doubt, it was good at creating strife and conflict, but not effective when building movements.

For people to come together, they needed to be recruited. And that meant, quite simply, picking them up where they were and taking them seriously. For example, no Black person in the rural South in the 1960s was going to just go and vote because someone "organized" him or her to do it. The organizer had to develop a relationship with people, talk with them over time, eat meals with them, learn about their situations. A community organizer in Chicago explained something equally true in the South: "I had to run with those cats, break bread with them, hang out at the pool hall. I had to lay down on their couch, in their neighborhood. Then I had to invite them into mine."[45]

Only then, within a relationship, could the organizer suggest taking the life-altering risk to go vote—or in the 1990s, to join a farmworkers' strike or march for LGBT rights in public. One could recruit people only by building a relationship and giving people something to fight for—a sense of possibility and a sense of community. Organizers had to acknowledge and respect community members in the full range of their experiences. They came to this remix of Ella Baker's approach organically—Baker died in 1986, and none of them had worked directly with her. Though certainly not inevitable, this mode of operating Baker-style brought a wide range of people into SONG's orbit.

SONG's sponsorship of the Mountaintop Festival was just one example. The festival was a "multicultural celebration of the many faces of Appalachian Lesbian, Gay, Bisexual and Transgender Culture." As one African American lesbian in Maryville, Tennessee, wrote, "This was the first gay festival I've ever attended." Its explicit goal was to "show [that] Appalachians, like all of us, are a racial mix"—not just one thing or another, not just white or straight. Indeed, difference is built into all of our communities, all of our families. And one can elect to celebrate it, right where people are. The African American lesbian from Maryville wanted the organizers to know "how much of a positive impact the festival had on me. Never have I felt such unity." Surrounded by other southerners, "I felt welcomed, loved, and a part of all the powerful energy!"—a necessary first building block to recruiting her into SONG's work. She affirmed, "It helped me to feel good about myself."[46]

For years to come, participants of the festival continued to use their experiences to soothe tensions and build coalitions in their communities. Members of one group, the Kentucky Fairness Alliance, stood by a Black church that had been vandalized by white hooligans. Attending service one Sunday, they heard the pastor condemn homosexuality. As it turned out, it was the last time he did. Having fashioned a mutual relationship of trust, the alliance members sat down with the pastor and simply shared their experiences of work and friendship with many gay and lesbian community activists. In particular, they made a case for how his exclusionary views played into the hands of those he knew "were most in need of saving."[47] If nothing else, exclusion of people on the basis of nothing other than whom they loved hardly satisfied the embracing spirit of Jesus.

Recruitment did not just happen around issues or grievances or demands. Significantly, it often happened around emotional connections, a sense of belonging and purpose. This, then, was the challenge SONG took on: how to get people together, and do so in a way that was empowering—educationally, spiritually, politically. The cultural obstacles were obvious and high. Few had ever tackled them successfully. Experimentation and failure would, no doubt, be part of the journey. But what were the alternatives? The promise of overcoming deep divisions, hatred, and ignorance made all of it worth it, even if it only happened one person at a time. In the end, the reward lay not so much in the tangible results as in the process of building a bigger vision of what individuals could do together. At base they worked to change what "politics" could be.

Over the course of the next two decades, SONG would initiate and experiment with a range of activities to bring people together around a common vision of justice. Some worked well, others sputtered along, and a few failed outright. Creating this new intersectional organizing model inevitably meant prioritizing some aspects of anti-oppression work over others. In the first year, Pam McMichael shared SONG's early planning with a mentor, longtime white anti-racist activist Anne Braden. Braden felt SONG clearly emphasized integrating LGBT work into other freedom struggles but thought "there wasn't equal emphasis on bringing anti-racist work to lesbian/gay organizing." Others wondered why so much energy was focused on gay and lesbian issues—how was SONG going to relate to environmental racism, for example? As Joan Garner recalled, SONG didn't want issues and people "pitted against each other." At the time when they were forming SONG, McMichael recounted, "there was a lot of controversy going on around the gay rights movement being compared to the civil rights movement. Black people did not want to be compared to white gay men. The gay movement then was primarily seen as white, gay men, and that was not the civil rights movement."[48]

The SONG founders responded to these critiques by practicing consistent reflection and reevaluation in order to refine their workshops. They were driven by the motivation to address what they perceived, at the time, to be the underlying problem of powerlessness and division. In what follows, we will dip in and out of their core initiatives on economic justice, racial equity, and cultural organizing to create an impressionistic sense of the early ways SONG put intersectional organizing into practice in the South.

THE ECONOMY, STUPID

Bill Clinton had won the presidency in 1992 amid a recession through his own southern strategy of attacking Black people like Sister Souljah and Ricky Ray Rector on the one hand and, on the other, consistently focusing his campaign on bread-and-butter issues. As his campaign manager repeated again and again, "It's the economy, stupid."[49] Economic justice structured and informed a good deal of SONG's early work. The reason was both simple and profound. Most people, regardless of their political leanings, had little clear information on the economy. Yet it affected so many aspects of everyone's lives. Who got to own and control what? And why? Where was the money going? And, perhaps most relevant to people's lives, what could a person do to address jobs moving overseas, or automation, or exploitative loans, and the resulting decline in income?

Scholars now write about a neoliberal economy emerging unevenly across the globe between the 1970s and 1990s. Yet what did neoliberalism mean in the daily reality of everyday Americans? Unions had mostly been obliterated—

more workers had to advocate one-on-one with their supervisors. Incomes had stalled since the mid-1970s, despite the fact that business profits kept growing and the efficiency of working Americans kept increasing. Jobs, meanwhile, seemed to become more precarious, or simply left the shores, faster than ever. President Ronald Reagan made famous the theory of "trickle-down economics," but the majority of Americans experienced a loss of real income. Those at the top saw their incomes rise. Rather than trickle down, in reality money and wealth were "percolating up." Indeed, the next twenty years would see a historically unprecedented redistribution of wealth from the majority of Americans to the top 1 percent. As SONG organizers stated on the ground at the time, long before the 2011 Occupy Wall Street movement popularized the idea that 1 percent benefited at the expense of the 99 percent, "We need to challenge this economic platform" and "build our own vision of our own economy."[50]

To generate a broad-based freedom vision, SONG ran economic justice education workshops throughout the South.[51] Capitalism needed to be challenged, the group argued, because it created jobs for its own needs but fell far short of addressing "human dignity and human needs."[52] When those needs weren't addressed, people became vulnerable to divide-and-conquer tactics like those brought to high visibility in 1990 with Senator Jesse Helms's "Hands" advertisement.

SONG workshops first explored what daily life was like for participants and then turned the lens to "what should be." For example, using half-completed sentences, leaders asked, "In Helms's North Carolina, lesbians and gay men are . . ." and then prompted people to write about *their* vision for the future. "In our North Carolina, lesbians and gay are . . ." They employed the same exercises around racial justice, economic justice, and political engagement. Such workshops not only provided teachable moments but also fostered crowd-sourced input from participants on "how to get to what should be."[53]

The workshops "showed the connection between the conservative social agenda and the conservative economic agenda," recalled SONG cofounder Pam McMichael. "Some people will say they are liberal socially, but conservative economically. Our premise was that one conservative agenda drives the other." For instance, "if you could get people to be homophobic, they would vote on ballot initiatives that hurt you if you were poor, [or] LGBT, [or] a woman, [or] African American." That reality reinforced SONG's determination "to always work intersectionally," recalled Suzanne Pharr. "We learned this from Black lesbians led by Audre Lorde and the Combahee River Collective."[54]

The scapegoating of Black people as "welfare cheats," immigrants as "job stealers," or gays as "unnatural parents" all effectively riled people up and deflected voters' attention from the real economic policy shaping everyone's lives. While citizens focused on abortion or the alleged crimes of marginalized people of color, the energy expended on such debates functioned like a shell game, distracting people at the base from the fundamental realities of corporate power moves: "deregulation in the environment and in business practices, the gutting of the social safety net." SONG's workshops were a way to fight for control of people's attention: they "got people talking about these issues, and we offered it all over North Carolina and other Southern states, always hosted by a local organization."[55] It was a reprise of Ella Baker's refusal of distraction and her ability to maintain a laser-like focus on getting to the core of an issue: "You don't pick around the edges. You go to the root, and make a new world."

After a particularly virulent campaign against welfare, for instance, Pam McMichael sent a two-page brief, "The Economy and Lesbigaytrans Liberation," (fig. 1). Both poor people and LBGT communities were scapegoats for "society's ills," McMichael pointed out. SONG believed that information "should lead to action," and in that spirit, the group offered these "suggestions for positive action lesbigaytrans organizers can take around welfare reform in your home community."[56]

Role playing, photographs, news articles—SONG used all of these in small group settings to encourage people to reflect on their current economic reality. Then SONG organizers encouraged people to imagine what daily life could and should look like. Following an exploration of basic facts of the current economy, they asked each workshop group to make a list of solutions offered by conservatives, such as lower taxes, fewer unions, less welfare, and corporate deregulation. In their 1994 "Contract with America," congressional Republicans had quite successfully pitted working Americans against each other, portraying immigrants or unions as threats to prosperity. It was a strategy that, according to SONG organizers, effectively kept the deeper causes of most social problems out of the limelight—such as growing corporate dominance without any oversight by everyday people or their representatives. SONG's workshops explored such divide-and-conquer solutions before they helped people develop "different solutions." A stronger social safety net, for instance, would actually offer "a line of resistance against corporate power."[57]

The feedback from workshop participants makes clear that the sessions had a genuinely clarifying effect. I "feel less crazed and overwhelmed," one participant responded. "I learned a lot about holes, my blind spots where [I] haven't thought of something," wrote another. One self-described "frustrated gay male" noted

FIGURE 1. SONG recruitment flyer, "The Economy and Lesbigaytrans Liberation," April 30, 1998. (Courtesy of Mandy Carter Papers, 1970–2013, David M. Rubenstein Rare Book and Manuscript Library, Duke University)

that after spending a great deal of energy on LGBT organizing, it was good to "get me back to the place I started, real life history around class." In general, people who knew how awful the economy felt in their day-to-day lives had a better grasp on the larger picture. At the same time, analyzing local needs made clear the immediate connections to bigger trends—losing local businesses due to multinational trade agreements, say, or serious financial stress on a family due to a lack of affordable health care. If nothing else, one woman noted, "I'm thrilled to connect with people [who are] passionately involved."[58]

Mandy Carter asserted that it was important for the six SONG founders to "take what we were working on and show it wasn't just about being a lesbian or a Southerner." To that end, SONG supported the Immigrant Workers Freedom Ride in 2003 and co-organized the Mount Olive pickle boycott. The group's message was this: being gay or being a person of color has consequences on every part of people's lives. Gay people and people of color worked; both needed economic justice. And farmworkers included people of color and people who were gay, bisexual, or transgender.[59] Quite simply, SONG had to illuminate common ground and get as many people to stand on it together as possible. That way southern "people power" could seriously challenge other organized groups' priorities—like those of corporations.

Thus during the first years of SONG's existence, organizers developed signature workshops on the economy, anti-racism, anti-homophobia, and privilege and on how to train other intersectional organizers. They supported specific campaign-based organizing on intersectional and single issues and directed their workshop participants toward such campaigns. Exploring issues and learning about how they fit together and fed on each other, combined with the "kinship" that participants in workshops frequently reported, strengthened a community of activists who emerged as central to southern organizing in the 1990s and early 2000s.

RACIAL JUSTICE ORGANIZING

SONG activists found a very common problem when working with whites for economic justice: whites often asked why they should be responsible for the misdeeds and racism of previous generations. Countless white people questioned why "affirmative action" should be applied to nonwhites and not poor whites. "I didn't own slaves," was a common refrain. Anne Braden had developed a clarifying response to this in the 1960s as a white woman in the civil rights movement: "What if your brother steals a car?" she asked white people who wondered why they should join the movement for racial justice. "Yes, you didn't steal the car," she would say, "but now you're benefitting from his ride." Much of American wealth was built on the backs of millions of African Americans and Indigenous people who were enslaved, robbed, oppressed, killed—and never paid. In short, "But I didn't steal the car!" simply did not address the reality of white lives in the 1990s, particularly when "the ancient stolen car" continued to allow a white person to get to school or work, to network, to have better opportunities all around.[60]

Since the late 1960s, unions, nonprofits, collectives, and other organizing groups had attempted to address the issue of multiple oppressions. Everyone who had been a part of a movement had examples of discrimination on the inside of justice organizations. SONG managed to address both realities by creating a unique environment for anti-racist organizing in the South.

SONG focused its early anti-racist workshops on LGBT groups. Across the region, organizers called on "white lesbians, gay men, bi, trans and straight allies" to sign up for workshops "that will increase our understanding of racism and white privilege and explore ways white people can become active allies in undoing racism."[61] Their primary task was to shake up people's day-to-day assumptions. Racism was not natural or normal but rather a result of deliberate decisions and "two very large subsidies to the modern economy: stolen Indigenous land and stolen African people." Initially, slavery had emerged from capitalist greed, not racist ideology. Only later had racism been used—in policies, songs, novels, journalism, laws, and ordinances—to exploit and restrict and segregate.[62] Black people were denied loans and access to jobs and educational opportunities; they were treated differently by the law; they owned merely 1 percent of national wealth. All of that did not just "fall out of the sky." Rather, it "was a choice" made by those with power.[63]

SONG's key insight was this: if people began to ask, "Who made those decisions?," then much of the political establishment, including Jesse Helms, would be under fire. They would have to defend themselves rather than continuously benefit from racist wedge issues. Racism was, above all, a product of politics. It still functioned effectively to keep people down, divided, and desperate. Only a freedom politics of coming together, based on a keen and shared awareness of a divided history, could create new spaces, fresh opportunities.

Pam McMichael saw the risks if this coming together failed. She had spent years as a community organizer in Kentucky. Born in 1953 to white parents who "talked and lived the golden rule," McMichael's early experiences led her to interracial friendships; she realized she was gay early on. As a young social services worker, she noticed white women on welfare had better access to cars than black women. Combined, these experiences led her to start attending meetings of the Kentucky Alliance Against Racist and Political Repression. "I credit those Black and white civil rights leaders with schooling me," she recalled. "I was growing by leaps and bounds, and I met people who were involved in international solidarity around Central and South America, particularly El Salvador and Nicaragua." Around the same time, she started going to Womonwrites, an annual conference of lesbian writers, and there she met white lesbian activists Mab Segrest and Minnie Bruce Pratt. Soon after, McMichael started the Woman's Place in Louisville to address a practical reality: without an intersection between feminism and the struggle for racial justice, women's movement work would reach only "predominately white women."[64]

Now, as part of SONG, she wondered what measure SONG might use to determine whether its movement culture effectively created anti-racist politics. The group stated at least one metric clearly: white people who did not actively challenge racism equaled support for white supremacy. Rather than count their numbers of friends and lovers who were people of color, SONG organizers suggested that whites count how many other whites they spoke to about racism. There were countless sites for this work: challenging a racist joke or conversation, lying down on a road to block concrete trucks delivering materials to a white-only construction crew, questioning the materials in the children's library at a local school.[65]

One SONG institute closed with a story about how such actions created possibilities going forward. A white gay man's mother and five aunts went on a road trip from South Carolina to Louisiana. Along the way, they stopped at the chain restaurant Cracker Barrel and ordered. All were in their seventies. As the food came, they each stood up, stating loudly, "We can't eat here! They discriminate against gays and lesbians!" They paid for the food on the way out and in clear terms explained their departure.[66] Such anecdotes inspired. Yet they also taught a hard truth. Everyone has the opportunity to learn from a workshop, retreat, or movement experience that fosters anti-racist consciousness. That doesn't mean everyone internalizes the lesson. Still, workshops were movement lighthouses, illuminating part of the path forward.

Very deliberately, SONG made space and supported people from multiple backgrounds. Growing numbers of southerners did not feel at home in the traditional straight-gay or Black-white dichotomies. Trishala Deb wrote in SONG's journal as "an Asian queer progressive woman" who remained an outsider to "progressive culture in the South." She, along with other Asian–Pacific Islander women she knew, had never managed to find full-time work as an organizer in the South. People tended to characterize her "in relation to" whites or Blacks. Few knew anything about being Indian or an immigrant, much less about the types of discrimination expressed through "model minority" stereotypes or slurs like "ch——nk." Alongside other SONG workshop participants, she realized that "navigating those differences and navigating solidarity within that has been an ongoing, important, and difficult route."[67]

Building on participants' "very heightened vulnerabilities" of their own situations and then expanding the net of understanding and empathy to others through role playing, group work, and personal interactions was part of the "slow walk of the trees" Toni Morrison wrote about in the 1970s. SONG's early organizers kept alive the promise of irrevocable and permanent change in the era between the social movements of the 1960s and those of the twenty-first century, like "the slow walk of certain species of trees from the flatlands up into the mountains."[68] And though this work was invisible *as politics* to those who debated politics in policy journals or to talking heads on cable news, it was the central locale of freedom movement politics by those who made up "the people"—whether it happened in Atlanta, in rural South Carolina, or in any SONG workshop across the South.

For many participants, SONG workshops were the first place they plunged into the messy yet exciting lived reality of what was otherwise hidden by a simple word like "democracy" or "diversity." As one participant described, she deeply appreciated "the small group discussions about what we do." She had time to unpack "what we bump up against," thinking and talking with others about "what we need [to learn] from this to know what we can do." Another workshop veteran appreciated the simple time "away from TV and other distractions." The entire environment and opportunity to meet so many people committed to similar values made a third feel "happy and overjoyed to be gay!"[69] At times the obstacles they uncovered felt overwhelming. Yet many walked away encouraged, emboldened by original insights, new colleagues, fresh ideas. The economic and anti-racism workshops were by nature short. SONG had not yet quite solved the challenge of follow-up. How to sustain the momentum?

WORKSHOPS, AND THEN WHAT?

Keeping people's energy in motion proved essential. How could SONG organizers make sure people's deep emotional commitments, developed during the workshops, didn't fade away? They did not want the void of "not knowing what to do" to drain participants' spirit or allow their newly gained understanding to drift into the confused barrage of largely meaningless twenty-four-hour news cycles. SONG's initial answer was to extend the workshops—to offer something longer, more intensive, and, perhaps most importantly, more practical, something that would fashion specific tools to take home—and to share some possible ways to translate ideas into action.[70]

Throughout southern organizing communities, the SONG retreat invitations became well known and, by many, highly sought after. In order to participate, one had to apply. The reason was straightforward and simple: retreats worked only with a group of interested participants from diverse backgrounds. Far from being cut-and-dried political organizing events, SONG retreats contained many components of fellowship.[71] "An important piece of the energy or glue of SONG events was [also] erotic energy," Mab Segrest recalled. "Flirtation, camp, an acknowledgement of the politics of desire." And SONG requested that each participant bring poetry, music, song, a dance, a game, a story, or photographs. Such personal gifts then allowed people to get to know each other but also turned into vehicles for explorations of serious topics. For example, participants were asked to create an art piece together as a means of exploring identities and priorities. Routinely, this activity was followed by joy and laughter but also by debate, pain, self-exploration, and, always, a broader sense of reality.[72]

Over many years, the consistent reality of SONG retreats was "a format that I can only describe as building family into the movement," Mississippi organizer Natt Offiah noted in 2015. "When you step into a SONG space it's like going back to your favorite aunt's house for a special family gathering full of the type of deep conversations and face splitting laughter you've longed for all year." It was as true in 2015 as it was in 2005 or 1995. One could "find family and build long lasting connections" as well as take part in "one of the most informative and growth invoking spaces I have been in this year." Importantly, people walked away with sharper tools, renewed commitments, and extended networks. A central part was strategic, "to collectively decide on the topics that we thought should be tackled next."[73]

Right from the beginning in the 1990s, such longer retreats "filled an important vacuum." As activist Cheryl Hopkins noted, they were a part of a range of organizations doing what no one else had yet done: "link up social justice organizing all around the South." Hopkins had been one of three participants from Greensboro, North Carolina, all previously unknown to each other. When her first SONG retreat ended, those three had become close friends, and over the next few years they brought an Art with Pride cultural series to the city, traveled to the Greenville (NC) Pride organization to share experiences, and developed a new Black History Month project. It was, literally, one of thousands of examples of people finding new ways to link their work to

SOUTHERNERS ON NEW GROUND

BUILDING ALLIES ■ CONNECTING RACE, CLASS, GENDER AND SEXUAL ORIENTATION

COPY

oard of Directors
aula Austin
ermain Kyles
onnie Leeper
Iatt Nicholson
'endi O'Neal
ernon Stokay

o-Directors
im Diehl
O. Box 268
urham, NC 27702
19) 667-1362
x (919) 683-6395
)NG4kd@aol.com

im McMichael
O. Box 3912
)uisville, KY 40201
02) 896-2070
x (502) 896-0577
)NG4Pam@aol.com

unders
andy Carter
an P. Garner
t Hussain
m McMichael
zanne Pharr
ib Segrest

April, 2001

Dear Friend,

SONG is proud to announce our Second Annual Retreat for Lesbian/Bisexual/Trans/Queer Women in the south. As a friend of SONG, we wanted to let you know about this important piece of our work. We invite your participation and/or ask your help in getting the word out.

SONG is hosting this skills and relationship building retreat for lesbian/dyke/bisexual/transgendered/queer women in the south to share our experiences as women organizers and cultural workers in the lesbigaytrans movement and the broader work for social change. This intentionally **multi-racial, multi-cultural** and **inter-generational** retreat will provide opportunities for conversations we don't have often enough as lesbitransqueer women working for justice.

We will gather July 6-8, 2001 at Honey Creek Retreat Center, Waverly, GA.

Activities and conversations will include: the issues of sexism we face as women in organizing; how we can help move our organizations around issues of sexism; the barriers of racism in building sisterhood; the issues between and among woman born and trans women; how we can better support each other; art and cultural activities; and even some hang out time at the beach.

The retreat will close with a session on concrete action steps that help us as women of all races and ages take our rightful place in organizing work.

Please find logistical information on the back of this letter. An application form is included. The application form should be submitted no later than May 31st to Pam McMichael: by fax to 502/896-0577, by e-mail to Pam@ southnewground.org, or by mail to PO Box 3912, Louisville, KY 40201. For more info, comments or concerns call Pam at 502/896-2070.

Looking forward to seeing you in July.

Kim Diehl   Pam McMichael
        Co-Directors

FIGURE 2. Call to SONG LBTQ retreat, 2001. (Courtesy of Mandy Carter Papers, 1970–2013, David M. Rubenstein Rare Book and Manuscript Library, Duke University)

others across the region, build new political relationships, and develop deeper programs.[74]

The August 1998 skills-building leadership retreat for people of color proved a milestone. SONG cofounder Mandy Carter led the retreat. Carter's first job as a political organizer began at eighteen, when she joined the War Resisters' League in San Francisco. Moving to Durham in 1982 for the league, she witnessed over three decades the many ways people who identified like her, "Southern Black lesbian social justice activist," had been forced to choose to bring only certain parts of their identity forward in political work. SONG heralded an important step forward, but even SONG needed to work on developing spaces where people of color could develop their ideas on their own, outside of a white presence. Carter determined to open up that space.[75]

The people of color retreat initiated conversation, developed new contacts in the eleven states SONG targeted, and produced a set of recommendations. Its exceptional significance, however, derived from its singular focus on gathering people of color who identified as LGBTQ. In the South, this group went to the heart of the bridge building necessary to address sexuality and race not only as equally important parts of one's identity but as interwoven. This made the impact "not just arithmetic . . . [but] geometric," as activist Barbara Smith reflected.[76] Simply combining single-issue political organizations together would not work. These LGBTQ people of color activists were experientially situated better than others to show how and why the categories of "sexuality" and "race" did similar work, both as pillars of identity and as causes of discrimination. They were often better positioned to identify precisely how and why race and sexual identity continued to offer the sharpest instruments in the toolbox to those who plied divide-and-conquer politics—and they were often the most astute in combatting those politics. Few were better equipped than SONG's LGBTQ people of color staff to serve as cross-community bridge builders, and they needed to develop more organizers in this mode.

It was the kind of work that existed nowhere else in the South. Eventually the LGBT people of color retreat was institutionalized as a yearly event. Reaching back to honor the work of a towering figure in the peace and racial justice movements of the 1940s, 1950s, and 1960s, organizers called it the "Bayard Rustin Project."[77] Rustin, a key strategist within the civil rights and labor movements, had worked with A. Philip Randolph to organize the first March on Washington in 1941 and served as the central organizer for its more famous successor march in August 1963. Rustin's intellect and moral compass made him a trusted adviser to people as politically divergent as Martin Luther King

Jr., Stokely Carmichael, and union leader Walter Reuther. The limiting factor on his political effectiveness was that Rustin was gay. And societal homophobia meant that many of the people he advised kept their distance from him, at least outwardly.

Invoking his legacy, the Bayard Rustin Project centered its work on bringing people "to work together who usually don't." The LGBTQ people of color retreat prioritized regular communication and site visits among organizers. From that point forward, at LGBTQ conferences, SONG hosted "Bayard Rustin Receptions." Reclaiming and highlighting Rustin's achievements, the group also determined to "explore the spirit behind his extensive civil rights and humanitarian work." Such deepened political relationships resulted in new visions of multi-issue organizing in conference host cities.[78]

By the end of SONG's first decade of organizing in the South, both its workshops and its retreats were as much about "unlearning" as they were about learning. Time and again, participants discovered the seemingly endless ways in which they, and everyone else in the room with them, had internalized assumptions that, more often than not, proved wrong. And these assumptions, they noted, were variously dangerous and unhealthy and almost always existed for no other reason than to serve undemocratic power. How else to explain the myth of "normal" sexuality or "superior" race? Or people's reliance on experts or beliefs in the rational actor model, in the efficiency and fairness of the market, or in the idea that one could take from the planet forever without wrecking it? Upon further investigation, SONG participants found none of these beliefs withstood even the most rudimentary tests of logic, much less experience. And yet, as deeply ingrained as many such assumptions were, they required sustained effort to be cracked.

The examples of false assumptions standing in the way of effective political organizing, of course, were endless: white people wanted to be anti-racist and democratic but then lost their cool when their leadership or authority was questioned by people of color. Men supported gender equality yet routinely and persistently interrupted women. Straight people of color questioned why LGBTQ rights should be part of the agenda. There was no shortage of nuts to be cracked, of bad assumptions to be pushed aside. The vision and the faith behind it all, however, was clear: SONG wanted to build a culture in which all members had the ability to fully participate in the decisions that most affected their lives.

It is worth reprising briefly the hazards of engaging respectability politics for each of these groups. Ultimately, if gay rights groups insisted that a central focus on racial justice risked alienating white gay people, or racial justice groups claimed that a central focus on LGBTQ rights might alienate Black conservatives, or women's groups risked alienating gay and racial justice groups by centering gender equity without an equal focus on racial justice and LGBTQ equality, such views endangered the activists at the most basic level by splitting their strength in numbers. SONG refused to re-create the environment Bayard Rustin experienced in the 1960s freedom movement. Organizers held that people must be able to bring "all of themselves" to the table. This strategy lit a path beyond the dead-end politics of divide-and-conquer.

SONG thus built fresh cultural channels that didn't exist before. In addition to workshops and retreats, in an era before widespread use of email and social media, organizers sent out mass mailings to let people know of marches, campaigns, and injustices that otherwise might be invisible. For example, Black communities might not know about a particular state policy affecting LGBTQ people's legal standing. LGBTQ people might not know that two southern Black churches were bombed or that the police were routinely harassing young Latinx and Black people outside of a particular DMV office. SONG's emerging database thus developed connections among people through this vital information chain.

"Through your involvement with SONG," one letter read, "we know you are committed to building alliances and interested in connecting people and issues. We knew you would want to know about this action if you didn't already." After a series of church bombings in South Carolina in the spring of 1997, SONG urged "justice minded folks" to gather with the Center for Democratic Renewal in Columbia, South Carolina, to "stand together to send a message" to the statehouse "that we will challenge hate in America in every form." The Center for Democratic Renewal had been formed by Black and white antiracist organizers after the Greensboro Massacre in 1979 to combat the resurgence of white supremacist violence in the wake of the civil rights movement. Even if a person couldn't join that particular protest, SONG listed six other actions that one could take to support the event.[79]

Information-sharing among people who felt isolated produced a sense of commonalty. To expand, SONG set out to map all the LGBTQ organizations in the South so that people could see how much activity and organizing was happening. To share ideas, the group began publishing a journal in 1996, "a twelve-page publication of analysis and education."[80] Both mapping and the published journal served to pool people's observations and paint a larger, inspiring regional picture. SONG's "need and willingness to continually and persistently look internally" also modeled a way to learn from the mistakes leaders made in their organizing. At board meetings, people took turns naming the tensions in their labors. This "major work" allowed them to place "simple and complex truths on the table."[81]

Vision, faith, and reflection, of course, were not enough. What SONG also revived in the South was a reactivation of Ella Baker's legendary ethos. Rooted in their respective communities, SONG culture workers continuously learned from each other and the communities they served. They built on the hard-earned wisdom of those southerners who had come before them. They helped people see each other, discover commonalities, and overcome stereotypes and prejudices. They built a culture of interdependence rooted in hospitality, mutuality, art, music, and innovative politics. They remained patient, a reliable presence. They did not instruct so much as they modeled. And they kept their eyes on the prize.

Two decades after SONG's founding, as the youth immigrant rights and Black Lives Matter movements emerged in the twenty-first century, a new cohort of young SONG leaders would build on the intersectional organizing framework laid down in 1993. (Their stories will be picked up in chapters 4 and 5.) Ella Baker, it is safe to say, would have been pleased. And encouraged.

THREE

Recruiting the Justice League

The Ella Baker Center Demystifies Youth Organizing

Darris Young knows about mass incarceration. For almost two decades, he experienced its ins and outs. Initially, he trained as a police officer. Then he served time in prison. He spent many years trying to keep young people from incarceration. He now works as a community organizer advocating the redirection of government budgets away from mass incarceration and toward education and jobs. His job is based at the Ella Baker Center for Human Rights (EBC) in Oakland, California.

Young's journey started early. In the mid-1990s, he lived in Northern California. He was a twenty-three-year-old African American man on his way to a career in law enforcement. The Berlin Wall had just come down, the Cold War had recently ended, and Nelson Mandela had been elected president of South Africa. At home, Anita Hill's testimony against Supreme Court nominee Clarence Thomas still reverberated through workplaces across the country, and Newt Gingrich and the Republican Party launched the "Contract with America." *The Silence of the Lambs* and *Forrest Gump* played in theaters, while Whitney Houston, the Fugees, and the Wu-Tang Clan pushed up the Billboard charts.

Raised in a middle-class family, Young grew up with the faith that if he worked hard enough and fought for his beliefs, he would succeed. At the Richmond, California, police academy, he successfully passed through a fourteen-week field training program. Everything seemed on course: he made friends; his peers elected him vice president of the incoming class. And then something happened that brought him up short. Without any official explanation, he was charged with dishonesty. "I didn't get an internal affairs investigation, I was just brought before this committee, asked a few questions," he said. It did not end there. "The next thing you know, I was terminated."[1]

When the training program was over, only two of the eight men of color made it—one Black man and one Latino. "Because I was looked at as a leader, they figured if they got rid of me, then they could get rid of anybody else," Young believed. Looking back from the vantage point of two decades, he realized, "It was at that point in my life that I began to struggle." Was it possible, he wondered, that the justice system, largely controlled by whites, would ever administer "justice to people who were not their own?" Wrestling with the crowded, sordid history of race in the nation, he "went through a big life struggle at the age of twenty-three," one that "led me down some very, very dark roads and alleys."

Young eventually crashed in his mid-twenties as the values he was taught to uphold appeared to fail him. Working hard was not enough. Being better prepared than anyone else was not enough. Being on time, dressing appropriately, and in general playing by the rules of respectability was not enough, either. The experience "brought home to reality [that] nothing matters." At a minimum, he felt that "who you are, your socioeconomic background, doesn't make you immune to racism." He came to a basic understanding of contemporary American life: "I am a Black man, and I'm going to face the same things that any other Black man has to face in this country." It carried him to some depressing conclusions: "If this is the way it is, what has all the trying done for me?" He had grown up believing in America. He had studied, had been diligent, and was hungry for success. He had been determined. All this, he thought, "should have got me further, and it didn't." He went through periods of disbelief, frustration, anger. In the end, he said, "I lost faith with the system, for what it could do for me."

Young started using drugs to numb the pain. From there it was a short path toward a series of crimes that allowed him to feed his drug habit. Yet living as an outlaw was more: it "was my way of lashing back out, trying to create fear within people—the same kind of fear that I had experienced." His unjust expulsion from the Richmond police had left scars. He could not find a constructive way to address it. Instead, he spent a significant chunk of his young adult life incarcerated.

In prison, Young began to hold study groups with younger prisoners. He loved to read: Nelson Mandela's *Long Road to Freedom*, Malcolm X's *Autobiography*, Nathan McCall's *Makes Me Wanna Holler*. Reading widely in ancient history, he realized that people from the African diaspora "were not these savage people that we were made out to be, or who I grew up seeing in Disney cartoons. We contributed like everybody else to the development of society."[2] He wanted to know more, to find out how all this made any sense. As he continued to study, he "began to pass these things along to some of the younger people that I would take under my wing and try to teach them. I realized that some of the things that I had been privileged to know," his younger peers in jail clearly did not know. The reason was quite obvious: "Most of them were going to prison at such a young age." In this way Young set out on his second career, this time as a teacher and community organizer within California's state prison system. Above all, he was "interested in stopping the flow of young Black men coming in and out of prison." It became his life's mission.

After his release, Young took on a succession of jobs—as a substance abuse counselor, as a domestic violence counselor, and in a group that worked on preventing youth incarceration. "I didn't think that it was possible to make holistic changes within society, where everybody's included," he recalled. "So my thinking was, 'I have to teach people how to work their way around these minefields without becoming destroyed by them.'" Then he saw an article about the Ella Baker Center in Oakland and its campaign to end mass incarceration. What did that mean, in real terms?

Young learned that the EBC was trying to tear down "laws that continually criminalize people and send people to prison for things that maybe you should get help for." It made sense, especially in light of what he had long realized: "If the playing field was equal, you wouldn't have so many African American or Latinos incarcerated." It was, of course, a realization echoed by millions of other people of color living in America, and one that the Movement for Black Lives would bring to high relief in the 2010s. By the 1990s, thousands of articles and hundreds of autobiographies and social science texts supported it. And yet, few knew how to change the realities on the ground.[3]

Since then, Young's work at the EBC has focused on exactly that: changing the realities on the ground in Oakland. It means making sure that money allocated to support previously incarcerated people's re-entry into society— money for medical services, housing, life skills—actually ends up where it belongs rather than in the pockets of law enforcement and parole officers. It means helping previously incarcerated people obtain sustained access to the County Board of Supervisors. And it means getting young people from the base of society *organized to be leaders* who can envision a different world, one without official fines and fees that have no other purpose than "to keep people permanently incarcerated." Since most low-wealth people "can't pay fines and fees, it just keeps them on paper and tagged."[4] Last but not least, it means creating solid and sustainable pipelines that allow present and future people to get into restorative justice programs instead of jail or prison.

This is the work of making sure those most affected by state and federal policies are at the table when those policies are being created. Legal scholar Michelle Alexander recently lifted up the labor of one such program, created by an indomitable community organizer, Susan Burton, in Southern California. "There once lived a woman with deep brown skin and black hair who freed people from bondage and ushered them to safety," Alexander observed. "She welcomed them to safe homes and offered food, shelter, and help reuniting with family and loved ones. She met them wherever they could be found and organized countless others to provide support and aid in various forms so they would not be recaptured and sent back to captivity.... Some people know this woman by the name Harriet Tubman. I know her as Susan."[5] Susan Burton, like Darris Young, is working today alongside many others to build, piece by piece, the infrastructure of the modern freedom movement.

FUNDI: PASSING ON THE ESSENTIALS OF SPADEWORK

Such political work is often invisible. It's not like a sit-in or a march or a political campaign. It is, again, what Ella Baker called the necessary "spadework"—the day-in, day-out work of building relationships, challenging people to develop skills so they can be their full selves, finding ways for everyday people to have a say in the decisions that most affect their lives. It is never high-profile. At times, it can feel downright tedious. Yet community organizers know that a fundamental element of democracy is to spend time and energy developing people at the base as their own leaders—one person at a time. It has its glorious moments, right there in the middle of people's messy and complicated real lives. Though the presidential administrations of the time—Clinton, Bush, and Obama—differed greatly in their policy aims, all three pursued top-down politics, that is, politics as practiced by established leaders operating in hierarchical modes. This chapter examines the lives of four people who worked from a different premise during the 1990s through the 2010s—bottom-up politics, associated with Oakland's Ella Baker Center. They worked in complementary ways to develop people at the base, one by one, as part of the demos. Like Ella Baker, they worked as *fundis*, growing youth leaders at the base, educating young people for citizenship—not prison.

Darris Young has spent his time since leaving prison in living rooms, waiting rooms, and prison visitation rooms and at church picnics. Day after day, he talks to people affected by incarceration—young students caught up in the school-to-prison pipeline, previously incarcerated people just released, family members whose lives have been forever altered by the incarceration of a parent or child or sibling. He knows all the nitty-gritty details—hardships caused by lack of money or health care, run-down facilities, racial profiling. He also knows about lame excuses and feelings of hopelessness. Above all, he knows that all the fancy concepts about the "war on drugs," recidivism, and the Three Strikes Rule have not improved people's lives or safety in his community. Instead, life has just gotten harder.[6]

It sometimes felt like navigating a terrain full of landmines. And most people had no maps. What was the Board of Supervisors? How did one talk to the members of that board? Or, more importantly, how did one get the supervisors to do what the community needed? What social services were available? Where did one have to go? What forms had to be filled out? Time and again, Young has seen that "when a family is affected by the criminal justice system, they don't know their rights" and don't know what to do.

Young has helped out wherever he could—sitting, listening, helping, facilitating, teaching. And when community members organized to go to the Board of Supervisors, learned how to speak publicly, and still got nowhere, well, Young said, sometimes we had "to step things up to a sit-in where people actually get arrested." His long-term goal remained the same: pry open the doors of opportunity that shut on him as a young person. He worked with others to make sure all the youth talent in the community could be developed so young people could become their best selves as adults. Rather than stay on the bench, he wanted them on the field, where their talents could bloom and they could contribute to society.

The work that Young and people like him do is work that depends on relationships—long and deep relationships. Without the necessary trust, people just find other things to do that they feel are more important. Without a relationship to the organizer, they simply won't come out—to a meeting or a rally or a board of education meeting. "But," Young noted in 2015, "at the end of the day," when people realize that "they're focused on the same thing you are—social justice for the most marginalized people in our society," a group can begin to coalesce. Young and the EBC asked people to come out not only for city council meetings but also for more social events like the Night Out for Safety and Liberation in Oakland. As one social media post advertised, "I don't watch my neighbors. I see them. We make our community safer together" (fig. 3). The annual block party worked to foster "a different conversation about public safety—one that is less grounded in fear and punishment, and focused on how we can build equality, power, opportunity, and prosperity

FIGURE 3. Ella Baker Center, Facebook post, July 23, 2014.

in our communities."[7] And though it's a cliché, it's still true: there is real power in numbers. Indeed, it may well be the only kind of power people have at the base of society.

The Ella Baker Center has operated since 1996. Its campaigns have shifted and its staff has grown, but its goal remains the same: training members of the community, particularly youth, to empower themselves. Block parties, door-to-door canvassing, legal aid, political consciousness-raising—all are tools in its quest for justice. To build community, "we promote seeing your neighbors without watching them with suspicious eyes."[8]

ORIGINS

The driving spirit of the early Ella Baker Center, Van Jones, was born in 1968 in rural Tennessee. Jones and his twin sister "were *in utero* when Martin Luther King was assassinated, Bobby Kennedy was assassinated." The country seemed a terrible mess—even "the Democratic convention was bloody," he later learned. "And I was born nine months into that," early on "intensely aware that there had been all this hope right before I was born, and then all these problems." As a young boy with a speech impediment and a distinct limp, he got bullied at school. At times, it was merciless. But then there was also the kind and determined love he experienced at home. For young Jones, the two merged into an early longing for some king of hero, someone like James Bond who could meet every challenge with grace, humor, and creativity.[9]

His dad largely fit the bill. Born into "abject poverty" in segregated Memphis, Willie Jones joined the military at a young age. It was his path to opportunity and college, growing into a lifelong dedication to education. After retiring from the military, Jones senior went to work at a struggling local middle school and "turned it into a great center of learning, and retired as an award-winning principal," his son recalled. His dad was "tough as nails, with the sharpest political mind of anybody I ever met." At home, it seemed, it was always about learning—and about politics. To the amusement of his teachers, young Van started talking politics in kindergarten. "We had these things called Weekly Readers where they would have little stories for us to read," Jones noted. "Anything that was about the Kennedy brothers or Dr. King, I would cut with my little round scissors and take it home. When other kids put superheroes or athletes on their wall, I had Bobby Kennedy and Dr. King." He changed "all my Star Wars figures' names to political people": Luke Skywalker was JFK, Han Solo was RFK, and Lando Calrissian was MLK.[10] His earliest political memory was watching Shirley Chisholm's 1972 speech at the Democratic National Convention with his parents. She was the first Black candidate for a major party's nomination for president of the United States and the first woman to run for the Democratic Party's presidential nomination.[11]

Jones's interest in politics, driven by his passionate desire for justice, never waned. He first gravitated to investigative journalism at the University of Tennessee at Martin in the mid-1980s, then to becoming a "legal gladiator" at Yale Law School.[12] The patterns of injustice were easy to see in New Haven, Connecticut, in much the same way they had been in the South. "Wearing combat boots and carrying a Black Panther book bag, an angry black separatist among a sea of clean-cut students dreaming of Supreme Court clerkships," Jones didn't hesitate to point out difficult truths. Drug policy provided a particularly glaring example. When white Yale students got caught with drugs, they typically got a slap on the wrist and were told to focus more on their studies. At worst, they were sent to expensive rehabilitation facilities before they returned to school. For low-wealth Black and Latinx youth, living a mere stone's throw away from the Yale campus, the story could not have been more different. A web of institutions with law enforcement at the center targeted these young people and carelessly tossed them into a downward spiral of school expulsion, incarceration, felony convictions, and the eventual closing of the doors of opportunity.[13] No matter how hard some of them tried to escape, the system sapped everyone's talents and spirits.

Jones joined the San Francisco–based Lawyers Committee for Civil Rights during the summer between his second and third years of law school in 1992, working as a legal observer in the Rodney King trial. A Los Angeles resident, King had been beaten without mercy by four police officers as he lay on the ground at a gas station. The whole thing had been filmed by a passerby and subsequently viewed by millions around the world. The video left no doubt that the LAPD officers illegally beat King long after he had complied. It was thus with utter disbelief that Jones, along with millions of others, heard the "not guilty" verdicts for the officers in April 1992. Days of uprising in Los Angeles and other cities followed.

After graduating law school in 1993, he moved to the San Francisco Bay Area to focus on prison reform and social justice. Eva Jefferson Paterson, the legendary civil rights lawyer at the helm of the Lawyers' Committee for Civil Rights, was the first to hire him and support his vision. "Eva was really my saving grace," Jones noted. "She understood that I was a little rowdy and difficult to deal with, but she tried to find a way for me to fit into her system. When she finally figured that plan wasn't going to work, she went way beyond the call of duty helping me start my own thing."[14]

And so, in 1996, Jones and San Francisco lawyer Diana Frappier founded the Ella Baker Center for Human Rights. The mission was simple: maximize human potential by creating alternatives to the "punishment economy" based on violence and incarceration.[15] Their work was part of a robust constellation of reform and prison abolitionist organizations working in California that included the Prison Activist Resource Center, the California Coalition for Women Prisoners, Mothers Reclaiming Our Children, California Prison Focus, and eventually Critical Resistance in 1997–98. The Ella Baker Center's slogan as a small, scrappy start-up was "This is not your parents' civil rights organization." Jones "wedged a desk and a chair inside a large closet" in the back of Paterson's office. He brought his "home computer and ran cables through the rafters to get the operation humming." He now had seen how the legal system worked on many levels. Armed with the law degree from Yale, he also relied on experiences from his dad, an MP in the military before becoming an educator, and his uncle who was a police officer in Memphis. A cousin worked as a prison guard at San Quentin. "That's why I was never afraid to challenge police abuse or stand up to the incarceration industry," Jones recalled. "I knew that law enforcement officers were neither devils nor angels, just public employees who need oversight and accountability like everyone else." He was aware that "most people would not guess that 'Van Jones's came from a law enforcement family,'" he laughed, "but I did."[16]

Jones's energy became legendary. He formed Bay Area Police Watch in January 1995. After San Francisco police officer Marc Andaya stomped and pepper-sprayed to death an unarmed African American named Aaron Williams in the city's Western Addition, Bay Area Police Watch mounted a two-year campaign to have Andaya fired. "This case became a question of not letting the authorities get away with this level of wholesale disrespect and disregard for human life and for the rule of law," Jones recalled. The pepper spray Andaya had used on Williams revolted Jones: "The resin sticks to your skin and it burns and it continues to burn until it's washed off," he explained. "The police never washed the resin off Aaron. And so this guy is beaten, he's kicked, he's stomped, he's pepper-sprayed, gagged . . . , and then left in a cell."[17]

"All of this was illegal and inhumane and yet it was going to be sloughed under the rug," Jones realized. It was a case that "was definitely a turning point in my life. I knew what kind of officer this was; I knew what the [Williams] family was going through and I just made a commitment inside myself that I was not going to walk away." Whether the Williamses won or lost, "this family was not going to fight by itself," he vowed. Andaya was fired in June 1997. "I'll never forget the look on the officer's face," Jones recalled.[18] Too many other police abuse cases since Rodney King had popped up for him to ignore the long pattern. Forcing Andaya out was not just a major victory; for Jones, it signaled hope for a new era of holding police accountable to the citizens they were sworn to serve and protect.

Jones worked not only on police accountability but also with another Ella Baker Center program called Books Not Bars, which aimed to "radically transform California's youth prisons into rehabilitation centers." For those youth already caught up in what later became widely known as the "school-to-prison pipeline," the program made sure they had better access to education and support. It was "radical" in Ella Baker's sense of "going to the root." The long-term impact of Books Not Bars, which joined a national network of books-to-prisoners programs that had begun in the 1970s, has been nothing short of transformative. By 2016, the program had worked with policy makers to reduce the California youth prison population by more than 75 percent and helped close five of the state's youth prisons where guard abuse had been the worst.[19] Such significant victories had a clear impact on the region. Young people in particular realized the EBC was the real thing, there for the long haul. Even more significantly, the EBC showed that sustained collective action was not only possible but powerful. Everyday people working together and organizing themselves could bear significant fruit.

Working to reform unjust law enforcement practices took an early toll on Jones, however. "I burned out after five or six years," Jones recalled of this time. "My journey toward trying to find more comprehensive solutions really came out of my exhaustion with trying to reform the incarceration industry." This echoed the analysis of John Clutchette, one of the Soledad Brothers, who wrote in the 1970s, "There is but one imperative—overhaul! [Reform] means changing the frame on the wall—but not the picture itself." Ten years before Michelle Alexander's pathbreaking book *The New Jim Crow* made such knowledge widespread, Jones followed Clutchette in highlighting the "perverse incentives" for profit within the criminal justice system.[20]

And profit was only part of the problem. As many who would join to form the prison abolition movement observed, Jones witnessed American policy makers, at the local, state, and federal levels, meeting the crisis of neoliberal fostered joblessness with "an increase in policing, an increase in incarceration, an increase in prison building instead of an increase in investing in our communities and addressing why we continue to permit the wealthy to get wealthier while the poor get poorer."[21]

To respond effectively, Jones realized the need "to push for jobs and economic development." Not only that, but jobs and development, in order to make any sense, had to point in the right direction. A low-skill job without a future, or economic development that created more problems than solutions—this was not the way to go. By early 2000, now armed with advanced degrees and years of on-the-ground experience, Jones developed not just in the Bay Area but "across this nation" a call for "green jobs, not jails."[22]

When it came to green jobs and a green economy providing jobs and a future, people had to find a way to work together. In low-wealth communities, activists focused on "social justice, political solutions, and social change."

Their work centered on people power—they endeavored to fix schools, improve health care, defend civil rights, and reduce the prison population. As such, their approaches included "lobbying, campaigning, and protesting," Jones recalled. "They were wary of businesses; instead they turned to the political system and government to help solve the problems of the community." In high-wealth communities in Marin County, San Francisco, and Silicon Valley, Jones witnessed activists who "had what seemed to be the opposite approach." First of all, they fought for very different things. "Their three focus areas were ecology, business solutions, and inner change." By going "green," they mostly meant addressing climate change, resource depletion, and melting glaciers. They wanted to protect the rainforests and endangered species. They were not as concerned with environmental justice—helping people directly suffering from pollution or having to live in toxic environments.[23]

Jones saw both communities as central. He was interested in organizing them to do things together rather than in one side winning an argument against the other. As someone who had credibility and legibility in each community, he worked to bring the two groups into sustained conversation. Initially each attempt "was a disaster—sometimes ending in tears, anger, and slammed doors." Sitting by himself at an abandoned hotel ballroom table after one such encounter, he realized he had witnessed "three binaries." He sat down and scribbled them on a napkin:

1. ecology v. social justice
2. business solutions (entrepreneurship) v. political solutions (activism)
3. spiritual/inner change v. social/outer change

Neither group viewed the approach of the other as particular useful, or even important. People saw reality as an either/or proposition. But what if reality could be better reflected by a both/and model?[24] The two groups could feed on each other, learn from each other. Above all, they could accomplish much more together.

While doing this coalition-building work, Jones confronted the trickiest question of all democratic movements: how to deal with "the polluter within, not just the polluter without." Relationships across and beyond traditional boundaries were key. But in building relationships around the complicated task of articulating common goals and strategies, "our egos often get in the way. Tempers flare." Most people have experienced a wide range of real or perceived indignities. Grievances around different group identities make it difficult to collaborate with other groups and "cumulatively . . . determine and limit the impact of our work itself."[25]

It was a central organizing experience for Jones: "the old politics" routinely take over—"naming, blaming, and shaming somebody else while concealing our own faults, flaws and hypocrisies." It had been a central problem for freedom movements since time immemorial and continued into the future. In 2018, Black Youth Project 100 leader Charlene Carruthers recalled scholar Beth Richie's "violence matrix," noting that "the levels of violence we face daily within our homes, communities, and society are off the charts. And there is no wall to keep this dynamic outside of our movement." The Movement for Black Lives would later put healing at the center of its work. Van Jones, addressing this problem in the early 2000s, suggested people start by confessing "our own weaknesses, our fears, our needs." That allowed everyone to be more open, more empathetic, and, most importantly, more willing to look for commonalities.[26] It was work Ella Baker had continuously done to keep SNCC in sync, bringing people together to focus on the larger goal at hand. It also opened possibilities to address the critique that some in the prison reform and abolition movements had made of Jones as the model of charismatic male leader that Baker had long criticized.[27]

Jones soon accepted a call to become President Obama's "Special Advisor on Green Jobs, Enterprise and Innovation." Yet Jones's blueprint, it turned out, was a bit too threatening for Washington prime time. Facing the largest global economic crisis since the Great Depression, the Obama administration retreated from "green jobs," seeking council among the very traditional elites who had almost sunk the ship.[28] People who brought innovative thinking to the table were pushed aside and marginalized, at least within the corridors of top-level decision making. The very views that had motivated and organized Obama's campaign at the grass roots began to be variously ignored by his policy makers. Worse, the movement that had brought Obama to power was effectively dismissed: on-the-ground organizers were shut out by top administration officials, who told activists literally to fall in line. Obama did not use his formidable gifts of communication to shed light on the role grassroots organizing had played in his own election. Freedom politics and movement building was sacrificed on the altar of high politics.[29]

In 2009, the front page of the right-wing Heritage Foundation website stated that "ending the myth of green jobs" was its number one priority. "And then they came after the idea, hammer and tongs, to obliterate it from public discussion," Jones noted.[30] An incendiary TV host on Fox News, Glenn Beck, called Jones a communist. Seemingly overnight, Jones moved from "visionary" to "outcast"—and the Obama administration did not see fit to have his back. People were forced to consider how expansive the political possibilities actually were, if the administration so fully and immediately caved to old-school racist red-baiting.

Less than a year into it, Jones was forced out of his Obama administration job. He resigned on September 6, 2009. Whether his ideas were too ahead of their time or simply too threatening to entrenched interests remains an open question. If nothing else, the Obama administration surrendered to politics as usual. As Baker had warned, one had to prepare for "the frustrations and the disillusionment that come when the prophetic leader turns out to have heavy feet of clay."[31] Disheartened but not defeated, Jones returned to grassroots organizing, helping to found several nonprofit organizations like Color of Change, Green for All, #cut50, and Rebuild the Dream. His presence in the world of the Democratic Party led by Obama, however, contracted.[32]

Meanwhile, Jones's first organization, the Ella Baker Center, continued its powerful work. In stark contrast to the top-down Democratic Party politics of Obama's top advisers, the EBC provided a vivid example of bottom-up organizing that functioned as a promising alternative. After quickly outgrowing its space in San Francisco, the EBC moved across the bay to Oakland, where Baker's legacy continued to be central, carried forth not only by the EBC but also by a significant contingent of community organizers and activists, including many SNCC veterans, who had settled in the city.

The EBC worked to keep alive the organizing tradition, introducing Baker's principles to hundreds and then thousands of young people in California. Baker's ideas have been applied systematically by EBC organizers to make sure that previously incarcerated people have an opportunity to be "a part of the planning process" for city and county budgets. The EBC also created possibilities for ex-felons to be trainers in Oakland's leadership development and hired people like Darris Young to build sustained relationships with nonprofit workers, city leaders, religious leaders, and youth leaders. At its best, this organizing work allowed those most affected by programs and budgets to be a part of the teams that design those programs and budgets.

Over the last two decades, it is possible to see the policy success of the EBC's work to organize people at the base. For example, the group compiled massive documentation of racial disparities in sentencing for crack and powder cocaine offenses. After years of pressure and organizing, on September 29, 2014, Governor Jerry Brown signed SB1010, eliminating these disparities in California law. The EBC had cosponsored the legislation. It also worked for the #EndYouthSolitary campaign for years, sped up the movement in the summer of 2015, and pushed the California legislature to end the practice of solitary confinement for incarcerated youth by the fall of 2016 (fig. 4).

FIGURE 4. Ella Baker Center, Facebook post, June 30, 2015.

And in the fall 2015, the EBC launched the #CaravanForJustice campaign to promote government budgets that reinvest in communities, not incarceration. The group opened a nationwide Twitter conversation on the costs focused on mass youth incarceration, #WhoPays. The conversation grew from a hashtag that raised people's consciousness to become a profound assessment of how incarceration bleeds whole communities of wealth and income and denies people the possibility to develop their talents. That fall, EBC organizers testified on Capitol Hill using the evidence they had collected (figs. 5 and 6). EBC organizers additionally worked in coalition with the California Green Stimulus Coalition and two dozen other nonprofits to create green job collectives. Ultimately this resulted in the California Green Corps, where young people lead the way in weatherizing homes, manufacturing cultural products, and creating new entrepreneurial opportunities.[33]

To make each of these campaigns come to life, organizers had to be "trained to effectively listen to peoples' ideas and facilitate a process whereby people

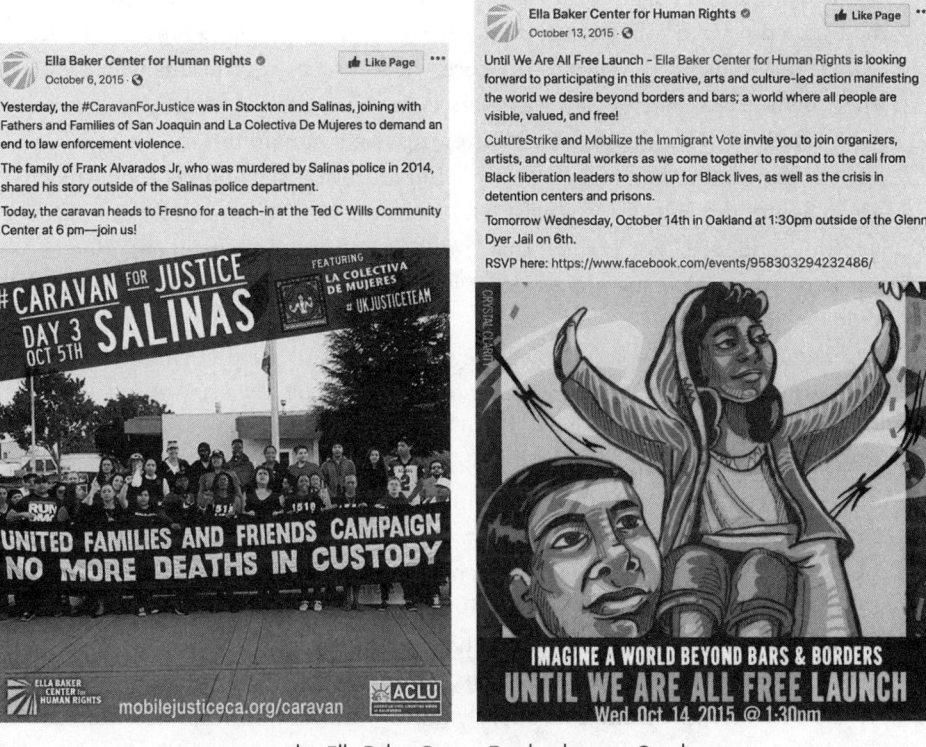

FIGURES 5 and 6. Ella Baker Center, Facebook posts, October 2015.

can dialogue about their problems and take leadership," local organizer Kwesi Tutashinda noted. "Then a process whereby each group's proposals are developed into concrete policy, either with community or city funds or both, has to be implemented."[34] These victories do not negate the reality that over the last two decades, the EBC has endured many defeats. Or that people have left because they burned out or grew restless and needed to experience faster, more tangible results. Yet the EBC's numerous successes cannot be dismissed. The organization grew youth leaders who pushed from the base to significantly increase resources for those young people in California's bottom socioeconomic quartile.

The EBC continually replenished itself between 1996 and 2016 by focusing on passing down the organizing tradition through youth leadership development. How did this work? The group made space for youth organizers from different parts of the country to come and spend significant time in Oakland at the center and also trained local young people. Lanise Frazier, from Boston, worked at the Ella Baker Center as an organizing intern from 2014 to 2015. She had grown up in a Massachusetts home where her mother, Dionne, and her aunts "raised us like hippies to the core," including as vegetarians who grew their own crops. Her family was Native American and African American, with relatives in Haiti and Cuba. "I grew up like a humanitarian," Frazier recalled. Her mother had instilled a pride in Lanise and her siblings about their Deep South and Haitian relatives: "Haiti was the first Afro-centered place to get independence." For Frazier, that "pride in culture that's been engulfed in my family has made me not afraid or hesitant about organizing in the sense of liberation."[35]

Frazier's organizing experience grew in scope and scale during her time at Gordon College in Boston, where she pulled people together as president of ALANA—African American, Latin American, Asian American, and Native American students and their allies. As an undergraduate in the early 2010s, she challenged faculty and administrators to provide a curriculum that stopped promoting racial ignorance and planned and carried out a symposium on colonization, trauma, and memory. Together with ALANA, she then organized and built programs that allowed students to overcome this racial ignorance when the administration didn't respond, a do-it-yourself curriculum rooted in programs like "Real Talk," "My Story," and "Beyond Color Blind Week." The administration frequently acted paralyzed in response, yet she continued on. After college, she spent time in both Brazil and Washington, DC, to expose herself to additional modes of organizing.[36]

Still in her early twenties, Frazier had developed the chops of an established organizer, rooted in a resilient extended family culture. Her mother in particular kept her grounded. Despite Lanise's experience as a person committed to liberation, she found that "I can still slip up into practicing white supremacy as a Black woman." Her mother's consistent presence kept a model in front of her of how to not only survive but thrive. One time, the two women were at a dance show where Frazier's brother was competing. They went to the restroom, laughing, having a good time. Two white women entered the facility and "looked at me with disgust." They said, "Can you move?" Frazier's "heart dropped" and she "stopped laughing. I looked down, and I actually said, 'Sorry,' in a small voice." Frazier recalled that this white microaggression jolted her back in time, as if she was "a little slave boy, growing up like [*Native Son* author] Richard Wright." It went back to the "training of how to be black in America, head down, 'sorry.'" Frazier "stopped my happiness for their comfort."

Her mother, Dionne, reacted swiftly as she came out of the stall and washed her hands. Lanise watched in the mirror as Dionne bit her lip. She "had something to say." For Lanise, it was "so over my head—this is just something that happens on an everyday basis. You engage with white people that think you are a threat. And so you try to do little things, to just end the moment." Lanise had apologized: "Sorry that I'm inconveniencing your existence. Sorry." The white women didn't "even give me any human consideration" as they washed their hands and left the restroom. "And so my mom came out of the stall," turned to Lanise, and said, "Never forget. Don't ever be sorry for who you are." Dionne clapped her hands together loudly. "Don't you *ever* be sorry for who you are." Her mother affirmed, "You have the right to laugh. You have the same right to laugh in this bathroom as they do." It was "just that simple": it was "OK for the white women to be uncomfortable."

Since that time, Frazier has tacked up a note on every wall where she stayed: "Don't be sorry, Be great." She no longer apologizes. She might say, "Maybe we can talk about altering our perceptions and have a conversation or a dialogue about how you might have been offended." Yet she determined to find other ways "to articulate myself," because saying sorry has "so much pain and suffering attached to that word."

Suffice to say that this strong early education was taken to a "whole new level," she recalled, when she got to the EBC in 2014. EBC organizers Maria Dominguez and Darris Young didn't just train her but treated her as an equal. They "introduced me as their colleague" when they took Lanise to meetings with others. They encouraged her to step in "to organize an actual conference, on my own." As she sat with people in the Oakland community as a representative for the Ella Baker Center, she learned something fundamental: "Nothing can happen" at the base of society "without organizing." She met repeatedly with the EBC staffer responsible for lobbying and the staffer responsible for national organizing and communications, and both were adamant: "National campaigning matters, policies matter, but if you cannot organize the people to come together, there's no movement. If you cannot mobilize, there is no movement."

Pressure was the only tool available for people at the base, without other means of power like money or military force, to change government and corporate policy. Over the course of her year at the EBC, learning the complexities of organizing people at the base, she felt such skills were essential to building people-power. It was both "just that simple" and an incredibly complex set of skills that was best learned by apprenticeship.[37]

Organizing young people meant supporting the development of activists like Frazier to go back to their communities and work with youth on the East

Coast, in the Midwest, and around the country. It also required working with multiple Oakland-area organizations in addition to the EBC. Nona Perry, a youth organizer for "Bay Peace—Better Alternatives for Youth," felt nurtured by EBC principles and organizers as well. Perry's job would be widely recognizable in Latin America as a "popular educator," someone who works with people at the base to develop their knowledge and insights based on their own experiences. At Bay Peace, Perry set up an intentional space for young people to think about their own experiences—at school, with the police, with social services. Once a person learns about an issue, Perry explained, "you go out there and you train the other youth about it. And teach them about it." It required action—"a movement of your feet. You have to get on your feet. You just can't sit down in the back of a classroom or an office and then take notes, and send them out." She and fellow organizers trained youth "to get their stories out" through practice, watching others, role playing, and public speaking. The organizers figured out which histories students wanted to learn and then taught them how to research it. Then Perry and her peers experimented: what were the best ways to get youth to act it out in role-playing?[38]

They called such workshops "The Gig." Young people "go into a community and give back [by] doing a workshop for another organization," Perry noted. If an organization was talking about immigration, Bay Peace took "The Gig" to them. The group made up a skit based on people's real-life stories, performed it, and asked the audience "to re-enact with us, and help us. That's how we help find our solutions." In addition to immigration, such skits might focus on sexual violence, school policies, or police brutality. Consciously drawing on the techniques developed by Brazilian activist Augusto Boal in the 1970s in what came to be known as Theater of the Oppressed, these young organizers "go out in the community and help other organizations with theater, [and through] political education."[39]

Perry and her peers found that many public schools served as holding pens rather than launching pads. John Dewey's idea of schools as a training ground for democratic-minded citizens has been alien to the experience of nearly all public school students at under-resourced schools nationwide for most of the twentieth and twenty-first centuries.[40] Perry recalled her own experience, not uncommon among many curious, ambitious, and talented students in under-resourced schools. After a long period of skipping class in middle school, she returned, intrigued by both history and science. She wanted to know more. "So I started challenging my teachers. I started going to libraries, reading about Martin Luther King, Malcolm X, Rosa Parks, Mother Teresa." Doing independent research on her own "revolutionary heroes," she started testing teachers in class—did they know about these people's full histories? This got her in trouble, and she remembered "getting kicked out a lot." Yet she felt that she was in the right: "When your actions are strong and you know the truth, [teachers are] gonna freeze up, and when they freeze up, what do they turn to?" In the time-tested manner of "batting down youth challenges," she explained, they most often turned to "adultisms" and said, "Oh, get out of my class. Go talk to the principal."

Such experiences made Perry "not want to go to school because we are supposed to go to school and get education, but the education is not accurately [reflecting] how we feel inside, and it's not connecting back to our culture. It's not teaching us where we come from as people." She called such behavior from teachers and administrators "adultism"—the act of minimizing or dismissing the good ideas of young people simply because they were young. Adultism, she reflected, repeatedly and continuously deflated students.[41] Adultism meant that children across the country entered school as one would enter prison rather than viewing it as a ticket to a wider world of experience and knowledge.

Kicked out of traditional public education, Perry ended up at an alternative school, Oakland's Emiliano Zapata Street Academy.[42] Administrators at her previous school warned her, "If you get kicked out of this school, you can't come back to the school system." She worried, "Then I'd just be a failure." She understood "that's what they want. The school to prison pipeline? That's the whole setup." When she got to Zapata, though, she loved it. It echoed her goal: "to actually walk in my heroes' footsteps. To actually learn, and then I can go out and teach my people," especially young people.

Perry saw a larger pattern: "We get stuck in this box" labeled "troublemakers." For her, the box represented the idea "You ain't gonna be nothing." It contained all the stereotypes about young people who came from the bottom quarter of the socioeconomic spectrum. It was a "violent circle. You become the stereotype. You start to believe it. So you go into the systems that punish those stereotypes. And then after you get out of that system," a person only had a narrow avenue to get out of the cycle. If you missed that small crawlspace, "you going back into the habit of the bad things." As Ella Baker had taught, you couldn't build a freedom movement without people who believed in themselves.[43]

Perry joined Zapata's "Resistant Art Class," where she learned the techniques of Boal's Theater of the Oppressed. She heard people describe what she later came to understand as the school-to-prison pipeline. She recognized that the class was "teaching the political education piece"—how one might respond to the eternal question, "What are we gonna do right now?" Susan Quinlan, a teacher and facilitator at Bay Peace, "saw a spark" in Perry. "You are really a strong leader," Quinlan told her. Quinlan "asked me to come to one of the staff meetings," Perry recalled, and asked Perry if she wanted a job working with young people, designing curriculum. "Their curriculum was basically organizing youth, to teach political education, to do Theater of the Oppressed, and then do poetry and rap on the side." Perry was in.[44]

One of the important democratic forms generated by freedom movements in the twentieth century was theater. This included the New Orleans' Free Southern Theater of the 1960s, started by SNCC veterans; the tradition of guerrilla theater started by the San Francisco Mime Troupe in the mid-1960s; and of course the Theater of the Oppressed, developed first in Brazil in the 1970s.[45] Perry and other youth activists in Oakland remixed these techniques in their own context in the 2010s to bring people out of a cycle where too many authority figures like teachers, police officers, and counselors told them they were not worth much. The struggle first was to make young people feel, from the inside, that they are worthy.

Perry laid out the situation she faced with her students: "Say a young boy, he was born to the oppressed system. His family probably don't believe in him. His mama on drugs, his daddy is nowhere to be found. So to actually deal with that, he don't know that he has these stereotypes of him—because he don't *know* he don't know anything." He was just growing up in the system. "But he's not aware of the stereotypes, so he's just being them." Perry continued to explain the overview of how the program worked. "He's a young boy. What do he turn to?" Most people turned to the streets. "In the streets, nothing but negativity. Some of it is positive, if you find the positive, like the movements, the organizations, but most of the people go to drugs, selling drugs, to try to get a job." If youth go to school, they often found more negativity from teachers and other authority figures, "so you like, 'F—— school. I'm not going there.' So you gonna live out these stereotypes. 'I'm gonna be a D-Boy, selling drugs.'"

Often the consequence of selling drugs was incarceration. "Now while you in jail or in prison, it's not helping you come out of this anger and this young boy . . . don't have family or don't have support, period." The unhealed trauma did nothing but hold him down. "So what is building inside of him is more anger," Perry noted. "Teaching him how to hustle more, and try to get out of the system, but get out of the system the wrong way."

Once he got out of jail or prison, few paths forward were visible. "The little road" looked like this: "'Okay, I'm out, I'm free. To get out of the system, I need to probably get a job, don't care about what people say, actually go to school, get my education, and move on.'" Yet it was so hard to see the road, "because nobody never taught him" how to follow the signs, "so he end up skipping over the road, and he end up going back to and doing the same habits that he know how to do. It's a recycle of that. Go back to prison, and then end up just coming out." Finding the "road less traveled" meant "joining an organization that will help you, heal you." The first step one had to go through was healing.[46]

Perry's job was to build this alternative road for Oakland youth and make it visible to them. "It's hard only because . . . the young people that we try to touch base with is from fourteen and up." Perry has found, like so many generations of teachers, parents, social scientists, and social workers before her, that "it'd be easy if you got them at age four, but since you're tackling the people that have already been through the oppression and they living in it, it's very hard to shake up their mind and actually tell them that they could make it."[47] They already don't believe in themselves or think they can make something out of their lives "because they already start believing in—and internalize—interpersonal and institutional" messages. It was made clear when teachers ignored their questions or schools had no art, music, or gym classes. It was clear in family settings where time and money were short. Foster care caseworkers reinforced this by leaving young people in abusive situations. The "institutionalized message is already [there]—they already got it, and they've been living it, and it's very hard to prove them out," Perry realized.

She knew the work to be hard going. Still, the key for her, like Ella Baker, was relationship building. She saw an earlier version of herself in the students she worked with. "If you wake up and look at yourself in the mirror and see you as one of those young people, and if you can look at yourself as one of them young people and say, 'I made it. I'm making it, so I know they can,'" one could find the energy, every day, to help them develop their own ideas, their own solutions, and their own leadership to bring about those solutions. "Basically," Perry concluded after a few years of the work, "you just gotta believe in yourself, one, and you gotta believe in them, and you have to love the work that you do."

How did Perry's theater workshops actually work? How did they train young people to solve their own problems as well as see larger political solutions? For example, if a community experienced crisis due to an increase in immigration raids, Perry and her students might make up a skit based on the real-life stories they researched among people in the community. Then they would take it back to the community and perform it. At that point, "we ask the audience to reenact with us, and help us, and that's how we help find our solutions. So the skit always ends out badly, because that's reality, it always ends out badly." They then would ask the audience to help find a better solution. "So for the audience to react with us, we try to find the positive solution, to get out of it." The skit encouraged people to see different points of view and imagine fresh ways forward.

Akin to the role-playing SNCC people used to prepare for nonviolent direct action in the 1960s, and to the retreats and workshops SONG organized to help people imagine a way to work together in the mid-1990s, the theater workshops in Oakland in the 2010s deepened people's political relationships and presented new ideas for public solutions. Once youth were trained in the theater techniques, "then we go out in the community and help other organizations with the theater part, or if they want a political education piece, we bring the curriculum in and teach whatever topic they ask us to come in and teach."

Perry loved the work, but her central insight remained: at fourteen, young people "already start believing in—and internalize—interpersonal and institutional [messages] that are oppressive." It made unlearning "very hard to prove [to] them." Nonetheless, modeling Ella Baker's patience and staying with young people while they learned, Perry persisted. Coming in just for a paycheck would not cut it. "Even though we are in the oppression, we live the poverty, you have to love the work," she felt. "It has to come from something very deep down inside of you, to actually do this work."

Spadework. Building relationships over the long haul through the work of people like Darris Young. Generating green jobs using a both/and rather than an either/or mentality through the work of people like Van Jones. Through it all, maintaining a pipeline to build youth leaders to have a say in the decisions that most deeply affect their lives. By supporting the development of youth organizers from across the country like Lanise Frazier from Boston, as well as developing young organizers like Nona Perry within Oakland, the EBC set up a long-term, sustained pipeline to train youth as leaders. It was vital to renewing democracy in Oakland and provided a model for the country as a whole.

The story of the EBC continues to evolve, but at the end of the second decade of the twenty-first century, the new storylines it has created through its work at the base can most vividly be seen through figure 7. The EBC wants to move the pathways for youth of color away from incarceration, police and extralegal violence, and hopelessness toward futures that provide innovation, green jobs, healthy communities, and democratic governance by people at the base. In many ways, the group's story of building a parallel institution instead of reforming existing ones mirrored that developed in the late 1990s and early 2000s by the DREAMers, immigrant youth activists chronicled in the next chapter. Many groups nationwide aspire to this but simply do not know how

FIGURE 7. Infographic from the Ella Baker Center, 2016. (Courtesy of the Ella Baker Center)

to build paths on the ground. In the true spirit of freedom movement veterans like Myles Horton and Paolo Freire, the EBC has made the road by walking it. There continues to be a consistent draw to the work of the Ella Baker Center: the reward of seeing unlikely organizations rally together to support the common good.[48]

As Darris Young pointed out, EBC's organizing work has "connected me with people who probably I would not normally have thought about a connection with." For him, Van Jones, Lanise Frazier, and Nona Perry, the greatest source of the nation's wealth is young people organizing at the base of society. Working with them and asking a few key questions is at the heart of protecting this wealth: "What makes a difference to you? What difference do you want to make for your communities? How can you organize around some of these things?"

Those in the EBC see themselves building a Justice League—teaching everyday people to be their own superheroes. If young people lack essential things like safety or functioning schools or recreation centers in their lives, the only way forward is to take to heart Ella Baker's premise that "the struggle must be engaged by the struggler." Or as Darris Young put it, "Organize. Come together as youth and be a powerful voice. Watch what you can get."

FOUR

Make Room in the Circle

Undocumented Youth Bridge Electoral and Movement Politics

> I was afraid of getting arrested and deported,
> but now that I confronted the President, I've broken
> through a chain of fear and shame.
> —Jennicet Gutíerrez, in an interview with Jorge Rivas

Some families easily stay together despite international travel because their passports and other documentation allow smooth passage across national borders for both work and vacation. Increasingly, global economic trends mean that a person with access to higher education might grow up in one nation, go to college in a second, and work in a third, fourth, or fifth country.[1] All the while, the education and wealth of these "cosmopolites" allow easy travel across borders to reunite periodically with family.

The vast majority of families across the globe face radically different realities. Without access to education and wealth, they cross borders undocumented. "No one leaves home" in this way, poet Warsan Shire writes, "unless home is the mouth of a shark."[2] They live on the run from law enforcement. They must find ways around bureaucrats in order to acquire driver's licenses, work permits, health care, education, housing, and visas. Undocumented, transnational children born elsewhere and raised in the United States have refused to stay in the shadow of second-class citizenship.[3] Their activism has forced the country to rethink who counts as the "we" in the constitutional "we the people."

In the three decades since Ronald Reagan called on the Soviets to tear down the Berlin Wall, the US has not followed suit but instead has increasingly raised the height and thickness of barriers between its own citizens and everyone else.[4] The rise of federal deportation powers has followed close on the heels of racist political campaigns at the local, state, and federal levels.

Why do such different standards exist between wealthy, educated families crossing borders and those of fewer means? Or between what the US asked the USSR to do and what it asks of itself? Since the 1980s, policy makers could have chosen to expand access to higher education, living-wage jobs, health care, and housing. Instead, American politicians have made all of these resources more inaccessible, redirecting tax monies to a massive state expenditure on the military, police, and prisons and to tax breaks that benefit people with higher wealth. The result: the US has the highest inequality of any developed nation worldwide. Compared to 1980, significantly larger numbers of Americans of all races and ethnicities feel left out—they have little access to global economic bounty, or to any bounty at all. Some 40 million US citizens live in poverty.[5] Quite predictably, in response, many of these citizens have circled the wagons, gravitating to politicians who shout "America for Americans," "America First!," and "Make America Great Again!" They work to restrict domestic public resources to those who count as "legitimate citizens." The consequences for transnational families without cosmopolite privilege are predictable and devastating.

Prior to Donald Trump, no politician soared higher on the hot anger of resentment than Joe Arpaio, Phoenix's six-term sheriff between 1993 and 2017. Arpaio directed his officers to police Phoenix's Maricopa County in a way that provided radically different opportunities for people, depending on their physical appearance and legal status. As one witness noted, when many older whites who gravitated to Phoenix as a Sunbelt retirement city saw "crime on TV, they see immigration. A guy like Joe symbolically saves them. It's kind of like he's a superhero." For Latinx people, in contrast, regardless of age or legal status, Arpaio stood as an urgent threat.[6]

Calling himself "America's Toughest Sheriff," on the job to keep the undocumented out of the US, Arpaio reinstated chain gangs and forced men in jail to wear pink underwear. Arpaio proudly established "a concentration camp" tent city for jail inmates in the summer of 2011, where temperatures climbed so high that people's shoes melted. Amnesty International, the ACLU, and Human Rights Watch all investigated Arpaio for racial profiling and inhumane treatment. Finally, in December 2011, US District Court judge G. Murray Snow, a George W. Bush appointee, ordered Arpaio to cease detaining people "based only on knowledge or reasonable belief, without more, that the person is unlawfully present within the United States." Arpaio ignored Snow. Children, students, and mothers all continued to be detained for weeks on end in sickening conditions and then, if they could not produce documentation, were deported by Immigration and Customs Enforcement (ICE) officers working with local law enforcement.[7]

By March 2012, a small group of six undocumented youth, aged eighteen to twenty-five, decided they had had enough. For years they had lived in Phoenix in fear. Friends and family members had been arrested, jailed, and deported. Few places in the county surrounding Phoenix seemed safe. Arpaio's officers could snatch a person after a routine traffic stop or catch someone during a workplace raid. Even schools and their own homes provided no safe harbor. Yes, as young people without any criminal record, they enjoyed some level of protection under the Obama administration. Yet whole communities lived under constant danger of family separation.

The youth planned to stare down that threat, and to do so in the most nonviolent and public manner possible. Drawing on the tactics used by 1960s civil rights activists, they planned a sit-in at a location symbolizing their plight: the roadway between a school and an immigration detention center. To ensure that the police did not get there before them and block access to the street, the young people designed their action carefully.[8]

In a single-story ranch house typical of Phoenix's post–World War II architecture, the group participated in a multiday training for the sit-in led by two activists from out of town. They role-played like the SNCC people had done four decades earlier, trying to imagine how they would react to provocation from outsiders. They discussed how to master their own anger and fear. They shared food and stories. They prepared themselves to respond nonviolently to whatever response law enforcement might bring.[9]

In a final ritual before the action, they went deeper into the ranch house, closed the door, and sat on the floor, forming a circle. One of the out-of-towners, Benito, burned some purifying sage and encouraged those in the group to close their eyes, relax, and connect with their ancestors as they remembered why they were there. He asked them to think about the dangers and hardship they faced crossing the US border. He reminded them of all the times they had been forced to lie in order to not be deported or to avoid putting other family members at risk. He asked them to imagine all the people who had played important parts in their lives and to focus on who they were that day, a group of young people who would stand up to Sheriff Arpaio's bullying and challenge him: "We've had enough, and now we're going to fight."[10]

As abolitionist Frederick Douglass famously noted in 1857, "Power concedes nothing without a demand." People abusing their power, precisely to the extent to which civil society allowed them to get away with it, runs like a noxious thread through modern history. Arpaio represented no particular exception. "Find out just what any people will quietly submit to and you have the exact measure of injustice and wrong which will be imposed upon them," Douglass observed. Injustices "will continue till they are resisted with either words or blows, or with both. The limits of tyrants are prescribed by the endurance of those whom they oppress." The six undocumented youth in Phoenix had endured enough. Quiet submission, they decided, was simply no longer an option.[11]

It was not an easy decision. They all understood civil disobedience posed life-altering risks. Arrest meant not just jail but likely deportation. Many had lived in the US for as long as they could remember and had few if any connections or relations in their country of origin. Everything they had hoped for, struggled for, learned—all was at stake now. Yet they all believed the alternative, a life in the shadows, was worse.[12]

The six young people—Viridiana Hernandez, Daniela Cruz, Jackie Sanchez, Stephanie Sanchez, Rocio Sanchez, and Hugo Sanchez—blocked Seventy-Fifth Avenue in Phoenix in front of Trevor Browne High School. They sat in a circle in the middle of the street, backs toward one another, facing outward. They locked arms. They began to chant: "Up, up with education. Down, down with deportation." As the nearby high school let out for the day, roughly 150 youth came out to support them, repeating along. A few called out, "Whose streets?," and the rest responded fiercely, "Our streets!" Huge signs lay on the asphalt: "Stop Arpaio!" Fists in the air, they chanted, "Undocumented! Unafraid!" Sixteen-year-old Jackie Sanchez sat by a protest banner and explained, "Arpaio is terrorizing our community and we're tired of it." His "only power is fear."[13]

Now, they announced, that era was over. For four hours, without cease, the chants and sit-in continued. Finally, one hundred police in tactical gear, helmets, and face shields moved slowly toward them in a line. The overblown police response was not lost on the six youth. One by one, the police lifted the protesters up and took them away. "Jail the worst you have?" read one poster. "Because our organizing starts in jail!" Each young person continued to shout, as the police took them away, "Undocumented! Unafraid!" Their work inspired and supported the wider network of Phoenix residents who formed Community Defense Committees to protect people from arrest and deportation.

Coming out of years of organizing against nativism and racism, the Phoenix civic protest symbolized a new era of youth action. No longer would undocumented youth lurk in the shadows, hoping to prove themselves good enough to gain US citizenship. They wore "Undocumented and Unafraid" T-shirts at public rallies; they took the mic and shared their stories with international media; and when federal ICE officers appeared, they yelled at them instead of running from them. "Those sorts of things were just unheard of before," reflected Ali, an undocumented youth organizer from the Midwest. Undocumented youth had "definitely taken ownership" of the movement for immigrant rights.[14]

Youth had tried electoral politics. They had experimented with movement politics. They had explored how it might be possible to organize on both fronts. Many "hard-core" activists had long associated electoral politics with liberals or with selling out. But these young people were bound by no such restrictions; they would use any tool available. They were clear and determined: young people were going to build their own doors to the future. This chapter explores how.

COMING TO AMERICA: YASMIN

To be sure, undocumented youth stories vary and are difficult to summarize or categorize. Yet there are central elements to most of them. Yasmin's journey is a case in point, shining a light on the challenges that hundreds of thousands of undocumented children face. (To protect Yasmin's identity, only her first name is used.) She was born in Veracruz, Mexico. Her family was proud and strong despite little wealth, with many of its members working in agriculture, railroads, or small business. She watched her elders struggle daily to provide for all family members. Her grandfather Pedro always had higher aspirations. He pushed Yasmin's mother, Rosalia, to get a good education, whatever hardship would cost the family. Many times, he told Rosalia that she would not inherit money or land, "but I want you to go to school, that's going to be your future."[15]

Yasmin's mother excelled in academics. In college, she studied accounting. Soon after graduation, she married and had three children. When her husband left, Rosalia simply worked harder, taking two jobs, and sent her first child to college in Xalapa. Still, she could not make ends meet. How could she provide for her children's education and their future, the way her father had provided for her? Faced with this harsh reality, she made the heart-wrenching decision forced on countless generations of migrants worldwide, including millions of subsequent US citizens: she left her children with her own parents, traveling to the US as an undocumented migrant to earn more money, and then sent for her children. Yasmin was nine when her mother left and twelve when Rosalia sent word that Yasmin and her older brother should come join her in North Carolina.[16]

Yasmin did not know what the journey would entail, though she had seen people hustle onto trains headed north from Veracruz. Her family had a long history of helping migrants—giving them food and clothing and arranging for them to get a shower and some rest in their church before moving on. Yasmin knew her mother had made the trek across the border. And she had found out that her mom was not willing to talk about it. Still, everyone knew that, back then, "it was not as bad as after 9/11," when border enforcement shifted from being a site of labor regulation to one focused on national security. After 2001, migration became "a lot harder."

Yasmin and her older brother, Cesar, only knew that they wanted to reunite with Rosalia. Prepared with little more than a backpack, a few dollars, and some cautionary advice from friends and family, they rode a bus to Mexico City, took a plane to Tijuana, and then rode another bus to the northwest Mexican city of Altar, due south of Phoenix. In hindsight, Yasmin almost incredulously recalls the fact that at twelve, "I didn't know about drugs, alcohol, and prostitution." Suddenly, at the border, she faced all of it.[17]

In Altar, people were everywhere. No one seemed to have a place to stay. There were no hotels or motels available. Coyotes—smugglers—approached as soon as people arrived, whispering, "I can cross you. It will cost this much. It's only an hour walk. A three-hour walk at most." The first night they slept in a house that rented "floor space" to sleep and then found a very small apartment where they were able to stay. The plan was to wait for the same man who years before had helped their mother cross. As they waited, Yasmin overheard men exploit women and girls: "Just let me do this, then I help you over the border." Others were raped. She saw small children, even younger than herself, on their own, trying to cross. The environment felt unbearably unsafe, yet some people demonstrated amazing feats of grace and support. She felt "naive. Just in shock." Her brother warned her: "You're not going to understand some things. You know what's wrong and what's right. Just follow your gut." It was more than she could comprehend. She was thankful Cesar was there to protect her.

The siblings' anxiety mounted as they waited. They were running out of what little money they had, eating "very bad things" to stay alive. They quickly grew exhausted from having to "wait for the right time to cross" due to border patrol. Finally their mother's guide arrived and led them on what became a harrowing trek. Small as Yasmin still was, she hid in a compartment under the car as they drove across the US-Mexico border. Passing landmarks on the US side, she heard others say, "After this place, we're going to be safe." Then their luck ran out. An hour into the trip, law enforcement pulled them over, took them to the detention center, and "in no time" transported them back to Mexico.

Back in Altar, Yasmin and Cesar together decided that they would not wait for another ride. With their last remaining funds, they bought book bags, extra clothes, and canned food. Along with a small group of others, they set off. Yasmin carried two gallons of water, one in each hand, and a backpack. Soon, the sun beating down, they came across the first evidence of migrants who had not made it: crosses in the desert, which marked migrant deaths, and old abandoned clothes and backpacks. "It was hard to realize," she remembered, "to make the connection to the people [jumping on] the train in Veracruz," her hometown. "They went through my state, they go all the way up, and then they have to walk. People have to cross many borders, and then they might not even make it. That was hard."[18]

To her great relief, their particular group of migrants was very supportive of one another. "No one [was] left behind; everyone helped each other." The informal leader of the group, José, knew Yasmin's mother, easing her fears. Still, she remembered moments that could have ended it all. Marching along the second night to avoid the heat or be seen, they first heard a helicopter, then saw its searchlights cross the desert terrain. "Quick, you have to run!" one in the group yelled to her. "I was really scared; you couldn't see anything," Yasmin recalled. "I felt someone grabbing my hand and pulling me down, hiding me in some bushes." For several minutes, which felt like an eternity, Yasmin lost track of her brother, Cesar. When the helicopter finally passed, they regrouped and kept moving. They walked for three full nights. On the fourth day, exhausted, sunburned, and scared, they arrived at an Indigenous homeland where they were allowed to stay hidden behind trees and bushes until a car came to drive them to a safe house. Yasmin remained there for three weeks to recover from bruises, thorns, hunger, and exhaustion. When she was ready to travel again, the group leader drove them to North Carolina to reunite with Rosalia.

The family reunion was exuberantly happy, and they quickly settled into a routine. They needed money. Rosalia found Cesar a job, then another. Both mother and son now worked two jobs. Yasmin, meanwhile, started eighth grade halfway through the year. She adjusted quickly.

Yasmin excelled in school and made friends. When she was sixteen, she completed driver's education in school and went to get her permit. It was a harsh reality, a legal smack in the face, when she learned that North Carolina no longer issued permits to undocumented immigrants. "I was really mad," she remembered. It didn't make sense to the teenager—all of her friends were able to get their licenses, even the ones who had cheated on the test. Yasmin had studied and easily passed without cheating. "I took the classes. I took the exam. I took driver's ed. I know how to drive. But now I cannot do it." It was the first time she personally experienced her limitations as undocumented: "Even if you can do [the work], there are going to be barriers." In rapid succession, more obstacles followed: she was an honors student in school but learned that community college was not an option for her as an undocumented student. She found out that she would have to pay out-of-state tuition for a four-year university. "All these little accomplishments that I've made, and now I cannot go forward."[19]

A slightly older student, Heriberto, took Yasmin to visit a nearby Quaker school, Guilford College, in Greensboro. As a student there himself, he told her about a scholarship program for students in financial need. She entered Guilford on a Bonner Scholarship. She worked hard. "I tried to do everything that I could, because there were many things I couldn't do. I felt I needed to make the best out of this time." Guilford seemed like a rare and cherished oasis: "I have access to resources, and I need to make it while I'm here, because in the real world, it might be hard." Yasmin wanted to study business but couldn't do a summer internship in a business or accounting firm "because I had no license, no social [security number], no ID, nothing. So I did my internships in nonprofits." She worked with Student Action with Farmworkers in Durham and the American Friends Service Committee in Greensboro.

Toward the end of senior year, after visiting her mother, she was on her way back to Guilford. Just weeks away from graduation, she felt good, confident of the future, proud that she had managed to work while going to college and keeping her grades up. She was pondering what she could do next when she heard a siren wailing behind her. Startled, she looked into her rearview mirror. A police cruiser signaled her to pull over. Her heart sank. "I saw my whole life go by in a few seconds," she recalled. "Walking the desert, coming here, struggling in high school, everything we did to get through college." Now six weeks from the finish line that her grandfather had worked for two generations to secure, her attempt seemed over.

The officer asked for her license and registration—she didn't have them. He looked at her in a way that she felt "he knew" that she was undocumented. He considered the car, noticing it was "full of things for school." Then he asked, "Where are you going?" When Yasmin answered truthfully, that she was on her way back to college for her last six weeks before graduation, he said, "Call someone to come get you." He drove off. Forty-five minutes later, her supervisor from the internship at the American Friends Service Committee came to pick her up. The woman and Yasmin made arrangements for Yasmin's car to be towed. Then Yasmin got into her mentor's car.

It was a story often told of the US: at its best, a young person can triumph in the face of many hardships, supported by members of the community. One could see it as a moment of solidarity, of opportunities provided to those who work hard, independent of creed or status. It was also a moment that showed authority in its best light, knowing how to distinguish between rigid rules and doing the right thing. Not least of all, it was a moment of human connection and compassion. Unfortunately, it was not a moment young immigrants in America could count on. Yasmin went back to college and successfully graduated, grateful for a community of support and to a police officer who found a way to listen to the better angels of his nature. Countless others have no such fortune—more than 6 million people have been deported since 1996, a dramatic increase over previous decades.[20] A destructive consequence: all too many are forced to live in fear, continuously anticipating what threat may lie around the next corner.

WHO COUNTS? THE BACKSTORY

Yasmin's experience echoes in every state of the union. There are an estimated 800,000 young undocumented immigrants who have recently graduated from the US public school system. As of this printing, only twelve states and the District of Columbia allow undocumented immigrants to obtain driver's licenses; only twenty have tuition equity laws that allow undocumented students the same access to in-state tuition as their peers. For undocumented youth in the majority of US states, without social security numbers, driver's licenses, or college options, opportunities to move on and up are few and far between. Another estimated 1 million undocumented children are currently enrolled in American public schools. They find themselves in limbo—not just legally and culturally but personally. None have a sense of safety or predictability in their lives. Even those who do all the right things in school and get high GPAs often find themselves locked out of opportunities for college. None of these young immigrants have a way to plan for the future, the only certainty in their lives being unpredictability.[21]

The political and cultural environment, meanwhile, has turned increasingly hostile to their presence. Prior to the 1965 Immigration and Naturalization

Act, a white supremacist "dual labor market" undergirded the US economy, where the federal government labeled European migrants "immigrants" and gave them access to legalization and upward mobility while categorizing Latin American and Asian migrants as "temporary workers" for railroads or for planting and harvesting crops or as day laborers. The US government denied the latter equal access to citizenship.[22]

After 1965, a new immigration system emerged, criminalizing the undocumented. As law, the system is color-blind—it eliminated the racist language of the Immigration Act of 1924. Yet in practice, the vast majority of those convicted of federal immigration crimes are from Latin America. Despite the fact that most Americans believe that immigration reform is vital, Congress has not managed to pass a single immigration bill since 1986. Paperless, and thus stateless, undocumented youth are unable to access most services, and most rights, that are commonly afforded citizens. "They can't vote, serve on a jury, work, live in public housing, or receive public benefits," notes scholar Aviva Chomsky, and their "stigmatization and exclusion create a vicious circle of further stigmatization and exclusion."[23]

As comprehensive legislation reform failed to emerge at the federal level, many states have stepped in to fill the void. From Arizona to Illinois, from California to New York, states with significant populations of undocumented people have pursued two contradictory strategies—the first in fits and spurts, the second with a vengeance. First, led by California, several states have attempted to create pathways for undocumented youth to become legal residents and then US citizens. These efforts favor those who came as very young people, who were educated here, and who claim a primary identity as a member of the United States. The second strategy centers on finding, prosecuting, and deporting undocumented immigrants. Widely reported in one dire story after another, this effort has wrenched apart hundreds of thousands of families, put children as young as three and four into detention centers by themselves and deported them alone, and has yanked thousands of children and teenagers out of schools. Among children who are US citizens by birth, some 4.5 million have one or more undocumented parents. In the climate ICE creates of "we can get you anytime," it is astonishingly hard for these children to feel safe and secure. When they can be picked up while waiting for a school bus, traveling with their sports team to an away game, or simply sitting in their own home, the resulting climate of fear is wholly debilitating. On any given day, over thirty thousand of these parents and children reside in detention centers. Even youth who have withstood gangs, sexual violence, and political threats, traveling thousands of miles all by themselves in search

FIGURE 8. Boy separated from parents at US-Mexico border, June 12, 2018. (Photo by John Moore/Getty)

of an opportunity to live and reunite with their parents, are now routinely put into detention camps shortly after being caught at the border.[24]

Law enforcement agents have increasingly refused to participate in such brutal policies. Antar Davidson quit the Tucson detention facility run by Southwest Key Programs when his boss told him to stop young children separated from their parents from hugging one another; North Carolina governor Roy Cooper recalled the National Guard troops sent to the US-Mexico border in protest. Cooper simply stated, "The cruel policy of tearing children away from their parents requires a strong response."[25]

Since the 1990s, some politicians have tried to find solutions within the political system. In 2001, a group of Democrats and Republicans first introduced to Congress bipartisan legislation called the Development, Relief, and Education for Alien Minors Act, or DREAM Act. Immigration activists as well as mainstream politicians believed it had a good chance of becoming law. It was distinctly middle-of-the-road, its clauses rewarding achievements that reflected common American values: students who had high grades or a good military record could become US citizens. Yet despite years of organizing and campaigning, the legislation failed to pass Congress in 2007 and again in 2010.[26]

There was, perhaps, a larger context for the failure. National legal systems have not evolved to keep up with global economics. Consistent, coherent immigration policies are largely absent in high-wealth countries worldwide. Goods, money, and people traveled across borders for millennia, but with the warp-speed increase provided by accessible air travel and the Internet, the rapidity and scale of trade, finance, and the movement of people inevitably translated into a loss of control and power by national governments. Global elites—the cosmopolites—increasingly float above and outside of the power of national governments. Policies intended to contain and police the majority of global migrants who can't access the wealth or education of cosmopolites are a way to reclaim national authority in a sphere where it is clearly waning. In the US, this has meant that immigrant youth are caught in the political sinkhole generated by leaders in both parties.[27]

As nations largely fail "to address the increasing numbers of non-state actors—transnational corporations, guerilla fighters, drug cartels, or transnational flows of migrants"—we have entered an era of global apartheid. Documents provide free passage to the few, while the many are locked into bottom-rung enclaves. Consisting of a mere 10 percent of the world's population, the seven largest advanced economies, also known as the G7, claim 40 percent of world GDP for themselves. The gap between the world's well-off and the world's poor remains stark and continues to widen.[28]

Increasingly, the democratic ideal of citizenship handed down by Western political theorists in the seventeenth, eighteenth, and nineteenth centuries, where increasing numbers of people are admitted to the circle of "free, enlightened individuals pursuing their own destinies," seems unworkable. This is true across the political spectrum. For those inside high-wealth nations who want to restrict citizenship, the Enlightenment view is simply too idealistic. They want to hold onto citizenship as a scarce resource and guard it. In contrast, for those interested in expanding the circle of belonging, the language trumpeting "you can be anything you want to be" and "you are in charge of your own destiny" is a problem. "There is no such thing as [individual] sovereignty," notes legal scholar john a. powell. There is only interdependence. "We are in relationship with each other—it can be a good relationship or a bad relationship, but we are in relationship to each other." Following the latter path meant a massive conceptual shift for Western jurisprudence. Neither nationalists nor advocates for global humanity felt like the five-hundred-year project of the Enlightenment was up to the task.[29]

Battered by these vast global shifts, students like Yasmin strive to be model citizens. The cold truth is that large numbers of nationalists, in and out of power, consider students like Yasmin as second-class—as people who are disposable, tolerated perhaps as cheap labor but only when needed, and certainly not eligible for first-class citizenship rights. It is true that since the 1982 *Plyer v. Doe* Supreme Court decision, all undocumented children are guaranteed access to K–12 education. Yet only fourteen out of fifty states expressly allow them in-state college tuition. Four states have explicitly banned undocumented students from receiving in-state tuition, and three states—South Carolina, Alabama, and Georgia—have banned undocumented students from attending certain public colleges and universities altogether.[30] Politicians passed such legislation by invoking the nonsensical specter of college-bound immigrant youth breaking the law—they were good, perhaps, for mowing the lawn or processing the chicken but not for higher education or the right to vote.[31]

Observing and describing dehumanization, of course, is quite different from experiencing it on a daily basis. At a rally for immigrant rights in Phoenix in 2009, hip-hop artist Zack de la Rocha choked up. The consistent dehumanization "inflicts in us a collective wound." Congress's refusal to pass the DREAM Act or any other immigration reform has left undocumented youth in the US with almost no options. They tried to lobby; they made logical cases to their elected representatives. But these legislators proved unable or unwilling to make a path for them to belong. "The only way to heal from those wounds and address those assaults on our dignity," de la Rocha stated, "is to resist."[32]

RESISTANCE CITIZENSHIP

Cristina Jimenez's world came to a halt in 2008. She and her fiancé, Walter Barrientos, had first met in 2004, working for the New York Immigrant Coalition. Now Barrientos was stopped on an Amtrak train in the Northeast while en route to an immigrant rights conference. It was 3 a.m. An ICE official came through the car, asking everyone with darker skin for identification. The brief encounter ended when Barrientos could not provide documentation. The officer pulled him off the train and detained him in Buffalo.

Learning about his incarceration by phone, Cristina went from shock to "fear—real in a new way." She had witnessed arrests and detentions many times. Most of her coworkers had family and friends who lived in a state of constant apprehension. She spent a majority of her waking hours helping people in the immigrant community—to find jobs or schools for their children, to get their papers straight, to interact with the authorities. Still, this was different. It hit home like never before. Walter was the man with whom she planned to spend her life. Now they were on the verge of a forced separation that could last years—even decades.³³

Building on her many connections, Jimenez and her friends immediately began to mobilize. Staying in fear, or frozen in place, was not an option. Instead, she said, "we organized." Hundreds in her network started putting pressure on law enforcement, calling, marching, and setting up vigils outside Buffalo Federal Detention Center in Batavia, New York. They made visible for anyone to see: here was another law-abiding immigrant whom ICE had detained for no reason other than missing documentation.³⁴

It paid off; "Barrientos was out in five days." It was a tremendous relief for Jimenez. She had witnessed firsthand the power of organized collective action. Movement power worked where electoral politics had failed—just like SNCC's "jail no bail" strategy in 1961. And yet fear kept nagging. She realized that solace for her trepidation could lie only in an organized community. The day Barrientos was released, she later recalled, was the day in which "I married the movement." No one, she decided, should "live through that fear of losing a loved one." Had they deported Barrientos, her plans, her dreams, and her life with him would likely have been over. And it was the power of an organized community that prevented his removal, at least for now. For her, the goal of the youth immigration rights movement was thus straightforward: "We organize our community to keep people together."³⁵

Describing this story later, in the fall of 2015 at a voting rights conference in Durham, North Carolina, Jimenez shared and two hundred movement activists listened carefully. People filled the room: youth from the Black Lives Matter movement and the Dream Defenders, activists involved in the budding Moral Monday movement, and, not least of all, veterans from SNCC and the Congress of Racial Equality, elders from the freedom movement. When it was her time to speak, Jimenez calmly pointed out that "all of you are gathered here at this conference to talk about citizenship and voting." For Jimenez, as managing director of United We Dream, the nation's largest youth-led immigrant rights organization, the world posed a different set of profound challenges. "Voting is *not* at the core of our consciousness at United We Dream." Instead, within the large community of young immigrants, "our daily experiences are full of fear of deportation." Their primary concern was keeping their families together.³⁶

Youth immigrant activists had to work in ways remarkably similar to those who participated in the nineteenth-century Underground Railroad—do everything possible to keep families intact or reunite them after forced separation. And like in the days of the early US republic, where African Americans, free and enslaved, had to build what historians Vincent Harding and Paul Ortiz called a strong "culture of resistance" through organizing churches, schools, and mutual aid societies, immigrant communities have done the same in the twenty-first century. (In response, where some poorer whites served in slave patrols and vigilante groups across the 1800s, they laid "claim to a tenuous white citizenship" earned "by the protection of wealthier white property." Similarly some low-wealth whites in the twenty-first century earn that badge by policing the border.)[37]

Jimenez now spoke to the inheritors of that resistance tradition. She described arriving in the US from Ecuador in 1998. She was just a child, but she knew, from day one, that plenty of people felt she did not belong. She learned to avoid authorities and that no place was totally safe. If she or others were stopped by the police, it could easily mean the end of their life in the US.[38]

This fear was built into her existence. Yet so was her resolute desire to end that dread—not just for her but for all young immigrants, and children in particular. She wanted to help overcome widespread ignorance in the larger population about the immigrant community. Questioning the weirdly contradictory nature of anti-immigrant rhetoric and policies, she noticed that many anti-immigrant voices originated with second- or third-generation US citizens. In the end, she wanted to challenge close-minded ideas about who belongs. What did it mean to be American? Who counted?

It was a question that had particular resonance for SNCC veteran Bob Moses, listening quietly in the back of the room. Now eighty, he had spent six decades working persistently with those who made up what he referred to as the "bottom quarter" of the nation's socioeconomic spectrum. He had long examined how US law and policy excluded the most vulnerable. One path to freedom he and fellow organizers had opened up in the 1960s was to bring "one person, one vote" closer to reality on the ground. Now he heard Jimenez calling to voting rights activists fifty years later to open up US society in a remarkably similar way.

Moses and Jimenez began to talk one-on-one and in small group settings over the four-day conference and then jointly presented their questions to the larger group. Were people in the room willing to open up US borders for the thousands who were desperate—fleeing poverty, persecution, sometimes the imminent threat of death?[39] Could they make space for those who had grown up in the US but, as undocumented youth, were frequently told that they were not equal? Moses and Jimenez asked the group assembled to listen to Bernice Johnson Reagon's 1968 recording "Room in the Circle," passing out a sheet of lyrics while the sound system played.

> Black people taken from an ancient land
> Suffered trials by cruel White hands
> In this circle, there's gotta be room for them,
> Move on over, make more (a little) room for them
> There'll be trouble if there's no room for them . . .
>
> Vietnamese fighting for their lives
> Fighting for their land, not standing by
> They can't make it if there's no room for them.
> Move on over, make more (a little) room for them
> It won't hurt you if there's more room for them . . .
>
> Little brown boy with straight black hair
> In India's land there's no food there
> He can't make it 'cause there's no room for him.
> Move on over, make more (a little) room for them
> There'll be trouble if there's no room for him . . .
>
> Seneca, Black Hawk, Cherokee
> Choctaw, Cheyenne, Sioux, Pawnee
> They can't make it if there's no room for them.
> Move on over, make a little room for them
> It won't hurt you to make a little room for them.
> Way overdue now, there's gotta be room for them . . .
>
> White man, we know you don't know how
> To save the circle, let me tell you how:
> Loose your hold, there's gotta be room for all.
> The circle will break, man, if there's not room for all.
> Move on over, make a little room for all
> In this circle, there's gotta be room for all.
>
> Save the circle, make more room for all
> In this circle, there's gotta be room for all.[40]

Encouraging everyone to sing these words together, Jimenez and Moses asked whether those in the room were committed to guarding the borders as people with the good fortune to be born inside. Or could they make room for Jimenez and others like her?

Jimenez pushed the group to imagine families ripped apart, dreams shattered, and individual lives disrespected and ruined. For some, "the immigration debate" could remain abstract. For her, the consequences were dire, both individually and for her community. In her shoes, organized resistance could be seen as not just the healthiest or most productive political response but also the most ethical.

THE UNAFRAID

Beginning in the 1990s, groups of undocumented students followed the rules of active citizens working within the electoral process. They lobbied members of Congress for years. Groups like the Latino Union of Chicago, Puente Arizona, the Asian American Justice Center, and the National Day Laborer Organizing Network carried out the spadework, passing down intergenerational knowledge and making space for later youth organizing. Some of the fruit of this largely invisible organizing could be seen in the spring of 2006, when millions of people went into the streets for weeks across the country, *manifestaciones* against the Sensenbrenner Bill. Young people did more than rally, however: they attended meetings and held hearings. They talked to the press. They documented for anyone to see what they brought to the table—stellar grades, immaculate military records, high work recommendations. And they did all this under the constant risk of deportation.[41]

After nearly a decade of strictly by-the-books efforts failed—Congress did not pass the DREAM Act in 2007 or in 2010—youth moved to nonviolent direct action. They announced publicly that they were left with no choice but to begin civil disobedience. They launched sit-ins, hunger strikes, and street blockades. And they continued their work within the electoral system, advocating and lobbying.

New coalitions now sprouted. Forcing a way forward out of a dire limbo, young people gathered themselves under a common call: "Undocumented and Unafraid."[42] Living in Chicago, Cynthia appeared shy, insecure in the presence of strangers. (To protect undocumented people from prosecution, many journalists and scholars use only first names or pseudonyms. Scholar Thomas Swerts used only Cynthia's first name.) At first bewildered upon hearing other youth coming out "undocumented and unafraid," she too began experimenting with sharing her story—first with her closest friends, then widening her circle to include teachers and classmates. It was strange to be "so open about something that you're not supposed to talk about," she noted. Yet the storytelling process was liberating. She found people to talk to and discovered new friends. Above all, it provided, for everyone to see, a clear sense as to who was ready and comfortable to stand up and do something.[43]

Critical for Cynthia was the discovery that she was far from the only one who suffered emotionally from a basic lack of safety and belonging. During a "die-in" in downtown Chicago in December 2010, she shared, for the first time, not only the difficulties of being undocumented but her "personal struggles concerning mental health and suicide." The very process of telling others the fear and trauma of being undocumented and hearing from others with similar experiences felt transforming. Above all, it allowed her to see beyond her personal travails. "Eventually," she noted, "it becomes not so much about you," but you begin to "realize this is about everyone else."[44] In a matter of months, Cynthia herself turned into a confident leader in the immigrant youth movement.

For many years, it had mostly been an individual crisis. Now it felt empowering to recognize one's crisis not as individual but collective. Building on rich Latin American cultural traditions of social democracy and on the LGBT movement's long practice of coming out, young people created safe spaces where the undocumented could share their stories. They were not alone. They called such sharing *testimonios*, and they used them as an instrument to both expose and fight against injustice.[45]

Transformative storytelling, used by groups like Cynthia's, the Immigrant Youth Justice League, emerged full force in marches and rallies all over the country—in Maryland, California, Texas, New York. The Immigrant Youth Justice League not only drew on the tools pioneered by the LGBTQ movement of the 1970s and 1980s to launch the first National Coming Out of the Shadows Day in March 2010 but also built on decades of spadework by campaigns such as those of Domestic Workers United, the United Farm Workers, the Industrial Areas Foundation, and hundreds of union locals and statewide campaigns fighting for dignity and justice. Lifting up the flag of those who paved the way, young people now stepped forward across the nation as "undocumented, unafraid, and unapologetic."[46]

It did not happen without strife or controversy. Many in the undocumented immigrant community found such declarations both alarming and threatening. As organizer Marisa Franco noted, everyone had been "taught to be ashamed of parts of who we are." And yet, she began to wonder, "how do we find each other if we're all in the shadows?" The concept of stepping out, she realized, was "about stripping away the things that make us hide. When it happens for many of us together, it's powerful."[47]

In Georgia, immigrant youth brutally excluded from higher education responded with "Freedom University Georgia"—a vibrant, voluntary educational organization. Invoking SNCC's Freedom Schools, volunteer teachers, professors, and professionals offered classes, provided advice, and, in collaboration with students, created an innovative environment of mutual learning.

In December 2013, Freedom University Georgia hosted a speak-out and exhibition at Atlanta's Hammond House museum titled *Documenting the Undocumented*. As participants stepped forward to share their work and address the crowd, they first announced, "My name is . . . —and I am undocumented." They presented their photographs and told their stories. On opening night, Cristian Osvaldo Flores showed a picture of a woman holding a banner reading "Queers, Immigrants, All of Us: Come Out, Destroy Fear, Unleash Power." He took a deep breath. The message was meaningful to him, he began, "because in addition to being undocumented, I am also gay."[48]

Queer activists have disproportionately taken leadership roles in the youth movement since 2010, invoking and remixing a range of intersectional organizing tools generated by the Combahee River Collective, Audre Lorde, Stonewall veterans Sylvia Rivera and Marsha P. Johnson, and the organizing of the 1980s and 1990s in support of people with AIDS, as well as tools formed within SONG.[49] The creation of organizations such as the Immigrant Youth Justice League and Freedom University provided the crucial free space in which undocumented youth could "be their full selves and reclaim their dignity as human beings."[50]

Public events provided key stepping stones for political mobilization: realizing the larger nature of one's predicament, beginning to see its broader structural and cultural roots, feeling empowered by sharing a common experience with many others in similar situations, and, finally, acquiring tools necessary to move ideas into action. From the outside, the *testimonios* may have looked like little more than sharing. In reality, such stories drew people into mutually accountable relationships that began to hold the larger movement together.[51]

Public visibility and successful mobilization brought with it a lot of pushback, both within the immigrant communities and from the larger society. The clarity and new confidence with which undocumented youth presented their demands clashed with all kinds of deeply ingrained assumptions. Their deliberate call to embrace the struggles of others who faced similar stigmatization, such as the LGBTQ community, provoked unease in a US culture habituated to separating and compartmentalizing people.

Into that apprehension stepped a fresh generation of leaders in SONG, now based in Atlanta. As SONG codirector Paulina Helm-Hernández recalled in 2015, "More moderate groups used to say, 'Never say "undocumented" or "transgender" because it will automatically polarize the conversation.'" In other words, more conservative immigration activists feared it could jeopardize wide support for immigrant rights if one made common cause with the LGBTQ movement's fight against oppression. Yet young people saw this strategic use of language as clear, strong, and uniting. Motivations varied, as did the level of analysis behind the strategy. Some youth talked about needing to be "more aggressive and more tenacious" in the face of Congress's failure to respond when youth played by all the rules. Others, like Tania Unzueta, who was part of a group of young immigration activists who participated in the National Coming Out Day in 2010, explained that young people explicitly decided "to adopt the terminology and strategies of LGBT activists," orchestrating a 'coming out' event where they publicly challenged the federal government to deport undocumented youth on the first "National Coming Out of the Shadows Day." For Unzueta, this approach had personal resonance: "To me, there was a very clear link at coming out as undocumented and coming out as queer." Of course, she too worried that bringing the two identities together might "derail legislative progress when an immigration overhaul seemed plausible and immigrant rights activists were hoping for Republican support."[52]

SONG also became the fiscal sponsor of Freedom University in early 2014. Freedom University's executive director, Laura Emiko Soltis, moved the organization from Athens to Atlanta "to connect the undocumented student movement with LGBTQ and Black Freedom Movement organizations and allies."[53] The moderates' strategy to push the notion of the "deserving immigrant" within the electoral system in order to win the hearts of more conservative congressional leaders had repeatedly failed. It was time to move beyond an approach of conciliation.

Instead of trying to resolve the human tragedy of family separation, many state and local politicians dug in. Georgia's policy provided a particularly demeaning example. In the fall of 2010, the Georgia Board of Regents passed Policy 4.1.6 and Policy 4.3.4, banning undocumented students from applying to the state's top five public universities. Simultaneously, the regents banned undocumented youth from qualifying for in-state tuition at any state school. The governor, perhaps unintentionally mirroring the actions of Mississippi, Georgia, and Alabama governors half a century earlier, appointed an all-white, all-male "Immigration Enforcement Review Board" that functioned in ways astonishingly similar to the white supremacist state sovereignty commissions of the 1950s and 1960s. The editorial board of the main paper in Atlanta's suburban Cobb County worried that "deserving Georgians are being turned away from attending" Kennesaw State University "while illegal, undocumented, ineligible-by-law people are being admitted and then given special treatment along the way." It was "the familiar lament of the subsidized white suburbanite," scholar Pamela Voekel wryly observed. Such narrow views may have driven legislators, but the irony probably escaped the regents when their discriminatory policies went into effect the same year as the University of Georgia celebrated its fiftieth anniversary of racial desegregation. It was not a parallel missed by undocumented students at Freedom University, who responded with a sit-in calling to "desegregate higher education in Georgia yet again."[54]

At Freedom U, undocumented young people between eighteen and twenty-eight can take courses and explore college options out of state. Freedom University mentors also help undocumented youth prepare applications for universities and the financial aid to attend. Using the same pedagogical tools crafted by a long tradition of activists, ranging from Latin American popular education to Myles Horton's Highlander Folk School to SNCC's Freedom Schools, volunteer professors emphasize a classroom of mutual respect and learning, and a curriculum that is relevant to students' own histories and identities. Since 2010, more than 250 students from Latin America, Africa, and Asia have received education, leadership training, and help getting to out-of-state colleges and universities through Freedom University. "One out of every five students who comes to Freedom U leaves with a full scholarship to a private university," reported Soltis. "So for many, Freedom U is the stepping stone and the determining factor between high school and college." The consequences reach well beyond education—for the Freedom University curriculum is not just, nor primarily, about expanded individual opportunities. People band together in solidarity, despite the lack of "any resources or institutional base," to develop the tools necessary for personal and community empowerment. Freedom U pushes young people to develop multi-issue, "autonomous, student-led organizations."[55]

At the same time that they created parallel institutions like Freedom U, youth were engaged in civil disobedience in places like Arizona, California, Illinois, Alabama, and Georgia, trying to stop deportations, sitting-in at detention centers, and disrupting businesses in downtown areas of major cities to educate the public. United We Dream worked together with DreamActivist, a "student action and resource network run by your fellow undocumented immigrants." Their theory was straightforward: "If we hide in the shadows and stay divided, it's easier to intimidate us. If we unite, go out into the light, and demand to be treated with dignity, we can fight for our rights."[56]

Dignity and human rights became conceptual anchors. Did humans cease to be human outside the protective wings of their respective national governments? Didn't it make much more sense to guarantee "inalienable rights" to people by virtue of their humanness? Weren't we all the same, with national boundaries little more than accidents of history? "Instead of seeing myself as undocumented—someone who is lacking, someone who is helpless," reflected

Maria, a young woman from Georgia, "I am able to see myself as an undocumented warrior: a warrior who was willing to fight for her human right to education." Iranian by birth, DreamActivist Mohammad Abdollahi emphasized his deep sense of solidarity: "Those of us who have crossed that line [to be out of the closet as undocumented] are privileged, and we have a responsibility to work for everyone else." Abdollahi echoed Jimenez when he clarified, "We don't need the legislators, we need each other. That's the heart of it." The activists "realized we could stop deportations just by being really organized."[57]

To train for civil disobedience, undocumented youth developed a consistent process between 2009 and 2012, putting their bodies on the line in what 1960s activists had called "dilemma actions." When SNCC youth engaged in sit-ins in 1960, they "won," whichever way the protest went: if they were seated at a segregated restaurant, they desegregated the lunch counter; if they didn't get seated, their protest publicized the unjust unconstitutionality of Jim Crow. Reverend Jim Lawson, instrumental in training the SNCC students in Nashville in nonviolent direct action between 1959 and 1962, now worked in the Southwest in 2009–12 with undocumented youth activists to train them in the same approach. The strategy in both cases had a simple yet profound aim: to build support through "images of students peacefully submitting to arrest, handcuffed and arrested while wearing graduation caps and gowns, blasted out across the country on mainstream media and social networking sites."[58]

To get a sense of how a person learned to do this work, we can circle back to the March 2012 action in Phoenix, Arizona, at the top of this chapter. Here, six activists gathered in a safe house and told each other their stories. Why did they feel a need to take part? What had they experienced that led to this moment? As they compared their experiences, the sheer number and variety of situations that frightened themselves and their families and friends mounted. One participant told of the terrifying visit of the housing inspector; another explained his dad's fear of losing everything when the police raided his construction site; yet another talked about the horror he felt deep inside when he witnessed ICE arrest a classmate right outside school grounds. And then there were the stories they had all experienced many times, like driving without a license, on constant lookout for the police. Daily tasks, so simple for most, were suffused with constant anxiety and the ever-present prospect of arrest. As Yasmin's story illustrated, being a law-abiding, hard-working, and successful member of the community provided no safety—all it took was being pulled over by a police officer for driving without the license that had been denied you, and the pursuit of your dreams for college, a good job, and a stable family life might vanish in a flash.

After the sit-in on Seventy-Fifth Avenue in Phoenix, the police charged the young activists with "disorderly conduct" and "suspicion of disrupting a thoroughfare." Supporters made hundreds of calls to ICE. The next morning, police released Rocio Sanchez and Jackie Sanchez, both under eighteen. The remaining four were released later in the week. ICE announced it would not deport the young people. "Upon further review, ICE has determined that these individuals do not fall under ICE's enforcement priorities and the agency has lifted the previously lodged detainers," the statement said. "ICE is focused on smart, effective immigration enforcement that prioritizes the removal of criminal aliens, recent border crossers and egregious immigration law violators, such as those who have been previously removed from the United States."[59] The updated "dilemma actions" from the 1960s sit-ins forced the press and the rest of the country to pay attention.

Young people's boost in assertiveness and public activity appeared to work. When Congress reconsidered the DREAM Act between 2010 and 2012, a slight but important shift took place in the way popular media portrayed undocumented immigrants. The increased strength of the activist community and members' repeated sharing of their stories as a positive part of the US civic body resulted in a wider affirming description of undocumented youth. This could most obviously be seen in journalism's and government's move away from use of the word "illegal" to describe undocumented people.[60]

Thousands of undocumented youth—from Seattle to Miami, San Diego to Chicago, Boston to Houston—kept up the pressure. As a new generation of SONG leaders came forward, they too began actions under the "Undocumented and Unafraid" call in the South. SONG organizer Salem Acuña noted of this period between 2010 and 2012 that youth "stepped up the organizing." They infiltrated detention centers, organized inside them, and pressured the Obama administration "to stop the lies and provide some relief. That's why Obama announced deferred action," a reference to a new policy, Deferred Action for Childhood Arrivals (or DACA), revealed by the Obama administration in June 2012. It allowed certain undocumented youth to get a work permit and temporary protection from deportation.[61]

SNCC, fifty years earlier, formed what Dr. King called the "opening wedge" to break apart Jim Crow; he had noted they were the "stormtroopers of the movement." Now, undocumented youth organizers played a similar role in the immigrant rights movement: they decided to act "as if" the right of family reunion trumped the state's monopoly over citizenship. They created a "platform for a group of non-citizens to appear in the public sphere," young scholar Joaquina Weber-Shirk noted. "They did so as DREAMers, articulating their right to politics, and acting on rights and performing citizenship that has not been granted by the state." They acted publicly as "members of the U.S. who belong and contribute to the national community, sharing an identity claimed by citizens."[62] "Would you let anyone take you from your home? From your family?" Lizbeth Mateo, a youth organizer asked of US citizens. "We have not, and neither should the many, many more like us."[63]

THE RESPONSE: PROFIT-BASED DETENTION

Any prison-style detention of nonoffenders who were undocumented threatened human rights. Yet privately run, for-profit detention centers for undocumented people proved flat-out unconstitutional. Rather than treat detention centers as a federal responsibility, the Federal Bureau of Prisons off-loaded them to private contractors out to make a profit, paying $5.1 billion in 2012 to these private prison companies for immigration detention alone. Financial incentive pushed prison companies to direct more of their profits toward lobbying for future contracts. For example, the Northwest Detention Center in Tacoma, Washington, operates under the Florida-based GEO Group, a for-profit company. Detainee hunger strikes at the Northwest Detention Center in 2014 and 2017 exposed GEO Group's human rights violations: inadequate food, health care, and shelter for the detainees. Investigative reporting further revealed where some of the money went: GEO Group spent massively on lobbyists to support Arizona's "draconian immigration laws" and "the maintenance of the 34,000-bed quota in federal detention centers." This quota mandate has resulted in a boom for the private prison industry, which "eagerly offers the bed spaces," a Seattle-based activist wrote in 2014. Armed with this information, immigrant rights groups have pushed GEO Group's investors to divest. Wells Fargo Bank, for instance, divested "seventy-five percent of its shares due to public pressure."[64]

Observers watching the massive shifts in public investment away from public education and infrastructure in the 1950s, 1960s, and 1970s and toward law enforcement, prisons, and border security between 1990 and the 2010s invoked several historical parallels. It was akin to the decline of the Roman Empire. Or the "new Jim Crow." Or perhaps Americans were living in a mashup dystopia of Huxley's *Brave New World* and Orwell's *1984*. It may seem obvious that community well-being generally increases in any society when it chooses schools over prisons, health care over border security, and jobs over law enforcement. Yet Baby Boomers who benefited as children from the heavy investment in schools, health care, and jobs in the 1950s and 1960s constitute the majority of lawmakers at the local, state, and federal levels from the 1990s to today. These historical analogies do not adequately explain their large-scale, overall shift toward fear-based investment.[65]

It was a shift that did not escape the attention of those who created Freedom U. They understood why Georgia legislators targeted undocumented students—even as it seemed like a farce, a huge Goliath aiming a howitzer at a tiny, defenseless David: they were "looking for a scapegoat to divert attention from the massive disinvestment in the university," reported Pamela Voekel, a faculty member at the University of Georgia and cofounder of Freedom U. Rather than raise the salaries of the state university system's least-paid workers or decrease the fees and tuition paid by families across Georgia, the legislators chose instead to target the 501 undocumented students who paid out-of-state tuition rates to attend university. *They* were the threats to the American way.[66]

INTERNAL TENSION

Detention posed one set of challenges for the movement. Inside, among undocumented activists themselves, an additional set of questions emerged with their shift toward "Undocumented and Unafraid": When and how to use direct action? How much to reveal to a public, and to authorities who had the power to prosecute them? How far and how fast to push for full citizenship rights, and do so not just for "model immigrants"? One bone of ongoing contention, for instance, was the public strategy that youth activists had put forth in the mid-2000s by arguing, "I'm not a criminal; I'm just like you."[67] It implied that so-called criminals should effectively be outside the arena of legitimate public demands for equal rights. Yet given the tenuous nature of immigrant life in America and the incredible challenges people faced to get an education, to drive legally, and to hold down a job without skirting the rules, who got to define what it meant to be criminal?

The answer, of course, was the US government—the very institution denying immigrants basic rights in the first place. Along with Movement for Black Lives and Indigenous youth, some young immigrant activists began to challenge the very distinction between legal and criminal. As the policy group Movement for Black Lives observed, "The criminal justice system has managed to create a pipeline from schools to prisons for Black and Brown communities," and, as such, "it has also been used as a tool of the state to delegitimize and neutralize people's movements throughout history." The point, of course, was to end the centuries-long pattern criminalizing all of these groups.[68]

Now, the same dynamic was playing out among immigrant communities. When undocumented youth invoked the idea that "I'm not a criminal; I'm just like you," it played into this "fixed game" by invoking sameness and solidarity with white middle-class norms. Instead, what about a level playing field for all and solidarity with all people of color? The immigrant blogger "ille the gal," an anonymous self-described "Asian illegal alien," laid out several points popping up throughout youth immigrant activists' communities: "As most are aware, the U.S. was developed by settler colonialists," she began. "Europeans decided to build over already existing communities of people whom they ascribed as 'primitive' in order to justify mass genocide and expansion over land." That made the US "technically an illegitimate existence that forcefully built over indigenous people's societies," societies that had existed for thousands of years and resisted colonization since Columbus's 1492 arrival. Thus, she continued, "the 'documented' are but less-recent immigrants who are also 'illegal' as their presence is unwanted, 'unauthorized.'" On whose terms was she "illegal" if people acknowledged that the US "illegally" settled on Indigenous lands? "If I choose to reject the U.S.'s classification of my existence, then I am technically an autonomous being living on indigenous land. I wish to be the sole sovereign of myself in search of self-determination."[69]

How to define who was in and who was out? Who was part of the struggle and who was deemed an outsider? These debates could lead to frayed relationships, and groups struggled to stay together. Fernanda, an undocumented activist from Pennsylvania, had been born in Peru and came to the US as a preteen. She first participated in civil disobedience in Montgomery, Alabama, in 2011. Chanting "Undocumented, unafraid!" she and a group of twelve other youth refused to leave a legislative building in protest against the state's punishing new law HB 56. The US Justice Department itself argued against the law, stating that it turned undocumented immigrants into a "unique class who cannot lawfully obtain housing, enforce a contract, or send their children to school without fear that enrollment will be used as a tool to seek to detain and remove them and their family members." The day before the action, Fernanda told journalist Eileen Truax that she was undocumented, but she did not define herself as a DREAMer. "The way [the DREAM Act is] written implies that I don't deserve to benefit from it because I wasn't a good student in high school." As a teenager, she had not been perfect. "We're like any teenager, any young person," she recalled. The government did not "have to ask us to be perfect as a condition to giving us a right. That's why I'd rather say I'm fighting for all immigrants," not just those eligible for the DREAM Act. Her brother Cesar concurred. He wanted to be an artist rather than a college student or soldier—the only two paths to citizenship made possible by the DREAM Act. Did such a career make him stateless permanently? "Because of that you don't deserve legal status? You could still contribute to your country doing other things," he noted. One didn't have to be perfect, he concluded; "you just have to be a person, that's all."[70]

Yet such debates also created openings for new coalitions. After the US presidential election of Donald Trump in 2016, more than fifty groups joined together to form what they simply called "The Majority." Patrisse Cullors of Black Lives Matter noted that "one place where you'll see depth in the conversation is around protecting our communities." All people of color needed to shield themselves, whether the threats came from ICE raids or from environmental destruction or from "further criminalization and violence." Marisa Franco, head of #Not1More and Mijente, pointed out, "We can't say, 'hey don't let ICE on your campus' and not call out over-policing of people of color on college campuses." Nor could movement people "celebrate local police who might consider not working with ICE but who over-police and won't make those same proclamations for other communities of color," Franco declared.[71]

MEASURING SUCCESS: IMMIGRATION REFORM IN PRACTICE

How much had undocumented youth activists accomplished in the first two decades of the twenty-first century? Context matters. To immigrants, government appeared in many guises, from the local sheriff, to ICE agents, to Congress, and all the way to the White House. At first, many immigrant youth activists met the election of Barack Obama with enthusiasm and hope. But reality soon set in. At the start of his first term in 2009, President Obama significantly increased enforcement at the US-Mexico border and the deportation of undocumented residents. He hoped this would give moderates room to maneuver on both sides of Congress for comprehensive immigration reform.

The results were sobering. Between 2009 and 2015, Obama's attempts at meaningful immigration reform failed repeatedly. Yet his "compromise" offer to the right wing through increased border enforcement and greater numbers of deportations succeeded spectacularly. At the conclusion of his second term, the Obama administration had managed to deport more human beings than the combined total of all nineteen presidents who governed the United States from 1892 to 2008—more than 2.5 million people. This was an astonishing 23 percent increase from the George W. Bush years.[72]

Evaluating the effects of twenty-first century undocumented youth organizers is thus a decidedly mixed bag. No doubt, US communities reengaged the long and complicated conversation about "who belongs" in response to youth immigrant activism. It is also likely that anti-immigrant sentiments in American culture would be both more widespread and more poisonous had it not been for the many actions by undocumented youth to share their stories in public. Still, comprehensive immigration reform continues to be missing in action.

Using *testimonios* and nonviolent direct action, creating alternative institutions and news sources—all of this work did create a major victory: a unique movement culture among the young activists. Their success can also be measured by their solidarity actions with other youth movements. Challenging the policing of brown and Black bodies initially led undocumented youth to work with the Dream Defenders and Black Lives Matter (BLM), both emerging out of the state of Florida's acquittal of the killer of Trayvon Martin in 2012. Through campaigns like #IfIDieInPoliceCustody, #SayHerName, and #JusticeForMikeBrown on social media and a range of on-the-ground tactics such as Freedom Rides, marches, Black Brunch protests, and civil disobedience, BLM challenged law enforcement's widespread lack of accountability for killing Black youth.

Cristina Jimenez and United We Dream stood with BLM early on, when, as she noted, "few Latinx organizations did." Jimenez "got hate mail from my own community." Yet she felt "young people have to lead—making that bridge for our communities." While detention centers imprison immigrant mothers and children in Texas, it is those same centers, she realized, "that profit from Black incarceration over many years." In both cases, people of color have been stripped of humanity and dignity. The message law enforcement communicated to "people like me," Jimenez recalled, "is that 'You don't belong, you need to be punished.'"[73]

The solidarity between United We Dream and BLM was simple but profound: "We are all fighting the same forces." If African Americans say, "Undocumented folks are stealing our jobs," Jimenez noted that activists could bring forward instead the idea that "the real enemy is corporations and government that steal our labor and lives." And as journalist Tina Vasquez noted, when Latinx people fail to speak out against anti-Blackness, "we are essentially saying our comfort is more important than the lives of black people." Jimenez recognized that one way to build mutual power was through voting. Yet in a situation where it could take ten to twelve years to become a citizen, undocumented youth looked for the power to create change in many additional ways. The overall strategy, she noted, was that "we fight criminalization of our communities." One of the most effective methods to harness internal conflict and use its energy in a positive way to fight this criminalization was "bridge-building" among movements, Jimenez noted.[74]

SONG organizer Hermelinda Cortés had been doing such bridge-building work for a decade. Raised in western Virginia, "I didn't grow up *down for La Raza*, shouting Brown Power, or reading about Cesar Chavez and Dolores Huerta," she recalled. "What I did have was an unhealthy obsession with Selena and singing 'Blue Moon' over and over again with my sisters," Cortés smiled. "I had hoop earrings, soda-pop bangs, and ponytails slicked back with limón. I had chicarrones, tamales and Jarritos on the side of dusty fútbol fields." Her identity formed in part by listening to her "father's deep belting renditions of rancheras on Sunday mornings." Akin to her African American counterparts in the state, "I had a fear of the police taking away those I loved, of bosses withholding pay, of white children taunting us with their racist jeers."[75] Working as a youth organizer in SONG throughout most of the early 2000s and into the 2010s, by December 2015, at a gathering in Chicago, Cortés looked out and reconsidered what had become possible: "What would it mean to present a united front of Latinx people embedded in the work of Black liberation, reproductive justice, trans and queer liberation, the death of capitalism and the defense of the Earth?" she wondered. "What would it mean to the billions of election dollars used to buy and con us, right wing and Democrats alike?" What would happen if "a people, por mi gente, to say *no* to the talking heads who claim to represent us but have no problem selling the most gender transgressive, the least papered, the blackest, the poorest, the most incarcerated among us down the proverbial river?"[76] That weekend in 2015, she and others formed Mijente, an organization where one could "imagine a movement that is not simply pro-Latino, but also pro-woman, pro-queer, pro-poor, pro-Black, pro-indigenous, pro-climate because OUR community is all of those things and WE care about all of them."[77]

Since 2013, thousands of joint actions have resulted from these strong intermovement relationships and intersectional organizations like SONG, BLM, the International Indigenous Youth Council, Mijente, and United We Dream. For example, a tidal wave of ICE agents descended upon North Carolina, Texas, and Georgia between December 2015 and January 2016. The raids targeted women and children from Central America. In Atlanta, SONG codirector and Atlanta Black Lives Matter leaders Mary Hooks and Paula Helm-Hernández of SONG spoke out: "It is deeply troubling for ICE to target mothers and children seeking refuge from persecution, murder, and torture in their home countries in Central America for deportation back to those same conditions and worse," they stated. The #Not1More coalition pulled together

Black and brown activists in the face of the Obama administration's actions. As SNCC participants used their bodies to block Jim Crow laws in the 1960s, #Not1More used civil disobedience to block deportation. They also spread the word, provided temporary safe havens, and advocated for immigrants' freedom across the country, together mobilizing thousands more people than immigrants' rights groups could have done alone.[78]

Another victory could be seen as ninety undocumented youth from twelve universities across the nation joined sit-ins to integrate classrooms for documented and undocumented students at Georgia State, Georgia Institute of Technology, and the University of Georgia on February 1, 2016. They chose the date intentionally—it was the fifty-sixth anniversary of the SNCC sit-ins in Greensboro. Freedom U organized the event over a four-month period. As Melissa Rivas-Triana, an undocumented student of Freedom U, noted, "We're taking our action to the classroom because we are determined to continue learning together despite the Board of Regents' insistent segregation." Her classmate Victor Morales said he was inspired to participate after learning the history of the Black freedom movement in the South: "The Greensboro Four showed me the power of being committed to a goal beyond myself and what it means to be free." Standing in solidarity with them was Tyra Beaman: "As a student of Spelman College who has had the privilege of attending an institution created to empower black women impacted by colonialism, sexism, and racism, it is my duty to ensure that all young people—regardless of their race, gender, or citizenship status—also have the opportunity to access equitable higher education." SNCC veterans and freedom singers Rutha and Emory Harris joined the sit-in. Rephrasing the song "Oh, Freedom" from the 1960s struggle, they sang together, "Oh, Freedom, Oh Freedom over me. . . . No more borders. No more borders, no more borders over me. And before I be a slave, I'll be buried in my grave, and go home, to my Lord, and be free."[79] SNCC's "jail no bail" and "fill the jails" strategy of the 1960s was a result of being pushed against the wall. When the federal government refused to end Jim Crow despite its unconstitutionality, SNCC forced the issue. Similarly, after Congress again failed to pass the DREAM Act in 2010 and a small group of hardline Republicans filibustered, undocumented youth had no choice but to come up with fresh ways to push people in power to make a legal pathway for them to equality in the country.[80]

Again and again, their direct action focused on reunifying families. It was the same unshakable drive that focused twelve-year-old Yasmin on the harrowing trek from Veracruz to North Carolina to reunite with her mother and mobilized Cristina Jimenez to devote her life to the movement after her

FIGURE 9. Freedom University, Twitter post, February 2, 2016.

fiancé's release from ICE detention. In March 2014, thirty undocumented immigrants planned to travel from the US to Tijuana, then immediately turn and cross the border back to the US, demanding the right of return and family reunification. It was "immigration reform in practice."[81]

Each attempt in the subsequent #BringThemHome campaigns became known by the number of activists involved: the Dream 9, the Dream 30. National attention followed. Youth activists publicly declared "unauthorized status at a legal port of entry" and asked for asylum. Some traditional immigration rights groups who supported the DREAM Act criticized these actions as "personally dangerous and counter-productive within a larger strategy for legislative immigration reform." But National Immigrant Youth Alliance organizer Rosario Lopez stated, "We don't want the families to rely on us, or on attorneys and politicians. We want them to recognize their own power."[82] Youth direct action again forced Americans to reconsider who belongs—and to make a choice.

The direct actions of undocumented youth activists—including putting pressure on ICE and detention centers to release loved ones, abiding by nonviolence at the border and high schools and other key deportation spots, and protesting on campuses—provided an alternative to the "dangerous immigrant" narrative so perniciously peddled by second- and third-generation citizens like Joe Arpaio. Perhaps equally important, youth activists made the term "illegal" an epithet. Throughout the political arena, if a person uses the term, that person is thus identified as a bigot and places himself or herself outside of respectful discourse. Instead, "undocumented" has become the agreed-upon terminology. "There is no such thing as an illegal human being," undocumented youth activists assert. Despite a desperate attempt by Donald Trump and his acolytes to bring back the bigoted vocabulary of "illegals," undocumented youth have changed the language of the nation.

Undocumented youth made blindingly clear that US constitutional law, an exemplar of democracies worldwide, had been outpaced by twenty-first-century economic realities. The US Congress's inability to address the human beings trampled underneath this economic blitzkrieg created a human rights disaster for millions of children in the heartland. Youth activists have not yet found a lever within the political party system to formalize their power or to sustain their foothold as political players. In other words, while they have the power to define the very terms of the debate, they have not yet figured out a way to create democratic forms that represent their politics in statehouses or in Congress. Work toward this goal took lower priority for many of them by 2017 as members of the Trump administration ratcheted up the rhetoric against immigrants and massively increased deportations. People in the youth movement felt forced to focus on keeping families together.[83]

Still, youth shifted the political terrain in a period of powerful opposition to immigration. They have forced a national conversation: Should a mother be separated from her child merely because of a piece of paper? Should a young person not be able to drive, get a job, or go to college merely because of a decision made by parents many years before that person was an adult? They dream of belonging to a United States that doesn't yet exist, a country in which the laws match a bigger ideal of who is American, where they fit into "we the people." This work challenges four centuries of liberal democratic theory, demanding "we the people," not states or the federal government or multinational capital and big corporations, need to "make a little more room in the circle."

FIVE

The Intolerable Price of Self-Respect
The Movement for Black Lives Organizes Urban and Suburban America

> This is the crime of which I accuse my country and my countrymen, and for which I nor time nor history will ever forgive them, that they have destroyed and are destroying hundreds of thousands of lives and do not know and do not want to know it.
> —James Baldwin, "A Letter to My Nephew"

Being Black in America often means to live in a state of simmering warfare with law enforcement. It is almost always a one-sided, asymmetrical war. From the earliest beginnings of American history, African Americans encountered people with and without badges who variously hunted them down, singled them out, and then sold, profiled, stereotyped, abused, harassed, and sometimes killed them. Granting all exceptions to this rule, it renders a kind of collective memory that shapes ongoing reality. During the last century, layered onto this collective memory in particular ways depending on region and city, an expanding police power and residential segregation often intensified this sensibility.

Many efforts at reform have been made since the 1960s. Cities across the country have installed Citizens' Oversight Commissions and revised their "use of force" policies, and, more recently, some police officers have been required to wear body cameras. Still, the largely unreformed bureaucratic habits of the working police of all races and ethnicities, accumulated over many generations, continue. Regardless of exactly how one inherits and inhabits the identity of being Black, it means having to live with the unreasonable expectation of unequal treatment. Being Black means that people who look like you continue to be stopped and frisked more often, jailed and sentenced more frequently and more harshly, shot and killed more readily, and seen as a threat more pervasively. It not only makes life more dangerous but also alters the very nature of citizenship for African Americans.[1]

This reality of anti-Black discrimination is a reality largely invisible to non-Black people—in power or out of power. Indeed, from the perspective of many Black citizens, the comforting tale of racial progress many other people tell themselves is a decidedly mixed bag, for it renders largely invisible the ongoing assault endured. The gruesome regularity with which young and older Black citizens are murdered at the hands of the police in this country is but the starkest reminder. No civilized country in the world engages in law enforcement practices as harmful to an entire racial group as does the United States. It is a reality that many Americans largely repress, both politically and culturally.[2]

This sustained experience has meant that local police departments across the country, as well as legal systems and sites of incarceration, have become transparent in ways they did not intend. Too many people hear leaders say "things have changed," then find out in actuality that it has not. When Darris Young was trained as a Richmond, California, police officer in the 1990s, long before he became an organizer at the Ella Baker Center for Human Rights, he swiftly encountered a deep-rooted cultural reality. He recalled police trainers telling him, during the very first week, "We don't want you to be here [as] a humanitarian." Instead, his superiors insisted, "[we] want you to have this attitude, train you with the attitude [that] it's you against 'them.'" Young was taken aback. This was not what he had expected to hear in a positive public servant approach. "If my attitude is indoctrinated and trained that it is 'you against me,'" he realized, then "almost from the outset, I am going to work expecting to come down on any enemy." That made no sense to him. People are citizens, he argued. Yet he was being trained to see them as "an enemy. And that is the way, unfortunately, too many cops are trained."[3]

Later, the more Young thought about it, the more things fell into place. US history was littered with case after case, example after example, of police violence against Black people. As late as the 1950s and 1960s, not just in the South but all over the country, "police officers—people who wore badges—were killing and lynching people." They got away with murder. It was a tragedy with a long history, which is why Young urged people to look at "*why* these things are happening." Yet most important for Young as an organizer at Oakland's Ella Baker Center was not just awareness but keeping the blatant injustice of racist discrimination and violence "in the public eye. Not let it go away. Because if it goes away, it never changes."[4]

In the US, there is a set of rhythms to racist violence. A story hip-hop artist Tupac Shakur told during a public interview in 1991 resonates with many Black people in the US. In his early twenties, Shakur recalled "walking down the streets of Oakland, minding my own business, and the police department saw fit for me to be trained or snapped back into my place." They asked him for identification "and sweated me about my name because my name is Tupac." The disrespect rankled. "My final words to them was 'F—— y'all.'" It was a response the Oakland police officers were not acculturated to tolerate. "Next thing I know I was in a choke hold passing out with cuffs on headed for jail for resisting arrest."[5] The tragedy lies in the routine nature of the tale. Many young Black people have experienced similar situations. Black women and femmes face particular challenges as a result of "misogynoir," or racialized sexism.[6] The larger culture can watch events like this unfold as daily fare on TV and across social media. And the standard cultural response is acceptance, however grudging it may be. People accept the unacceptable—until they don't.

What is almost entirely missing from the conversation is any reflection on how exceptional, and specifically how exceptionally brutal and counterproductive, this type of policing is. In virtually all other highly industrialized nations—countries such as Japan, Great Britain, Canada, and Germany—police officers are trained to de-escalate confrontations whenever possible. Many are unarmed on patrol. The point is to resolve, not to intensify. Indeed, things like shoot-outs, car chases, and stop-and-frisks are almost exclusively American brands, eagerly sold by Hollywood to a spectacle-intoxicated world but not a lived reality in democracies outside US borders. Indeed, even brutal autocratic regimes in Russia or China arrest and imprison fewer people than does the presumed beacon of freedom. With less than 5 percent of the world's population, the US is home to an astonishing 25 percent of the world's prison population. One should note that other highly industrialized nations also have significantly lower crime rates in general and, more specifically, that the number of people killed or incarcerated is a mere fraction of what it is in the United States.[7]

Common policing practices in the US often leave people in appalling disbelief. Social media has helped spread this shock and distrust. Actor and activist Jesse Williams's five-minute BET Awards speech on national television in 2016, for instance, forced many in his broad-based Grey's Anatomy audience to acknowledge this outrage and to decide which side are you on? "'You're free,' they keep telling us," he noted. "I don't want to hear any more about how far we've come when paid public servants can pull a drive-by on a twelve-year-old playing alone in the park in broad daylight, killing him on television and then going home to make a sandwich," he recalled of Tamir Rice. "Tell Rekia Boyd how it's so much better to live in 2012 than it is to live in 1612 or 1712. Tell that to Eric Garner. Tell that to Sandra Bland. Tell that to Dorian Hunt," he continued. "She would have been alive if she hadn't acted—so free." Of course, Williams pointed out, there are alternatives. "Police somehow manage to deescalate, disarm and not kill white people every day," he noted. So, "we're going to have equal rights and justice in our own country." Otherwise people will have to stand forward and "restructure [the police] function."[8]

At the bottom of the criminal justice system in America lies a stark reality: Black and white are not treated the same. Period. And this is true regardless of status or position. "Our degrees won't save us, our middle-class status won't save us," noted Melina Abdullah, the head of the Pan-African studies department at California State–Los Angeles. When she looked back at those killed by police, their parents were often "college-educated, middle-class people." Seven-year-old Aiyana Jones was killed by police, "sleeping on her grandmother's couch." Abdullah realized that even though she risked professional censure, she couldn't stay on the sidelines. "I have two little girls. How can you sit back? That's how a lot of us feel. We're really facing wartime conditions."[9]

The Movement for Black Lives (M4BL)—the groups loosely associated with the Black Lives Matter movement—emerged to address this reality blistering the heart of American society. This chapter is not an overview of the movement—a fool's errand given how large, diverse, and expansive it has become. Instead, I examine its attempt to organize everyday people at the base in cities and nearby suburbs. If SNCC organized among rural citizens for the vote in the 1960s, M4BL looked for a way to organize urban and near-urban Americans at the base.

TRAYVON MARTIN AND THE DREAM DEFENDERS

Centered prominently on the coffee table in the middle of the Florida governor's office was a can of iced tea and a bag of Skittles candy. The objects held significance beyond the everyday: these were the items seventeen-year-old Trayvon Martin had gone to purchase from a Florida convenience store on February 26, 2012. He still clung to them as he was shot to death by George Zimmerman. Zimmerman, a twenty-eight-year-old vigilante living in a gated community in Sanford, accosted Martin because the teen "looked suspicious."[10] Martin, whose father lived in the same community, was simply walking home with a snack.

The iced tea and Skittles represent an undeniable and terrifying truth: if you happen to be Black, the most basic of activities can get you killed in today's America. In most cases, the killers walk free. Law enforcement and the legal system muster elaborate rationales, and leaders of the major institutions of the culture look the other way. James Baldwin's observation is as pertinent today as it was when made in 1962: his countrymen, he recognized soberly, "have destroyed and are destroying hundreds of thousands of lives and do not know and do not want to know it."[11] In the end, almost no one is ever held accountable for the routine killings happening on the streets of America. Particularly for young Black citizens, this fact is a blunt daily reminder that for far too many in power, Black lives do not matter.

A spark flared on July 13, 2013, when George Zimmerman was acquitted on all charges in the killing of Trayvon Martin.[12] For many, it was this generation's "Emmett Till" moment. How could society let free someone who had killed a young person in cold blood—a person who could have been any one of them? Some experienced it as simply the worst day of their life—an utterly unimaginable lack of accountability for a blatant murder. "How do we explain this to our children?" people asked across the country. At first, it seemed as if the usual responses would unfold: press conferences and marches were held; veteran activist Al Sharpton and his National Action Network organized rallies in New York City and one hundred other cities across the country on July 20.[13]

A day after the verdict, a group of young Black citizens from Martin's home state proclaimed an end to quiet submission. They talked and planned. Then they marched to the Florida governor's office and staged a nonviolent occupation. They were determined that this time, they would be heard. If the governor ignored their pleas, they would occupy his office. Police brutality and the random murder of Black youth had to end. And if elected officials were unwilling to respond and help, they would hold "People's Hearings."[14]

Elected officials in Florida did in fact refuse to respond to the youth. And so these young people held public hearings on their own, broadcast from the governor's office they had nonviolently occupied. As if to say that the iced tea and Skittles represented a judgment against the state, they put these two items on the governor's coffee table and testified over them—witness to what it is like, as a young person of color in today's America, to be profiled, to be met with suspicion and hostility in school, on the streets, in stores. They talked about how it felt to be singled out, to fear the constant harassment by the authorities, to know, deep down, that your life is cheap. They recalled learning from mothers, fathers, grandmothers, and uncles about the many things to avoid when stopped by the police. They discussed living with the horrifying prospect of unexpected death—your own or your friends'. "I have to be invisible to survive," one student from Tampa said in a tone of resignation. He had been stopped and frisked so often that he had lost count. Another Black teen remembered, when he was still a child, once waving at a police officer from his mom's car. He certainly did not anticipate what happened next: the officer stopped the car, screamed at both child and mother, and threatened to arrest the child for making an "obscene gesture." It made no sense. "I was devastated," the teen testified. Until then, he had thought the police were superheroes.[15]

College students and older teens were not the only ones to participate; some children determined to take part as well. Jamaya Peeples was ten years old when she showed up at the state capitol in 2013. She told a reporter, in a clear and unwavering voice, that she had to be part of the Tallahassee sit-in so there won't ever again be "another Trayvon Martin killed." Just in case anyone doubted her resolve, the fifth grader said that she would stay "until the governor calls a session. If school starts before then, I will come back on weekends and breaks."[16]

For thirty-one days, the young people engaged in the sit-in. Hundreds of high-school- and college-age students participated in Tallahassee. If the government wouldn't protect the American dream of life, liberty, and the pursuit of happiness, they would. Someone had to. They called themselves the "Dream Defenders."[17]

As they sat and debated and testified and learned from each other, the youth concluded that what Florida really needed, urgently needed, was something they called "Trayvon's Law"—a law to protect young people by ending racial profiling, repealing the state's "stand your ground" law, and removing zero-tolerance discipline policies in schools. Rather than provide for their education and safety, these laws had generated unacceptable consequences for youth of color, channeling them out of school and into the criminal justice system and putting them at risk on the streets of their own hometowns.[18]

The injustice, of course, was not restricted to Black youth. All nonwhite youth were in danger. They knew this from their neighborhoods, their schools. Their first group T-shirts thus read "Can We Dream Together?"—not just in English but in Haitian Kreyol, Spanish, and Arabic, reflecting some of the predominant languages spoken in their Florida communities.[19]

The central goal of the group occupying the governor's office was a "full legislative package to challenge the criminalization of our generation," as Dream

Defender and Florida A&M student Steven Pargett explained. "We are conducting our own hearings, taking testimony from community and expert witnesses with court reporter transcription, and getting the word out."[20] If the governor and the legislators refused to do their jobs, the Dream Defenders would generate the evidence for them.

The young people's occupation of the capitol created a stage where the clash of values became clear. Politicians decried their takeover. The mainstream media, taking their cues from established leaders, largely dismissed the young people and their "strident" demands. Social media, on the other hand, lit up with comments and discussions and declarations of support. The young people themselves, meanwhile, learned from 2011's Occupy Wall Street movement, creating committees for community outreach, committees for meals and sleeping arrangements, even a committee to make sure "everyone is exercising, resting and staying clean." Meals were organized to prioritize the perishables first, and the youth kept tabs on when food was donated.[21] In all of this early work setting up public testimony and ensuring people had what they needed, they discovered something one often has to experience to understand: nothing is more empowering than becoming an active participant in your own life.

Take the speech by Lucky Thomas, an African American studies major from Vero Beach. She had never played a prominent role in public life. Yet here she was, stepping forward into the middle of a circle of her peers, in a formal state building, in the capital city. All but a hundred pounds, she took a deep breath, her eyes revealing her determination, and said, "I'm going to talk about our dreams right now." Then she paused and looked around the Florida statehouse. "I'm with some of the most beautiful faces I've ever seen." In one sentence, she expressed the kind of affirmation that went to the heart of their protest. Heads around her nodded. "All right," they said. "We here." Then Lucky (pronounced Lou-key) began to explain why they were all "here"—one reason, really. "We're here gathered for justice. Not just for Trayvon." Her jubilant expression then turned somber and thoughtful. "Justice for all of our Black and brown kids." Amid supportive calls from those in the circle, she then addressed those young people directly: "We want to make sure that they know, 'You shouldn't be scared because [others might be] scared of you.'"[22] It was a goal both radical and basic: she wanted to be able to raise her children to get to their twenty-first birthdays alive "here. In the state of Florida. Here in America, period."

Her fellow activists outwardly represented a range of identities in mainstream America—young, some with braids and head wraps, others in business attire. All cheered her on. "Give our kids a chance!" she demanded. "Because they *matter*." She pointed around the circle. "These kids here? They *matter*. They matter to me." She took another look, beyond the circle. "They matter to Florida. And Governor Rick Scott," she called to the dethroned health care executive and venture capitalist, pausing to make sure the governor could hear clearly, "they think they matter to *you*."[23]

The clarity, hard-won experiential knowledge, and passion of women like Lucky Thomas drew young people from across the country to the Tallahassee sit-in. First students from around the state joined. Then young people traveled from Baltimore, Philadelphia, Charlotte, and New Orleans. On the last Friday of the month-long sit-in, with their powerful voices echoing off the statehouse's marble halls, the group invited in faith leaders. Prayers were offered by a "rabbi, an imam, and representatives from Baptist, Catholic, Episcopal, Lutheran, Methodist and Presbyterian communities," recalled one reporter. "Isaiah, Gandhi, Jesus, the Torah, the Bible and the Koran were all invoked as the crowd held hands around the Florida state seal." The Reverend Brant Copeland prayed "for a person to be able to walk in their neighborhood and not be accosted by armed people who make judgments of them. People of faith should stand here together because we are all pointed in the same direction."[24]

Thirty days later, the sit-in ended. The Dream Defenders had catapulted their issues to the national stage. Trayvon Martin's death would not go unmarked. And the time of quiet submission was over.

As citizens from around the country witnessed the young people's call to Governor Scott to "give us a seat at the table," the wheels of traditional power set in motion the routine procedures of stonewalling, sidelining, ignoring. Speaker of the Florida House of Representatives Will Weatherford agreed to call a session on "stand your ground," but, of course, not before the fall. Meetings took place in which youth activists got to talk to representatives of the Florida Department of Law Enforcement and the state's juvenile justice leaders on racial profiling and disproportionate contact with youth of color. Yet when it came to actual results, nothing happened. In a stunning failure of electoral politics, representatives of the people verbalized all the usual platitudes, practicing the politics of vague and distant promises. The governor himself publicly refused to call a special session. His suggestion for addressing systemic violence against Florida's youth of color? A "day of prayer." In the legislature, only forty-two lawmakers of the ninety-six necessary voted in favor of holding the session. Ninety voted against the session and twenty-eight did not participate.[25] Standing up and making your voice heard was essential, the Dream Defenders had learned. Yet it was not sufficient. It had not translated to political accountability for lawmakers, no matter how righteous or commonsensical the demands.

Regrouping, the Dream Defenders vowed to move forward. Ten days later they rode buses to Washington, DC, for the fiftieth anniversary of the 1963 March on Washington. Dream Defender Phillip Agnew—with short black hair and intense, gentle brown eyes—stood forward at Howard University on the eve of the march, his voice holding a quiet lilt that pitched lower with emotion. Excitement and exhaustion from the thirty-day sit-in at the Florida state capitol was still visible as he spoke. Love meant action, he stated. "We come here to act, and that's how we love you." The truth for Agnew, standing on the hallowed ground of the 1963 march, was that "America is a do-it-yourself project, and we are the people with the tools to do it." Black youth, he recognized, always "started from the bottom."[26] Now, the Dream Defenders had come to the nation's capital, the very center of power, to stand *their* ground.

The next day, on the steps of the Lincoln Memorial, as tens of thousands of people gathered, the Dream Defenders broke into a freedom song: *"What side are you on my people / What side are you on?"* The reply: *"We're on the Freedom Side."* As the chant passed around the circle, two young women Dream Defenders stepped up to name points of contact with the longer freedom movement: *"Ella Baker was a freedom fighter, and she taught us how to fight. We gonna fight all day and night until we get it right."* The group replied: *"Say what?"* They called: *"What side are you on my people, what side are you on?"* The group reply: *"We're on the Freedom Side!"*[27] They continued, evoking Fannie Lou Hamer, Harriet Tubman, Assata Shakur. The variations drew forward a many-sided freedom vision, carried on rhythms both ancient and fresh.

Agnew moved to the podium on the white marble steps. Building on the energy among those assembled, he proclaimed, "If you're a young person in the struggle, I want you to say 'Get ready!'" Thousands replied, "Get ready! Get ready!" He continued, "I want to take two minutes to tell you who we are."[28]

Young people were "the forgotten generation," Agnew began. "We are the illegals. We are the apathetic. We are the thugs. We are the generation that you locked in the basement while movement conversations were going on upstairs." The son and grandson of Chicago preachers, Agnew's intonation drew people in. As the future of the nation, "we came to love," he called, to join in "a conversation that will shake the very foundations of this capital." The young and the previously marginalized were here to join the center. "And so I will ask for the final minute of my conversation with you to be dedicated to the young people. Stand with your fists in the air." Thousands raised their arms in a fist. "Join me in a call and response that will shake the vestiges of democracy. I believe that we can win. Repeat after me, 'I believe that we will win.'" Voices all over the mall then echoed together, "I believe that we WILL WIN!"

Much like the young students who had formed SNCC, the Dream Defenders mobilized around a particular issue. SNCC had formed around the sit-ins, a concrete way to refuse Jim Crow. The Dream Defenders emerged in response to the murder of Trayvon Martin, sitting-in at the state capitol to reject laws that criminalized young people of color and led far too often to their unpunished murder. Both groups used the tools of nonviolent direct action to organize and to focus attention on the need to reform the society's structure. Now elders themselves, SNCC veterans such as Zoharah Simmons, Charlie Cobb, Judy Richardson, and Courtland Cox worked as *fundis* with the Dream Defenders. Trayvon Martin's death was no isolated incident in an otherwise well-functioning system, just as Jim Crow was not a glitch in the American tale of freedom and equality. Both formal segregation and repeated violence against Black youth were merely symptoms of deeper institutional corruption. Those patterns became visible in racial profiling, police violence, unequal sentencing, disenfranchisement, and many other forms of discrimination that legal scholar Michelle Alexander aptly summarized as the "new Jim Crow."

#BLACKLIVESMATTER

Trayvon Martin's death was as tragic as it was unsurprising. For millions of young people of color, it served as a gut-punch reminder of the precarious nature of their own lives. It was not a local story—it was a national agony. As if he was a family member or close friend, in Black communities across the country, people simply referred to him as "Trayvon." "If I had a son," President Barack Obama said, "he'd look like Trayvon." And so the responses to the Zimmerman acquittal came not just from Florida's Dream Defenders but from young activists across the country.

Friends Patrisse Cullors, Alicia Garza, and Opal Tometi had been active in multiple movements over the years—in Los Angeles, in Oakland, in New York. Their work had prepared them in practical terms for the news of Zimmerman's acquittal. Yet none of them could get "over" it and just move on. Zimmerman killed Trayvon in cold blood and walked out of court a free man. Patrisse Cullors described her afternoon after the acquittal as if in a daze, scrolling through Facebook posts, looking for information, trying to make sense of it all. Then she came across a powerful letter from Alicia Garza, a friend from Oakland. Garza's letter read in part, "B[y] t[he] w[ay] stop saying that we are not surprised" at the verdict. "That's a damn shame in itself," she posted. "I continue to be surprised at how little Black lives matter. And I will continue that." She urged, "Stop giving up on black life" and pledged, "Black people, I will NEVER give up on us. NEVER." "Black people. I love you. I love us. Our lives matter."

Cullors immediately reposted Garza's letter, responding with the hashtag #BlackLivesMatter. And thus a long-understood Black reality crystallized in new form.[29] Activist Ash-Lee Woodard Henderson later summed up its impact: "That Alicia Garza could write a love letter to black people," she said in 2018, "and remind us on one of the hardest days of our lives, and on literally one of the hardest days of my life, that I mattered to her, and that all Black people mattered to her," simply "transformed how we understand our blackness in the twenty-first century political moment."[30]

In the immediate aftermath of Zimmerman's acquittal, social media posts tagged #BlackLivesMatter provided a platform for hundreds of thousands to gather online, a centralized digital place to express disbelief and outrage and demand action. Observing this groundswell, Cullors, Garza, and their New York–based friend Opal Tometi decided to create an organization around "a call to action for Black Lives Matter." The women brought together extensive experience from the immigrant, labor, and police-prison reform movements, aiming to build on-the-ground chapters and "a network online" that could respond to "the anti-Black racism that permeates our society and also, unfortunately, our movements." Tometi developed "all the initial digital components." The three women were determined, Cullors reflected later, "to take public this basic concept: That our lives mean something. That Black Lives Matter." Meanwhile, the hashtag #BlackLivesMatter continued to connect others to the central argument of Garza's initial post. The hashtag created a powerful way to unite disparate video footage and testimony under a clear claim.[31]

Cullors called people to a meeting at her Los Angeles home a few days after the Zimmerman verdict. They talked about what they envisioned: "We deserve another knowing, the knowing that comes when you assume your life will be long, will be vibrant, will be healthy. We deserve to imagine a world without prisons and punishment," where they were not even needed, "a world rooted in mutuality."[32] Meetings of a similar kind were held in Black communities across the country—and, indeed, organizing efforts remained remarkably decentralized. A few characteristics about Black Lives Matter (BLM), however, require emphasis. Though often later dismissed by casual observers as a mere hashtag, what would grow into chapters in over forty cities across the US and Canada represented more than a single organization. It was the embodiment of a new *organizing* model, building on experiences of the past and on experiences from a variety of diverse, intersecting movements. Scholar Kim TallBear (Sisseton-Wahpeton Oyate) remarked, "As a Dakota feminist and supporter of BLM," she saw "women who lead the movement as *sharing* ground with women" from the Indigenous movements organizing around the Dakota Access pipeline and Idle No More. For TallBear, Tometi, Cullors, and Garza were "caretaking their peoples and others as they defend bodies marginalized in a brutal anti-Black, antitrans, anti-immigrant, and antiworker world."[33]

The reader may wonder how to distinguish the official work and statements of BLM chapters from people posting material online and connecting it to the broader movement using #BLM or #BlackLivesMatter hashtags. The movement itself has both tightly knit groups that operate largely through face-to-face relationships, and at the same time, many organizers and activists learn and teach one another and outside observers by linking material through social media. The latter work is not filtered by chapters, and online postings sometimes challenge stances taken by BLM chapters. Yet the massive number of people who have taken part in posting material with the hashtag and in engaging the ideas underlying it must be seen as evidence of the movement's wider societal impact. The hashtag campaign is part of what 1960s activists called "consciousness raising," for it links people to one another, changes their individual and collective understanding, and provides a wealth of information, insights, and perspectives that would otherwise not be available.

Above all, Cullors, Garza, and Tometi aimed to build an inclusive *organizing network* that both unified and empowered people who had felt harassed, disrespected, ignored, or otherwise marginalized and brutalized by local, state, and national institutions. Responding to isolated incidences, they thought, was no longer sufficient. As Tometi created "the architecture for our first website and Twitter accounts, our Facebook and Tumblr," they intentionally aimed to avoid "disaster tourism"—they didn't want organizers descending on the next city to experience the shooting of yet another young Black person.[34]

Instead, they wanted to address a simple reality: all "respectable" politics—working to change laws, institute voting rights, elect a Black mayor or police chief or president—had not changed the fact that Black lives, in the most existential way, still did not "matter." Black lives were much more likely lived in poverty, in dismal educational institutions, in jail; Black lives were shorter, often more brutal, and regularly stereotyped; and, quite simply, being Black—and particularly being young and Black—embodied a life of permanent danger. What people within the long freedom struggle sometimes called "the politics of respectability"—fitting in and playing by the rules—made little sense if the rules were stacked against you. As Cullors put it, "We've chosen the tactic of disruption. We've chosen the tactic of challenging respectability."[35]

This challenge worked on multiple levels. First, Black Lives Matter organizers aimed to reshape the most powerful institutions in the US: governments and corporations. They put their bodies in the way of business as usual. They laid down in highways and freeways at rush hour in the Bay Area. They marched in the streets of Atlanta, Philadelphia, Phoenix, and countless smaller towns, chanting, "No justice, no peace. No transphobic police," and "No justice, no peace. No racist police." They interrupted arts performances, city council hearings, sports events, and Sunday brunches all over the country. They blocked entrances to shopping malls and corporate headquarters. At each intervention, activists continued to assert that until all could experience the right to live peaceably, they would interrupt others' peaceable lives. On Los Angeles's Rodeo Drive, "where the wealthiest and mostly white people shop and socialize," Cullors (writing as Patrice Khan-Cullors) wrote, "we want to say before those who do nothing about it, what it means to live your whole life under surveillance, your life as the bull's-eye."[36]

At the same time, the leaders of BLM centered Black, queer, feminist ways of looking at the world, or as historian Barbara Ransby wrote, BLM took root, both politically and ideologically, squarely within the "US-based Black feminist tradition." BLM organizations emerged as distinct from Black organizations dominated by men, those that excluded members of the LGBTQ community, or those that followed a rigid, hierarchical top-down structure. In addition to Tometi, Garza, and Cullors's experiences in the labor, immigrant rights, and prison reform movements, all three women identified as queer. They insisted on an intersectional organizing frame for their work from the start, bringing it to prominence in both the national and international imagination.[37]

This frame centered the experiences of queer women of color. They articulated the specificities of their lives and demanded accountability and justice within the society *and* within the movement. Many forebears of Black feminist thought and experience could be seen in their work—including Anna Julia Cooper's 1892 *Voice from the South*, the National Black Feminist Organization, the 1977 Combahee River Statement, the writers of the 1983 anthology *This Bridge Called My Back*, and the Black queer political innovators of the 1970s, 1980s, and 1990s like Barbara Smith, Mandy Carter, and Audre Lorde.[38] The marginalization of these thinker-activists in previous decades contrasted with BLM, now arguably the *center* of the movement and founded by three queer Black women.[39]

This freed up Black organizers internally. "It's beautiful not to have to apologize for claiming liberation for all parts of your Black identity," New Orleans organizer Mwende "FreeQuency" Katwiwa noted. "All of us had been doing organizing before this happened," she said of work carried out under the banner of Black Lives Matter. "A lot of times I would find myself having to conform to different types of organizing and different definitions of Blackness." Her organization, Black Youth Project 100 (BYP100), formed in response to the verdict that found George Zimmerman not guilty in the killing of Trayvon Martin, drew thousands of young people to events across New Orleans. Katwiwa witnessed how this changed the dynamic with older Black organizers who earlier resisted the inclusion—much less the centering—of LGBTQ and feminist perspectives. Watching youth bring thousands of new voices to the table, the elders said, "'Alright, alright. We see y'all. We're gonna meet you on your level.'" It was, she noted, "a beautiful thing"[40]—and a major shift in the center of gravity within the freedom movement.

BYP100 also popularized Fresco Steez's (Angie Rollins's) phrase "unapologetically Black" to signal in part that members were no longer caught up in yesteryear's cultural wars about respectability politics and class, or gender and sexuality identities that had so often bedeviled older civil rights organizations and some corners of the Black freedom church. Unapologetically Black "exists as the ultimate antithesis to white supremacy [as] the ideological anchor of racial capitalism," reflected historian Barbara Ransby. Indeed, BYP100 made it clear to all other Black-led organizations: those who wanted to collaborate with BYP100 had to accept the inclusive nature of its organization. No more discrimination inside a race justice organization. BYP100 centered its work on peoples' ability "to take their own power" and draw on the resilience, resistance, and collective survival practices of the Black freedom struggle.[41]

BLM, with its action-oriented and inclusive organizing strategy, managed to embrace and energize youth from around the country. As Povi-Tamu Bryant, a Los Angeles activist, pointed out, unlike many other organizations, "we're not saying you need to leave your gender identity at the door, your college education at the door. We're saying, 'Bring all of you.'"[42] This included collaboration with many other independent organizations that emerged in the aftermath of the Zimmerman verdict, like the Dream Defenders and BYP100. It reenergized SONG, which began to organize alongside Black Lives Matter chapters in cities throughout the South like Atlanta, Durham, and Richmond.

This visibility encouraged others to come together in small towns and mid-size cities nationwide. Black Lives Matter "opened up space for new organizing," noted Garza. The collective pressure of marches and nonviolent direct action showed signs of success: by the fall of 2015, for instance, forty new laws had been proposed in twenty-eight states to reform criminal justice policy.[43] BLM raised questions. It offered opportunities for engagement. It experimented with organizing beyond "respectability politics." And there was the hope, however slight, that it would make a dent in public awareness, raise the bar for egregious police transgressions, and stem the tide of racist violence.

Then came Ferguson.

FERGUSON

To understand what happened in Ferguson in August 2014, it helps to pull the camera back briefly, perhaps to see the reality of American racist violence through the lens of, say, someone from outside the US—from a culture that generally subscribes to the idea that all lives matter and should matter equally. In most postindustrial nations, police escalation and provocation are simply not respectable law enforcement tactics. Representatives of the state are expected to serve citizens rather than treat them as submissive subjects. State authorities need to follow the same rules every other citizen has to— indeed, authorities have a special duty to do so. And within places like Finland, Germany, and Japan, those who do not follow their own laws and regulations or those who apply them differently, depending on skin color, have no legitimacy.[44]

Much has been made of the fact that Ferguson citizen Michael Brown allegedly stole from a convenience store—that he was not a model citizen. Leaving to the side the question of whether or not he transgressed, unless one believes that shoplifting or being disrespectful should be punishable by death, the facts remain brutal and nearly incomprehensible: an eighteen-year-old recent high school graduate, Michael Brown, a few weeks away from his first day of college, was killed by a police officer, shot in the back while unarmed.

On that sweltering summer day, in a display signaling profound disrespect, police left Brown's body lying on the street in partial view for a full four hours, the sun pounding down. The delay resulted from a number of factors, some within the St. Louis police's control and some not. The police defended their actions, yet community members and outside police experts joined a chorus of the wider public: no one's child or parent should be treated this way. Ferguson committeewoman Patricia Bynes recalled that the treatment of Brown's body, more than anything else, "sent the message from law enforcement that 'we can do this to you any day, any time, in broad daylight, and there's nothing you can do about it.'"[45]

The outrage expressed by people in the streets and across the country came not just in response to out-of-control law enforcement. In Ferguson, it evoked a specific history of white police as fee collectors from low-wealth Black people. And for Blacks across the nation, the treatment of Brown's body called to mind a long history of enraged whites putting tortured Black bodies on public display in response to Black self-assertion. In 2014, the behavior of a majority-white police unit in Ferguson resulted in a visceral reaction from millions of Black Americans that harkened back to lynching. For over a century in the US, thousands of postcards and then photos had circulated of smiling whites, sometimes with their small children, gathered around Black bodies swinging from trees. As Ida B. Wells observed, "Whenever a burning is advertised to take place, the railroads run excursions, photographs are taken and . . . the lynching mob cuts off ears, toes, and fingers, strips off flesh, and distributes portions of the body as souvenirs among the crowd." Rarely if ever have majority-white school districts taught this history in the intervening decades. In this way, it was a visual text largely illegible to white Americans under sixty in 2014.[46]

By the testimony of the officer who shot Brown, he made no attempt to de-escalate the confrontation with Brown or prevent deadly force. He neglected to handle the situation with the respect every citizen deserves—and by law is entitled to. This raised obvious questions: What role did the segregated neighborhood and school system play in this death? What role did the larger criminalization of young Black men play? Would the killing of Michael Brown have happened if he had been born the child of white parents?

Such are the realities of militarization and racism in contemporary America. If one needed further indication of the blatant double standards followed by the police, the August 2017 events in Charlottesville, Virginia, provided a garish contrast: heavily armed white supremacist vigilantes were allowed to roam through a calm college town—without being challenged by police. When one white nationalist actually fired a shot in the direction of a nonviolent racial justice demonstrator, the police, standing in line a mere twenty feet away, did not so much as move.[47]

From the outside, Ferguson illuminated a gigantic racial divide. Four months of mass protests ensued between August and November 2014, with activists joining from around the country. Ferguson images were nearly incomprehensible outside of international war zones: heavily armed police in riot gear and armored vehicles, preposterously overmilitarized, carrying semiautomatic weapons trained against peaceful protesters. Except that it was more like a pseudo-military coup. Regular police, excessively armed, seemed

FIGURE 10. Ferguson, Missouri, 2014. (Photo by Scott Olson/Getty)

to have declared war on Black people. For those aware of racist continuities in American history, it brought back images: first to Bull Connor's police tackling civil rights activists with dogs and fire hoses in Birmingham in the spring of 1963, then further back to police chief John Gustafson refusing to protect the wealthiest Black district in the nation, where whites killed over 300 Black people in the Tulsa Race Riot of 1921. Or further still to white police ignoring white rioters who started New York City's Tenderloin riots in 1900, yet clubbing and arresting Black residents still asleep in their beds. There were two stark differences: unlike Birmingham, Tulsa, or New York City, this time the police came in full military gear. And second, everyone had cameras and broadcast both still images and video around the world immediately. Global humanity could thus see Ferguson's local police, armed as if entering combat. Civil society it was not.[48]

Inside the movement, Ferguson was a turning point of another kind. It made clear for all to see that the tragedy of persistent violence against young Black citizens was not an exclusive domain of big cities—Los Angeles or New York or Chicago. Rather, it was a daily phenomenon in Heartland, USA. One twenty-eight-year-old teacher and public school administrator, DeRay Mckesson, kept coming back to Ferguson, week after week, unable to stay away

FIGURE 11. DeRay Mckesson, Twitter post, December 14, 2014.

(fig. 11). Mckesson would emerge in the next few months as a major spokesperson of the movement, who, it should be noted, more than once has been criticized for behavior contrary to Ella Baker's horizontal political practice.[49] Yet his observation is no less true. Ferguson changed what happened in large and small cities. It changed what happened in towns and suburbs. It initiated, quite literally, a national and global phenomenon. Exceptions existed only in places that, for all intents and purposes, had no Black presence.[50] This was not one biased jury in Florida who whitewashed George Zimmerman for killing Trayvon Martin. Youth response to Ferguson illuminated for thousands and then millions of Americans the structural bias of multiple institutions—the police, yes. And the municipal courts, school systems, health care entities, and bank and real estate institutions.

Sustained activity in Ferguson highlighted the interconnected nature of the challenges Black Americans faced. As it served to bring organizers from all across the country together, it allowed people from different cities and towns to build deeper face-to-face relationships. For example, it was at Ferguson that Patrisse Cullors met Phillip Agnew (then Umi Selah) and BYP100's Charlene Carruthers for the first time. "I feel like I am meeting long-lost family," she recalled.[51] Organizers who had been working in local #BlackLivesMatter campaigns arrived in Ferguson from everywhere—they met, they exchanged experiences, they stood in solidarity with local residents as they faced a militarized police. And they shared pain and sorrow, trying to articulate a path forward.

Collectively, these activists grappled with a persistent current of American culture, refusing to go away. The president was Black. Some of the police involved in the violence were Black. And yet, for all who cared to look, it was unmistakable: at its core, police violence was fed by anti-Black attitudes—sometimes open and explicit, often so deeply rooted that its practitioners seemed no longer aware of its debilitating control.[52]

As more details emerged from Ferguson, people came together in Missouri because the Brown shooting echoed dynamics they saw and experienced far too often in their own hometowns: police officers almost itching for deadly confrontation. Police are unlike public servants at such institutions as hospitals, schools, or libraries, scholar Keeanga-Yamahtta Taylor observed. In contrast to these other occupations, police face few if any consequences for gross malfeasance. And because they have the awesome power of life and death, "astronomical sums of taxpayer money" have gone to pay compensation to victims of police brutality and misconduct across the US since 1960. Public schools have routinely been shut down when money got tight, yet "rarely, if ever, are police rebuked for costing cities millions of desperately needed public dollars." Instead, police historically and currently in the US are "universally lauded by public officials and shielded from any consequences—including for killing or brutalizing civilians."[53]

"The free rein of police is a critical component of urban governance today," Taylor reflects. Certainly, for millions of Black and brown Americans, indiscriminate police brutality is an all-too-familiar routine. Time and again, activists gathered in Ferguson from across the country realized that "everybody here is representing a family member or someone that's been hurt, murdered, killed, arrested, deported."[54] Police violence against people of color was not isolated—not by place or by time. On the contrary, it was a persistent pattern of abuse of power, fed by implicit bias, affecting millions.

Youth sprayed the images in Ferguson across social media: of police in heavy body armor aiming rifles and dogs at women, at children, at the elderly. They were picked up by media from around the world. Reporters and activists came to witness. Many joined demonstrators chanting "I can't breathe," "Black Lives Matter," and "Michael Brown—Emmett Till / How many Black lives will you kill?" Reporters of color experienced firsthand being singled out, getting manhandled, arrested.[55]

Law enforcement's abuse of power in Ferguson overwhelmed and outraged local residents and global onlookers alike. It caused indignation. Upon reflection, it was sobering, almost debilitating. What could Ferguson residents or anyone else do in response? Bearing witness, showing solidarity, and asserting a physical presence by standing up to law enforcement's disproportionate response was essential. Yet it was not enough to prevent violence and abuse, not enough, above all, to prevent the killings of Black youth.⁵⁶ Even a multitude of creative actions did not suffice. As people drifted out of Ferguson after a few weeks, more and more activists concluded that the Black Lives Matter movement badly needed fresh approaches, including a permanent organized presence—one that reached across geographical boundaries as much as one that overcame confines of identity or faith.

Ferguson highlighted the massive fault line of racism in the heartland. Yet in this town, that could hardly be separated out from economics. In the words of Ferguson's Reverend Starsky Wilson, the police state on the streets of Ferguson seemed similar to the Roman occupation under which Jesus lived. A great chasm had opened up in the US between the "have and have-nots, those who get—and those who get forgot."⁵⁷ The problem was more than just absurd degrees of inequality. Increasingly, the very apparatus used to keep a boot on the necks of poor people was financed through the exploitation of these very same poor people. Across America, the redistribution of wealth from the many to the few had left communities "cash-starved," struggling to pay for basic services. Ferguson, like thousands of other similar communities around the country, relied on police and courts "to extract millions in fines and fees from its poorest residents, issuing thousands of citations each year." The citations and tickets plugged "a financial hole created by the ways in which the city, the county, and the state have chosen to apportion the costs of public services." As the reverend reflected, "Like the Jews under Roman rule, those in Ferguson stayed poor due to laws levied on them." Or as Patrisse Cullors reflected, the police "stole from the residents and then used that money to buy the tanks, tear gas and machine guns that on August 9 would be turned against those very same residents."⁵⁸

Reverend Wilson's sermon highlighted a widely ignored reality visible in plain sight: depending on their race and economic status, Americans experienced two different realities—one hopeful and full of progress, the other one of precarious steps forward amid a persistent pull down. Not surprisingly, affluent white citizens were often clueless about the day-to-day realities that Black people faced: profiling, the lack of respect, the broken ladder of freedom. If you were poor and Black, the police acted frequently as an occupying force, and courts generally did little more than rubberstamp injustice. For too many Blacks, whites were often people, in the memorable phrase of Dream Defender Phillip Agnew, who "can play our jazz but can't stand our blues."⁵⁹

In this kind of environment, the hashtag #BlackLivesMatter served as a powerful shorthand. First of all, it "says to people that 'I mean something,'" Agnew reflected. But it was more than a defensive claim. It was a plain assertion that

"I deserve more. I am human. And I'm going to force you, whether it's by blocking the road, whether it's by dying-in, whether it's by interrupting the shopping season, to acknowledge that, even if it's uncomfortable for you."[60]

MOVE OVER, NIGHTLY NEWS: THE ROLE OF SOCIAL MEDIA

Social media platforms made it easy for people to collectively gather evidence that the signs of crisis were everywhere by 2014. Twitter in particular had "become a special kind of public square for African Americans," noted movement historian Barbara Ransby. But the movement could grow strong only if it had solid and reliable internal lines of communication. This had been as true on the ground for tenant farmers organizing in the 1920s in Alabama as it was for autoworkers striking in Michigan in the 1930s or for SNCC standing up against Jim Crow in the 1960s. Problems developing internal channels of communication led to misunderstandings and infighting among those participating in American freedom movements, as well as among Indians protesting British rule in the 1930s, Polish workers striking in the 1970s, Zapatistas in Mexico fighting for their land in the 1990s, and Indigenous groups defending their land across the world against repeated corporate encroachment in 2016.[61]

Plenty of evidence existed: any movement could easily be broken by authorities if everyday people could not talk among themselves and keep the lines of communication open. In the 1960s, SNCC held frequent workshops and retreats and, in the days before long-distance telephone calls were routine, used CB radios and the long-distance Wide-Area Telecommunications Service (WATS) line to keep one another informed. Lech Walesa solved this problem for the Poles on the first morning of their general strike in 1980 by demanding that negotiations with the authorities be done over the loudspeaker so everyone could hear, preventing those in the movement from the fear their leaders were selling out. Occupy Wall Street adopted this tactic in 2011. The Zapatistas held frequent meetings and retreats to keep their internal lines of communication strong. Indigenous groups at Standing Rock relied on both new and old practices—social media, workshops, and physical encampments—to mobilize support, build internal solidarity, and maintain a strong physical presence.[62]

In the 2010s, Twitter became one vital way to overcome the central problem of how BLM organizers could stay in communication and in sync. It is much harder in the social media era to have government or corporate media monopolize information or impede all communication, at least within the

US.⁶³ As scholar Mark Anthony Neal noted in September 2014, "There were over one million tweets using the hashtag #Ferguson before CNN started any coverage of Ferguson." It was a fresh insight: "Young folks are now using technology to be able to cover information on the ground that drives mainstream corporate media to those instances."⁶⁴ Social media also changed the politics of representation. "In the past you could look only to movies or TV or music or celebrities in order to feel like you had representation," young actor and activist Amandla Stenberg reflected. "Now you can go on Instagram and you can see a girl who looks like you who is killing the game and expressing herself. Just being able to see that is so affirming."⁶⁵

Black communities had created a whole range of strategies and tactics over centuries that became part of a culture of resistance to white supremacy—including work slowdowns, noncooperation, sabotage, retention of African cultural traditions, escape, outright rebellion, and building maroon communities. The limiting element had been that few people in any one region were in a position to publicly share the widespread nature of this protest and resistance. In the 2010s, Twitter hashtags intensified the scope and scale of work that the Black press and music had long done. The new platform overcame an old problem: people saw not only what was happening in their community on social media but also similar patterns in other communities. And everyone knew it was "see-able" across a public format—social media. Two generations after the 1964 and 1965 civil rights acts, suddenly the entire population could learn how disaffected from law enforcement millions of people in Black and brown communities had become.⁶⁶

#BlackLivesMatter, posted by Patrisse Cullors in the immediate aftermath of Trayvon Martin's killer going free, was shared on Twitter fairly frequently, about fifty times a day, between July 2013 and August 9, 2014. Yet one can see its escalating usage: by the end of August 2014, the hashtag was used 52,000 times. And in the first four hours after the Ferguson grand jury decided not to indict Darren Wilson on November 24, 2014, it was used 92,784 times. The hashtag both generated and reflected a sense of urgency across the entire city, state, and nation—and got people to show up in the streets.⁶⁷

In this way, the hashtag provided crucial internal communication linking the movement and educating Black and non-Black publics. It also revealed the massive collective memory that is largely exclusive to Black people in the US. Gross police abuse in the cases of Rodney King (1991), Abner Louima (1997), Amadou Diallo (1999), and others each precipitated local, and some national, protest. Michael Moore's 2007 seven-minute film, *The Awful Truth*, began to present this consciousness to larger numbers of non-Black people.⁶⁸ Yet one post on Twitter by Candice Price, (@MidwestSkit,) represented a new scale of analysis and information-sharing invisible to most non-Blacks prior to the killing of Trayvon Martin. Responding to those who claimed a Black person would not have been shot if only they had acted differently, she listed the blatant truth:

> Run = you die (#WalterScott)
> Stay & get arrested = you die (#FreddieGray)
> Lay down while handcuffed = you die (#ericharris #Oscar Grant)
> Fight back = you die (#TrayvonMartin)
> Mind your business = you die (#JohnCrawford)
> Put your hands up = you die (#MikeBrown)
> Proclaim your innocence = you die (#EricGarner)
> Getting married = you die (#SeanBell)
> Pants sagging = you die (#ErvinEdwards)
> Beg for your life = you die (#ThaddeusMcCarroll #CedricBartee)

The tweet continued to list the ways Black people's various responses to police interaction made no difference to the outcome of a massive structural problem. This information was now visible to everyone and available publicly. Hashtags made it "findable." Learning across racial, ethnic, and geographic lines became easier than ever.[69]

Philosopher Charles Mills wrote in 1997 that mainstream US institutions promote "racialized ignorance" despite the cost of this ignorance to civil society.[70] This can easily be seen in the fact that prior to #BlackLivesMatter, most whites did not know about police brutality in communities of color unless they had close friends or family across the color line.

Historians provided little help, noted Nathan Huggins in 1991, as the majority wrote history as if white supremacy, race-based slavery, and segregation had been aberrations instead of "the most flagrant contradiction" at the heart of the nation's political life. Schools and universities have taught ignorance of the bare facts of race in US history from the eighteenth through the twenty-first centuries. Part of what people refer to now as "white privilege" meant simply not having to know about the dangers of "driving while Black," or the terror of walking through certain non-Black neighborhoods while Black, or the uncertainty of shopping in stores while Black. One could see this racial ignorance rise to high visibility when white New York City police officers reacted with intense anger to white mayor Bill de Blasio's public explanation in 2014 of how he educated his son, Dante, to handle police contact. Dante de Blasio's African American identity put him at risk for violent profiling. Fathers of white children don't have to know this. Fathers of Black children do. Activists, organizers, and observers on Twitter thus began to "unteach" the racial ignorance that many US institutions promote. People could ignore this reality, or they could fight against it daily, as did white nationalist trolls. In line with a long history of whiteness in the US, they could claim ignorance and innocence. Twitter's vast global audience and its command of media attention made such claims increasingly hard to sustain.[71]

Social media fostered ways for movement activists to talk to one another across time and space—Palestinian activists tweeted to Ferguson activists, for example, their tips for minimizing the impact of tear gas. On social media, young people could stay in ongoing conversation with movement elders around tactics, strategy, and analysis. In ways that carried forward the independent media traditions of the early twentieth century—the Black press, independent publishers and bookstores, and Third World Liberation media services—social media also "gives us a space to birth and control narratives," Ash-Lee Woodard Henderson, codirector of the Highlander School, reflected in 2018. "It gives us a space to tell our truths in our own voices. It gives us a space to actually practice what it is to center the most marginalized voices." And even when activists knew that government agents were "literally collecting data that they're going to use against me," Woodard Henderson stayed on social media platforms for a very straightforward reason: that's where the people were. "What's real is that my brother is there, and I can talk to him there. That regular black people are using it."[72]

Social media also came with serious limits and dangers, but rarely was there space to talk about the issue of social media and activism outside of a "for it" or "against it" framework. Woodard Henderson summed up the challenge: "I don't think the polarity of the way that we talk about social media is useful to grassroots communities." As an organizer, she wanted to see "a nuanced conversation about using it as a tool, not a replacement, to grassroots organizing."[73] If people had personality clashes or fights, social media magnified those disagreements and put them out in public in ways that seldom led to greater clarity or positive outcomes. Yet one had to suss out the enriching, community-building components of social media and figure out how to separate them from the dangers of social media stardom and its resulting disfiguration of young political groups.

To open that more nuanced conversation, youth activists generated creative strategies. The Dream Defenders decided that during the second half of 2015, they would conduct a "social media blackout." Organizer Nailah Summers recalled, "Some of us were reflecting on the fact that we want to be on the ground, doing the work, not just on Facebook and Twitter." Movement scholar Clarence Lang reflected that social media amplified the destructive myth that movements popped up "spontaneously"—it seemed as if all it took was a few viral tweets to bring hundreds of thousands of people into the streets. Or as Barbara Ransby noted in 2015, "Twitter is personality-driven, anonymous when convenient and an opportunity for spectatorship as much as engagement. We don't know how many of our followers are actually supporters, just as we don't know if all our Facebook friends actually like us." She recognized, moreover, that these new technologies "are also the site for ever more sinister and sophisticated forms of government surveillance."[74]

Observers who wanted to create or join movements thus did not have the chance to learn that underneath such mass mobilizations were thousands of hours of "agenda setting, constituency building, recruiting, political education." In addition to these concerns, the Dream Defenders grew wary of the celebrity profile of some of their leaders. Social media had been crucial to getting people active and to the education of its members, but the Dream Defenders determined to take a reflective pause. After the blackout, they used social media as a microphone rather than as a primary site for their organizing.[75]

"Millennials are not a monolith," Woodard Henderson reflected. And neither were their elders, veterans of the civil rights and Black Power movements. Addressing the latter, she remarked, "You taught us that 'By any means necessary' meant by all the means." Social media was a tool, "neither perfectly good nor perfectly evil," and "young people are savvy enough to know that. Trust us." No youth activist she knew was saying, "It's this great thing and it's making organizing perfect for us." Nor did those in Black Lives Matter "have a meeting and say 'oh, now we're digital organizers only.'" It was "an addition, not a replacement, and as a Southerner," she continued, invoking ideas of hospitality and face-to-face organizing, "I take that seriously." Woodard Henderson, the Dream Defenders, and others in the Movement for Black Lives now move at what veteran activist adrienne maree brown called "the speed of trust. That's as fast as our movements can go."[76]

Controlling this self-created environment of information sharing, learning, and transfer was necessary, but not sufficient, for movement organizers. Activists also needed to develop means by which to disagree without setting back the movement. Charlene Carruthers, the founding national director of Black Youth Project 100, noted that members of her group had to change their internalized expectations of political behavior. Most of them came into the movement wary of internal disagreement. Given so little movement history to base their own work on, they feared recreating what they understood to have happened in prior political groups in the 1930s and 1960s, where dissent could mean the group broke apart. Instead, BYP100 created an intentional environment, "part of a broader democratic process," where "we work on challenging ourselves to make sure we are inclusive in our leadership development, and invest in people." Such work echoed Van Jones's insight from his green jobs campaign in the Bay Area during the early 2000s, of "battling not just the punitive, unforgiving jailers on the outside" but intentionally taking care of "the punitive jailer within, the hurt and angry part of ourselves who can't forgive our coworkers and allies for shortcomings and disappointments."[77]

BYP100 members knew everyone made mistakes or had incomplete knowledge, so "challenging ourselves is important." They carried out continual trainings—on prison abolition, on anti-Blackness, on putting their struggle in a global context. "We have to make connections among ourselves," Carruthers asserted. As an activist, member-led organization of Black eighteen- to thirty-five-year-olds, this new style of what older generations called "political education" was essential "to creating justice and freedom for all Black people."[78]

A strange reality surfaced. Analyses like those offered by adrienne maree brown, Ash Lee Woodard Henderson, and Charlene Carruthers verified the depth of the movement's experiences and political sophistication. Yet the less one knew about police brutality's impact on Black communities over the previous six generations, the more "impulsive" the #BlackLivesMatter movement seemed. The media and various commentators described the movement as "spontaneous," even "an outbreak" or "a miracle."[79] These were descriptions from afar, from people who were distant observers. For those who had long known and lived these collective histories, the movement was only the most recent form of the long American freedom struggle.

Perhaps the single greatest accomplishment of the first year of the Black Lives Matter movement was that it organized people to combat the politically visible problem of police brutality in the public sphere. They made it so that images and experiences of police brutality broadcast on social media could no longer be unseen or repressed. The dramatic nature of the deadly police behavior and the raw vulnerability of the targeted human beings affected everyone who saw such images. The urgency created through social media posts brought people out into the streets to make their voices heard.

ORGANIZING AND DEMONSTRATING

For BYP100, as well as the Dream Defenders and BLM, marches and civil disobedience were the most visible actions to those outside the movement. Yet street politics were only part of the struggle. Organizers used less-observable tools like small meetings, trainings, and community organizing campaigns to do the hard work of maintaining internal communication and to train new people at the base to be their own leaders in local communities. "Ella Taught Us," featured on a poster one BYP100 activist held up at their 2016 convening, encapsulated this truth. Following Baker's lead, though, involved an ongoing and multigenerational struggle long into the future. If anything, Ella Baker's organizing model was not about quick fixes.

The mindset and habits of democratic action did not happen after one convening, or even as a result of a few really good organizers showing up in each town or city. It is useful to recall that Ella Baker reorganized her entire life so that she could live among SNCC people for over four years in Atlanta—a hub where many SNCC workers stayed for extended periods of time. She got to know the young SNCC workers as people and built resilient relationships with them. She went to their small and large meetings. She sat through endless group discussions and, for the most part, stayed quiet but fiercely determined. At key moments, her interventions and questions to the larger group allowed them to remain united—and focused—on a few central ideas: "We can do *both* voter registration *and* direct action." "Strong people don't need strong leaders." "Local people need to be involved in decision making." And she connected SNCC youth to longtime local leaders who had been organizing for decades, like Mississippians Amzie Moore and E. W. Steptoe, Alabama's Amelia Boynton and Lillian McGill, Georgia's Dolly Raines and the Christian family of Albany. Those local people then put SNCC workers into networks that *they* had. This work allowed SNCC to stand on the platform built by the generations before them.[80]

People staying with the youth of BLM to provide support Ella Baker–style have emerged in multiple places. Jamala Rogers from St. Louis, Makani Themba in Jackson, Mississippi, and Chicagoans Cathy Cohen and Barbara Ransby were but a few elders connecting to prior Black feminist movement, labor movement, immigration rights movement, and anti-war movement histories to build concrete ways for younger generations of Black organizers to learn about the history of the organizing tradition.[81] It meant that BLM activists did not have to start their work from scratch as they experimented in something that is completely unfamiliar to most Americans: fresh ways to make government bodies accountable to people at the base. SNCC activists Bob Moses, Zoharah Simmons, Jennifer Lawson, Courtland Cox, Judy Richardson, Charlie Cobb, Betty Garman Robinson, and others worked hard to create ongoing relationships with BLM activists as they created a series of platforms to share their own history. They hosted multiple conferences and created a "Today" section of the SNCC Digital Gateway to foster connections with youth organizers. During a multiyear project, the repeated gatherings with young people from the Dream Defenders, BYP100, BLM, and other youth organizations included not only formal meetings but often sessions that ran late into the night over food and libations, recreating an intergenerational movement culture to sustain young people's struggle.[82]

BALTIMORE

Trayvon Martin's killing provided the impetus for this generation's "sit-in" moment—when Black youth across the country began to organize in large numbers against police abuse and the school-to-prison pipeline and to demand that the powerful institutions of the nation reinvest in the potential of youth of color. Momentum had been building through the previous two decades—the Rodney King, Amadou Diallo, and Sean Bell traumas; responses to Hurricane Katrina; the case of the Jena Six in Louisiana and of Troy Davis in Georgia.[83] Yet it was after Trayvon Martin's killing that youth stood forward in a way that could no longer be ignored. Ferguson then brought the organizers in local movements together for the movement's first sustained national BLM gathering: they saw themselves *as* a group doing work across the country, in many contexts, and could compare notes. They learned from one another, exchanged ideas, and built stronger face-to-face alliances. Some unraveled the role of fines and fees in holding poor people down and then shared that nationally. In Ferguson, activists educated mainstream journalists and learned how to effectively use social media to share their stories more widely.

Then in April 2015, in North Charleston, South Carolina, police officer Michael Slager shot Walter Scott in the back, killing him. Two weeks later, Baltimore police severed 80 percent of Freddie Gray's spinal cord after his arrest for possessing a knife. He died a week later. It had happened again. Black men killed by police in situations where deadly force could not be justified. Baltimore residents rose up, and like Ferguson, the country witnessed months of sustained confrontations between Baltimore citizens and police.

The killing of Freddie Gray opened a third phase of organizing. The murder in Baltimore was clearly not reducible to a Black-white issue. Something else was at work. In Selma in February 1965, Martin Luther King Jr. had argued that "if Negroes could vote, there would be no oppressive poverty directed against Negroes."[84] Yet as Baltimore in 2015 made clear, the promise of the 1965 Voting Rights Act—putting Black elected officials into office—was not sufficient to protect Black people from institutional violence. Scholar Keeanga-Yamahtta Taylor reflected, "When a Black mayor, governing a largely Black city, aids in the mobilization of a military unit led by a Black woman to suppress a Black rebellion, we are in a new period of the Black freedom struggle." The Freddie Gray killing, Taylor continued, "exposed Black elected officials' inability to intervene effectively on behalf of poor and working-class African Americans."[85] How could the movement hold Black officials in Baltimore accountable to those at the base of society?

Racism alone could not explain this problem. Hundreds of thousands of Black families had moved into the middle and upper classes since 1965. Yet in cities across the country, Black politicians seemed unable to fix majority-Black schools that failed children. They were not able to implement policies that created equal-opportunity loans for Black entrepreneurs or homeowners. When gang activity dominated specific areas of Detroit, Washington, Houston, Los Angeles, New York, or Baltimore, as legal scholar James Forman Jr. illuminated, Black leaders of police forces relied on the same strategies as those of their white predecessors: mass incarceration.[86] The uprising in Baltimore in the spring and summer of 2015 forced a movement and societal reckoning. Marches, protests, political education, and social media education, while essential, were also not sufficient. Movement strategists searched for policies to make life better for the majority of Black citizens bypassed by the gains of the civil rights–Black Power era.

POLITICAL PLATFORM:
THE MOVEMENT FOR BLACK LIVES

To respond to this reality in the year following Baltimore, hundreds of Black and brown organizers from more than forty organizations affiliated and allied with Black Lives Matter gathered repeatedly, starting in Cleveland—a kind of "Holy Ground, the place where little Tamir Rice has been killed"—to create a comprehensive policy agenda. They engaged in an immensely complex process of sussing out and coming to agreement on both goals and the best way to achieve them. In an ideal world, they would have had more time.[87] Yet people were suffering immediate threats, and police continued to kill young people at an alarming rate.

One issue in particular stood out. Yes, the stories of police brutality were becoming more widely known. Still, "they never talk about the women and girls." It was a statement whose stark truth, said in grief, sculpted the freedom movement's agenda going forward. Chicago police officer Dante Servin went on trial in 2015 for killing Rekia Boyd, a twenty-two-year old Black woman. Activists gathered to support Boyd's family in court. Angela Helton, Boyd's mother, sat grief-stricken in the courtroom. "They never talk about the women and girls," Helton told Charlene Carruthers of BYP100. Servin's case was dismissed, but the Movement for Black Lives (M4BL) refused to let this go. Mervyn Mercano, Patrisse Cullors, Maurice Mitchell, and Thenjiwe McHarris reached out to Carruthers to ask how they could help. Scholars Andrea Ritchie and Kimberlé Crenshaw had created a powerful report on police violence against Black women and girls; they too contacted Carruthers to see if it made sense to release their report in conjunction with Servin's police board hearing.[88]

"The nexus of Black women's intellectual labor and grassroots organizing led to powerful actions across more than sixteen cities in the United States on the same day," Carruthers recalled. "The moment Rekia's mom joined the Chicago action, I looked at her and said, 'Ms. Helton, I remember sitting in the courtroom with you that day, and you shared that no one ever talks about Black women and girls. Well, we're changing that all over the country today.'" #SayHerName National Day of Action brought out people across the country, and campaign activists showed up at every Chicago police review board meeting for a year. Their first victory occurred when Servin resigned before the police review board made a determination on him, but the activists didn't stop there. The movement would keep pushing to "advance structural changes," Carruthers noted, "so that no more families have to go through what Rekia's family continues to cope with today."[89]

Social media's capacity for information sharing meant millions learned of the #SayHerName campaign. And more broadly, people knew immediately as soon as law enforcement beat, humiliated, or killed anyone. Groups large and small gathering to figure out a larger strategy for the movement felt increasing pressure in 2015–16. Society-wide tensions became unbearable, and the drumbeat to "do something, anything," quickened as Philando Castile and Alton Sterling were killed on camera by police in July 2016. When Diamond Reynolds, Castile's partner, began live-streaming the police stop on Facebook, the world could see the incredible calm and composure both Castile and Reynolds showed, while Officer Jeronimo Yanez appeared to wholly lose his, shooting Castile at close range without cause as both Reynolds and her four-year-old daughter sat, terrorized, in the vehicle alongside Castile.[90]

A few days later, a Black sniper in Dallas killed five police officers and wounded seven.[91] Self-described conservative media outlets, which had framed BLM since its earliest emergence as a war on police, goaded ever-higher tensions with

FIGURE 12. Joe Walsh, Twitter post, July 7, 2016.

headlines such as the *Drudge Report*'s "Black Lives Kill." Radio host and former congressperson Joe Walsh published incendiary posts on Twitter (fig. 12). Rush Limbaugh alleged on air that Black Lives Matter was "a terrorist group committing hate crimes" and that this was the "deadliest attack on law enforcement since 9/11." The FBI would largely follow right-wing radio's lead in the subsequent year, introducing "Black Identity Extremists" as a new "terror threat."[92]

BLM activists experienced this time as if under siege. Organizers felt pressure to do something, but it was not clear within such a compressed time frame what could be done. The pace of work that had begun in individual groups and between organizations over the previous year had to speed up. Finally, members of over sixty groups aligned with BLM announced comprehensive policy demands on August 1, 2016 (fig. 13). It was a powerful, detailed answer to those across the political spectrum who had repeatedly asked, "Well, what does Black Lives Matter want after all?"

The careful deliberating process these groups had engaged in set a high bar and a clear path forward. First, they called for an "end to the war"—the criminalizing and killing—of Black people. They also demanded policies that aimed to repair the harm done to Black people over the last three centuries. Additionally, they pressed for control over investments in Black communities, shifting funds from surveillance, policing, extractive industries, and incarceration to education, health, and well-being. In order to make such policies possible, they insisted on a shift in political and economic power, calling for collective ownership over economic entities in Black communities, community-accountable institutions, and political self-determination.

FIGURE 13. Movement for Black Lives platform, published August 1, 2016. (Courtesy of Movement for Black Lives)

The coalition announcing this policy platform, M4BL, included the Black Lives Matter network, as well as the Ella Baker Center, SONG, the Dream Defenders, BYP100, and over forty other groups. Participants did not focus solely on police accountability, as had earlier platforms like Campaign Zero. Instead, the combined groups announced the creation of an "M4BL Policy Table" to "focus on supporting the development and implementation of visionary and uncompromising local, national, and international policy objectives aimed at ending state-sanctioned violence against Black communities."[93]

The M4BL platform made plausible multiple ideas that many throughout the US had previously deemed "impossible." Adherents demanded community control and political power for a simple reason: the practical relevance of the M4BL platform was verified every time a police unit trampled on the rights and dignity of young teens. Every time a Black or brown driver was pulled over and addressed with cynicism or met with brutality. Every time a school or hospital could not adequately serve its constituents. Every time a Black or brown person was slammed to the ground in the course of going about daily errands. Every time a boss stole time or wages from a low-income worker. Every time another unarmed person was killed by a police officer using extreme force. Each time a civilian complaint was waved off by police organizations, police administrations, or party functionaries in city councils, state legislatures, or federal agencies. Every time corporate leaders, mayors, and school officials greeted demands for basic human rights with helpless shrugs and then expected people at the base to respond with ingrained deference to long-term patterns of disrespect. Every time something like this happened after August 1, 2016, the only end point that made any sense at all was the idea of a government accountable to the citizens it policed and governed. This is what the M4BL policy platform offered.

At the root, of course, it was quite a simple idea, one that had a long tradition in US history. It was about democracy: how to keep policy makers in touch with and accountable to those who lived at the base. Thomas Paine, Thomas Jefferson, and Charles Macune had called for such a government and economy among white men of all classes in the eighteenth and nineteenth centuries, and visionaries like Harriet Tubman, Angelina Grimké, and Anna Julia Cooper expanded the vision beyond white males. In the twentieth century, the sit-down strikers in Michigan as well as those who lined up for soup kitchens by the hundreds of thousands in the 1930s forced federal and state policy changes that emerged as part of the New Deal. The nation's "Second Reconstruction" during the civil rights–Black Power movement, the liberatory movements of women, and the LGBTQ, environmental, anti-war, American Indian, and Brown Power movements all expanded the nation's call to respond to everyday people's need for "liberty and justice for all."

The organizational challenge for M4BL was how to take these policy ideas "out of the kitchen" and into the governing bodies of the cities, hamlets, and suburbs of the nation. The Dream Defenders inspired "a nation of organizers," Patrisse Khan-Cullors explained, "bringing direct action back into the fore for our generation."[94] Now those gathered under M4BL needed to force major policy change.

The fact that the Ella Baker Center for Human Rights and SONG worked within the M4BL platform coalition bears note. For many years—in the case of SONG since 1993, and in the case of the EBC since 1996—these organizations had tirelessly worked on a series of interrelated movement issues: racial justice, workers' rights, LGBTQ rights, women's rights, immigrant rights, and labor (SONG), and an end to mass incarceration, police accountability, and the right to quality education and green jobs (the EBC). Here at the M4BL Policy Table, all of these issues came together. The Policy Table testified to the power of the decades-long, patient organizing of people at the base within a group-centered leadership model. It was a concrete policy manifestation of Pat Hussain's 1990s assertion, "I'm no longer going to choose between my ovaries, my skin, my lover Cherry, or my checkbook. Because they're all equally important to me. So I line those issues up one, one, one, one; rather than one, two, three, four. This is a conscious break in the way we've been taught to think."

The early innovations of M4BL were obvious. The movement resuscitated nonviolent direct action as a viable twenty-first-century political tool for Black equality. Participants developed sophisticated face-to-face and social media networks to strengthen internal lines of communication. They prioritized healing justice practices "that demonstrate that as we all seek to care for communities," Khan-Cullors shared, "we must also care for ourselves." "Young Black people in the United States have once again shifted the center of gravity in politics, kitchen table conversations, and mainstream media discourse," BYP100 leader Charlene Carruthers stated. "From Ferguson to Chicago, Charlotte, and Baltimore, uprisings of young Blacks have put the world on notice that something is shifting in the United States." The M4BL activists opened "doors" to the movement for allies from Latinx, Indigenous, Asian American, and white racial justice groups to work alongside them within an "unapologetically Black" framework. They lifted up the egalitarian ground rules pioneered in previous generations by Black feminists and people of color within the LGBTQ movement, centering "the voices of those not only made most vulnerable but most unheard, even as they are on the front lines at every hour and in every space: Black women—all Black women." They "repurpose[ed] university resources to instruct themselves and one another—to self-radicalize," in the words of Black intellectual Robin Kelley.[95] They systematically assessed the work still to be done in the wake of the 1960s freedom movements and put forward a set of concrete policy proposals.

In addition to these national achievements, local and statewide victories came when BYP100 won its campaign for reparations for victims of the Chicago police, making that city "the first municipality in the history of the United States to ever provide reparations for racially motivated law enforcement violence." BYP100 won participatory budgeting for citizens in Durham, North Carolina. Seven additional states joined the twenty-eight states working to reform their criminal justice policy, a big victory for all organizing within M4BL. The Dream Defenders also experienced a huge electoral win in 2018 with Amendment 4, restoring the voting rights of over 1.5 million people convicted of a felony in Florida.[96]

As with every movement, these innovative democratic forms emerged mixed together with errors; and certainly, authoritarian tendencies popped up among individuals and some organizations. Yet perhaps the most pressing unanswered question remains before the coalition: how will the Movement for Black Lives organize in communities over the long haul? In the 1960s, SNCC dug in to rural areas in Mississippi, southwest Georgia, and Alabama, ultimately using the Mississippi Freedom Democratic Party to force the national Democratic Party to reform. Yet attempts by SNCC, the Southern Christian Leadership Conference, the Congress of Racial Equality, the Black Panthers, and other Black liberation organizations in the 1960s and 1970s to bring alive the organizing tradition in urban areas failed to take root. The vacuum meant that ordinary people at the base lacked an effective way to hold their leaders accountable over the next five decades. Campaign-based organizing in the 1990s by SONG in the South and by the Ella Baker Center in the Bay Area has not generated a reliable, transferable urban community-organizing model. This central question for M4BL remains: practically, can it continue to organize everyday people to rally around its platform? If activists and organizers are able to bring people-power pressure to bear on local, state, and federal government agencies to implement fully the M4BL platform, it will perhaps build the next rung on freedom's ladder.

SIX

Mní Wičoni—Water Is Alive

Indigenous Youth Water Protectors Rekindle Nonviolent Direct Action in Corporate America

> Some things can't be sold.
> Some things can't be replaced.
> She's your mother;
> the fresh water is her veins.
> —"Stadium Pow Wow," A Tribe Called Red

The youngest among them were only thirteen and fourteen. "Water is life!" they chanted. "Protect our mother!" Their voices and drumbeats filled the air. They knew how young they seemed, how few in number. The central question was how to make their voices heard. Huge amounts of money were at stake: transnational oil companies were fighting to increase the Northern Midwest's Bakken Region oil profits. Corporate interests pushed forward construction of a $3.7 billion, 1,172-mile pipeline from North Dakota through South Dakota and Iowa and eventually to Illinois, estimating it could deliver 500,000 barrels of crude oil every day. The young people knew their chants were likely to be further drowned out by the summer 2016 presidential election campaign between Hillary Clinton and Donald Trump, stomping and sputtering its way across TV screens and news headlines. Still, the handful of Indigenous young people banded together, several tiny Davids aiming slingshots at corporate oil's Goliath.

On the clear, cool morning of July 15, 2016, they started to run from North Dakota toward Washington, DC. Wearing brightly colored T-shirts and shorts, holding flags and prayer sticks and singing, they began in relay-run format, carrying a petition with 140,000 signatures to demand the US Army Corps of Engineers stop the Dakota Access Pipeline (DAPL). Each runner completed anywhere from one mile to ten miles at a time, moving steadily from Cannonball, North Dakota, to Lafayette Square in Washington, DC. "We run!" shouted one young man as they started. "We run!" responded the fifteen or so people running alongside. "For our brothers!" he continued. "For our brothers!" they returned. "For our sisters! For our people! For Life! For Water!"[1]

Along the two-thousand-mile journey to Washington, others witnessed their trek and asked, "Why are you doing this? What do you think you could possibly accomplish?" Some decided to find out more; others ran alongside for a few miles or joined for the remainder. The young people, calling themselves "water protectors" in contrast to "protesters" or "activists," deftly used YouTube, Twitter, and other social media platforms to elevate "our campaign into national awareness" and attract media coverage. "I'm running to let America and the world know we do not want the Dakota Access Pipeline built through our land," asserted Bobbi Jean Three Legs (Standing Rock Sioux). She had a two-year-old daughter, Chloe, whom she wanted to protect. For Danny Grassrope (Kul Wicase Oyate Lakota), twenty-five, "I never thought there would be as many people as [ended up joining] the run, because we were just bringing awareness." He "didn't expect people to come up and fight beside us." Yet come they did. Twenty-one-year-old Lauren Howland (Navajo/Apache) observed that the #NoDAPL run covered such a long distance that it caught people's attention. Exactly how far and how hard were youth willing to push to stop the Pipeline?[2]

Some Indigenous elders seemed skeptical of the young people's work to rebuff the Dakota Access Pipeline, recalled then-nineteen-year-old Jasilyn Charger (Cheyenne River Lakota). Elders' long memories included the many ways outsiders had violated treaties, attacked communities, and ignored Indigenous rights. Some elders supported the cause, but several doubted the method's effectiveness. Yet Charger rose to the challenge: "It was important to make the adults see that if you're going to sit there and argue, we're gonna go wake up our brothers and sisters."[3]

Runs like these had deep cultural roots. Before Europeans brought horses to the continent, relay runs were a primary method that members of the Oceti Sakowin (the Seven Council Fires, the people commonly known as Sioux) used to communicate between scattered members of the nation. Could the fight for clean water unify them? Charger, Three Legs, and Joseph White Eyes set up the relay's itinerary to pass through as many Oceti Sakowin lands as possible.[4]

The run lifted up a central reality invisible to large parts of the general US public: the Oceti Sakowin, whose homeland included Standing Rock, wholly rejected the Pipeline. They didn't think it would bring jobs or economic health. Instead, they warned it would bring ruin and waste. As the young people ran through South Dakota, Iowa, Illinois, and Ohio, they recruited new young people to defend Indigenous rights. They stayed in people's homes, community centers, churches, and women's lodges along the route. They talked with elders as well as youth, sharing stories about the old ways and the camp upriver at Standing Rock where those ways were being revived. Both outsiders and Indigenous youth were really "caught . . . off guard," Jasilyn Charger recalled, when "they saw youth like them doing it."[5] Similar to the 1960 sit-ins, youth putting their bodies on the line forced the rest of the country to notice. Perhaps most important, they put out a compelling challenge to other Indigenous youth: *Will you stand with us to protect land and water?*[6]

Upon their return from Washington, DC, Charger and the other runners found "thousands of people" at Standing Rock.[7] "It's powerful to see" how this small group of people—"there was less than ten of us when we started"—had suddenly turned into a "whole movement," said twenty-three-year-old Terrell Iron Shell (Oglala Sioux).[8]

The Pipeline reflected a long tradition of insider politics at work—and young activists simply refused to accept business as usual. A Lakota elder remembered that the Pipeline was initially "scheduled to go way north of here," where it would threaten the water in Bismarck, the urban-settler core. "So they just moved it down here, assuming, 'Well it's a reservation, no one is going to say anything.'" It had been done many times before to Indigenous, Black, and Latinx communities across the continent. The assumption was historically verifiable, the elder admitted: "A lot of our elders and older people, we couldn't [challenge] it." They had been beaten, betrayed, lied to, and pushed aside too many times. "It took the spark of the youth, the young people's willingness to step up and say we've had enough, and then do something," he said. And, as if reaching back to the day when he felt the fight in him as well, he added, "And we're so proud of them."[9]

The Oceti Sakowin youth water protectors embodied the Lakota proverb borrowed as a common refrain by the majority-white environmental movement: "We do not inherit the earth from our ancestors, we borrow it from our children." As journalist Desiree Kane (Miwok) observed, the youth of

Standing Rock are "the ones who really started the whole movement."[10] This chapter charts the ways youth water protectors initiated and shaped the work at Standing Rock and how that struggle connects with the organizing tradition represented by Ella Baker as well as with that of Indigenous elders.

A BIT OF THE BACKSTORY

What ultimately drew tens of thousands of people to Standing Rock in the summer and fall of 2016 and media from all over the globe? Once home to millions of Lakota, Standing Rock in the twenty-first century included fewer than nine thousand of their descendants. At the movement's height, for eight months between June 2016 and February 2017, those descendants and their allies lifted up for the world to see a simple, essential reality: everyone deserves clean water.

Each morning the camp awoke with beating drums filling the air as more and more people arrived to bear witness to the water protectors' quest. The land, water, and sky are "our original Bible, that comes down from on high," recalled Cannupa Hanska Luger, a New Mexico–based artist who was born on the Standing Rock homeland. While "everyone else sees a pipeline and 'progress,'" those from Standing Rock see "someone going through our Bible and editing things without any care, ripping a line straight through that story." For Luger, "this is why we say this is not a protest, why we are water protectors. We're not just in protest of a pipeline. What we are trying to do is maintain a cultural practice." It was a story not many people outside of Indigenous cultures understood. "Obviously if they did," twenty-six-year-old Eryn Wise (Jicarilla Apache/Laguna Pueblo) noted, "we wouldn't be getting beat up by police to protect the most basic and beautiful thing." While many generations came to Standing Rock as water protectors, youth saw themselves taking a unique role. Ome Tlaloc, thirty, recalled that "an old Sioux prophecy says that a black snake will come to destroy the world at a moment of great uncertainty—unless the youth stop it."[11]

How a person viewed Standing Rock depended on where one stood. Observers sympathetic to youth water protectors often saw them as part of a "long lineage of protectors." The Pipeline sat square in the way of the youth goal: a basic human right to clean drinking water. On the other hand, those sympathetic to corporate leaders' seventy-year pursuit of billion-dollar profits might have understood Standing Rock as simply part of "a lineage of obstructions to great fortunes."[12]

Standing Rock marked a highly visible moment in the ongoing movement for Indigenous rights in the Americas. A few years earlier, in 2012, one could see the rekindled movement as Indigenous women started #IdleNoMore in North America. Setting up actions at malls and state buildings as twin symbols of capitalism and liberal democracy, they forced people to recognize that both were built on land illegally taken by the Canadian and US governments. The women in #IdleNoMore pointed out that instead of representing freedom, both malls and government buildings enacted settler colonialism. It was a fact that proved hard to swallow for people who saw shopping and voting as the behavior of good citizens. As education professor Shauneen Pete (Cree) noted, #IdleNoMore "foretold the ways in which resistance to the expansion of development" of oil and gas pipelines would be met with nonviolent force by Indigenous people.[13] In another example, Kānaka Maoli, Native Hawaiians, organized in 2015 to protect Mauna a Wākea, or Mauna Kea, from the Thirty Meter Telescope, a $1.4 billion, eighteen-story industrial piece of technology. Official responses, in these as in many other similar cases, included the time-tested technique of criminalizing activists for standing in the way of progress—or what Indigenous water protectors defined as resource extraction and exploitation.[14]

People continued to contest the terms used to describe the struggle itself. Increasing numbers of activists and scholars drew attention to US and Canadian societies as settler colonial cultures. While the Dakota Access Pipeline owners promised jobs, energy independence, and safer oil transportation, Phil Wanbli Nunpa, the Sicangu Lakota Treaty Council's executive director, explained that neither this western development framework nor the western environmental movement fully captured the reasons underlying the Standing Rock movement. "Water is alive: we call it mní wičoni, water is life." The idea that water possesses personality or personhood "defines our cultural response" to the Pipeline, stated Edward Valandra (Sicangu Titunwan of the Oceti Sakowin Oyate). "Our definition challenges the West's anthropocentrism, which accords person/peoplehood only to humans. Hence, the Western way of life would both deny and defy water as having personhood." Valandra, founder of the Community for the Advancement of Native Studies, pointed out that the US government lacked both consistency and coherence in defining personhood. On the one hand, it denies personhood "to humans who become subject to the Thirteenth Amendment's slavery exception"—those who are incarcerated are legally allowed to be enslaved. On the other, it treated "fictional entities like corporations as legal persons." Even under US constitutional law, in short, who or what is considered a person with full legal rights has changed over time and, from the perspective of different cultural or legal frameworks, is neither clear nor coherent.

Water is treated as property under US law. This concept stands in clear violation of Indigenous cultural worldviews that consider water not only as essential to human life but also as part of the Great Being that provides the foundation of life itself. As Valandra explained, the "Oceti Sakowin Oyate's original set of instructions requires us to be good relatives to the natural world." This view—that humans' relationship to the water required responsible, respectful interaction—is in profound contrast to the typical American view that basic resources like water are a commodity endlessly exploitable by humans. Such an idea includes other-than-humans having a voice in political language, as the Ecuadorans have set forth in their recent constitution. In Ecuador, where Indigenous politicians have played a significant role, Pachamama (source of life, or nature) has political rights. One can see this emerge in North American Indigenous cultural thought when artist Prolific the Rapper sings, "She's your mother; the fresh water is her veins." When people think together of how best to develop societies, in short, one Indigenous question becomes "What responsible conduct does water expect from us?"[15]

However alien the question seemed to those driving the DAPL project, that was how Valandra and many Indigenous thinkers framed it. All human life comes through the waters of the womb, Bobbi Jean Three Legs noted. "Water is our first medicine for many tribes around Indigenous communities. And it all goes back to being a mother. Your baby is first coming from water, so it's very sacred. And your babies are in water for nine months before they even breathe their first breath of air."[16] Within this way of understanding, the young people at Standing Rock didn't talk about their work as protest. "Everything that is done is about ceremony," one ally from the Denver BLM chapter, Angela Maxwell, reflected. "The acts of protection are prayer acts." Youth came together to say, "You know, we don't want this [pipeline] here!" recalled Dakota Eagle, who grew up on Standing Rock and now lives in Bismarck. "And [youth] weren't doing it in a violent way. It was a ceremonial way. The focus wasn't on the Pipeline, exactly. The focus was on the power of people coming together and being prayerful."[17]

Kyle Hill, from Turtle Mountain, Bear Clan, recalled that his grandmother, a judge, wrote the first law code for American Indian communities in the US. "I want to say she was an activist," he noted, but "as Indigenous people it's not looked at as activism, it's just who you are . . . you fight for the environment and for the rights of your people."[18] Another young person summed up, "We are protectors, not protesters. We're here to protect water, not to scrap with the cops."[19] What those outside of an Indigenous context commonly understood as "nonviolent direct action" was at the heart of prophecy that underlay the movement: "Should the Oceti Sakowin or their allies resort to violence, they could be wiped out."[20]

The practical and philosophical reinforced one another. "They're going to do everything they can to instigate you," musician Nahko Bear (Apache, Puerto Rican, Filipino) told young water protectors after law enforcement sicced dogs on protesters in September 2016. "Remember what we're here for. We're here to create for our Mother; we're not here to create more violence."[21] Charles Pierce, a veteran journalist watching from afar, noted it was "easy to dismiss this kind of talk as some kind of vestigial quasi-religious incantation instead of serious policy proposals." Yet talk of protecting Mother Earth, Pierce noted, "makes at least as much sense as letting a foreign company with a terrible safety record run a pipeline full of the world's most poisonous fossil fuel through some of the most arable farmland in the world."[22]

In the middle of this clash, Indigenous youth drew from and innovated within sacred traditions. Their "media messaging, digital engagement and rapid mobilization techniques" created "crucial blueprints for other movements around the world." Their information sharing made it possible to stall or stop industrial projects that threatened water supplies, arable land, and Indigenous burial grounds in over three hundred communities worldwide. Rallying against them were energy companies and governments with access to huge teams of technocrats—those trained to harness the law, big data, technical expertise, and traditional political power.[23]

Indeed, Lakota elders' suspicions proved true: the Army Corps of Engineers had rejected an early proposal for DAPL to run through Bismarck, forty-five miles north of the Standing Rock homeland, for fear it could harm Bismarck's municipal water supply. Bismarck is 92 percent white. This stood in stark contrast to the fact that any Pipeline leak threatened Standing Rock's main water source, Lake Oahe, where more than 10 million people, many of them living on Indigenous homelands, drew their water.[24] As Standing Rock Sioux chairman David Archambault II told a reporter, "There's always this attempt to say, 'We can make this the safest pipeline ever,' but if they can do that," he asked pointedly, then why not leave the pipeline running through Bismarck?[25] A shocking statistic often buried is that oil companies have caused over 3,300 oil spills and leaks in the US alone since 2010. In this time period, Sunoco Logistics, operator of the Dakota Access Pipeline, has experienced more crude spills than any of its competitors. In 2017–18 alone, Energy Transfer

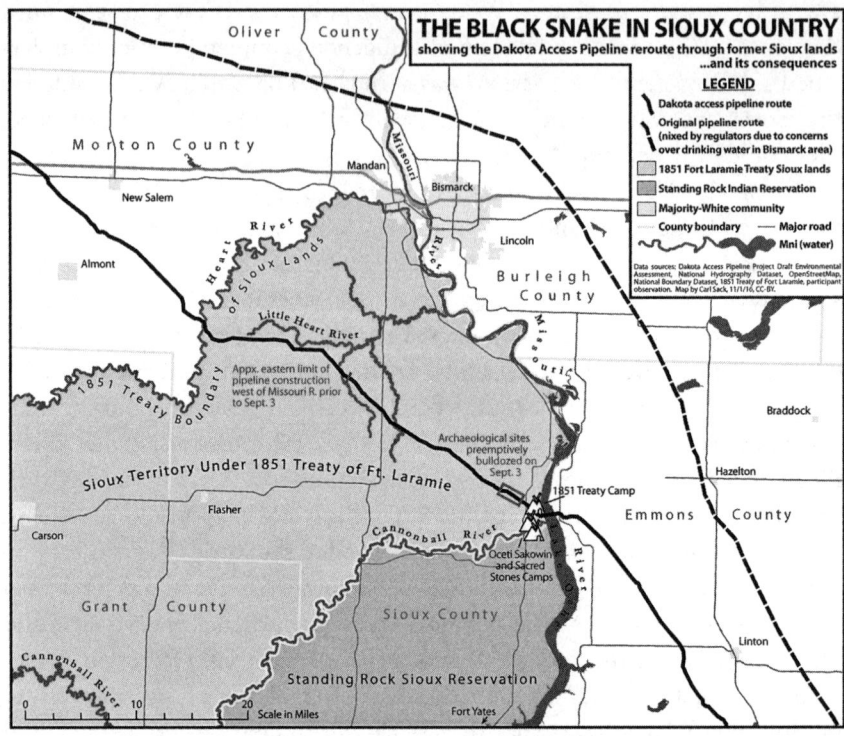

FIGURE 14. Map showing the route of the Dakota Access pipeline. (Map by and used with permission from Carl Sack)

Partners (ETP, one of the corporations building the Pipeline) and Sunoco were issued six stop-work orders by state agencies and the Federal Energy Regulatory Commission because they were violating regulations protecting streams, rivers, wetlands, drinking water, historic sites, and public safety.[26]

Furthermore, the corporate entities who constructed the Pipeline built it on land they do not have legal title to. The current Pipeline cuts through areas that belong to the Sioux nation under the Fort Laramie treaties of 1851 and 1868. Despite these legal realities and a 1980 US Supreme Court decision affirming the 1851 boundaries, the Army Corps of Engineers claim sole jurisdiction, a thunderous downbeat in the repetitious rhythm of centuries, the naked power of the US government trampling the rights of Indigenous Americans.[27]

Settlers, dams, and pipelines—battles over how to live on the land began early as Sioux fought off European settlers in 1803 when Lewis and Clark came through to survey the lands of the Louisiana Purchase. "For the next hundred years," scholar Nick Estes (Kul Wicasa, Lower Brule Sioux) wrote, "the U.S. led various unsuccessful military campaigns to suppress, annihilate, and dispossess us of our rightful claim to the river and our lands." It soon culminated in General George Custer's 1876 defeat at Little Big Horn. That year, the Sioux won the battle but lost the war, as the US Congress passed the Indian Appropriations Act of 1876, abolishing "treaty-making with Native Nations, and then pushed through the Black Hills Act of 1877," Estes continued, "which illegally ceded the Black Hills and created the present-day reservation system."[28]

One hundred years later, Indigenous youth created the Red Power movement of the 1960s and 1970s to champion Indigenous self-determination. The American Indian Movement (AIM) occupied Wounded Knee on the Lakota Pine Ridge homeland in 1973 and created culturally relevant institutions like schools, community centers, and legal advocacy groups. Then, in 1974, the International Indian Treaty Council formed at Standing Rock. It was an important milestone for "more than ninety Native Nations from around the world" who joined together. This foundation led to forty years of work at the United Nations, where they expended themselves to articulate and defend the rights of Indigenous people within an increasingly rapacious global economy dominated by multinational corporations. The work started in 1974 at Standing Rock, Estes wrote, became "the basis for the 2007 Declaration on the Rights of Indigenous Peoples," a decisive turning point in international legal norms.[29]

For those familiar with this longer history, it seemed to come full circle in 2016, when more than three hundred Indigenous nations sent representatives to witness and protect the Missouri River at Standing Rock. Yes, this international bloc came to "challenge and redefine" the specific legal jurisdiction claimed by the Army Corps of Engineers. But on a larger scale, they also directly challenged all legal claims that currently "legitimate settler sovereignty."[30]

Indigenous rights remain precarious in both international and US legal courts, where European norms of property rights, including the right to exploit and profit, take overwhelming precedence. Yet even within its own intellectual, moral, and legal frameworks, over centuries of signing treaties with Indigenous people, the US government has left behind an almost perfect record of illegality, breaking those treaties. No international legal body has been able to hold the US to account. Indigenous people have claimed "this land is our land," but US legal institutions and law enforcement have not upheld the claim. At base, this can be seen as a case of might makes right. The long history of corporate and government power makes the youth water protectors' innovations that much more remarkable.[31]

THE INTERNATIONAL INDIGENOUS YOUTH COUNCIL

As Indigenous youth continued their relay run to Washington to promote the #NoDAPL campaign, they received bad news on July 26, 2016: President Obama's Army Corps of Engineers would allow the Pipeline construction to proceed. Undeterred, the youth continued. Adult allies in the Indigenous Environmental Network called for people across the world to follow the lead of the youth runners and come bear witness at Standing Rock. By the time the young people returned to North Dakota in August 2016, hundreds and soon thousands of people joined them. Over the next few months, roughly 100,000 people passed through Standing Rock in support.[32]

The flood of new people proved essential: the only way to stop the Pipeline was by drawing recruits and demonstrating people-power. However, recruiting also posed a huge, immediate challenge. What if those recruits didn't share the Oceti Sakowin youth's long-term worldview, including their deep commitment to nonviolent approaches? Youth water protector Lauren Howland (Apache/Navajo) noted that the Indigenous youth "will always continue to be about prayer and peace." No matter how "violent they get, we don't hate them, the cops aren't our enemies, the Pipeline workers aren't our enemy, they're just doing their job." Howland and the other youth members banded together to form the International Indigenous Youth Council (IIYC). If the multinationals appeared focused and determined, IIYC members would match them: "We pray for everybody. We want it to remain prayerful and peaceful." That was "how we're going to win. We're not going to win by being violent back" to law enforcement or to private security for multinational corporations or to construction workers.[33]

The IIYC was one of many groups at Standing Rock, but it played an essential modeling role. First, it had been the one to get people literally moving. Thousands, and then tens of thousands, came to Standing Rock in response to the IIYC relay run. Equally important, the youth set and held the standard, holding people to nonviolent behavior. As events from the Arab Spring (2011) to Occupy Wall Street (2011) to Charlottesville (2017) demonstrated, this was frequently a near-impossible task. Highly visible events brought together people with varied backgrounds and beliefs, even if they shared a common goal. If one person broke nonviolent discipline by pummeling a counterprotester, that could ruin the effort of thousands. The IIYC youth worked with ceaseless regularity to educate and train recruits and thus promote nonviolence within the movement.

Similar to activists who used the tool of nonviolence in the civil rights, immigrant rights, and Black Lives Matter movements, the IIYC's insistence on nonviolence not only had cultural or philosophical roots but also was a recognition of a basic political fact: unless the movement held to nonviolence, people like Donald Trump could say there was violence on "both sides," a false equivalence between treaty violators and water protectors, or between white supremacists and racial justice advocates.[34] Second, hopelessly outgunned by law enforcement, the youth in an armed struggle did not have any chance of succeeding. Perhaps most importantly, violence fundamentally contradicted the very philosophy the water protectors represented. By training and then holding thousands of people to strict nonviolence, the IIYC youth continuously reminded the movement of the vision of the world they were fighting for.

Three key moments stand out where youth water protectors had to innovate and model nonviolent direct action in response to stunning levels of violence from law enforcement. In the first week of September, then October 26–November 7, and finally on November 20, 2016, the youth water protectors remained nonviolent despite their opponents' recourse to pepper spray, tasers, water cannons, and rubber bullets. The IIYC's strength, creativity, and illumination of how to hold to nonviolence showed a democratic way forward—no matter how difficult.

September 2016

In early September, three bulldozers hired by Enbridge, Inc., a Canadian multinational energy corporation that was part of the DAPL project, tried to continue to build the Pipeline. Water protectors lay in the dirt, putting their bodies in the way. Dogs controlled by Enbridge's private security contractors bit at least twelve people, a fierce visual reprise of Birmingham's civil rights demonstrations against Jim Crow in 1963 (figs. 15 and 16). Raina Crow, a member of #IdleNoMore–Duluth, participated in the nonviolent direct action. She watched as the water protectors forced construction crews to leave on September 3. "I hope we've accomplished letting Enbridge know that the people of this nation and the people of this world, tribal or otherwise, have withdrawn their social license to pollute water," Crow stated. "They need to find an honest, nonviolent way to make a living."[35] As disbelieving journalists crowded into Standing Rock, drawn by the dog-biting footage circulating virally on social media, one observed that "over the next 12 hours, I watched as grandmothers with red feathers in their hair, Oglala elders in ceremonial

FIGURES 15 and 16. "Yes that's the blood of peaceful protestors on this dog's mouth" (Shadi Rahimi). (Top photo used with permission from and courtesy of Democracy Now!; bottom photo of Charles Moore, May 1963, Birmingham, AL, courtesy of the Steven Kasher Gallery)

regalia, and teens astride horses were teargassed, tased, and arrested." Police "fired rubber bullets at protesters and blasted them with ear-splitting whines from Long Range Acoustic Devices." As law enforcement moved down the highway, the crowd confirmed in echo the chant of Black Lives Matter protesters in Ferguson, Missouri, two summers earlier. Arms held high above their heads in the air, they shouted in unison, "Hands up, don't shoot!"[36]

As the days went on, a mix of local, state, and National Guard law enforcement officers stood on one side of the river, while water protectors stood in the river itself, in prayer. Violence threatened to erupt as a few protectors began taunting the police. IIYC member Danny Grassrope jumped into the river and swam to them. The protectors had "forgotten why we're here," Grassrope recalled. "So we need to continue to remind them why we're here." Making his voice heard above the din of rubber bullets, tear gas, and screaming, he calmly raised his voice: "Everyone! You're here to pray! You're not here to antagonize the police officers." If they did so, he asserted, "you're hurting your own people. Do you understand?" His reminder came at a vital time to prevent the breakdown of nonviolent discipline. For the movement to keep going, "you've got to stay positive, and peaceful and in prayer," he reflected later, "because this is a ceremony, and we have to protect what we have here, and that's our prayer. That's one thing that can't stop."[37]

October 26–November 7, 2016

Between the end of summer and early November, the number of people at Standing Rock grew fivefold, and then doubled again. The IIYC had to address two major hurdles within the protectors' camps. First, it had to navigate a challenge from some elders who felt the youth needed to step aside in the face of so many outsiders coming in. Some elders thanked the members of the IIYC and essentially said, "'You did your part. You're relieved. We got this.'" It was hard: "When all the people came, the youth got swept aside," Jasilyn Charger recalled.[38]

The second challenge came as the chilly fall temperatures descended and many witnesses became impatient as the Pipeline construction continued. IIYC members made sure to be a visible, audible presence at every action to stop construction and worked hard to de-escalate conflicts between law enforcement and protectors. Terrell Iron Shell of the IIYC recalled, "We knew how they felt," he said of the people who wanted to retaliate against aggressive law enforcement. Yet "we can guide them as youth," he noted. The IIYC members started by telling their allies, "'If you're fighting for my future, do it this way, just back off, you don't have to be angry, cuss at the police, throw anything at them.'" During the actions in September and October, "we just kind of talked them down," Iron Shell continued. "After that it got peaceful." In the face of the challenges both from elders and from impatient people, the IIYC reminded those at Standing Rock that it was an Indigenous youth-led movement, Lauren Howland noted in October 2016. "People forget that, that the youth are here fighting."[39]

The IIYC turned people's focus back to protection and prayer again and again. Between October 26 and 28, 2016, hundreds were arrested as law enforcement shot nonviolent protesters with rubber bullets and tased those preventing construction. Some police aimed hot pepper spray directly into nonviolent protectors' eyes. In those circumstances, members of the IIYC realized that not everyone was able to stay true to nonviolence or prayer, including themselves.

Nonviolence was hardest, they realized, when law enforcement attacked people one loved. It had been the same in SNCC, and among undocumented youth activists, and within M4BL. Watching her younger sister maced by law enforcement through a Facebook Live feed, IIYC member Eryn Wise "raced to the scene and threw herself at the police." Quickly three IIYC members put their arms around her, pulling her back. Her brother, Alex Howland, was also engaged in nonviolent protecting. He kept saying, "We'll pray for you, we'll pray for you!" to law enforcement, even as they sprayed his face with tear gas. This incredibly poised and determined action, the fact that "he was still praying for [the law enforcement officers] . . . brought me back," Wise noted.[40] Prayer grounded the young people. After all, the camp began in April 2016 as a place where ceremony—song, dance, prayer—was their most powerful activity. Standing Rock's inhabitants had gathered to assert and collectively honor their "sacred duty. In ceremony their power coalesces . . . pray[ing] this protection into being."[41]

Immediately following the October 26–28 confrontations, the members of the IIYC decided to hold a Forgiveness March. The action aimed to restore a sense of harmony and behavior rooted in ceremony. "When we are confronted with hatred, it is so tempting to get revenge," spoken word artist Lyla June Johnston (Diné) related during the Forgiveness March. "We don't want to become the very thing that is hurting us." To prevent this, they would "confront hatred with love." IIYC member Jacquilyn Córdoba deeply appreciated how the November 6, 2016, march unfolded. Careful not to violate any traffic laws, they walked silently to the Morton County police station, stayed on the sidewalk, and created a huge circle around the law enforcement complex. As police officers came outside, the water protectors put their hands out in greeting and began to sing. "This is a great opportunity for us to connect to the police officers on a human to human level," recalled Córdoba. "We're not fighting against the police or the sheriff's department. We're here to stop a pipeline, and we're here to protect water."[42]

After lighting sage—an ancient purification ritual—and blessing the space, Lyla June Johnston began to speak. "On October 27, a great many of our friends and family were very severely hurt," she noted. "At this time, we must also say that we are not perfect people either." She recognized "that we did things, and we said things on that day that were not in alignment" with their goals. She pointed to a huge banner the group had created: "LOVE | PRAYER | FORGIVENESS | WÓAKIKTUNŽE." "Wóakiktunže," she continued, pointing to the sign, "does not only mean 'I forgive you.' It also means, 'I'm asking you to forgive me.'" The large group stood "here today acknowledging that both sides stepped out of their center." Forgiveness, she clarified, "does not mean that what happened was okay. Forgiveness means that we choose to respond to hatred with love."[43]

Youth actions to bring the movement back to its core principles continued the next day. The IIYC led a second prayer march, this time on the Standing Rock homeland, "to remind people why we're here," Terrell Iron Shell explained. "We did a silent march. It wasn't to silence ourselves. We've already been silenced." Rather, it was to "show discipline, humility." "You couldn't hear a sound," he recalled, astonished. There were four hundred people marching behind him, several holding flags aloft. As they reached a police barricade at the Breakwater Bridge, the group of four hundred sat silently in the road. Iron Shell and four other IIYC members slowly approached the police. Iron Shell introduced himself and his friends. "We prayed with the police there," he recalled. "We offered them water." Only one of the five officers accepted. They thanked him publicly, realizing that "it showed us that the officers are also human, but it also showed a lot of humility and courage on the officer's part. By taking that water and praying with us, he knew that the other officers would treat him differently." Iron Shell vowed to never forget how unified young people were on that day. It returned them to a sense of their broader and deeper purpose. It demonstrated how they wanted to act in the world.[44]

November 20, 2016

Then came November 20. It was a mere two weeks after Donald Trump's presidential victory, ricocheting around a stunned world and emboldening corporate leaders and law enforcement nationwide. "The new Selma, that's what I saw there," noted UN environmental justice advocate Catherine Flowers about Standing Rock. Flowers had grown up near Selma, her parents hosting civil rights workers from SNCC in their home in 1965 when she was eight years old. Now fifty years later, she traveled to Standing Rock as an internationally recognized advocate for the human right to water and sanitation, working for the UN Sustainable Development Agenda. "All these people from across the U.S. willing to put their lives on the line to protect water," she marveled. "We make sure everyone becomes a water protector. No water, no life." Yet as she arrived in Standing Rock, she encountered "the most militarized police force I had ever seen in my life." Law enforcement blocked communication with outsiders; they "interfered with signals, they were monitoring everything, breaking into people's social media accounts and putting out false accounts through Facebook."[45]

And then law enforcement moved on the ground. Starting November 20, they began to clear a bridge occupied by nonviolent protesters. They fired incendiary rounds and tear gas and shot people with rubber bullets. "We were there from seven p.m. to four in the morning," recalled Liz George, a Detroit resident who had come as part of a peace delegation. "There was a girl standing there dancing, getting sprayed down by mace." On the front line, nonviolent activists held up plastic shields while police hosed them down with freezing water in twenty-five degree temperatures. They shot nonviolent protectors with rubber bullets. George could hardly believe what she was seeing. She focused on one young Indigenous girl in particular, whose stamina seemed surreal. "Every time she'd pull down the shield, one police officer in particular would aim rubber bullets at her," George noted, and "she'd raise the shield again, and pull the tarp over her head." When the girl would peek out, "he'd aim at her face again." After hours of this back and forth, the girl and her friend "decided to take off their goggles and masks, lower their shields, and look him in the eye." They were just two young girls, and it seemed to humanize them. "He put down his gun." Yet until then, they'd "held up the shields all night, getting hosed down" in the below-freezing temperatures.[46]

In a federal affidavit, former Baltimore police commissioner Thomas C. Frazier reviewed law enforcement conduct on November 20, 2016. Other than at Standing Rock, he stated, "I have never seen in any other American city or county, the use of water hoses or a water cannon against a United States citizen for any reason although I have read about this occurring in the early 1960s against civil rights marchers." He testified: "The brute force of the impact of the water jet is a force option that would not be considered appropriate by most modern police chiefs or sheriffs, or tolerated by their citizenry," he declared. "In this case, the use of this device in sub-freezing temperatures, in my opinion, serves no reasonable purpose and can only be considered a retaliatory and punitive action."[47]

November 20 knocked the wind out of many water protectors. It scared and exhausted them. It enraged others. The sheer police brutality was impossible to grasp. And with it came an increasing realization of the danger of the moment: growing numbers of participants were questioning nonviolent tactics. When deputies on horseback trampled Selma activists in 1965, Congress moved with uncharacteristic speed to write and pass the Voting Rights Act—within months. Yet the eerily similar scene in 2016 at Standing Rock prompted no such congressional or presidential action. There was no obvious movement whatsoever to recognize the rights of Indigenous Americans from outgoing President Obama or the Congress or Mr. Trump. The contrast between 1965 and 2016 was quite revealing, representing a new low point. On the ground in the Dakotas, the federal bipartisan nonresponse led to a movement dilemma: what to do next to protect people's right to clean water?

Questioning nonviolence was easy to understand, but for the IIYC, the wrong way to turn. Another clear signal had to be sent. When the Morton County sheriff's office issued a call throughout the state for North Dakota citizens to bring its tired, cold, stressed, and underprepared officers supplies, IIYC youth stepped up again. On December 2, 2016, they trekked from Standing Rock to the sheriff's door, Costco-size cartons of Gatorade in hand. Lauren Howland knocked first.

The first person to come to the door was one she recognized from the police line the night she was hurt in November. "We love you guys. We give this to you," she began, Gatorade in hand. The law enforcement officers, surprised, opened the door. "Hey, you might try and cut off the supplies given to us," IIYC member Jacquilyn Córdoba said. "We're still in prayer, and we're still going to be giving our heart and souls to those in need. If you guys need stuff, here it is." Lauren Howland concurred. "No matter how violent they get, we don't hate them," Howland told the group. "That's how we're going to win. We're not going to win being violent back to them."[48] The men from the sheriff's office stood back and welcomed them inside. For a while, the two groups simply sat together and talked, person to person, reaffirming a mutual humanity.

"YOU DAMN SURE BETTER NOT GO TO STANDING ROCK WEARING FEATHERS"

The IIYC's work was complemented by other youth working at Standing Rock. "Part of what made Standing Rock difficult was the constant swelling and receding of numbers—sometimes there were as many as seven thousand people there that all needed tents, access to toilets and medical care," noted Dr. Kalamaoka'aina Niheu, an ally from Hawaii. The full effort "involved hundreds of thousands of people, offering support and sending supplies and donations."[49] Yet perhaps the hardest item to distribute to incoming allies was an ethos: Standing Rock members required non-Indigenous people to adapt to

Indigenous practices. Each ally received an information packet upon arrival and had to participate in an orientation run by youth organizers from the Indigenous People's Power Project (IP3).

The IP3 worked with the IIYC to develop ground rules. They included "Follow Indigenous leadership," "Understand this moment in the context of settler colonialism," and "Never attend a ceremony without being expressly invited." Los Angeles–based artist Andrea Bowers noted, "It's a whole different reality out there" at Standing Rock. "It's a different set of rules. It's based on Native prayer and spirituality, and there's a different hierarchy of power, so it's necessary to just step back and be in service." Or as Susanna Battin, another Los Angeles artist noted, "The media coverage has been about the conflict and confrontation." Yet some of the deeper work of the mobilization remained largely invisible. It was "a historic cultural moment—the collaboration, the listening, the breaking down of colonial misconceptions, the style of leadership that we in middle-class white America just haven't experienced."[50]

As Andrea Bowers recalled, everything changed through "the nature of group dynamics motivated by respect." She witnessed Indigenous and white military veterans in arguments, then saw them talk it out. "In the end, I'd see them hug each other," and then the Indigenous protectors said, "'You're here, you are family now.'" It was "not the way we do things" in broader US society, she continued. "This was a respect to culture and the process—everything embodied that."[51] Her point was echoed by thousands of other witness-visitors. "As a country, we're not going to move forward unless we as a people unite in one voice," said Christopher, a white volunteer from Kentucky with the nonprofit Red Road Awareness. "And it's not going to start unless us white people start with the people we stole the land from."[52]

IP3 trainings were clear, direct, and impossible to ignore if a visitor wanted to stay at Standing Rock. "We are here as guests, these are sacred grounds, if somebody tells you to stop singing, or stop banging a drum, this is not a revolutionary personal experience," IP3 trainer Eva Cardenas instructed. Allies were not at Standing Rock to save others. Instead, "we need hands on deck, we need support." If anyone in the group was here with a savior mentality, Cardenas pointedly continued, "please pack up and go back."[53] The IP3 asked Denver's Black Lives Matter 5280 chapter to assist at the camp with these trainings, to teach newcomers "how to participate in ways that were helpful, not hurtful, to the cause." Indigenous activists expressed frustration toward "people who came as if this was a festival," Denver BLM activist Jumoke Emery-Brown recalled. "This is not a party. This is not a place where you go only because you want to say, 'I was there.' And you damn sure better not go to

Standing Rock wearing feathers. You don't go in a costume. You don't go to set up your Burning Man tent." Still, people did show up who wanted "to put on makeup and dance and throw a rave," and time and again the IP3 worked persistently with them until they either followed the guidelines or left the camp.[54]

Whites unaware of their surroundings or their white privilege were akin to people walking around with an invisible eight-foot-long two-by-four on their shoulders, Pat Hussain had recognized in her work with SONG. It was as true at Standing Rock in 2016 as it had been in SONG in the 1990s or in SNCC during the summer of 1964. Whites turned and knocked people down and then said, with innocent astonishment, "What's the matter? What's wrong?" When those people didn't go home or were "unaware that their actions might produce negative consequences," it took time and energy to educate them. Denver BLM member Angela Maxwell recalls how one young white woman noticed a remote-controlled drone flying overhead during a prayer ceremony, likely belonging to law enforcement or corporate security. She gathered rocks and threw them at the drone. Yet she did not appear to realize that if she found her target, both drone and the rock would fall right on top of those gathered in prayer. She did not take into consideration that police and media would likely portray this incident as "Indigenous people attacking government property." Certainly, no one in the wider media would likely bother to clarify that a non-Indigenous participant had committed the action.[55] It took a lot of time to explain to people like this the complex dynamics of the work the Indigenous water protectors set for themselves and the stakes if anyone allied with them screwed up. And as in the civil rights movement of the 1960s, it would be the Indigenous people left to clean up after the ally-witnesses returned home.

The attitude the protectors asked people to bring to training, Eva Cardenas clarified, could be summed up as "This is a ceremony. Act accordingly." Would you go into a church "playing a drum or dancing, or acting all hooligan?" she asked. And if so, would your grandmother be OK with you acting like that? Cardenas requested of each visitor, "Act like your grandma is with you all the time."[56] In the face of tens of thousands of visitors in a six-month period, the IP3's trainings proved essential to keeping the protection ceremonies intact.

SOCIAL MEDIA, ART, AND TECHNOLOGY

Oceti Sakowin youth expertly used hashtags throughout 2016—such as #NoDAPL, #ReZpectOurWater, and #StandWithStandingRock—to link Standing Rock to other communities across the English-speaking world. Hashtag campaigns also garnered support from high-profile citizens like climate scholar

Bill McKibben, actress Shailene Woodley, and actor Leonardo DiCaprio. Krystal Two Bulls, an activist with roots in the Oglala Lakota and Northern Cheyenne nations, reflected that "technology has helped movements around the world to unite under one banner; to realize that it's the same story, just different locations. And we've never had access to that before. It was a major game changer and it will continue to be moving forward." Twitter reported that between October and December 2016, over 5 million tweets included #StandWithStandingRock, and to misdirect law enforcement surveillance, thousands "checked in" at Standing Rock on Facebook.[57]

Eryn Wise, media liaison for the IIYC, noted in October 2016 that social media storytelling campaigns provided not only ways to recruit but ways to protect the movement, saying, "Facebook Live has really helped shape this movement." After her younger sister was maced by law enforcement on Facebook Live and Eryn immediately responded by running up to the site of confrontation, she pointed out to the officers that everyone could see this abuse. "I was screaming at the police officers," Wise said. "I was telling them, 'You know, I just watched you on a video with 32,000 other people.' And they seemed pretty shaken by that. I think Facebook Live has really threatened their ability to hide." The same reality appeared when Diamond Reynolds broadcast her partner Philando Castile's killing by police officer Jeronimo Yanez in Minneapolis in 2016. Facebook Live worked as "a tool to bypass the mainstream media in order to spread a message to tens of thousands of viewers in real time." While it could be used by corporate security and police to surveil those in the movement, it also served as a potent nonviolent weapon, tracking corporate security and law enforcement as they interacted with peaceful protectors and protesters.[58]

Social media not only provided a way for millions to see what was happening but also rekindled visible solidarity among Indigenous people worldwide. IIYC members taught elders to use social media "in a way that will help share their story," Wise noted. "We need people not only to see our side of things and have our story told," she continued, "but for *us* to be the ones that tell it." To this end, they made sure to make hard copies of everything posted so that technical faults or Facebook editors could not shape or control their stories. They studied Facebook's algorithms intensely over an extended period of time in order to share information quickly and effectively with those outside Standing Rock.[59]

Indigenous youth making their own media meant they countered the centuries-old falsehood that refuses to die: that Indigenous people are disappearing. Within the cultures of academia and journalism, practitioners have

FIGURE 17. Cannupa Hanska Luger's mirrored shields at Standing Rock, showing the police what their own violence looked like. (Photo by Cannupa Hanska Luger)

long resorted to portraying Indigenous people as part of "static cultures on the verge of extinction," scholar Anne Spice recalled, "despite fervent and powerful efforts to resist erasure and assimilation." As one group of allies wrote from Standing Rock, "Live media of Indigenous agency is crucial to the writing of anticolonial history from the viewpoint of those who are risking their lives to be and remain anticolonial," even "in the wake of state and corporate terror."[60] Documentary work by Indigenous youth—of their thinking and actions within the movement—was itself activism. Indigenous youth finding ways to portray themselves, rather than relying on others, opened up new ways to think forward.[61]

Artists also made important contributions. Cannupa Hanska Luger created dozens of mirrored shields from Masonite and reflective vinyl (fig. 17). The shields not only served to shelter frontline water protectors but became "bright works of sculpture" that forced law enforcement to look in a literal mirror, to bear witness to their own brutality in real time. Local artists had created a similar piece, *Mirror Casket*, in Ferguson in 2014. It innovated on a classic nonviolent direct action tactic.[62] Vocal artists performing on site like Nahko Bear and Lyla June Johnston used the sounds of prayer ceremonies, song, and testimony, reframing how individuals might experience their own participation.

Sometimes the total sensory experience shifted how people made sense of their own lives. South African martial artist Nic Gabriel, traveling to an ayahuasca ceremony in Peru years earlier, noted that it had happened to him. Picking up on many mainstream cues, he had previously thought of Indigenous ceremonies more like a "hippy concept," a cliché about people coming together to affirm "the earth is your mother, man." All this changed when he experienced the ceremony, when he saw and heard people living and expressing a distinct perspective so clearly different from his own. At its essence, it was a view of the commons—people as community and as part of nature—versus what he was used to, a view of individualism and competition. He began to see what later became a lifelong shift: "We don't have to compete. It's not about me, it's about *everybody*."[63]

The larger Art Action Camp at Standing Rock affirmed this idea through its artists, media, legal team, and action team. Here people created patches, banners, and silkscreens. Journalist Sarain Fox (Anishinabe) noted that each morning, this was first place she would head. One of its most affecting messages was simply "Mní Wičoni." She realized that the single image of "a woman holding a feather or a thunderbird that says, 'Water is life,' or 'Protect the sacred'" had taught "millions of people one simple phrase in [the Oceti Sakowins'] language." To have all these people from around the world "use it is profound and impactful and something we've never seen before in terms of ally-ship." Indigenous artists Christi Belcourt (Michif) and Isaac Murdoch (Ojibwe) created the slogan, and "mní wičoni" soon became a worldwide rallying cry (figs. 18 and 19).[64]

Art and social media used to orient and train newcomers into a broader sense of community meant that young water protectors inspired a wide range of creativity that drew others. Whether the water protectors could sustain it was not yet clear, but it had all the makings of a new kind of family. Different people took on distinct roles and brought with them singular skills. In the end, everyone contributed to the creation of the emerging movement culture.

For the IIYC youth, this community turned out to be affirming and sustaining in a way few had experienced before. Not only did it help them overcome their previous cultural invisibility, but forming a new "chosen family" in an environment of immense creativity also served as a balm for the disruption, personal violence, and structural inequalities many had faced.[65] Jasilyn Charger explained that the central work they realized they needed to do was to take full measure of what had happened to themselves and to previous generations—then let it go in order to spare those to come: "We don't want our children to inherit this depression." In practical terms, it meant using

FIGURES 18 and 19.
Posters by Joey Montoya and
Tomahawk Grey Eyes.

art, social media, and activism not just to forgive "the white man" but also to forgive the parent who beat them, or the missing caregiver, or the abusive relative. The process proved intense. And yet, by fashioning a family of choice amid the life-giving energies unleashed within the movement, they began to learn about themselves and each other. It was, in many ways, reconnecting to a long cultural history. As such, some re-formed bonds to biological family members as much as to Indigenous traditions. To call such a process "transformative" would barely scratch the surface.[66]

Eryn Wise, for example, in her twenties, "grew up in an Anglicized society." Before Standing Rock, Indigenous cultural practices seemed "weird to me. It was still pretty foreign." Raised a member of the Jicarilla Apache Nation and Laguna Pueblo Nation in New Mexico, she wondered, "Why do I have to do [these ceremonial practices]? Why do I have to listen to this, or why does my mom believe in this?" After being a part of the movement, where she worked as media liaison for the IIYC and media coordinator at Sacred Stone Camp, her attitude shifted. "Now, I just feel bad for giving my mom a hard time because I'm older," she reflected. "I get it. I get why it is we pray for the birds and why we pray for the sky, why we pray for the earthworms and why we pray for the grass. All these different things; I understand why there's so much beauty in the day-to-day things."

Wise's brother Alex Howland arrived from New Mexico in mid-August 2016, planning to stay at Standing Rock for a week. Soon he realized months had gone by. "I've grown so attached to this place, I've grown attached to the people, I've grown attached to the land, the water, the air. It's because of the Lakota and Dakota people that I now have new eyes to view the world that we live in, and to get back into that sense of tradition and prayer." Howland's and Wise's stories illustrate how becoming a water protector took on meaning well beyond advocating for clean water. Yes, "we are made up of water, we are born in water, we come from water. Water is an essence of our being," Howland stated. Yet "a lot of people don't see it," the many ways "we are connected to that water. We are water. That's why a lot of us are here. That's what water means to us: it means life, it means unity." In the course of protecting the water, they forged secure bonds of family and community. Water, Wise said, "means one people."[67]

GENDER AND THE MOVEMENT

The role of Indigenous women, girls, and people of "two-spirits" in creating this family culture within the movement deserves particular note.[68] "It began with the water," sang the group One Tribe. "And a Woman. LaDonna Tamakawastewin Allard, and a prayer to protect water." Elder LaDonna Allard served the Standing Rock movement in ways akin to Ella Baker within the civil rights movement. She linked the freedom struggle of prior generations to the current moment and at the same time encouraged young people to develop their own perspectives. One Tribe's song told part of the story: "The Oceti Sakowin youth heard her. And so the core of those who would become the IIYC ran across the land to carry her message into the world." They became "the peaceful warriors of our generation."[69] It was a sentiment familiar to the elders at Standing Rock and also would have been recognized by the elders of the civil rights movement: peaceful warriors of a new generation carrying the message to the world.

LaDonna Allard owned the property on which the first camp set up against the Pipeline. As a historian for the Lakota, who saw herself as one in a long line of strong women, "We stand up," Allard later noted. "We will not let [DAPL] pass. We stand. Because we must protect our children and our grandchildren," she continued. "If you respect women, you respect Earth and you respect water." It was that simple: "This whole fight, it has nothing to do with being an activist, but it has everything to do with being a mom." Her son was buried on her land "so that he would be right there to watch the mouth of the Cannon Ball and the Missouri Rivers. And when they told me they were going to build a pipeline," she refused in a way any mother could understand: "I can't allow that, I can't allow anybody to put a pipeline next to my son's grave."[70]

Women like Allard as well as gender nonconforming people raised up explicit connections between their experiences and the extractive fossil fuel industry. The Standing Rock Two-Spirit Nation Camp held space for "all to be their full authentic selves." They were "creating and fostering a safe space for everyone."[71] "In recent years my reservation, Fort Berthold, has become part of the oil boom," noted Zaysha Grinnell (Mandan, Hidatsa, Arikara). "As a young person, I noticed the differences taking shape all around me due to this extraction project—in the environment, the lands, the people." She witnessed "the lands that I had grown up on getting destroyed little by little, drill by drill." People she "grew up to love and care for were being sexually abused and sexually harassed on a daily basis" when the oil companies came in. Men working in the camps brought "violence and sex trafficking. Indigenous women and girls near the camps are really affected by this and we are not going to put up with it."[72]

Many young people gathered at Standing Rock connected this pattern of sexual violence with natural resource extraction. Mary Kathryn Nagle (Cherokee), a lawyer from Tulsa, explained: "We as Native women know that any time a corporation or a government is trying to conquer our lands and our water, Native women's lives and bodies will suffer." It had been true since the earliest contact. "From Columbus to the Sand Creek Massacre—part of the war that was perpetrated on these lands was a specific attack on Native women," Nagle reflected, "because the U.S. military and other governments that were attempting to conquer the land understood that the way you destroy a nation is you destroy its women." Statistics reinforced this observation at nearby Fort Berthold: the increased rates of extraction of oil in the Bakken Region meant an increase in the rates of violence—sex trafficking, violence, rape, murder. "What has not increased," Nagle noted, is the federal or state government's policing of these crimes."[73]

Those who experienced this firsthand stepped forward as leaders. "As a young Indigenous woman," Zaysha Grinnell explained, "I can feel the suffering of my people. I always remember this feeling—even speaking to you about it right now, I remember it—the hurt in my heart seeing this happening to my people." Parallel to the way women like Rosa Parks advanced the civil rights movement through work on behalf of Recy Taylor and other Black women raped and sexually assaulted by white men, Grinnell began to organize on behalf of women and girls raped and sexually assaulted by men working on the Pipeline. For Grinnell, "everything that my people value and care for is at great risk of being harmed."[74]

Still a teen, Grinnell created a youth group called the Modern Day Warriors, collected eight thousand signatures on a #NoDAPL petition, spoke at rallies, recruited people to support Standing Rock, and spread information via social media. "The elders pass on their wisdom to us so we are able to do these things, and we will keep going until our lands are permanently protected against destruction," she vowed. "The more youth that come and join us, the more power we have and we are reclaiming the resistance that comes from our ancestors." It was a recognition of a larger truth that increasingly pervades not just Indigenous struggles but the environmental movement at large. "This is the time of the seventh generation, a time when the young take a stand for the future. We are leading everyone in a good way and showing people how to live a better life."[75] Women and gender nonconforming people stood forward to lead central parts of the work.

MOVEMENT BRIDGES

The water protectors realized that to be heard, they had to both revive and build networks across cultures, as much as across age cohorts. People coming together at Standing Rock resulted from generations of patient organizing. As earlier chapters have explored, youth activists of color picked up legal scholar Kimberlé Crenshaw's term and called this "intersectional organizing." It meant organizing at the intersection where issues overlapped—like labor rights, women's rights, Indigenous rights, and environmental justice. Visually one could see this intersection as 350 First Nations from all over the world came to stand in solidarity with Standing Rock. "When you go into the camp, you see hundreds of flags," recalled American Indian Movement elder Isa Barajas de Benavidez. "Just to see the diversity of the support amongst indigenous peoples—along with the support of those from different backgrounds—is incredibly powerful." Fellow AIM veteran and founder of Women of All Red Nations, Madonna Thunder Hawk, saw grassroots people like her coming "from all corners of this country and the globe" to hold the line. It was "decolonization going on right in front of us." Hāwane Rios, a youth activist from Hawaii who stood at both Mauna a Wākea and Standing Rock, reflected, "We've made so many connections; this feeling of solidarity comes to me very naturally." Also present were activists from the Black Lives Matter movement, Latinx youth organizers, environmental activists, reproductive justice advocates, and a range of other youth organizations around the US.[76]

All shared an understanding that self-determination, human rights, and water had to be protected for coming generations. Hāwane Rios explained, "There's an unspoken promise, now, to back each other up." Raven Chacon, an Albuquerque-based artist who is an enrolled member of the Navajo Nation, recalled, "What you saw was truly a global community, but with the majority of them being American Indian people. That was something I'd never seen in my life."[77] The Lakota people "put out the call," Jeanne Dorado explained. For her, it felt like "Native folks around the world—we're all finally, we're just done. We've played the game, we let you think that it worked, we got to where we are. Now we're all sick, now the planet is dying, now we're running out of natural resources. Now I think it's time to listen." It proved a turning point "in the way nations stand together. The native folks here have never come together like this in agreement over something beautiful, which is love and spirit," Dorado realized. They shared a common future, "which is the children."[78]

In August 2016, the Oceti Sakowin invited Black Lives Matter's global network to join their opposition to the oil Pipeline. BLM demonstrated solidarity by centering Indigenous sovereignty to stand with the water protectors. "There is no Black liberation without Indigenous sovereignty," the group posted on its website.[79] Denver's Black Lives Matter 5280 chapter decided to send four members to Standing Rock in November 2016. Before leaving Colorado, they met with the American Indian Movement of Colorado to learn how to act more fully in solidarity. AIM gave them a list of supplies to bring and noted that women might bring skirts to wear at all ceremonies. When asked by others, "What does BLM have to do with #NoDAPL?" the BLM members were clear: "For us, the same law enforcement that's being employed to brutalize sovereign [Indigenous] nations is simply an extension of the forces being used to brutalize and terrorize [Black] communities," Jumoke Emery-Brown recalled. "We do not believe that the history of stolen lands is separated from the history of stolen labor, so while we're not centered in this fight, it is absolutely something we are proud to be a part of, because our histories are intertwined."[80]

"There are so many fights going on simultaneously, at this moment, everywhere," noted activist Krystal Two Bulls. She cited the Mauna Kea telescope, Palestine/Israel, and the Tohono O'odham at the Mexican border, preparing to resist efforts to build Donald Trump's proposed wall. She also saw continuities: struggles against the construction of new refineries being proposed near Philadelphia, the Trans-Pecos Pipeline between Texas and Mexico, the Plains Pipeline in Oklahoma, the Sabal Trail Pipeline in Florida. The San Carlos Apache were facing water pollution from copper mines at Oak Flat. Indigenous grassroots groups had emerged in the Vietnamese Mekong Delta and the Indian Brahmaputra River, as well as the Myitsome Dam project in Myanmar/Burma, to fight for clean water.[81]

It seemed as if everywhere around the world Indigenous people were often those most negatively affected by water contamination. This was affirmed by Chanse Adams-Zavalla, twenty-two, who came to Standing Rock from his home on the Maidu homeland just north of Santa Barbara, California. A burst oil pipeline decimated the coastline near his home in the spring of 2015. "It's disgusting what happened to my people," he declared. He came to Standing Rock to prevent a rerun.[82]

This common set of problems fostered intersectional organizing. Joel Garcia, codirector of the Los Angeles arts nonprofit Self-Help Graphics, traveled to Standing Rock over Thanksgiving 2016 with a group of Chicano artists, many observing Indigenous traditions as part of their Mexican heritage. "I don't know anyone whose life wasn't changed by being there," he noted.[83] One group of scholars and cultural workers represented Chicana, South Asian, white, and Indigenous perspectives. "Any effort to build new fossil-fuel extraction and transportation infrastructure is an implicit violation of the Paris agreements," they asserted. "The fight against fossil fuels is a fight for our planet, for justice, and for a livable future. Standing Rock is standing for the planet, and we must stand with them." Interconnections made them sturdier. "With the Trump Administration, we're anticipating that the resistance will grow that much stronger," Two Bulls recognized. "We have to build a solid platform for us all to stand on together."[84]

LAW ENFORCEMENT

The youth story at Standing Rock centers on the IIYC. Still, their innovations cannot fully be appreciated without recognizing the law enforcement decisions between August 2016 and February 2017. The ominously disproportionate response of law enforcement, with no modulation from the state house or governor in North Dakota, or Congress or the president at the national level, gave young people few options.

On August 17, 2016, for example, after a month of increased nonviolent actions by youth to stop Pipeline construction, Morton County sheriff Kyle Kirchmeier made a widely disputed public statement claiming that the water protectors were compromising safety: "They were preparing to throw pipe bombs at our line," he stated to the international press corps gathered in North Dakota, also alleging "M80s, fireworks, things of that nature, to disrupt us." As reporters gathered from across the globe in his hometown, he asserted, "And that in itself makes it an unlawful protest."[85]

It was a claim made without any evidence. Further, it was a claim that completely contradicted what journalists and bystanders observing the activists' camp experienced on a daily basis: while the occasional member of the camp might have spat or thrown a punch, all "preparations" happening in the camp were geared toward nonviolence, the standard that the IIYC, the IP3, and others worked so hard to maintain. Indeed, how little credibility the sheriff's statement carried even within his own ranks became obvious when his officers, after a full two days of arresting nonviolent activists, took off their hats out of respect as Lakota prayer songs began at Standing Rock. Many bowed their heads to join (fig. 20).

Nevertheless, beyond Morton County, the sheriff's inflammatory statements had their intended effect. In a matter of days, Governor Jack Dalrymple began to escalate the state's response, first by making an emergency declaration on the basis that public safety was presumably at risk. Then, a few weeks later, the governor called out the North Dakota National Guard. At no point did the governor make attempts to independently verify the sheriff's assertions or to reach out and engage a dialogue with his constituents. "I wish [Governor Dalrymple] had consulted with the tribe before making today's declaration,"

FIGURE 20. Members of law enforcement remove hats and join the circle for morning prayers at Standing Rock. The photographer, Mniluzahe Berg, served in the military and later became a police officer due to a dream he had of his brother, who was killed by a police officer in 1999. He came to Standing Rock to support the water protectors "because I seen the way the police were treating our people at Standing Rock and felt I could possibly help."
(Photo by Mniluzahe Berg, courtesy of Indian Country Media Network)

Standing Rock chairman David Archambault II recalled, "because the tribe has its hand extended in the spirit of partnership and cooperation." For leaders at Standing Rock, Archambault continued, "we look upon this situation as an opportunity to work together."[86]

Sheriff Kirchmeier never made clear why he opted for escalation. It seemed uncertain whether he did it on his own or upon orders from others. Did he believe his own claims, or did he invent them to cover other motives? A wide range of explanations are possible. The outcome, however, is indisputable: Morton County law enforcement turned "very aggressive" over the course of the late summer and fall of 2016.[87] All possibilities the IIYC might have had for dialogue, negotiations, and de-escalation were effectively thrown out by law enforcement in favor of belligerence and a wholly disproportionate militarized confrontation. The parallels to Ferguson two years earlier proved uncanny and unmistakable.

Police escalation began a spiral of intensified action and reaction. In short order, the National Sheriffs Association initiated close cooperation between law enforcement throughout the region to support the Cass County and

Morton County sheriff's departments. North Dakota law enforcement also invoked federal legislation to bring in other agencies, including the Emergency Management Assistance Compact, a group originally intended to help states during environmental crises. In many ways, it seemed a classic take from Machiavelli's playbook—maintain the status quo through overwhelming force and outright deception. State politics and law enforcement worked in lockstep with corporate interests, determined to "keep public order" in the face of a crowd of everyday people who lacked legislative or financial force. Everyday people did not wear suits or uniforms, they did not carry official titles, and they did not bring large amounts of money to the table. Indeed, with no apparent sense for tragic irony or historical continuities, Morton County subsequently promoted their aggressive confrontation with #NoDAPL protesters as national "best practice."[88]

If Ferguson police in 2014 looked like a modern replay of whites beating and killing Black people during the Atlanta race riot of 1906, or in Tulsa in 1921, or in Detroit in 1943, the Morton County sheriff's department beat, maced, tased, and tortured Indigenous water protectors in ways strikingly similar to the brutality wielded by "Sharp Knife" Andrew Johnson in the First Seminole War in Florida, or by US cavalry leader Nelson Miles driving Chief Joseph and the Nimi'ipuu (Nez Perce) out of their homeland in 1877, or by FBI snipers killing local Oglala Lakota citizens at Wounded Knee in 1973. Militarized escalation was just one side of the coin, however. The other included a concerted effort by one of the corporations building the Dakota Access Pipeline, Energy Transfer Partners, to destroy the protests. Again, there is no publicly available evidence that could shed light on precise intentions behind ETP's dabbling in privatized warfare. What is clear now, documented in *The Intercept*'s investigative journalism, is the fact that ETP hired TigerSwan, a US military and state department contractor based in North Carolina, to monitor, surveil, and disrupt the water protectors. Documents leaked by a TigerSwan insider in spring 2017 showed that these mercenaries worked with law enforcement to spy on and target the nonviolent Indigenous-led youth movement.

Standing Rock so far had been a domestic political issue involving citizens publicly debating and organizing around their ideas for how best to live. When ETP hired TigerSwan, a private corporate security firm, the latter brought to the table instruments and skills honed in warfare in places like Iraq and Afghanistan. TigerSwan changed the terms of engagement. The fossil fuel–based wealth versus sustainable well-being debate turned a clash of ideas to one of guerrilla warfare. In the company's internal documents, TigerSwan repeatedly referred to youth protectors as "insurgents" and to the movement as "an ideologically-driven insurgency" comparable to "jihadist terrorists." A report from February 2017 notes that for TigerSwan, the water protectors "generally followed the jihadist insurgency model while active." It was not the first time veterans of US wars abroad used the language and logic of warfare against domestic citizens, nor was it the first time the language and logic of state terror arrived in the Dakotas.[89]

It was hard to grasp for peaceful youth activists. IIYC member Jasilyn Charger noted in astonishment that TigerSwan and law enforcement "are saying we are radicalists, we are savage, we are disobedient when we're protecting our water." What the youth protectors came to understand all too well, and all too quickly, was that this precise militarized corporate framework allowed men, women, and children to be mauled by dogs, shot, beaten, and arrested, "just for occupying a space."[90]

Slowly, non-Indigenous North Dakotans started to realize this as well. "We are using public and military employees to do the private work of a pipeline company," explained North Dakota Democratic state senator Tim Mathern. This, too, had a peculiarly dense and lengthy history in the US, going back at least as far as the Pinkerton Agency. For over a century and a half, Pinkerton had been in the business of repression, coercion, and enforcement at the behest of the highest private bidder. The privatization of law enforcement in the Dakota Access Pipeline conflict, serving corporate interests, went hand in hand with a wave of legislation passed by states since 2016 aimed to criminalize constitutionally protected protest.[91]

Rarely debated in public, the combined effects of these attempts can only be described as chilling to those interested in democracy. They range from sending protesters itemized bills for law enforcement, to labeling boycotts "economic terrorism," to removing liability from drivers who "accidentally" hit or kill protesters. The latter was particularly striking, given the obvious parallel in time to trucks driven by people labeled "terrorists" into crowds in Nice (July 2016), Berlin (December 2016), London (March 2017), and Charlottesville (August 2017). Of course, as Senator Mathern also noted, the costs of the enforcement of policies repressing citizens are shouldered by citizens. North Dakota borrowed $28 million from the Bank of North Dakota to fuel the hyper-militarized police presence. "The North Dakota taxpayers are at risk for paying the bill of a multinational corporation that's extracting our resources," warned Mathern.[92]

Together, the militarization of unchecked police combined with dubious privatized "security" pose fundamental threats to constitutional freedoms, as well as to basic rights for citizens. Not only did "the leaked materials . . .

highlight TigerSwan's militaristic approach to protecting its client's interests," *The Intercept* report notes, but also the thousands of documents "show the company's profit-driven imperative to portray the nonviolent water protector movement as unpredictable and menacing enough to justify the continued need for extraordinary security measures."[93]

One can trace these tactics of TigerSwan to those long used, often illegally, in the US government's history of domestic intelligence gathering, infiltration, and repression of citizen activism since at least the Civil War. Nick Tilsen, executive director of the Thunder Valley Community Development Corporation and a citizen of the Oglala Lakota Nation on the Pine Ridge homeland, labeled law enforcement at Standing Rock "the modern form of COINTELPRO."[94]

COINTELPRO, or the disgraced "Counter-Intelligence Program" run by the FBI and other federal agencies in the decades immediately following the Second World War, had been exposed after the US Congress's public Church Committee hearings in 1975. Until then, under the guise of legal law enforcement, those in COINTELPRO used anonymous letters, warrantless taps, provocateurs, conspicuous surveillance, repeat arrests, and other forms of intimidation to disrupt, misdirect, discredit, and neutralize political groups like the American Indian Movement, the Puerto Rican independence movement, and the New Left and groups like the Black Panther Party that they called "Black Hate Groups." The latter were singled out for particular focus: police and police infiltrators killed forty Panthers between 1960 and 1971.[95]

The Church Committee highlighted law enforcement's violation of the Constitution, and for a while, the public, the legal community, and legislators tilted in favor of citizens' rights. Yet since the late 1970s, and especially in the wake of Osama bin Laden's attack on the US in 2001, COINTELPRO tactics resurged. Tilsen recognized in 2016 the long arm of COINTELPRO, first deployed in South Dakota against Pine Ridge in the early 1970s. Law enforcement worked with private contractors, using "all of the lessons that they have been building off of fighting terrorism, but using it on their own people" in the US. Water protectors saw "security officers and police who knew us by first name, who knew where we came from, who knew where in the camp we were staying." The Dakota Access Pipeline corporation hired Delta Force veterans from TigerSwan, who then used "counterintelligence tactics against peaceful water protectors who are expressing our constitutional rights."[96]

For Tilsen, it was an outrage. "The movement has to be diligent in recognizing that this is a reality," he stated, and those who support Standing Rock "have to recognize what we're fighting against." Water protectors "show up with our prayers. We show up with our bodies. We show up with our children and our

INFORMATION CONTAINED IN THIS REPORT IS PROPRIETARY AND SENSITIVE
DO NOT RELEASE OUTSIDE OF AUTHORIZED AND APPROVED RECIPIENTS

"This doesn't stop us, this is not going to stop us. We're going to go somewhere else and continue this fight."

— ▆▆▆▆▆▆

There is a clear determination, expressed by prominent figures in the Standing Rock anti-DAPL indigenous movement, to continue fighting pipelines in other places now that the fight in North Dakota is all but over.

This is to be expected. What the anti-DAPL protesters have called an "indigenous decolonization movement" was, essentially, an externally supported, ideologically driven insurgency with a strong religious component. And, as it generally followed the jihadist insurgency model while active, we can expect the individuals who fought for and supported it to follow a post-insurgency model after its collapse.

The archetype of a jihadist post-insurgency is the aftermath of the anti-Soviet Afghanistan jihad. While many insurgents went back to their pre-war lives, many, especially the external supporters (foreign fighters), went back out into the world looking to start or join new jihadist insurgencies. Most famously this "bleedout" resulted in Osama bin Laden and the rise of Al Qaeda, but the jihadist veterans of Afghanistan also ended up fighting in Bosnia, Chechnya, North Africa, and Indonesia, among other places.

We have already seen this "bleedout" happen with the ideologically driven pipeline fighters from Standing Rock, as several of them are in the process of moving to Iowa, including high-profile drone flyer Dean Dedman Jr. Additionally, other camps are being set up and are actively recruiting Standing Rock diaspora, such as the Two Rivers Camp in Texas fighting the Trans-Pecos Pipeline.

We also saw bleedout happen in the aftermath of the collapse of the Mississippi Stand group in Iowa in late-2016. Former members have surfaced in New York, Florida, and Arkansas protesting pipelines and proliferating the knowledge they gained from their anti-DAPL efforts in Iowa. For example, Alex Cohen provided non-violent resistance training to activists in Arkansas. Additionally, ▆▆▆▆▆ is currently supporting the anti-Sabal effort in Florida. Recently, she posted on Facebook in support of two pipeline activists arrested in Florida who had locked themselves inside of a pipeline, a tactic Mississippi Stand group used at the Des Moines River HDD in November 2016.

▆▆▆▆▆▆ a key original supporter of the Mississippi Stand group, provided an insightful analysis of why the MS group failed to a small group of protesters in November, 2016. He said there were three basic causes, 1. not enough people (protesters) quickly enough, 2. ideological divides within the protesters, but most importantly, 3. DAPL was able to radically increase security measures at key nodes and do so far faster than the protesters were able to conduct effective shutdown or sabotage actions.

FIGURE 21. Excerpt from TigerSwan's "DAPL SitRep," February 27, 2017. Over a hundred documents leaked from TigerSwan to *The Intercept* are available at https://www.documentcloud.org/public/search/projectid:33327-TigerSwan.

families to these protests. And these guys are showing up with all the technology that's possible and all the weaponry that's possible." Protecting water, it became clear, was not just about water. It meant a clear and direct "fight over the future of this country."[97]

The proverbial wisdom may be true, that "he who strikes the first blow admits he's lost the argument." The Dakota Access Pipeline, however, was not about winning an argument. Being correct or having evidence on one's side, even being on the right side of morality, meant very little when arrayed against the collective might of wealth and state power, or what some at Standing Rock came to call "settler-colonial capitalism." The youth water protectors were playing on the field of right and wrong; the oil corporations and state government were playing on the field of win and lose. As scholar David Uahikeaikaleiʻohu Maile (Kanaka Maoli) wrote, it is the state with this win-lose mentality that must take responsibility for violence, "not the people who are challenging the inherent injustices perpetrated by the state."[98]

The violence came fast and furious: Sheriff Kirchmeier used all available tools to punish, beat back, and arrest #NoDAPL protectors in the second half of 2016. The open, direct violence, in turn, played out in the context of an even larger, more insidious form of "slow violence." People of color, particularly African Americans and Indigenous people, are far more likely to be poor, unemployed, incarcerated, or killed by police than the national average. When North Dakota, along with eighteen other Republican-run states, began to pass more laws limiting the rights of free expression, journalist Sandy Tolan detected more than "a nod to Jim Crow." In 2016, the state saw significant increases in felony convictions for minor infractions, criminalization of peaceful protest, and an attempt to make it legal for motorists to "unintentionally" run over and kill protesters in the road. These were all tactics previously employed by white supremacist leaders in the South during the civil rights era of the 1950s and 1960s and intermittently resuscitated ever since, with murderous results in Washington State, where a white man ran over twenty-year-old Jimmy Smith-Kramer, and during the antiracist protests in Charlottesville in 2017, when a white supremacist killed antiracist activist Heather Heyer.[99]

Not only did law enforcement choices at Standing Rock echo 1960s white southern sheriffs and the US cavalry in the 1800s, but local law enforcement and corporate security forces advanced a militarized attack on peaceful protesters unlike anything the nation had seen since the era of US government support of genocide and slavery—at least unlike anything the nation had seen outside Ferguson, Missouri, in 2014.[100]

FIGURES 22 and 23. A consistent tool against freedom movements: a white motorist threatens to run over civil rights activists in Chapel Hill, NC, 1964 (photograph © Jim Wallace), and a hate crime by a motorist in Charlottesville, VA, in August 2017 results in the death of Heather Heyer (video still courtesy of CNN). Additionally, Jimmy Smith-Kramer (Quinalt) was killed in a hate crime by a motorist in Donkey Creek, WA, in 2017 (not pictured).

VICTORY: "I GOT MY FUTURE BACK"

The excessive law enforcement made the IIYC victory all that much more remarkable on December 4, 2016. After more than five months of the IIYC's nonviolent direct action, the Army Corps of Engineers announced it would not grant DAPL a permit to continue digging the Pipeline at Standing Rock. Six months earlier, "when the youth ran to D.C., that's when this really got started," Standing Rock chief David Archambault II exulted to the crowd that gathered to celebrate. People lined up to shake the hands of the young people who started the movement as runners. Archambault continued, "We all came here to stand for something greater than whatever we did at home."[101] When author Naomi Klein interviewed thirteen-year-old Tokata Iron Eyes on Facebook Live that day, with over one million people watching, Iron Eyes said, "I feel like I got my future back." Then she broke down in tears.[102] They had won. And young people had pulled it off.

Archambault immediately asked those who came to Standing Rock to disperse, telling them not only had they won, but their work was done. For youth activists, this was a blow. "Dave Archambault doesn't speak for our entire generation," Jasilyn Charger replied. "When he dies, my grandchildren are going to be here, and nobody can speak for them but me."[103] Given the history of the conflict between Indigenous people and resource extractors, IIYC members were right to be skeptical that the Army Corps's ruling would mark the end of the conflict.

And by this time, "home" for the members of the IIYC was complicated: they had come to experience a safe home, some for the first time, collectively at Standing Rock. The entire experience had pulled people together based on "opposition to forces operating at the behest of the government and big oil, and they will succeed only through people power," noted Dr. Kalamaoka'aina Niheu.[104] Anticipating events to come, Chanse Adams-Zavalla asserted that "even if somehow, someway, they build this pipeline, they've inadvertently sparked a whole generation of us indigenous folks and everyone who wants to stand with us to fight for Mother Earth. We're going to inherit this planet," he continued, "and everyone's welcome to inherit it with us if they want."[105] With concentrated state and corporate forces arrayed so openly and blatantly against them, it was no longer enough to play by rules increasingly stacked against a defense of nature and, by extension, the seventh generation to come.[106]

Where to go from here? As scholar Audra Simpson (Kahnawake Mohawk) described the dilemma, "How, then, do those who are targeted for elimination, those who have had their land stolen from them, their bodies and their cultures worked on to be made into something else, articulate their politics?" The Standing Rock nation had preexisting political traditions to draw on. Yet how might youth consistently speak from those traditions, when most people are familiar with ideas on how to be a citizen that are drawn from Enlightenment ideas of individual rights? Many simply refused "to consent to the apparatuses of the state," Simpson continued. At bottom, this was a refusal to act as if the playing field was even or fair. If nothing else, the experience of Standing Rock confirmed that the state of North Dakota and corporate entities continued to push for an enduring logic of settler colonialism, operating "like a grammar and posture that sits through time." The refusal of the US government to honor its agreements with Indigenous peoples meant that when citizenship as a concept was reduced to voting and paying taxes, Indigenous people moved out of what Simpson called "their own sovereignty" and "into settler citizenship and into the promise of whiteness."[107] Many didn't want this form of citizenship. Instead, they wanted sovereignty to protect the water and defend the land.[108]

How then to understand the IIYC and its role? The youth-led movement "wasn't just a year long period of activism, a blip on the political radar," stated scholar Anne Spice (Tlingit member of Kwanlin Dun First Nation). "These movements may appear to be *interruptions* of the normal progression of relations between settler states and Indigenous peoples," she continued, but "are in fact *continuations* of hundreds of years of Indigenous resilience and resistance."[109] Standing Rock might also herald a new kind of relationship between Indigenous-led movements, white-led environmental groups, and environmental justice groups headed by African Americans, Latinx people, and Asian-Pacific Islanders. For many decades, Indigenous groups had combined a focus on environmental protection; recognition of treaty rights; justice for Indigenous young people and women within the legal, education, and health care systems; and an end to non-Indigenous environmental activists who ignored or reproached Indigenous people. Bill McKibben, one of the most visible public intellectuals of the environmental movement, highlighted this shift with a tweet after the 2016 election, lifting up the work of IIYC media coordinator Eryn Wise and Standing Rock elder LaDonna Allard (fig. 24). They continued to build coalitions, particularly after the November 2016 election of a president who, to a degree greater than any other before him, embodies the naked interests of the fossil fuel agenda.[110]

A mere four days into his presidency, Donald Trump signed an executive order that obliterated the visible accomplishments of the water protectors. It

FIGURE 24. Environmentalist Bill McKibben promotes work of IIYC media coordinator Eryn Wise, with Bernie Sanders and LaDonna Allard, on Twitter.

showed a remarkable ignorance of the youth at the base of the movement. "I approved" the Pipeline, he smiled. "It's up. It's running. It's beautiful. It's great. Everybody's happy. The sun is still shining. The water is clean." He seemed surprised: "I thought I'd take a lot of heat. And I took none, actually none. People respected that I approved it."[111]

Trump's reference to the people's respect was a "total lie," said Nick Tilsen. A hundred thousand people had stood at Standing Rock against the Pipeline. "We sacrificed our freedoms to protect this water. We sacrificed everything that we had," Tilsen recalled. "And it was women and children and families, and indigenous people with our allies from all over the country and all over the world."[112] Once again, two stories clashed—Trump's self-serving story of a small but powerful elite versus the story of organized people. And, as always, the former had more outlets than the latter, even though it represented far fewer Americans.

The water protectors, however, were determined to continue. Everyone understood it was an uphill battle. Indigenous peoples and their allies were certainly familiar with temporary setbacks. In many ways, future steps of organized resistance and mobilization were as uncertain as the erratic nature of governance emanating from the White House. And yet there was now a common experience to build upon, and a shared set of principles that activists would not compromise.

"Despite that it's the day after the Trump election, we have to stand up and be heard," twenty-two-year-old Morgan Brings Plenty (Cheyenne River Sioux) said. "We can't be fearful, because that's what people thrive on—fear. This country was built off stolen land and fear. You shouldn't let fear be who you are." "As an Indigenous person growing up on this land you feel like nobody sees you," noted IIYC member Thomas Lopez. "You feel like people don't want you around. If you just disappeared, everybody would just be happy."[113]

Yet Lopez did not feel deterred. He and his *compañeros* had forced the Army Corps of Engineers to stop the Dakota Access Pipeline in December. It was a formidable victory no one could deny. It felt "good to be acknowledged as a human being," Lopez recalled. Facing down forces far more brutal and stark than anyone could have foreseen, he predicted it would be only the first major victory for the Indigenous youth water protectors. "If you think you're going to endanger the lives of *any* human being, indigenous or not," Lopez warned, "you have to go through us first. *We* protect this earth. And you *will* have a very difficult time doing this."[114]

CONCLUSION

Citizens of a World Not Yet Built

> There were some positive things in the conceptualization
> of this country. They are matched or over-matched by the evil
> that is in the creation of the country. —Howard Zinn

> I am citizen of a world that has not yet been built. —James Lawson

In the early summer of 2018, the Trump administration separated youth from their parents at the US border and put children as young as three years of age behind bars, alone, in detention camps. The world could only shake its collective head in shock. What had happened to the quintessential American claims to fairness and decency, to protecting the dignity of all?[1]

On another level, it was business as usual—and good business at that. Politicians scored points by craftily playing on popular fears around security and jobs—Trump's approval rating among Republicans reached 90 percent. Government agencies found further justification for their bloated expenses. And private prison and logistics corporations profited mightily—hundreds of millions of dollars in security, surveillance, and detention. Good business, all. This was true despite the fact that the US had no actual immigration crisis. Even mayors from Texas border towns assured the nation that all was well.[2] Yet the fabricated, though no less heated, debate about the alleged imminent threats from immigration effectively shifted the attention of the American public. Many very real problems—climate change, escalating inequality, corporate lobbyists stomping on the remnants of US democratic forms, the widespread disappearance of good work at a living wage—once again disappeared from view, crowded out by the latest con. Traumatized children, inhumane detention centers, militarized immigration officers, shady corporations on the take—it seemed that the veneer of rationality and maturity, otherwise a mainstay of elite politics in America, was peeling off.

"The people" did not remain quiet. A wave of outrage built on social media, followed by marching in the streets, as letters and phone calls to elected officials piled up. In restaurants and other public spaces, everyday citizens, and young people in particular, rebuked administration officials in peaceful direct actions that Trump administration officials and centrist pundits quickly characterized as "violent." Though no physical force was used by activists, they did "violate" the rules of the game, for they refused to be bamboozled. Instead, they made clear, in thousands of ways, that the self-interest of the administration's policies did not represent them. The groups Mijente, #Not1More, and United We Dream intensified their #AbolishICE campaign, building on years of work by Puente in Phoenix, the Georgia Latino Alliance for Human Rights in Georgia, Juntos in Philadelphia, the Asian American Justice Center, the Organized Community Against Deportation in Chicago, the New Orleans Congress of Day Laborers, the Northwest Detention Center Resistance in Washington State, and the National Day Laborers Organizing Network and some of its members. "We started as a disparate set of local groups, working with different constituencies inside immigrant communities, discouraged by a national landscape devoid of demands that had meaning or real aspiration for our bases," reflected three organizers involved in the campaign. "#Not1More was a call for a moratorium on deportations," they noted. The heart of it was the "notion that ICE should be abolished." The idea went to the root of the problem—"that no one should be subject to the harm of immigration enforcement." Over the previous few years, #Not1More had issued a call to "dismantle government agencies that exist solely to bring terror, harm, and violence to communities of color."[3]

Activists from many backgrounds—Black, Indigenous, immigrant—understood that this was hardly the first time the US government had forced family separation and trauma. Slavers had stolen and then sold millions of children from Black families over at least twelve generations; white office holders had removed eight generations of children from Indigenous homes and put them into boarding schools and non-Indigenous foster care.[4] It was now 2018, and, across the country, young people of color decided to step up and try to stop those who profited from creating human misery through family separation.

An obvious target was the public-private partnership between the federal agency ICE and the international corporate giant GEO Group. GEO's business model was straight out of a Hollywood horror movie: privatize and make

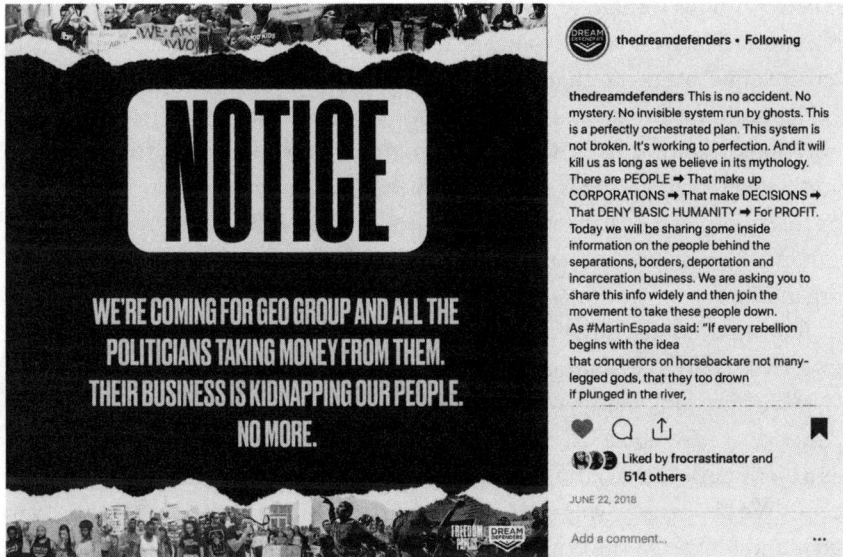

FIGURE 25. Dream Defenders, Instagram post, June 22, 2018.

"more efficient" government services. It profited from every additional child detained, prison bed filled, or mental health patient locked away. Targeting government officials who "legalized" family separation, the Dream Defenders started a campaign on June 22, 2018 (fig. 25). "We're coming for GEO," they declared. "And all the politicians taking money from them. Their business is kidnapping our people. No more."[5]

The Trump administration's actions deepened the collapse of the distinction within the freedom movement between movement organizing and electoral organizing. No longer did it feel to movement organizers that only movement politics were real and those doing electoral work were just "playing politics." As one organizer, Nse Ufot, reflected a few months later, "The policies that we are pushing for, we use elected officials and government agencies to enforce them." As head of the New Georgia Project, she reflected, "It is important to have our people, or people who are accountable to our communities, in those [elected] positions. It's our [tax] money." The logic was indisputable. Every time citizens bought "a bag of Doritos, or paid a payroll tax," they helped support government, funding the very civil servants tasked to execute "programs for the public." It was thus only reasonable and right, Ufot asserted, to expect officials to "do my people's work, and do work on behalf of me and my family." Electoral politics was not separate or distinct from people's lives.

If communities wanted to have a say, if they wanted to be heard by their representatives, they needed to engage in politics. A critical first step was to help "create equal access to that electoral system."[6]

Neither movement politics nor electoral politics alone would suffice. Corporations profiting from incarceration, politicians benefiting from division and hatred, civil servants defending their positions rather than serving the people—these were cancers at the heart of civil society that required pursuit of a kind of "freedom politics"[7] in both electoral politics and community organizing.

Tearing children from parents once again brought to the surface two Americas, two separate strands of history, two diverging visions for the future. Neither blue nor red, neither exclusively Republican nor Democratic, these two Americas differ, above all, in their faith in people. The conflict could be seen as a birthmark of the nation as much as it is solidly enshrined in the Constitution. "We the people" was a revolutionary departure from resting authority in gods and kings. On the other hand, some founders believed "the people" to be an unnerving mob that needed to be ruled and contained. One America embraced an expansive vision of widening freedoms, best symbolized by people like Frederick Douglass, Ella Baker, Bobbi Jean Three Legs, and, at his best moments, Thomas Jefferson. The other represented a sober account of dangers and limits, often cloaked in the posture of cool-headed realism and maturity, symbolized by a long line of leaders ranging from James Madison and Alexander Hamilton to Mitch McConnell and Bill Clinton.[8] The first strand can be characterized as freedom politics and the second as elite control.

Over the long haul of American history, both strands have seen significant victories and defeats. "The people," first envisioned by the constitutional fathers as white propertied men (6 percent of the population in 1789), later came to include Black men, then women and Indigenous people, then successive waves of immigrants. Collective freedom struggles ended slavery, lifted millions out of poverty, and secured standards for safer working conditions, old-age benefits, the right to bargain collectively, and legal guarantees against discrimination on the basis of race, religion, gender, and sexual orientation. And yet, as a democratic presence, "the people" have also been disenfranchised, surveilled, segregated, impoverished, and, if all else failed, locked away, deported, or killed. The arc of the moral universe bent toward justice, it seemed.[9] Except where it did not.

When generations of historians have, at long last, unscrewed the lens of elite control and popped on a more granular lens that revealed "the people," they began to discover the seemingly relentless rationale of power accumulated through wealth, violence, and the logic of the market—the ruthless extraction of resources and exploitation of people. The long march of elite control slowed or stopped in its tracks only when people organized to stand in the way, resisting its cold philosophy of efficiency and accumulation, raising their voices on behalf of dignity and self-determination.

Young people have consistently stood on the front lines of these struggles. All too often, youth found unacceptable the quiet tolerance of the intolerable that mature adults had swallowed. By default, young people had not yet internalized the pruned moral compass of "reality." Why, they asked, should they accept vile morals that hide behind technocratic logic—like the deportation of DREAMers to "keep America great"; the building of oil pipelines to secure the flow of energy; the incarceration of people of color to keep America safe; the violent exclusion of people based on race or religion or sexual identity or gender in the name of Christian values; wars of extraction in the name of democracy; or escalating inequality as a presumed consequence of merit?

Most recently, this determined stance was on display at Marjory Stoneman Douglas High School in Parkland, Florida. After fourteen of their peers were murdered, the halls of their high school sprayed with bullets, the students came together, organized, and told their governor, as much as the rest of the world, "Enough."[10]

Young people don't like running into the line of fire any more than they have some inherent proclivity to get in trouble. Instead, time and again, a morally compromised and socially unacceptable reality, passed down from their elders, forces those into resistance whose entire futures still lie ahead. Take the young Black students who enrolled in college in the early 1960s, excited for new experiences, ready to expand their minds, only to find themselves refused service at libraries, lunch counters, and department stores. Rather than accept inequality, they engaged in sit-ins and formed SNCC. Time and again, it is young people who, after running into realities that give a lie to what their culture professed, raise their voices, put their bodies on the line, and attempt to create new realities. Young people who found themselves profiled, beaten, and incarcerated in the school-to-prison pipeline, or forced to lie to get a job or drive a car because they are undocumented, or who stood in the Missouri River in twenty-five degrees to preserve their access to clean water. Young people who formed the Ella Baker Center, United We Dream, the International Indigenous Youth Council, the Dream Defenders, the Movement for Black Lives, and hundreds of other groups that must be added to the country's collective understanding of its history.

Youth activism appears when the rules young people are expected to follow reveal foul realities, yet grown-ups in positions of authority profess ignorance or, worse, enforce rules, no matter right or wrong. The results have been documented in countless essays, books, films, and documentaries. Eight people in the US now have as much wealth as the bottom 165 million Americans combined; happiness and health and security are declining across the board within the richest country on earth; Americans incarcerate a far greater proportion of their own people than any other country on earth, including authoritarian states like Saudi Arabia and Russia; we make up 4 percent of the world's population yet use some 30 percent of its resources; we exceed the per-person carbon emissions necessary to leave behind a livable planet by a factor of eight; we are in the midst of tearing the culture apart over allegiance to two parties that share in common the distinction of having contributed to the crimes mentioned above. And too many US politicians and diplomats try to sell all this as a desirable model for people around the world.

Young people come to these realities without yet being resigned to the everyday pathologies inherent in the tension between striving for freedom politics and the push for elite control in American life. We see this when a young child asks his grandmother, "Why can't I use this water fountain?" Or when an eleven-year-old wonders, "Why did the police stop me, and then curse me out on the way to school today?" We hear it when Tokata Iron Eyes, at thirteen years old, reminds us, "[Doesn't] everything and everyone need water to live?" And we listen to the primal terror in a six-year-old's voice as she is torn from her parent's embrace by adults in uniform at the US-Mexico border and cries, "No! Why?"

These are the right questions. Except at key junctures in the nation's history, it appears very hard for the adults in the room to recognize "right," blinded as they routinely are by the false realities of age posing as wisdom or, in many cases, by elite control posing as maturity.

Over the last three centuries, we have seen rulers sell success as amount of territory conquered, or number of people under the sway of a particular version of God, or the purity of "das Volk" that will bring about the thousand-year "Reich." All claimed to be nominally serving "the people"; none consulted them.

The Enlightenment and the creation of democratic republics publicly proclaimed a change to all that—government by, of, and for the people, not government by inheritance, title, wealth, or privileged connection to God. From the perspective of many regular citizens, it was progress, even if not all citizens counted equally and some were excluded altogether.

Still, democratic republics have effectively replaced the rule of kings or emperors or religious leaders with their own internal logic: the rule of the market. The papal edict or the decree from the führer has been superseded by an ongoing racial capitalism driven by cost-benefit analyses, stock market ratings, and economic growth predictions. In all cases, the well-being or will of the people is reduced to purely functional value: the degree to which they serve the rules of the system. Rather than politics or economics serving people, both people and nature serve the needs of the racialized economic market logic. "Utility maximization" leaves no room for ethics of justice or equality, any more than it allows for democratic debates about the good life. In our current era, astonishingly enough, we do not even have a wide-ranging public discussion and debate about what a sustainable life might look like.[11] "Politics" thus has shriveled to be a handmaiden of market logic—the economy must grow, or we risk falling behind.

Yes, universities and nonprofits could serve as vital sites of what scholar Robin D. G. Kelley has called "fugitive study." Here people working in the tradition of Ella Baker, Walter Rodney, Myles Horton, and Paolo Freire could pass on the organizing tradition and "*think* together, to plan." Yet it cannot be the only place that happens. Whether they are in school or not, many young people hear constantly they should consume content, for fear of missing out. Young and old, blue and red, most feel that we don't have time, but we must keep taking in information. Not knowledge—but information. Despite the fact that most media content is mindless, young people absorb this as the way they are told to engage society. As Dream Defender and poet Aja Monet recently reflected, "Today consumption is what collects people." People group themselves by what shoes they wear, what apps they use, and what clubs, restaurants, or weekend leisure they can afford. "We're not just facing the deaths of Black and brown bodies," she stated. Young organizers also have to combat the idea "that capitalism can save us from that."[12]

One might call it neoliberal citizenship, the branding that capitalism is cool. "How do we politicize people on why that's not freedom?" Monet asked. "What is organizing, beyond this thing you hear Obama did?" To recruit more youth to their cause, organizers must struggle against the norms of much of society, because so few young people are taught to see how freedom politics might work among everyday people. Youth activist Sunny Osment noted in 2018, There is a "militancy for capitalism, instead of militancy for the [freedom] movement." It is not that people aren't interested in reading or debating with one another; "it's that we don't have time in a way that is imaginable to us. We are in debt; we have two jobs." Young people feel they are supposed to be always hustling. "Just financially, it's inescapable to think, 'I can read a book,' versus numb ourselves for thirty minutes watching a Netflix show."[13]

And how to get beyond this small group?, Monet asked. If groups like Black Lives Matter or the Ella Baker Center or SONG or the IIYC are largely led by academic, middle-class people and intellectuals of color, "how do we get to the poor folks who are not in the place of having these conversations?"[14] The culture promotes individualism and consumption. This creates a profound challenge to those who want to adapt the tools and knowledge subsequent generations need for a basic education in freedom politics.

Within the deeply embedded logic of the economy, every citizen has a role to play in creating more goods and more services. Within this hubbub of business and productivity, the young people raising profound questions about values and about the viability of our common future appear to most responsible adults—politicians, journalists, and scholars—as little more than annoying noise. Indeed, for most adults in general, the questions of young people simply reveal an insufficient appreciation of the realities of life.

Again, we run into freedom politics versus elite control, ordinary people versus people in the service of a systemic philosophy. Here is what has changed: even by its own criteria, the economic growth logic no longer works. Indeed, the only thing we can't continue doing, the thing that is demonstrably unrealistic, is what the realists tell us is the only thing—keep growing, keep investing, keep expanding.[15] Idealism may be the new realism. The striving of freedom movements—making people and their well-being the center of politics and economics—not only is the most desirable but also seems to be one of the few viable options.

What we learn from the young people in these pages is that striving within freedom movements is not about finding better representatives or parties or organizations to govern "the people." Instead, we should experiment with ways for people to govern themselves. Yes, "we the people" is messy, full of conflict, and sometime agonizingly slow. And no one, as scholar Teresa Phelps observed, "is immune from wanting a master narrative" or, for that matter, "from wanting to be comforted by coherence" or by tradition.[16] But this comfort is simply not possible on a routine basis in a democracy where multiple conflicting points of view must be reckoned with.

Citizens of societies today are generally no more accustomed to that particular form of public messiness as they are comfortable with multiple, conflicting voices. We have much to learn about how to the put the well-being of people and the earth at the center of our politics. People want to belong, to be treated with respect and dignity, and they want a sustainable world where that reality encompasses everyone. From the smallest units of the family, to worker-owned cooperatives, to participatory processes holding city and state governments accountable, all the way to national and international political negotiations, millions have already experimented with people-power. Their histories provide a wealth of insights.

Freedom movements seek to address large imbalances of power. The challenge is severe, the expectations of performance are high, and people's tolerance for error is low. The odds are stacked against any kind of systemic victory. Failure is much more common than success. In American culture, guided by Hollywood and electoral campaign narratives, failure is scorned and an absence of a happy ending to be avoided at all cost.[17] The "evidence" that historians and social scientists routinely use to assess political progress is not particularly helpful in understanding the movements described in this book. The reason is quite straightforward: most scholars use today's metrics of success—parties formed, elections won, legislation passed, jobs created, growth rate increased. Often, however, those are not the sole or even primary goals of young people pursuing freedom politics. Young people not only want to win elections or change policy but also want to hold accountable both politicians and policy makers to the people most affected at the base of society.

Striving within freedom movements is a fundamentally different process than gaining access to the halls of elite power. As a result, freedom movements' milestones are often missed. The people driving the movements in the 1960s, 1990s, and 2010s pushed democracy far beyond what, in mainstream culture, is generally associated with the term. Rather than see democracy as a spectator sport, confined to inconsequential commentary or the picking of choices prefabricated by others, they acted, collaborated, listened, argued, struggled, resisted, argued some more. In the process they formed, changed, and reformulated who they were and what they wanted. They moved from spectator to player, even when they did not know all the rules.

The young people documented in these pages performed much more democratically than they had been taught to in schools, families, or workplaces, and more democratically than they had often believed they could. In this sense, the movements they created served as freedom labs.

The internal goings-on—the recruiting, the debating, the growing, the building—is precisely where most historians, political scientists, and anthropologists, and many journalists, lose the thread, often without realizing it. Rules of evidence focus on sanctioned groups of historical and political actors. It is culturally accessible for scholars and journalists to study the written

FIGURE 26. "Organize!" poster. (Courtesy of Pixabay)

words of university-educated intellectuals—to read pamphlets, listen to oratory, or follow established leadership. Yet when it comes to unearthing the inner workings of freedom movements, many of these same scholars and journalists don't know where to look or what to ask. As a result, youth activists in freedom movements like the ones described in this book either disappear from the stage of history-making, or their roles become disfigured as hotheads or idealists in attempts to force them into the straitjacket of mainstream politics. Many simply remain invisible.[18]

The elite inability to see and explore the inner workings of freedom movements has a long tradition. Few understand that the cake tells us little about the bakery—the visible product doesn't say much about who produced it and how they did so, much less how it might have altered them in the process. Thomas Jefferson was a rare voice when he realized that "a great deal of knowledge about the revolution is not on paper, but only within ourselves."[19]

One of the biggest black holes of information about freedom movements is the question of recruitment: how to move from a broad set of ideas and perceptions—a grievance—to a specific set of particular and tangible actions. It is a long and complicated process for which no ready-made template exists. And as the experiences portrayed in this book show, it is also a process that happens almost entirely behind the scenes and, even if successful at first, is very difficult to maintain.

Shared grievances, expressed in personal conversations or public pamphlets or tweets, are a necessary but by no means sufficient condition that get people to move. For movements to happen, many things need to be put in place, chief among them a community of people and practical ideas about what to do. The basic truth is that it's a lot easier to agree on what's wrong than to figure out what to do about it and then find people to do it with. SNCC engaged in sit-ins and then co-created the Mississippi Freedom Democratic Party and the Lowndes County Freedom Organization. The IIYC created a 2,000-mile relay run from the Dakotas through the Midwest to Washington, DC. Undocumented youth and BLM activists marched and sat on highways. It got their work off the ground.

Unlike most pursuits in life—getting an education, buying a car, applying for citizenship, landing a job—there are virtually no models or guidelines readily available for those attempting to build a movement. Activists operate by necessity in uncharted territory, breaking out of received wisdoms, challenging, exploring, and, quite often, simply inventing things on the spot.

As conversations with activists reveal, time is the most precious—and the most scarce—resource. Movement building requires enormous time that needs to be diverted from people's everyday lives of paying bills, raising children, pursuing a career. Whether young or old, most people don't like to waste their time, which puts a continuously huge burden on movement organizing. Does it make sense to spend time on this effort? Could I be doing something better? Will this ever lead to anything? Why can't we agree on things? How long will this debate take? Should we not act, now?

More than time-consuming, organizing is also inherently experimental. The new cannot be created with the tools of the old. There is no comfort or tradition to follow. On the contrary, frequent failure is an inherent component of trying something new. Ideally, organizers find ways to act, think about what worked and what did not, refine their thinking, and act again. Realistically, they often run out of steam.

The most fortunate organizers in this book found guides in elders who had gone through similar struggles. Ella Baker, LaDonna Allard, and Bob Moses all served as freedom movement builders and healers, modeling how to move in what Toni Morrison described as "the slow walk of the trees." Young people then remix the ideas, songs, and political forms at hand to create new possibilities, speaking back to and through their predecessors.[20] The next generation beyond millennials is already coming forward. The tip of these freedom movements can be seen in the March for Our Lives after the Parkland mass shooting in March 2018 and in fifteen-year-old Greta Thunberg's rousing call to action at the UN's climate change conference in December 2018.[21] In order to chronicle this work, journalists, scholars, and activists themselves have to learn to trace both evolving action and movement participants' evolving *thinking* about what they do. Otherwise they will continue to miss both substance and significance of youth-generated freedom movement.

Political moderates historically compound this problem by their unrealistic standards of protest—nonviolent or otherwise. Moderates dominate every society. What defines a person as moderate shifts over time, as one can see in the deeper truth under comedian Dick Gregory's joke from the 1960s: "A moderate is a cat who will hang you from a short tree."[22]

This helps to explain a recurring historical abnormality, social movement scholar Lawrence Goodwyn noted: "While the occurrence of injustice in human societies is constant, the number of large-scale movements in history is quite low. In most times and places, the demands of movement building are simply too great. People live their protoinsurgent lives in the privacy of their kitchens and never find a way to connect with the larger society."[23] One astonishing measure of success by young people in the previous chapters is simply that they got "out of the kitchen."

Their initiatives can—but don't always—start a freedom process. It begins when people start to question all the forms of submissiveness and resignation they have inherited. To be sure, not all debates inside SONG, the EBC, the immigrant rights movement, or BLM or among the water protectors would count as egalitarian conversation. How could they? Hierarchical thinking is a hard habit to shake, especially in a culture shot through with it. Think of how many times children are not asked, "What do you think?" but are told instead to "sit down and be quiet." Activists in all freedom movements inevitably struggle with authoritarian habits within themselves. They have learned them at school, from family, from religious organizations, from interactions with bosses or law enforcement.

Time and patience are required to sort out what is "innovative and democratic" and what is simply a different version of old hierarchical habits. It requires room for experimentation, what Bob Moses called "crawl spaces," or what scholar-organizers Harry Boyte and Sara Evans called "free spaces." Routinely, this kind of democratic experimentation runs into conflict with the desire "to act," and act now. When people are arrested, deported, beaten, or even killed by police or white supremacists or ICE officers, the desire for action is not just understandable but inevitable. Yet too often, activists sate this desire for action with authoritarian speed.[24] Debates get cut short; sisters and brothers in the movement get interrupted or disrespected. Left unaddressed and unresolved, the outcome is predictable: people leave, and "people-power" dissolves. The movement stops moving.

Often such authoritarian moves reveal a powerful reality: everyone is so innocent and ignorant about what is needed to create free societies grounded in functional democratic forms that they don't share a common set of understandings. Small-*d* democracy itself is an insufficient term to describe this reality. Studying the forms in which freedom movements organize reveals the many layers of this dilemma. What is a minimal consensus for coming together? How does one not only listen but hear? What are forms of compromise with each other that do not jeopardize people's self-respect? How, in the end, does a person find ways to overcome deeply ingrained hierarchical assumptions in his or her own mind and behavior?

When movement organizers do their job and open space for everyday people to articulate what they want, freedom movements often issue demands that range over wide sectors of life. Together, organizers and everyday people create a powerful commentary on existing economic conditions and social relations. We can see this in SNCC's call for "one person, one vote," or SONG's Pat Hussain assertion that "I'm no longer going to choose between my ovaries, my skin, my lover Cherry, or my checkbook." It was undoubtedly "a conscious break in the way we've been taught to think." We see it when EBC demanded the state of California invest in youth education and health rather than in detention and prison. Or when immigrant youth called to "abolish ICE." The Movement for Black Lives platform and IIYC's insistence on protecting the rivers, land, and sky in the Dakotas may seem unrealistic or unfeasible to those pursuing traditional power. Yet one of the most electrifying actions freedom movements perform over the course of history is that they critique the public policies that sustain existing economic conditions and social relations.

Freedom movements uncover startling roadblocks to the most basic goals for a decent life—good health, work, housing, and quality education. Yet to those in power, their calls routinely appear naive at best. Demands such as "Don't kill unarmed citizens," or "Don't deport young people who have grown up in the US," or "Do not put a teenager in prison for life," or "Don't run the pipeline under our water source" represent an obvious bottom line to activists. Without fail, however, those in positions of authority dismiss such calls as unrealistic, and often dangerous, for they question the very essence of how power works in modern societies.

Media commentators trying to understand movements often talk about democracy and freedom as abstract ideas, not as a lived reality that groups like SNCC, the IIYC, SONG, or the EBC demand. Journalists and scholars see fragments of these politics as they witness a demonstration, or participate in Standing Rock's prayer ceremonies, or sit in the back of a church meeting during an uprising like Ferguson or Baltimore. When young people suddenly appeared in Phoenix in 2012, Tallahassee in July 2013, or Standing Rock in September 2016, almost no media commentators possessed the vocabulary to describe where youth activists came from, what they were trying to do, or why they were acting. Almost without fail, commentators recruit abstractions like "anger" or "pent-up frustration" in order to describe such seemingly "spontaneous" eruptions. Completely missing from the picture are the people, the meetings, the discussions, the organizing.[25] And so people outside the movement, and young people learning about these movements in school weeks or decades later, make do with misleading fragments—slogans and iconic images that take the place of deep historical knowledge.

The consequences are stark. Adult society fails to see and acknowledge the innumerable contributions young people have made to political life since the 1960s. Not helping matters is what organizer Nona Perry called "adultism"— the formidable condescension of most adults who tend to minimize or dismiss the good ideas of young people simply because they are young.

And yet, it was the young people of SNCC who learned how to move idea ("stop Jim Crow") into action in restaurants, in workplaces, and at the voting booth. When it became clear that the civil rights movement had not quite managed to drag segregation behind the barn and shoot it to death, others stepped in and picked up the fight. SONG created some room to move in the vital crawl spaces across the South in the 1990s, to model intersectional organizing that came to full bloom in the 2010s. The Ella Baker Center in Oakland has spent the better part of three decades figuring out how to grow successive generations of youth organizers to redirect public monies toward education, not prison. Youth immigrant organizers have taught the nation to value family emancipation and reunification as an essential right. The Movement for Black Lives and youth water protectors at Standing Rock shone a brilliant spotlight on the mounting reality of government and corporate authoritarianism— surveillance, beating, shooting, warrantless taps, repeat arrests, mass incarceration. All of them have advanced visions for a just and open society, doing so where adult society had dismally failed. In each case, it has been young people, not corporations or established parties or law enforcement, who pushed the nation a step further toward its self-proclaimed ideal of "liberty and justice for all."[26]

History does bear out Frederick Douglass's observation that power concedes nothing without a demand. Yet one might add that, even when power is forced to become more inclusive, no victory is permanent. All movement triumphs generate their own fierce backlash. The 1954 *Brown v. Board of Education* Supreme Court decision outlawing racial segregation immediately led to the Massive Resistance movement. Seven decades of struggle later, some schools have been temporarily desegregated; others closed. Only a fraction of US students have experienced full integration. Established power allowed massive educational inequality to prevail under a new context. Today, public schools in the United States are more segregated by race than they were in 1954.

There are more examples of backlash than can adequately be discussed in these pages—the reemergence of white nationalism, the rollback of labor and environmental regulations, the erosion of the minimum wage, the reversal of progressive taxation, the abandonment of immigrant and refugee rights, the reinvigorated dismissal of rights for Indigenous peoples, the regressive disintegration of women and girls' access to reproductive justice, and, not least of all, escalating attempts to disenfranchise entire groups of citizens.[27]

Meanwhile, leaders in the US, from Washington and Jefferson to Clinton, Bush, and Obama, exhibit a persistent loyalty to hierarchical power. In times of greatest crisis, they have sided with elite power, whether by enshrining slavery in the Constitution, putting welfare out of reach for millions, invading Iraq, or bailing out banks rather than people. Time and again, one can observe our most visible political and military leaders as they seemed to skewer themselves on a present they could not understand, and on a future they could not contemplate, because they renounced the capacity for honest reflection. Or because they sided with elite power. These were tragic junctions in history when everyday people suffered or died because leaders lacked the vision of their own people.

On all issues of greatest concern to the well-being of the nation—peace, justice, civil rights, environmental protection—it was often young people who started the conversation and forced the country to reflect on the errors of formal leaders. Here I have documented some of the ways they tried to set the country on a better path.

In the end, the actors in this book defy easy categorization. But they raise in common the question at the heart of all free societies: are "the people" willing and able to create political forms that allow ordinary people to have a say in their own lives?[28]

This is not to say that young people always get it right. Yet they do raise questions that need to be addressed, collectively, in order to build a more perfect union of human well-being and dignity. If we choose to see young people and tell their stories, as James Lawson observed, we may yet become citizens of a world that has not yet been built.

WHO'S THE EXPERT?

An Essay on Evidence and Authority

As I began research for this book, I was teaching college students and raising young kids of my own: the nerd researcher, not the organizer working in the community or activist in the street. I listened carefully, took notes, and tried to grow by understanding the different approaches young people took to changing the world.

My physical location dictated how I documented youth activism, dramatically impacted whom I could be in consistent reciprocal relationship with, and affected how those relationships informed my work. In 2003, teaching history at Virginia State, a historically Black university, I quickly became involved in a community-based project that reimagined a badly injured public school system. It was the undergraduate and high school students in this program who led—they were young, of course, many from modest to low-wealth backgrounds. Their fierce dedication meant that once they started their first after-school program for public school students, they would not let go. Their creativity and determination humbled me.

I watched them design an innovative math literacy program within the local public school system that improved the Algebra I passing rate of ninth-graders from 11 percent in year one to 76 percent in year five. The experience forced me to rethink much of what I had learned in elite educational settings. Who makes change happen? Clearly, change came not only from the top and was rarely initiated by elected or appointed leaders. And yet it was easy to see why many thought so. No one was recording the efforts of these VSU students; no newspapers gave them credit for their stunning work.

One had to document their achievements to set the record straight. When I shared my plans, the students told me I was crazy—a fool. Who would care about what they were doing?, they asked. Who, after all, they reminded me, recorded the Jena Six march on campus? What journalists told the story of how VSU students brought Hurricane Katrina survivors to campus and made a place for them, promoting their well-being and healing? And plus, what did it really mean in the larger scheme of US freedom and democracy?

Their responses reflected a larger reality: almost none of them had seen examples of people their age or background changing their communities, much less bringing the US closer to its democratic promise. On rare occasions, their textbooks included a brief mention or photograph of the 1960 Greensboro sit-in or the 1968 high school walkouts in Los Angeles. Otherwise, young people were absent from K–12 history texts. Young people's political work was also largely missing in the media and in Hollywood movies.

This book on contemporary youth activism emerged as a response: I wanted to share with students a larger tradition, denied to them, that demonstrated the ways young people impacted history.

To avoid taxing activists already interviewed several or even ten or twenty times, I drew on others' interviews with activists. Yet particularly for the Ella Baker Center and undocumented activist chapters, I interviewed people who were a part of these movements. I reached out through mutual acquaintances or emailed them directly. I explained that my work with college students led me to realize that K–12 textbooks had few to no examples of young people changing the world. I'd scoured fourth-, eighth-, and eleventh-grade US history textbooks and found no one under twenty-five but the Greensboro Four, which seemed a form of educational malpractice. I asked if I could interview them about their work.

After building these sources into a rough draft, I experimented, imperfectly, with different ways to make sure activist cohorts had the opportunity to "talk back" to the written record assembled here, before publication. Those I quote had the right to clarify, disagree, and make sure I was representing their words fairly, of course, and such a process also increased the chances of me learning nuance and insight about internal movement dynamics that are only available to participants. Critically, this makes clear that the activists are *creating knowledge*, not simply sharing experience.[1]

It is no great insight to observe that work with people on the margins of power and wealth is not straightforward. Yet it does have clear consequences on who and what "counts" as part of the evidential record. Some people have been taught that both their lives and their stories are of no value. Thus, the concept of documenting and recording their stories seems irrelevant, much like a waste of time and energy. Many young people said, "Why are you asking me for my story? It's not that important." This included a nineteen-year-old who gave me one of the most insightful and powerful interviews to shape this work. In addition, for many on the margins, the formality and requirements of the academic and institutional world seem burdensome and unnecessary, and the balance of power in the negotiations is unequal, often grossly so.

This results in a conflict between two worlds. University-based researchers don't always find people willing to tell their stories. Activists often "move so fast the dross burns off," as one put it, making it difficult to track them down for permissions or further decision-making. Activists may be impatient about archival processes or not have the time to catalog and put their materials in context. Sometimes, activists see reviewing academics' work as just more unpaid labor or not worth the time it would take to correct. Above all, activists are often justifiably suspicious of the extractive processes used by scholars or institutions that want their papers, interviews, and ephemera—and then use them for purposes not helpful to movements. Many scholars of social movements do not feel accountable to activists and their communities but instead hew to the norms of their discipline, or their university's tenure and promotion committee, or simply their own sense of determining what happened.[2] As a result, activists' experiences with scholars are not just mixed but often quite dismal.

This reality leads globally to a gross imbalance: there are many more cubic feet of papers in the world's archives that preserve the records of centrist and conservative politics than the tiny number of archives that document freedom movements. This limits collective historical knowledge of small-*d* democratic social processes. Subsequent generations of activists often feel they have to reinvent the wheel in their own time because they don't have access to prior freedom movement traditions or innovations.

There are also many studies of social movements written by scholars who put forward inaccurate facts or less-than-useful interpretive frameworks because they did not or could not get feedback from activists. I learned just how much I'd gotten wrong after I published *Many Minds, One Heart*, on SNCC, in 2007. Prior to publication, I spent a decade of research in a dozen archives, traveling widely to gather oral histories, pouring over microfilm of newspapers, tracking down every written source I could before publication. After publication, SNCC activists sent mail and email telling me where the book was inaccurate. Or they'd show up at book readings and let me know, "This part isn't what I said."

I was determined to do better the next time. One important step toward sharing power was to open my work more widely before publication to pushback and feedback by those who made the history. In 2017, I used the notation software available at Genius,³ put an early version of each chapter of this book up on the web, and asked those quoted to review and annotate. Many of my university colleagues looked at me like I was little more than ridiculous. *What are you going to do if different activists have different memories of the same event? What if you don't agree with some of the edits they suggest? How will you maintain your professionalism—aren't you allowing the subjects to have too much influence over your interpretation?* The skepticism from scholars pushed me to define my approach more clearly: I shared that given my first book experience, feedback from activists before publication was likely to lead to a much more insightful and accurate book, and if there were contradictions in the record either between activists or between an activist and the documentary record, I would include those discrepancies in the text itself.

These colleagues raised other legitimate questions. They reminded me that the whole enterprise of history is an impossible task—there are eternally other interpretations, always partial or missing evidence. Did I really want to add additional variables to the already-challenging work of the historian? Others wondered how scholars and activists could work in truly collaborative ways, without scholars simply becoming cheerleaders "trying to find the win" for David against Goliath, or scolds who disrespect movement attempts without knowing movement terrain themselves.

Another way scholars voiced this range of issues was to express concern for the work's rigor. The audience may demand the victory of a specific "David" be chronicled, they reflected, but that was not the real role of scholars. Through many conversations with activists who were also searching for more exacting and informed critiques of movements, activists often asked, "How do we develop a thorough role for critique coming from an informed, transparent, and bighearted place?" Inside their own organizations, activists by the mid-2010s found one another increasingly demanding that rigor in order to become more effective. How might scholars put their tools to good use in this struggle for clarity? Given the arrogant manner in which many scholars had traditionally offered feedback to movements, activists asked to explore what roles there might be for scholars to offer hard critiques that come from a place of informed respect.

With all these threads of conversation in mind, I had high hopes that the response rate from activists in 2017 would be greater than it was in 2003 when I printed out and mailed chapters to forty SNCC activists prior to finishing that book, along with self-addressed stamped envelopes to return the chapters to me within two months. For the SNCC book, many didn't respond at all. Some wrote back, "Not interested in correcting the record," but twelve gave me some feedback, either written on the rough draft itself or verbally. I hoped online feedback might be easier. Yet I'm not sure it was: I put up the material for this book in September 2017 and again in March 2018 for feedback. I gave a smaller window for response, as some SNCC people told me, "Two months was too long, I kept putting it off and forgot about it."

The response rate this time was about the same as the SNCC book. There were many reasons. I'm paid a living wage to do this kind of research, but the activists aren't. Frankly, the work of sifting through my writing would have taken time some didn't have or want to take. Some felt that if they were going to spend time writing or editing, it should be focused on writing their own account on their own terms rather than on correcting mine. Some didn't feel comfortable with the length or formality of the language I used. The sign-up process for Genius in order to annotate can be a barrier; one has to feel comfortable with the idea of annotating and must spend time on it that might be better used for other work. Some got back to me months after I'd sent the request to review, asking, "Am I still able to send feedback?"

At this point, I'm determined to find more accountable and effective ways to collect accurate information about freedom movements. During the second half of the decade I was working on this book, I participated in a parallel project with SNCC activists to build the SNCC Digital Gateway (snccdigital.org). We activists, archivists, and academics learned and grew on all sides about how to build history together. We experimented with how to merge and meld the very different priorities of activists with those of archivists and scholars. It became obvious that it's not enough to share my material with activists *after* writing a rough draft. We worked from the beginning of the project to build a joint framework of understanding and a mutually respectful and accountable process for decision-making on budget and direction at all levels of the project.

Establishing collaborative practices between movement scholars and activists is not primarily about being kind and respectful; instead, these are important collaborations because they create more accurate information, and the analysis those collaborations generate is more effective for supporting democratic initiatives today.[4] Yet for *On the Freedom Side*, started in 2006 and built over time, I didn't know enough yet to engage that kind of process from the beginning.

Exploring the largely unarticulated terrain of how to build accurate accounts of freedom movement organizing illuminates several central realities. First, current university and foundation funding systems often fail to address the fact that PhDs are not the only intellectuals creating knowledge in the country. Activists are not simply acting; they are engaged in an iterative process of thinking, doing, and then rethinking. Activists are an essential political and intellectual force. Since our society values knowledge production, it benefits us if we figure out how civic activists can document their knowledge sustainably, on their own terms, over time.[5] Second, to see how people moved their visionary hopes for society into reality, one needs a trustworthy guide. The documentary form of oral history is essential, but surely not sufficient. A now infamous example from oral history's canon teaches us that in the 1930s, freedwoman Susan Hamlin shared wholly different stories about her past enslaved experience when approached first by a white female researcher and subsequently by a Black male researcher:

> She shared this with a white interviewer: "I don't know about slavery but I know all the slavery I know about, and the people was good to me. Mr. Fuller was a good man and his wife's people been grand people, all good to their slaves. Seem like Mr. Fuller just git his slaves so he could be good to them."
>
> Yet she shared this with an African American interviewer: "When any slave was whipped all the other slaves was made to watch. I see women hung from the ceiling of buildings and whipped with only something tied 'round her lower part of the body, until when they was taken down, there wasn't breath in the body. I had some terribly bad experiences."[6]

Those working to train journalists and scholars would produce better knowledge-creators today if they explicitly acknowledged and worked to lessen these known, ongoing hazards. Third, as Robert Coles noted, "a machine can both record what is going on and shape it." Fourth, when scholars pull back the curtain further, showing readers how we frame, edit, and omit evidence (and also examining our own standpoint), everyone has a stronger plot of ground to stand on when they judge the insights and limits of the resulting book.[7]

To this end, self-study while researching youth activism seemed a vital intellectual task. I built from the Confucian axiom "Real knowledge is to know the extent of one's own ignorance." While it may be true that "all good historical practice is reflective," historians hardly agree on the wide range of methods we use to hold ourselves to this idea.[8] If I was asking of my many sources "Who made this document and for what reason?," I needed to track and examine how *I* was learning, changing, and thinking as I documented these youth groups.

In the wake of the last three decades' worth of pathbreaking work in critical race theory, feminist and queer theory, Indigenous and postcolonial studies, and critical ethnography, it's clear that "who tells the story" is central to the process of knowledge creation. We experience our humanity in specific bodies defined by time, place, race, class, gender, sexuality, physical body, age, and political and social cultures. These form a unique social location for our experience. Our awareness of that unique social location allows us to become more responsible for our perspectives and for what we can and cannot see.[9] As civil rights scholar Nishani Frazier recently commented, many times we try, like the Wizard of Oz, to stand behind the curtain of "scholarly detachment" to cover or hide exercises of identity and power not at all "detached."[10] Theoretical physicist Lisa Randall also observed that science has frequently been misshapen by the fact that "most people mistake their own perspective, shaped by their subjective and limited perception, for the absolute reality of the external world." For her, questioning one's assumptions has been crucial to advancing "research on dark matter" as well as "the only thing that has ever advanced human empathy. Recognizing the limitations of our senses and the subjectivity of our experiences," she noted, "is the only route to transcending them."[11]

Both Frazier and Randall called me to grow awareness of my own limits as well as the limits of my sources. I'm a middle-aged US academic who benefits from white privilege. I've lived large parts of that time as a heterosexual mother nourished and socialized into university life largely by diverse Black colleagues at a historically Black college and simultaneously anchored by SNCC activists whose experiences taught them to be skeptical of academic communities. SNCC people dramatically shaped my early thinking and approach to documenting activism by giving me an alternative to the university-based epistemologies (more on this below).

My scholarship was further sculpted by a decade of undergraduate students at Virginia State University, where Black cultural and epistemological diversity flourished. These young people—especially Anki Jones, Jewel Princess Johnson, Nikki Wilson, Reese Chenault, Afua (Asibey) Ahwireng, Jessica Hennegler, John Wiley, Chantel Williams, Kacey Morgan, Jeffrey Herring, and David Young—challenged, experimented with, and creatively enhanced my research on social movements. It was not enough for them that these movements happened; they wanted to understand *why* people got involved and how they came up with tactical and strategic innovations. When I couldn't answer the questions, I brought activists to campus to talk with them in small groups and learned much more than I previously knew from my archive-dives and interviews. I was deeply influenced as a young scholar by activist friends in the anti-WTO movement who challenged me to "find out if you don't know";

by Darlene Clark Hine's call for historians to "all [be] doing each other's history" as a way to "register meaningful progress in the war against racism, sexism and class oppression"; and by Eduardo Bonilla-Silva, Tufuku Zuberi, and Charles Mills calling for an end to "white methodologies" and "epistemologies of ignorance."[12]

Time and resources, however, were hard to come by when I began the book in 2006. I had a heavy teaching load; my university couldn't fund much travel and research; my income could not sustain the work. I laid out the foundation of four chapters. And then I started working at Duke in 2013. The institution was historically white, a private university with abundant resources for research. One challenge was that I was no longer around many of the very people whose powerful contributions and efforts I wanted to document. A second challenge was moving from a university on the margins to one at the center of academic power. How could I take the horizontal values that informed the freedom movement into this starkly hierarchical space? It was a shift symptomatic of the larger society—vast inequalities in opportunities, a glaring disconnect for students between what educational resources they deserve and what society gives them, and cultural chasms separating different communities.

VSU students and my mentors in SNCC had also taught me that scholars of all backgrounds, races, and genders have a profoundly checkered record of accountability to the communities they study. That record is almost uniformly exploitative, despite intent.[13] Few scholars of the freedom movement had found ways to change this. And people growing up white find many prior generations stumbling into the countless traps of well-meaning white scholars telling stories about people of color. To avoid some of those, I tried to walk in the paths laid out by movement scholars like W. E. B. DuBois, John Hope Franklin, Vincent and Rosemarie Harding, Howard Zinn, Alice and Staughton Lynd, Roxanne Dunbar-Ortiz, Cathy Cohen, and Barbara Ransby, putting underrepresented voices at the center, making oneself transparent and accountable to those communities, and ensuring those sources are available to the public.[14]

Self-study involved two primary things: exploring how my experiences limited my perspectives and working to transform the unjust realities I encountered.[15] I tried to lay bare the power dynamics of documentary and scholarly production. Could I make power more reciprocal in interviews? How? What about in the process I used for getting feedback from people on the chapters? I reflected on my systems for tracking social media conversations and cross-referencing those with traditional archival research. Self-study also meant reflecting on which scholars I was in conversation with, which scholars I was reading and citing, how I made sense of which evidence "counted," and whether some evidence counted more than others and why.[16]

Centering women of color in the text and drawing on much scholarship pioneered by women of color, I'm mindful at the same time of the ways white women like me, both historically and presently, do not consistently center and/or do not give credit to colleagues of color, particularly women of color.[17] It's been important to eat humble pie along the way. Scholars often use their credentials, title, or position as a shield to deflect challenges to their approach, demeanor, lack of transparency, or lack of accountability. I've lowered and then tried to put down altogether that shield to learn, grow, and do better.

Being vulnerable to activist pushback is challenging. I had learned the protocols for quantitative history, archival work, and oral history release forms, but I didn't learn how to make myself open to activist pushback in graduate school, nor did I observe senior scholars engaging activists in this way. Obtaining feedback from activists before publication is logistically hard to set up, and intellectually and emotionally, it can unsettle. Despite scholars' oft-cited desire to create new knowledge, in PhD programs, few teach younger scholars the resilience and frameworks necessary to cope with this intellectual and emotional unsettling that can result. I've learned this unevenly, over a long period of time. These reflections all shape the ways I write, cite, and structure this work. As a process, it remains a work in progress about which I'd be grateful for dialogue, feedback, and critique.

For humanities researchers studying the recent past and present, the US research university system rewards extraction of information from "subjects" for archives and production of monographs by PhD-trained scholars. Sometimes this results in brilliant work. Yet it promotes a "power-over" mindset: individual *over* community, giving the scholar control *over* the stories of the still-alive history makers. In the 1990s, within a PhD program, I learned to work with archives, primary and secondary sources, and quantitative and qualitative data. At the same time, the 1960s activists offered me an ongoing *relationship* within which I could learn through experience. They possessed significantly different intellectual models from the PhD program of how to transmit the lessons of the nation's organizing traditions. SNCC people have consistently provided an anchor for the values I aspire to embody as a freedom movement scholar.[18] From my earliest interviews with Judy Richardson and Casey Hayden in 1995 through working with Dave Dennis and Bob Moses on the Petersburg Algebra Project (2004–9) and now more recent work since 2013 with Judy Richardson, Courtland Cox, Jennifer Lawson, Charlie Cobb, Ivanhoe Donaldson (rest in power), Geri Augusto, and Bruce Hartford on the

SNCC Digital Gateway—these relationships proved essential and life-giving. Learning within this double tradition often leaves me with more accurate and complex layers of information to share with the wider scholarly and activist communities.[19] It has also given me a sense of responsibility to center youth activists' ways of knowing, working, and learning. SNCC workers have taught me that I need to be accountable to the knowledge they have shared over three decades in two ways: first, by making room for youth activist perspectives within mainstream educational institutions and publications, and second, by spending a significant portion of my time supporting youth activists as they document their own history.

Though I am trained as a historian, this short book encompasses more documentary tools than historical ones. My colleagues at Duke's Center for Documentary Studies have been intensely and routinely generous, sharing with me vital insights on how stories or documents get made, how they form people's ideas about themselves—and how to honor the impulse to critically evaluate one's own part in crafting the story. The idea of getting close and telling stories from the "inside out," privileging the voices of those engaged in youth activism, means that I have to figure out as a documentarian my relationship to the people whom I'm interviewing or documenting. A more traditional documentarian isn't necessarily going to give creative control or editorial control to anybody else, particularly the subject(s) of the story. Yet in watching my younger colleagues, especially filmmakers Kenneth Campbell, Ambria McNeill, Amber Delgado, Rahi Hasan, and Wilson Land, I've seen how much one can learn by including activists in the process of documentation itself.[20] These filmmakers have the capacity to welcome everyone to the table, empowering each perspective. Documentary is a mode synthesizing the creative and critical. It opens and encompasses all sorts of ways of knowing communities. While I've been surprised by a certain level of routine condescension among university-based scholars toward documentary as a field, using its self-reflexive tools alongside those of a historian has proved vital to the accuracy of this work.

During this project's evolution, digital documentation technologies have transformed rapidly. These sources on nontraditional historical actors are complex and deeply instructive. The availability of technologies that make recording and correspondence accessible in the social media era means that citizens can now build their own public archives and platforms. Still, digital storage can fail, people stop maintaining sites or archives, and access to community archives remains uneven. In these chapters, I have drawn on three forms of primary sources. First, I used memos, minutes, and other printed material (chapters on SNCC, SONG). Second, I drew on the oral histories and interviews I and others have done. For the last four chapters, I relied heavily on social media, documentary media, and web-based sources to document organizers' activity. Is a blog equivalent to a published first-person account? What about a tweet, or a post on Tumblr, Facebook, or Instagram? Should a blog post carry the same evidential weight as an oral history or a letter in an archive? In an era where "the content of websites can be easily modified, tweets are frequently deleted, the number of social media comments and likes can be artificially boosted through click farms, and dubious sources spreading misinformation can be disguised as reliable news organizations," how can we discern what is legitimate?[21] How does the legitimacy historians assign to each piece of evidence relate to the field of power in which all of these testimonies are deployed?

In addressing these kinds of questions, I'm particularly grateful for Bergis Jules and the innovative group Documenting the Now, which works to establish ethical practices for those using and archiving social media content.[22] Nishani Frazier, Christy Hyman, and Hilary Greene's work on Black digital humanities calls each project to "summarize restrictions of use, determine impact on living persons, and establish ethical rules that give living persons power to include or exclude materials pertaining to them and yet balance this with other questions like access, activist usage, and asserting black epistemological narratives." They ask historians to pose "one fundamental question when considering a project. Will this do harm to individuals or the black community in such a way that open access becomes dangerous, damaging, or hurtful?" Combined with Wolfgang Ernst's call for us to rethink the way that memory works in conjunction with our phones, tablets, and personal computers—the micro-archives surrounding us—it is clear from work like Frazier, Hyman, and Greene's that historians of the twenty-first century will need to expand our practice to think more critically about preserving, citing, and corroborating social media, oral history, and documentary evidence.[23]

The territory of "shared authority" that oral historians have done so much to explore in the last two decades seems only partly mapped.[24] Doing oral history with activists and drawing on activist autobiographies is not enough.[25] If scholars hope to lay out the interior dynamics of freedom movements as well as the ways those movements shape the larger political culture, we have to invent new knowledge-creation pathways. What our social science and humanities-based disciplines are doing right now is important but not sufficient.

My experience points in one clear direction: if scholars work with activists and archivists to create new institutional and individual pathways for activists themselves to engage in the formal knowledge-creation, knowledge-preservation, and knowledge-dissemination processes, we will have more accurate information about freedom movements and more sophisticated analytical frameworks to understand them. Both will improve the ability of everyday people to hold their governments accountable.

ACKNOWLEDGMENTS

Organizers have pushed my thinking and helped me ground this project in a range of sensibilities that reflect their work. For their time and insights, I'm grateful in particular to Phil Agnew, Rebekah Barber, William Barber III, Cynthia Brown, Mandy Carter, Charlie Cobb, Courtland Cox, Sarah Cross, Dave Dennis Sr., Ajamu Dillahunt-Holloway, Lanise Frazier, Bruce Hartford, Casey Hayden, Ash-Lee Henderson, Faith Holsaert, Jennifer Lawson, Akanke Mason-Hogans, Deborah Menkhart, Ben Moynihan, Bob Moses, Maisha Moses, Tema Okun, Sunny Osment, Nona Perry, Judy Richardson, Mab Segrest, Laura Emiko Soltis, Hope Tyson, and Darris Young and to the many undocumented activists I interviewed who chose not to be on record or only have their first names included, especially Brenda, Nadia, Vianey, and Yasmin.

Several Virginia State University students, now alumni, encouraged the early phase of this project, and their thinking structured key pieces. I am grateful to Anki Jones, Jewel Johnson, Nikki Wilson, Reese Chenault, Afua (Asibey) Ahwireng, Jessica Henggeler, John Wiley, Chantel Williams, Kacey Morgan, Jeffrey Herring, and David Young.

Exemplars of public intellectual work at its finest who gave me a north star to aim for include Carol Anderson, Charlie Cobb, Shalom Goldman, Bill Grieder, Judy Richardson, Madonna Thunder Hawk, Patricia Williams, and Peter Wood. Gina Streety's powerful reminders in person and online and Tim Tyson's Tuesday Morning Poetry in the Cornfield served as enchanting life rafts on the high seas of a roiling administrative calendar. Lynn McKnight and Greg Britz are shipmates I could not do the work without, keeping the course steady with enormous determination over decades—I am grateful.

Young people's work—their ideas and actions—are central to the chapters in this book, but much of the intellectual grounding for this project to illuminate their work has been laid by at least five generations of activists and scholars. In particular, I walk gratefully in the wake of Wini Breines, Bill Chafe, Jennifer Nez Denetdale, John Dittmer, John Hope Franklin, Paolo Freire,

Larry Goodwyn, Linda Gordon, Rosemarie and Vincent Harding, Darlene Clark Hine, Robin Kelley, Alice and Staughton Lynd, Charles Payne, Francesca Poletta, Barbara Ransby, Bernice Johnson Reagon, James Scott, Vandana Shiva, Linda Tuhiwai Smith, Ponna Wignaraja, and Howard Zinn. Broadly speaking, the collective forty-plus-year conversations, layered by brilliant minds in each generation working in critical race theory, colonial-postcolonial subaltern studies, gender/queer studies, ecofeminism, contemplative studies, and working class–labor studies, have enabled me to see in fresh ways how people act with self-determination while situated within larger inequitable structures. This collective tradition allows people to see ordinary people not solely stooped by oppression and not wholly free from institutionally oppressive structures, but visible nonetheless—people who are able to band together to put forward a vision of justice that is comprehensive and complex rather than piecemeal and parallel.

A web of sustaining relationships kept me focused and helped me to move forward. I am humbled by many practitioners who have shared their work with documentary tools in the last few years. They have deepened my understanding of how to think responsibly about the moral dilemmas that face us as people who tell others' stories. I'd particularly like to thank Geri Augusto, Kamal Badhey, Whitney Baker, Kathryn Banas, Britany Barbee, Eric Barstow, Michelle Benham, John Biewen, Sarah Borst, Lou Brown, Natalie Bullock Brown, Harlan Campbell, Kenneth Campbell, Roxane Campbell, Steven Cheek, Allen Creech, Jamila Davenport, Amber Delgado, Alexa Dilworth, Jordana Dym, Chris Everett, Gail Exum, Katie Fernelius, Tamika Galanis, Lana Garland, Mara Guevarra, Mike Gulley, Deirdre Haj, Adrienne Harreveld, Alex Harris, Gary Hawkins, Iris Tillman Hill, Katie Hyde, Candice Jansen, Caitlin Johnson, Nancy Kalow, Shambhavi Kaul, Jenna Kruger, Aaron Kutnick, E. B. Landesberg, Savannah Lennertz, Worth Long, Xaris Martínez, Lisa McCarty, Quadiriah McCullough, Lynn McKnight, Ambria McNeil, John Moses, Paul Newman, William Page, Dan Partridge, Liz Phillips, Angie Potiny, Rahi Hasan, Tom Rankin, Courtney Reid-Eaton, Sandra Rodriguez, Sarah Rogers, Sherrill Roland, Margaret Sartor, M. J. Sharp, Lani Simeone, Chris Sims, Ernest and Camryn Smith, Sam Stephenson, Ishan Thakor, Charlie Thompson, Sadie Tillery, Maria Varela, Naomi Walker, April Walton, Greg Weaver, Joanna Welborn, Melinda Wiggins, Kristina Williams, Marco Williams, David Wong, and Ramon Zepeda.

Beyond the documentary community, many colleagues have provided inspiration and furthered my thinking in the decade it took to pull this project together. I take sole responsibility for the limits of my perspective and analyses here but am grateful for the fellowship of Antar Abraham, Bill Adair, Cheryl Adeyemi, Anne Michaeux Akwari, Kelly Alexander, Paul Alkebulan, Viv Benesch, Lou Brown, Linda Burton, J. Kameron Carter, Ellen Cassily and Frank Konhaus, Guy Charles, Chris Chia, Robby Cohen, Sarah Cross, Sandy Darity, Sally Deutsch, Laurent DuBois, Laura Eastwood, Elizabeth Englehardt, Bill Ferriss, Cora Fisher, John French, Gustavo Furtado, Bryan Giemza, Thavolia Glymph, Lauren Goodwyn, Wade Goodwyn, Aaron Greenwald, Andrej Grubacic, Alexis Pauline Gumbs, Jarvis Hall, Michael Hardt, Bernie Herman, Sharon P. Holland, Guo-Juin Hong, Amy Howard, Deborah Jensen, Candice Jimerson-Johnson, Sarah Nicole Johnson, Joy Kasson, Blair L. M. Kelley, Randall Kenan, Ranji Khanna, Bob Korstad, Max Krochmal, Jo Kuykendall, Pedro Lasch, Peter Lange, Michelle Lanier, Adriane Lentz-Smith, Lisa Levenstein, Sarah Loose, Malinda Maynor Lowery, Nancy MacLean, John Martin, Rhonda Mawhood Lee, Louise Maynor, Sucheta Mazumdar, Chuck McKinney, Charmaine McKissick-Melton, Julie Morris, Todd Moye, Kirsten Mullen, Mark Anthony Neal, Ted Owenby, Laurie Patton, Nimmi Ramanujam, Ben Reese, Lia Scholl, Ted Segal, Rachel Seidman, Mark Shapiro, William Sturkey, Priscilla Wald, Corey Walker, Mike Wiley, and Peter Wood.

Molly Bragg, John Gartrell, Valerie Gillespie, Deborah Jakubs, Laura Micham, Naomi Nelson, Will Sexton, and Kelly Wooten surpass my zaniest nerd dreams of how archivists can preserve and move forward a whole body of activist thought and action and allow us to discover and explore them. I am grateful for their help with this project but more broadly for the work they steer within the Duke University Libraries to get activism on the record.

We scholars who work to stay accountable to the values and people animating the long freedom movement find ourselves on a strange path. I've been fortunate along the way to learn from Curtis Austin, Dan Berger, Leslie Brown, Beth Castle, Emilye Crosby, Kaley Deal, Roxanne Dunbar-Ortiz, Jelani Favors, Karlyn Forner, Nishani Frazier, May Fu, Hasan Kwame Jeffries, Bergis Jules, Chuck McKinney, Tiyi Morris, Paul Ortiz, Anh Pham, Robyn Spencer, and Annie Valk. I'm also deeply inspired by young scholars whose work has taught me so much: Nicole Burrows, Jaskiran Dhillon, Ajamu Dillahunt-Holloway, Nick Estes, Ashley Farmer, Katie Fernelius, Adrienne Harreveld, Christie Hyman, Anki Jones, Shirletta Kinchen, LaTasha Levy, Eliza Meredith, Alexandria Miller, Isabell Moore, Allison Raven, Chloe Ricks, and Jakobi Williams.

Editors and their teams can make or break a book and its author. The tenacity, kindness, and astute judgment of Mark Simpson-Vos is something to behold in wonder. I am grateful to Mark and Lucas Church, Jay Mazzocchi, Cate Hodorowicz, Julie Bush, and Dino Battista at the University of North Carolina

Press. Dirk Philipsen and Tim Tyson's edits carved my prose into more readable form. And I'm permanently indebted to the insight and depth provided by two anonymous readers who patiently, generously, and thoroughly commented on two revisions. Xaris Martínez, pure and simple, gave this book room to breathe.

A posse kept me afloat while writing. Briana Boyer, Beth Warsharsky Ricanati, John Wagner and Susan Scovill, Tim Tyson and Perri Morgan, Renée Afanana Hill, Oliver Hill, Liz Kieff and Tom Levinson, Wolfram and Gabi Nieradzik, Rainer Blaisius and Lila Schweins, Veit Hannemann and Andrea Brandt, Nina Philipsen, Laurie Patton, Leoni Philipsen-Vida, John and Ana Castro Srygley, Leff and Jenny Lefferts, Anne Akwari, Jenny Colleton, Robin Veenstra-Vanderweele, and Danita Mason-Hogans—thank you for being chosen family I can always call on.

SNCC people taught me to acknowledge the work of those who came before, who made the road by walking. My path emerged from a fierce, justice-seeking Scottish great-grandfather, John Wesley McWilliams; his son John Wesley McWilliams Jr., who loved history; and my mother, Merritt McWilliams Andruss, who tirelessly found ways to support my work on this project. My sister, Samantha Wishnack, inspired with both her courage and encouragement. Thomas J. Hogan III made sure I grew up knowing I could do anything. SNCC women pushed me forward, held me accountable, and taught me how to move—thank you, Judy, Jennifer, Faith, Casey, and Zoharah.

This book is dedicated in four directions. First, to the young activists whose work at VSU and beyond chronicled here: May this book heighten the profile of the freedom movements you've built and learned from. Second, to Briana Boyer and Danita Mason-Hogans: You kept my feet on the floor and my mind focused on the horizon. Third, to Cloë, Sven, Shamus, and Nik, the young people who lived with me for large parts of the writing: It was your verve that carried me, your presence that reminded me to center young people, and your BS detector that kept me honest when I strayed toward demonization or idealization. Finally, Dirk Peter: We built an environment in which the work could unfold, and it was your kindness, joy, and brilliance that lit the path. Thank you.

NOTES

ABBREVIATIONS

Carter Papers
    Mandy Carter Papers, 1970–2013, David M. Rubenstein Rare Book & Manuscript Library, Duke University, Durham, NC
SNCC COH 2016
    SNCC Legacy Project Critical Oral History Interviews, 2016, David M. Rubenstein Rare Book & Manuscript Library, Duke University, Durham, NC
SNCC COH 2018
    SNCC Legacy Project Critical Oral History Interviews, 2018, David M. Rubenstein Rare Book & Manuscript Library, Duke University, Durham, NC
SNCC Fortieth Anniversary
    SNCC Fortieth Anniversary Conference, 2000, David M. Rubenstein Rare Book & Manuscript Library, Duke University, Durham, NC
SNCC VRC 2015
    SNCC Legacy Project Voting Rights Conference, 2015, David M. Rubenstein Rare Book & Manuscript Library, Duke University, Durham, NC
SONG Papers
    Southerners on New Ground Papers, 1993–2003, David M. Rubenstein Rare Book & Manuscript Library, Duke University, Durham, NC

INTRODUCTION

1. On young people as the future of democracy, see Cohen, *Democracy Remixed*, especially chap. 4; MacLean, *Democracy in Chains*; and Levine, *Future of Democracy*.

2. On the Jena Six, see Flaherty, *Floodlines*, chap. 10.

3. Teaching for Change, "And the Youth Shall Lead Us," *Medium*, Feb. 23, 2018, https://medium.com/@teachingforchange/and-the-youth-shall-lead-us-83f30428f5df. On Remond, see Coleman, "Like Hot Lead." On Torres, see Romo, *Ringside Seat to a Revolution*, 228–33; and A. Stern, "Buildings, Boundaries, and Blood." On the Green Feather Movement, see Alison Kysia, "The Green Feather Movement," Zinn Education Project, 2013, https://zinnedproject.org/materials/the-green-feather-movement/ (accessed Mar. 2, 2018). On Johns, see Branch, *Parting the Waters*; and

Olson, *Freedom's Daughters*, 79–82. On Nash, see Halberstam, *The Children*; and Hogan, *Many Minds*. On AIM, see Castle, *Warrior Women*. The Tinker siblings' case background can be found in C. Ross, *Lessons in Censorship*. For Kimberly Burwell, see Brooks Berndt, "A Case for the Mother of the Environmental Justice Movement: Dollie Burwell," United Church of Christ, http://www.ucc.org/pollinator_a_case_for_the_mother_of_the_environmental_justice_movement (accessed Dec. 2, 2018). Gay-straight alliances can be found in Miceli, *Standing Out*.

    4. See McGuire, *At the Dark End of the Street*. On people driven out of movements, much of this "evidence" is not written down but shared in conversation. For a few overt references, see Alice Walker's fictionalized civil rights movement book, *Meridian*; K. Anderson, "We Made the Change"; Holsaert et al., *Hands on the Freedom Plow*; Berger, Boudin, and Farrow, *Letters from Young Activists*; and Spencer and Hogan, "Telling Freedom Stories." One of the most promising pathways forward has been charted by Movement for Black Lives' activists. See for example Carruthers, *Unapologetic*, Kindle locations 362–448 and 838–54.

    5. Harris-Perry, *Sister Citizen*, 16; Springer, *Living for the Revolution*, introduction; Joan Garner interview by Rose Norman. This approach has not always been standard in American historical writing. Darlene Clark Hine noted that because Black women have "always occupied the bottom rung of any racial, sexual and class hierarchy . . . few scholars deemed this segment of the population worthy of intellectual inquiry." Hine, *Hine Sight*, 51.

    6. For more on the Young People's Project and the Algebra Project, see Moses and Cobb, *Radical Equations*; "History," the Young People's Project; Fenton, "HuffPost's Greatest Person of the Day"; and Goode, "Young People's Project Empowers Youth with Math Skills."

    7. Who gets to tell the story? What counts as historical evidence? These are deceptively simple questions and so vital to knowledge production that I've written an essay at the end of the book that addresses them more thoroughly. Such inquiries lead to thornier issues underneath: who gets to establish what does and does not "count" as documentary evidence on democratic movements? Activists engaged in pro-democracy movements in Latin America, Poland, China, the US, and South Asia and across Africa have developed parallel processes to those of scholars for establishing bodies of knowledge concerning what "is true" and what is not true about democratic forms they have invented while they are engaged in activism. They sometimes later create oral histories and other sources of archival knowledge through donating their papers or writing memoirs. There is often a rift—sometimes a pothole, and sometimes something that opens up wide enough to seem like a chasm—between what activists see as "knowledge" and "evidence" and what scholars see. This book aims to address these gaps in part by highlighting where they exist so that readers can judge for themselves. It might make for imperfect and awkward narration, but the topic seems too important to sidestep through evasion; thus it is more fully addressed in the essay that follows the conclusion. On social studies textbooks more broadly, see both the bibliography and the text of Gordy and Pritchard, "Redirecting Our Voyage through History"; Wade and Everett, "Civic Participation in Third Grade Social Studies Textbooks"; and Hass, "Analysis of the Social Studies and History Concepts."

Dorsey is quoted in Field and Mulford, *Freedom on My Mind*. The titanic pressures to forget and omit were inspired by McKinney's speech "Teaching the Civil Rights Movement."

8. Wilentz, *No Property in Man*, 97. See Huggins, "Deforming Mirror of Truth."

9. Audra Simpson has encapsulated this as "Indigenous peoples are grappling with the fiction of justice while pushing for justice" in "Consent's Revenge," 333.

10. Ransby, *Ella Baker*; J. Grant, *Ella Baker*. "The wisdom of the pinched toe and empty belly" was a phrase SNCC organizer Charles Sherrod used frequently. See Hogan, *Many Minds*, 201.

11. SNCC in the 1960s created the Lowndes County Freedom Organization, or LCFO, with Black Alabamians. Their work "gave rise to what I call freedom politics," Hasan Jeffries wrote in 2010. "This new kind of political engagement combined SNCC's egalitarian organizing methods with people's civil and human rights goals. Freedom politics was a substitute for the undemocratic traditions that defined American politics, which ranged from disenfranchising poor people to choosing candidates exclusively from the propertied and the privileged." When local African Americans embraced the LCFO, they "transformed local black political behavior. More importantly, they created a model for exporting freedom politics beyond the black community to democratize American politics." Jeffries, *Bloody Lowndes*, 5, 177–78, 243–45.

12. See Jackson, *More Than a Game*; and Jackson with Delehanty, *Eleven Rings*; as well as Crawford's depiction of Davis in *World beyond Your Head*, 131–34.

13. Baker, "Colloquium Session III." Thanks to Emilye Crosby for helping me track down the source of this in the unprocessed Voices of the Civil Rights Movement collection. "Ella's Song," written by Bernice Johnson Reagon and other members of Sweet Honey in the Rock, made Baker's words—which she repeated about young people in many different settings in the 1960s and 1970s—well-known in many wider circles of the Black freedom movement and the women's and LGBTQ movements. See Sweet Honey in the Rock, "Ella's Song." Schuyler quoted in Ransby, *Ella Baker*, Kindle location 1320–24. For a fascinating portrait of what Black political life individually and collectively looked like in the immediate years after the Civil War that may well have shaped Baker's sense of what "democracy" looked like and what she thought possible, see E. Brown, "Negotiating and Transforming the Public Sphere."

14. There are important exceptions to this exclusion of youth from serious academic study, but they too are often marginalized. See Cohen, *Democracy Remixed*; and DeSchweinitz, *If We Could Change the World*.

15. McKinney, "Teaching the Civil Rights Movement during a Time of Universal Deceit."

16. The framework of a mixtape is inspired by Mark Anthony Neal. In 2017, he gave the inaugural Trinity Distinguished Lecture at Duke, titled "My Mother Gave Me This Big-Ass Name: A Black Scholar in the Mix."

17. Three recent books that provide important context for remix culture in the digital age are Clayton, *Uproot*; Cohen, *Democracy Remixed*; and Gunkel, *Of Remixology*.

18. Rancière, *Hatred of Democracy*, 2. See also MacClean, *Democracy in Chains*.

19. "Everyone is important," quoted in Solnit, "Loneliness of Donald Trump." As scholar Ponna Wignaraja observed, "There is little need to criticize the dangers of centralized power, repressive state structures and absolute power that corrupts." We have acres of libraries full of books cataloging these realities. We are short on models that work: "What needs to be elaborated is the concept of participatory democracy and the building of countervailing power, initially within the political spaces that are already available." Wignaraja, *New Social Movements*, 10. Teaching for Change provides one important counterbalance, making resources of popular democratic movements available to K–12 teachers. See http://www.teachingforchange.org.

20. Russell, "Free Josh."

21. Reagon, "Solidarity of Past"; Janelle Monáe, Instagram, August 2015, https://www.instagram.com/p/6VNc3hn_m1/ (accessed July 4, 2016). See also Lebron, "Janelle Monáe for President."

22. Mokoena, "Janelle Monáe Leads Protest." Bernice Reagon, in an important speech in 2010 ("Solidarity of Past"), articulates the vital nature of collective song in public spaces instead of individual singing:

> If you begin to make movies about it and you begin to tell the story of the civil rights movement and you turn it into a story of the leaders, and the soundtrack is a solo voice with a band behind it, you actually are not passing the material we need in the future to the next time. . . . Many of us didn't understand the freedom songs as resistance songs until they locked us up in jail. And those were the songs that we sang, flipping only a word here and there, to make it totally contemporary and specially not realigning the structure of the song—and the statement was contemporary. It was the same system, it was the same urgency, it was actually serving a new situation.

23. I follow here in the steps laid out by organizer Maria Varela, who pointed out, "I want to work against the grain of the popular narrative that the Black civil rights movement spawned or provided the template for" Latinx, Indigenous, and Asian movements. Clearly, synergy with the Black freedom struggle provided valuable energy in these movements, as well as exchange among them and common work together. Yet the latter movements too drew on many genealogies within their own long freedom struggles. Varela, email to the author, Aug. 10, 2016, in the author's possession. See also "#WeStand" video, 11 Jan. 2017, https://www.youtube.com/watch?v=XCF9MDxliAg. This book consciously works against a tradition of highlighting leaders only: "Many books by and about activists often drown out the grassroots." Berger, Boudin, and Farrow, *Letters from Young Activists*, xxviii. Shelley called poets the "unacknowledged legislators" of the world in "A Defence of Poetry," first published in 1840 (see https://www.poetryfoundation.org/articles/69388/a-defence-of-poetry [accessed Dec. 1, 2018]).

24. King, *Truth about Stories*, 153. One could also invoke Muriel Rukeyser here: "The universe is made of stories, not atoms" ("Speed of Darkness," 111). Stories open up possibilities for the future through retelling stories of the past—"not by reestablishing the illusions of coherence of the past, control over the present, and predictability of the future, but by making it possible to carry on without these illusions."

Brinson *Aftermath*, 104, quoted in Stauffer, *Ethical Loneliness*, 110. Recently, writer Rebecca Solnit reflected that she was on the search for better metaphors, better stories. "I want more openness," she noted. "I want better questions." Questions and stories were tools to contend with "the amazing possibilities and the terrible realities that we face." Too often, we have "clumsy, inadequate tools" that failed to open our eyes or shed light. "They don't lead us to interesting places. They don't let us know how powerful we can be. They don't help us ask the questions that really matter." Solnit interview, "Falling Together."

CHAPTER ONE

1. Diane Nash quoted in J. Lewis, *Walking with the Wind*, 149. See also David Halberstam, *The Children*, 271, 322. For more detail, see Hogan, *Many Minds*, chap. 2; and Arsenault, *Freedom Riders*, 127–29.

2. Jack Chatfield interview by the author.

3. The first comprehensive treatment of SNCC was Carson, *In Struggle*. A dozen or so monographs have followed where SNCC organizing work is centered, including the pathbreaking work of Dittmer, *Local People*; Payne, *I've Got the Light of Freedom*; and Greenberg, *Circle of Trust*. A wide range of movement memoirs then emerged, including Moses and Cobb, *Radical Equations*; Curry et al., *Deep in Our Hearts*; Carmichael with Thelwell, *Ready for Revolution*; Holsaert et al., *Hands on the Freedom Plow*; and Watkins with McInnis, *Brother Hollis*. In the last decade, Jeffries's *Bloody Lowndes*, Moye's *Let the People Decide*, and my *Many Minds* have been joined by Cobb's *That Nonviolent Stuff'll Get You Killed*, Sturkey and Hale's *To Write in the Light of Freedom*, and Sharon Monteith's forthcoming *SNCC Stories*.

4. For a recent thorough, important examination of the misuses of King's legacy in particular, see Theoharis, *More Beautiful and Terrible History*.

5. See Katznelson, *When Affirmative Action Was White*; Darity and Myers, *Persistent Disparity*; Conley, *Being Black*; Reddy, *Freedom with Violence*; and Rana, *The Two Faces of American Freedom*.

6. The material in this short summary is taken from my monograph *Many Minds*, chaps. 1–7. While the GI Bill did make home ownership and college affordable for many, Katznelson has demonstrated that those individuals were overwhelmingly white. Katznelson, *When Affirmative Action Was White*. Hitler did in fact approve of prewar US racial policies; see Whitman, *Hitler's American Model*.

7. Baker used the term "democracy," and so did SNCC organizers and local people like Amzie Moore, Fannie Lou Hamer, and Annie Pearl Avery, to describe the aspirational goals of the freedom and justice movements of the time. This is visible in speeches, memos, and interviews. However, there is a vibrant discussion among social science and humanities scholars today that builds on Walter Benjamin's observation that there is no documentation of civilization that does not simultaneously document that very society's barbarism. These scholars question the use of "democracy" as an analytical term, exploring whether it is an Enlightenment construct that cannot encompass the restorative justice required to address the genocide of Indigenous people in the Americas by European settlers or the nation that those settlers built on the basis of stolen land as well as on enslaved African labor. See for example

A. Simpson, *Mohawk Interruptus*; Rana, "Goodbye Cold War"; Reddy, *Freedom with Violence*; and Coulthard, *Red Skin*. Similarly, within critical ethnic and race studies, postcolonial studies, and queer studies, the idea of sovereignty operates in recent scholarship on multiple levels, including those of self and self-determination as well as various constructions of state sovereignty in and outside of Western epistemologies.

8. For more on Baker, see Ransby's biography, *Ella Baker*; as well as J. Grant, *Ella Baker*.

9. Sit-in literature at this point is quite deep. Starting with Chafe's 1981 *Civilities and Civil Rights* through Cohen and Snyder's *Rebellion in Black and White*, one can find a wide range of information on how the sit-ins transformed not just the urban South but the political calculus of the two national political parties operating in the large shadow of the Cold War.

10. Anne Braden, tape 6, SNCC Fortieth Anniversary.

11. Carson, *In Struggle*, 20.

12. See Ransby, *Ella Baker*, chaps. 2–6.

13. "Diane Nash Remembers Activist Ella Baker."

14. Baker, "Bigger Than a Hamburger." As Julian Bond noted, "I remember it being an eye-opener to me, because I really had not thought about much more than a hamburger. We were doing lunch counter sit-ins, we wanted to integrate the lunch counters, and that was the deal. I knew that racial problems extended far beyond lunch counters. But I didn't see *us* doing anything like that, til she mentioned it there. So it was a real eye-opener, a real big step, a big leap for me. And I think it was for a lot of the other people too." Julian Bond in Hampton and Fayer, *Voices of Freedom*, 63.

15. In hundreds of newspaper articles, white southerners in positions of authority noted that "their" Black citizens were happy with things as they were and did not want to vote. The Mississippi Freedom Democratic Party, Bob Moses later noted, was a response to show that Black people in Mississippi were not happy with disenfranchisement. They used their ballots to prove the "demand side," that Black Mississippians indeed wanted to vote and were denied. Moses and Cobb, *Radical Equations*, 129.

16. Judy Richardson, tape 1, SNCC Fortieth Anniversary.

17. Joyce Ladner, tape 9, SNCC Fortieth Anniversary.

18. Victoria Gray Adams, "The Power of Women," in Holsaert et al., *Hands on the Freedom Plow*, 231.

19. On Amzie Moore, see Dittmer, *Local People*; Payne, *I've Got the Light of Freedom*, 54, 62–65, 142, 239; Moye, *Let the People Decide*, 92–107; Curry, *Silver Rights*, 37–57; and Charles and Cobb, *This Nonviolent Stuff'll Get You Killed*, 86–91, 121, 136.

20. Moses, "Address at 75th Birthday Celebration."

21. Moses, "Address at 75th Birthday Celebration." See also Carson, *In Struggle*, 26, 46; Dittmer, *Local People*, 102; and Payne, *I've Got the Light of Freedom*, 63.

22. The Mississippi Freedom Democratic Party was central to the drive that led to the Voting Rights Act of 1965 but certainly not alone. Campaigns in Jacksonville, Texas, Virginia, South Carolina, and Georgia and of course the movements in and around Birmingham and Selma in Alabama between 1963 and 1965 were key. The

literature on both local and regional movements for the vote is extensive. We await an updated thorough literature review, but for a few key texts, see Lawson, *Black Ballots*; Branch's trilogy *Parting the Waters*, *Pillar of Fire*, and *At Canaan's Edge*; Berman, *Give Us the Ballot*; Landesburg, *Free at Last to Vote*; and May, *Bending toward Justice*.

23. Charles Jones, tape 8, SNCC Fortieth Anniversary. On various articulations of the "beloved community" and its critics in SNCC, see in particular J. Lewis, *Walking with the Wind*; Greenberg, *Circle of Trust*; and Holsaert et al., *Hands on the Freedom Plow*.

24. Joanne Grant, "Peek around the Mountain," in Holsaert et al., *Hands on the Freedom Plow*, 309. For more on the way collective singing held the movement together, see Reagon, "Solidarity of Past."

25. "Diane Nash Remembers Activist Ella Baker."

26. "Diane Nash Remembers Activist Ella Baker."

27. Adams, "The Power of Women," in Holsaert et al., *Hands on the Freedom Plow*, 231; Grant, "Peek around the Mountain," in Holsaert et al., *Hands on the Freedom Plow*, 308; Reagon, "'Let Your Light Shine'—Historical Notes," in Reagon and Sweet Honey in the Rock, *We Who Believe in Freedom*, 20. Also see Ransby's comprehensive exploration of Baker's practical philosophy of organizing people in *Ella Baker*, 13–14, 284, 293.

28. Joyce Ladner, tape 9, SNCC Fortieth Anniversary.

29. Victoria Gray Adams, tape 9, SNCC Fortieth Anniversary.

30. Adams, tape 9, SNCC Fortieth Anniversary; Baker quoted in Ransby, *Ella Baker*, Kindle location 4993–95. For one critical look at the challenges faced by those in the "helping" business, see D. Wagner, *What's Love Got to Do with It?*

31. Adams, tape 9, SNCC Fortieth Anniversary.

32. Braden, tape 6, SNCC Fortieth Anniversary. Baker and Braden first met in 1956 and were lifelong colleagues. See Ransby, *Ella Baker*, Kindle location 3292.

33. Braden, tape 6, SNCC Fortieth Anniversary; Ladner, tape 9, SNCC Fortieth Anniversary.

34. Victoria Gray Adams interview by Joseph Sinsheimer.

35. Braden, tape 6, SNCC Fortieth Anniversary.

36. Jean Wiley, "Letter to My Adolescent Son," in Holsaert et al., *Hands on the Freedom Plow*, 521.

37. Annie Pearl Avery, "There Are No Cowards," in Holsaert et al., *Hands on the Freedom Plow*, 459.

38. In comparing Ella Baker "to Gramsci and Freire—two men, one European and the other Latin American"—Ransby does not do so in order to legitimate Black intellectuals in light of their white peers. Baker did not learn from them or imitate them but "through her own process of political evolution arrived at a very similar place." This set of ideas, refracting the work of Lewis Gordon's *Existentia Africana*, has been very helpful in contrast to the way Black intellectual life has often been framed. Ransby, *Ella Baker*, 419. Sexism within various civil rights organizations has been the subject of hundreds of scholarly studies. To what degree it was present in SNCC remains a point of debate among SNCC activists. The majority of SNCC women echo Jean Wiley's sentiment. See Holsaert et al., *Hands on the Freedom Plow*,

for the most comprehensive portrait, as well as "SNCC, Women and Stokely," and "Women and Men in the Freedom Movement."

39. Morrison, "Slow Walk of Trees."

40. Morrison, "Slow Walk of Trees."

41. Bob Moses, tape 12, SNCC Fortieth Anniversary. See also J. Grant, *Fundi*.

42. Moses, "Address at 75th Birthday Celebration." To see the enormous range of SNCC veterans' subsequent activity, see "Profiles," SNCC Digital Gateway, http://snccdigital.org.

CHAPTER TWO

1. For resources on Atlanta that spanned the twentieth century, see Du Bois, *Souls of Black Folk*, 63–65; Mixon, *Atlanta Riot*; Godshalk, *Veiled Visions*; Kruse, "Politics of Race and Public Space"; and Brown-Nagin, *Courage to Dissent*.

2. Craig Washington to 2ndsunday-atl@egroups.com, "Organizers Harassed at Atlanta Gay Pride Event," email, July 6, 2000, box 1, SONG Papers. This was a phenomenon that people of color in Pride marches often experienced across North America, from the first Pride marches in the 1970s. In 2016, Black Lives Matter–Toronto Pride marchers stopped the Pride parade, demanding that the mostly white male Pride leadership respond to their demands for a more inclusive event. See Khan, "Black Lives Matter Toronto Co-founder Responds." See also this post on Twitter: https://twitter.com/BLM_TO/status/749754649951948800?ref_src=twsrc^tfw (accessed Nov. 2, 2016).

3. Craig Washington to 2ndsunday-atl@egroups.com, "Organizers Harassed at Atlanta Gay Pride Event," email, July 6, 2000, box 1, SONG Papers.

4. On the relative fluidity of identity, I have adapted Gyan Pandey's eloquent phrase "identities we inherit and inhabit." It is a deft shorthand for thinking about the complex interplay between what we experience (internal identities) and what is imposed on us by others, as well as how these change over time. See Pandey, "Politics and Democracy in Our Time," 60. John Hope Franklin's corpus of historical work of more than fifteen books eloquently and painstakingly documents this reality in US history. He also made numerous attempts in political work to illuminate the reality he experienced into the late 1990s: "In spite of my work as a professor and writer, I am just another black face, often mistaken for the waiter or valet at some of America's finest restaurants and hotels." See Franklin, "Talking, Not Shouting, about Race."

5. The primary sources and secondary literature on the abolitionist, women's rights, and labor movements overflow with examples. Sojourner Truth's "Ain't I a Woman?" speech is probably the most well known in US history. See also Allen and Allen, *Reluctant Reformers*; McCarthy and Stauffer, *Prophets of Protest*; Brah and Phoenix, "Ain't I a Woman?"; and Cooper, *Beyond Respectability*.

6. Nicholas von Hoffman, "Finding and Making Leaders," 1963, reprinted in Schutz and Miller, *People Power*, 74–86.

7. "SONG: Southerners on New Ground," n.d. [1994], box 31, Carter Papers. Segrest called them "lesbian," and Pat Hussain in her interview by Lorraine Fontana said "dyke" fit her better:

I felt like a feminist. I felt and thought that women were deserving of everything that men believed to be their purview. I had been raised in a country that felt like we were second-class, with a father who didn't think I was. That presence of self was always there, and not wanting to be denied, and pushing back against that. Being a "lesbian-feminist" always got in my way. I didn't want to belong to an organization that was predominantly white, because there's always that push. It's kind of like swimming through molasses. That there's so much unintentional harm done, that I didn't feel like doing that any more. I just didn't want to do it. I didn't want to be a "lesbian." Again it becomes about race. The Isle of Lesbos, a Greek island—I don't think my folks came from there. "Dyke" fit me better than anything else. "Queer" is perfect for me. Dyke went to the Harlem Renaissance, Ma Rainey and Bessie Smith.

8. Similar groups formed across the country from the late 1960s through the 1990s. See for example Jones and Eubanks with Smith, *Ain't Gonna Let Nobody Turn Me Around*, especially section 6; J. Williams, *From the Bullet to the Ballot*; and Sonnie and Tracy, *Hillbilly Nationalists*. The challenges to social movements internally had consistently been present in US history. See for example Boggs, *Living for Change*; or Allen and Pam Allen, *Reluctant Reformers*. In every region in the US, activists struggled with the challenge of single-issue versus intersectional organizing approaches.

9. Lorde, *Sister Outsider*, 138.

10. The Combahee River Collective Statement is likely the first use of "identity politics" in the current historical era. Combahee River Collective, *Combahee River Collective Statement*; Jones and Eubanks with Smith, *Ain't Gonna Let Nobody Turn Me Around*, especially chap. 3. See also Taylor, *How We Get Free*; Crenshaw, "Mapping the Margins"; and Collins, *Black Feminist Thought*, 5, 18, 60.

11. Crenshaw, keynote address.

12. Crenshaw, keynote address.

13. Cooper's recent work *Beyond Respectability*, 58, 88–89, traces Mary Church Terrell and Pauli Murray as two of these early formulators of intersectional thought and organizing. See also Bambara, *Black Woman*; hooks, *Ain't I a Woman?*; Giddings, *When and Where I Enter*; and White, *Too Heavy a Load*.

14. Barbara Smith interview by Virginia Eubanks, in Jones and Eubanks with Smith, *Ain't Gonna Let Nobody Turn Me Around*, 43–44, 52.

15. On Alinsky and the IAF, see Schutz and Miller, *People Power*, especially 3–5, 326–29. For an important account of what IAF, the Midwest Academy, and other similar organizing omitted for black and brown community organizers, see Carruthers, *Unapologetic*, Kindle location 1447–60.

16. In 2012, the national NAACP voted to support marriage equality for gays and lesbians. Former head of SNCC communications Julian Bond later became chair of the NAACP board and advocated strongly for adding a platform for LGBTQ equality in the early twenty-first century. See Michael Barbaro, "In Largely Symbolic Move, NAACP Votes to Endorse Same Sex Marriage," *New York Times*, May 19, 2012, http://www.nytimes.com/2012/05/20/us/politics/naacp-endorses-same-sex-marriage.html.

17. The list of such feedback litters the papers of SONG, as well as interviews and public talks by the SONG founders. For a particularly eloquent elaboration, see

M. Carter, "Justice or Just Us?" Since SONG's founding in 1993, it must be noted how significant the changes have been to address these former blind spots within GLAAD, the National Gay and Lesbian Task Force (NGLTF), the NAACP, and other organizations originally founded around "single issue" politics. GLAAD's current website page describing the organization's work has specific emphases on Spanish-language and Latinx media, the South, and global voices (https://www.glaad.org/programs); the NGLTF's Creating Change conference includes a full-day racial justice institute and an intersectional framework (https://www.creatingchange.org/faq/); and the NAACP Board in 2012 voted to support marriage equality (https://donate.naacp.org/news/entry/naacp-passes-resolution-in-support-of-marriage-equality).

18. Hussain's quote on not choosing between her identities is in untitled notes, box 2, SONG Papers. To date, no book-length treatments of Mandy Carter exist, though surely if there is justice in the historical world, such studies will soon emerge. Carter has coedited a collection with Martinez and Meyer, *We Have Not Been Moved*. See also Roy, "Arundhati Roy on the Rising Hindu Right."

19. Pat Hussain interview by Lorraine Fontana.

20. Hussain interview.

21. Hussain interview.

22. Mandy Carter interview by Rose Norman.

23. On Joan Little, see McNeil, "'Joanne Is You, Joanne Is Me'"; Greene, "'She Ain't No Rosa Parks'"; and McGuire, "Joan Little and the Triumph of Testimony." On the Greensboro Massacre, see Bermanzohn, *Through Survivors' Eyes*; Waller, *Love and Revolution*; and Jovanovic, *Democracy, Dialogue and Community Action*. Helms's work in the 1990s will be discussed later in this chapter. On banks in Charlotte, see Graves and Smith, eds., *Charlotte NC*; and Gitterman and Coclanis, *Way Forward*.

24. Hussain interview by Lorraine Fontana. On Segrest's evolving thinking on NAFTA, see Mab Segrest interview by Rose Norman. On Segrest, see also Powell, "Look What Happened Here"; 91–102; Enszer, "Night Heron Press"; and Segrest, *My Mama's Dead Squirrel* and *Memoir of a Race Traitor*. The quote from Segrest is from *Memoir of a Race Traitor*, 1. Mab Segrest, note to author, Sept. 9, 2017.

25. Mab Segrest, note to author, Sept. 8, 2017; Suzanne Pharr interview by Rose Norman.

26. Segrest interview by Rose Norman.

27. Segrest, *Memoir of a Race Traitor*, 1; Segrest interview by Rose Norman.

28. Notes from "North/South Dialogue on Poor People's Movement Building," n.d. [October 1997], box 2, SONG Papers; SONG Application to the Astraea Lesbian Foundation for Justice, Feb. 15, 2006, box 81, Carter Papers. On the longer strands of hospitality within the freedom movement, see Harding and Harding, "Radical Hospitality."

29. "It was intentional that we started with three black and three white women. It was intentional that we looked for intersections of -isms." Carter felt that was the key. Carter interview by Rose Norman; Hussain interview by Lorraine Fontana.

30. Notes from "North/South Dialogue on Poor People's Movement Building," n.d. [October 1997], box 2, SONG Papers; SONG Application to the Astraea Lesbian Foundation for Justice, Feb. 15, 2006, box 81, Carter Papers.

31. The US Census splits the population into four regions: West, South, Midwest, and Northeast. For 1990s data, see the US Census Bureau website, https://www.census.gov/history/www/reference/maps/population_distribution_over_time.html (accessed July 31, 2017). For data since 2000, see https://www.census.gov/popclock/data_tables.php?component=growth (accessed July 31, 2017). The "heart of the iceberg" comment by Bob Moses is in Carmichael with Thelwell, *Ready for Revolution*, 319.

32. Pharr, "Gift of Grace"; SONG, "Report to Unitarian Universalist Veatch Program at Shelter Rock, for period Jan. 1–Oct. 30, 1996," pp. 7–8, box 32, Carter Papers.

33. On the South as a center of reaction, see MacLean, *Democracy in Chains*; Mayer, *Dark Money*; Cullen and Wilkison, *Texas Right*; Kruse, *White Flight*; and Crespino, *In Search of Another Country*.

34. Pharr, "Gift of Grace." Pharr is the author of over fifty articles and two books, *Homophobia: A Weapon of Sexism* and *In the Time of the Right: Reflections on Liberation*. See http://suzannepharr.org/about.

35. SONG, "Report to Unitarian Universalist Veatch Program at Shelter Rock, for period Jan. 1–Oct. 30, 1996," pp. 7–8, box 32, Carter Papers; Taylor, *From #BlackLivesMatter to Black Liberation*, Kindle location 1286–88. On Nixon's Southern Strategy, see Phillips, *Emerging Republican Majority*; Kruse, *White Flight*; Lassiter, *Silent Majority*; E. Miller, *Nut Country*; and Kotlowski, *Nixon's Civil Rights*. Divide and conquer, James Madison privately summarized a month before penning *Federalist* Number 10, was, "under certain qualifications, the only policy by which a republic can be administered on just principles." Madison to Thomas Jefferson, Oct. 24, 1787, in Hutchinson et al., *Papers of James Madison*, 10:20–22, quoted in Holton, *Unruly Americans*, 11.

36. Thrift, *Conservative Bias*, chaps. 5 and 6; Dan Carter, review of *Conservative Bias*.

37. On Helms, see the senator's own account of the "Hands" ad in *Here's Where I Stand*, 191–92; Link, *Righteous Warrior*, 371–85; and Thrift, *Conservative Bias*.

38. The "Hands" advertisement can be seen here: http://www.pbs.org/30second candidate/timeline/years/1990.html. For commentary on the polling, see *The 30-Second Candidate*, PBS, 1998, http://www.pbs.org/30secondcandidate/timeline/years/1990.html (accessed Jan. 8, 2015). The creator of the ad, Alex Castellanos, reflected on its racist impact decades later in Fang, "RNC Adviser Alex Castellanos Admits." Helms maintained that the ad was not intended to be racist: "Minority classifications were not limited to race, and we had no more interest in a race-based vote than we did in race-based jobs. This campaign was never about Mr. Gantt being black; it was always and only about him being a liberal" (Helms, *Here's Where I Stand*, 191). See Link, *Righteous Warrior*, 378–80.

39. Garner dated her involvement as an activist in women's, lesbian, and antiracism causes to her time as head of the Fund for Southern Communities. See Garner interview by Rose Norman; and Pam McMichael, *Southern Stories*, pamphlet, [n.d.], box 1, SONG Papers.

40. Minutes from the Feb. 1995 Hopscotch House retreat, box 237, Carter Papers. The SONG codirectors, Pat Hussain (Atlanta) and Pam McMichael (Louisville), and Mandy Carter (Durham), Mab Segrest (Durham), Joan Garner (Atlanta), and

Suzanne Pharr (Arkansas) served as the initial board. When asked if any one of the original six founders was a ringleader, Joan Garner said no. "There really wasn't a 'ringleader,' per se. We all had a role, and it was a collective role. It was about all of us, our collective wisdom. Now we knew we had to designate key people to run the organization. When we got our first grant, Pat Hussain and Pam McMichael became co-directors, working full-time on SONG. We all became founding board members." Garner interview by Rose Norman.

41. McMichael continued (in an interview by Rose Norman):

> We were doing a lot of listening. We were going to different conferences where gays and lesbians were present and exploring things with people there. And we were finding that many people were really interested in talking with us and hearing what we were trying to do from vision-based organizing that was crossing these lines of difference and building a movement where people didn't have to leave their identities at the door. We all saw coalitions and alliance-building as a way to liberation for all of us, that no one group was strong enough to get there on their own. We're also not just one thing in our identities as lesbians. We're also women, we're working class, we're people of color, we're differently abled.

42. Mab Segrest, "Pam Notes," n.d. [1996?], box 1, SONG papers; Segrest note to author, Sept. 9, 2017.

43. Pharr interview by Rose Norman. On Handcox, see Honey, *Sharecropper's Troubadour*. See also Hudson, *Narrative of Hosea Hudson*; and Kelley, *Hammer and Hoe*. On Clark, see Clark, *Ready from Within*; Charron, *Freedom's Teacher*; and Payne, *I've Got the Light of Freedom*, 68–77, on her and Horton.

44. Facilitators' Agendas in boxes 1 and 2 of the SONG Papers give a strong sense of these cultural innovations. This particular one is from SONG's Higher Ground retreat, Feb. 25–27, 2000, box 1, SONG Papers.

45. Bob Lee, quoted in Sonnie and Tracy, *Hillbilly Nationalists*, 77.

46. "Mountaintop Festival" program, [1995], box 32, Carter Papers; SONG, "Report to Unitarian Universalist Veatch Program at Shelter Rock, for period Jan. 1-Oct. 30, 1996," pp. 3–6, Box 32, Carter Papers.

47. SONG, "Report to Unitarian Universalist Veatch Program at Shelter Rock, for period Jan. 1–Oct. 30, 1996," pp. 3–6, box 32, Carter Papers.

48. Garner interview by Rose Norman; Pam McMichael to SONG Sisters, May 6, 1994, box 32, Carter Papers; Suzanne [Pharr], "Hopscotch House," n.d. [Feb. 3–5, 1995], box 237, Carter Papers.

49. Bill Clinton's 1992 campaign manager, James Carville, infamously posted a sign in campaign headquarters to remind those within the organization of the major issues they needed to focus on: "Change versus more of the same. The economy, stupid. Don't forget health care." Kelly, "1992 Campaign"; Berry, *History Teaches Us to Resist*, 131.

50. "SONG Training-Reduced to 3 ½ hours," n.d. [1996?], box 31, Carter Papers. The literature on neoliberalism as well as that on income inequality since the 1980s is vast. For an overview of neoliberalism in the wake of the Cold War, see Harvey, *Brief History of Neoliberalism*; and D. Jones, *Masters of the Universe*. On income

inequality, a recent work that looks at the phenomenon in historical context is Lindert and Williamson, *Unequal Gains*.

51. SONG was not the first to offer workshops exposing people to antiracist ways of understanding the world—people coming out of the civil rights, women's liberation, liberation theology, and gay liberation movements had been running antiracist workshops in every part of the nation since the 1960s. As Sarah Burgin writes, there were multiple ways "white activists addressed racial injustices and racialized ignorance within their own movements, and yet had a sense of the effects of these efforts on the larger U.S. society." Workshops on oppression had been operating in the country since at least the late 1960s. By the late 1970s and early 1980s, anti-racism workshops in the North and West had become "increasingly common both inside and outside of social movements." For example, Black and White Men Together, a multiracial organization for gay men formed in New York and San Francisco in 1980, spent its early years examining racial discrimination and how campaigns for gay assimilation tended to reproduce class and race hierarchies. The group not only looked at the history of race but also shifted toward reflexivity and examined how one contributed through one's own experiences. White Kentuckian Anne Braden had engaged this work since the 1950s; see Braden, *Fight against Racism*; Fosl, *Subversive Southerner*; and Burgin, "Workshop as the Work." Mitchell Karp, a long-term member of Black and White Men Together, asked white men in a 1986 article to not collapse differences in the pursuit of LGBT aims or coalition building. Moreover, the way some women's studies classes are taught today collapses early women's liberation movements into a single blob: "Those white women were racist." While many were, it doesn't help us to more accurately understand the significant innovations that emerged at that time by erasing them from the historical record. They were not numerous, but the pioneering women like Chude Allen whom Burgin has begun to bring back into the historical record are important innovators. Burgin, 162, 276, 94–95, 277. See also Mitchell Karp, "The Challenge of Symbolism."

52. Carter interview by Rose Norman; "SONG Economics Training, Teresa Amott, March 6, 1996," p. 3, box 31, Carter Papers; SONG, "Report to Unitarian Universalist Veatch Program at Shelter Rock, for period Jan. 1–Oct. 30, 1996," box 32, Carter Papers.

53. For the Jesse Helms "Hands" advertisement, see http://www.pbs.org/30second candidate/timeline/years/1990.html (accessed Dec. 5, 2015). SONG Economics Training, Teresa Amott, March 6, 1996," p. 6, box 31, Carter Papers.

54. McMichael interview by Rose Norman; Suzanne Pharr quoted in Acuña, Woodson and Pharr, "Race, the Election and Regenerating Our Democracy." Pharr noted in 2013, "Every day in my work, I talk about intersectionality, and where did I get that idea? I got it from the Combahee River Collective Statement." Pharr interview by Rose Norman.

55. McMichael interview by Rose Norman.

56. SONG Economics Training, Teresa Amott, March 6, 1996," pp. 7–13, box 31, Carter Papers; Pam McMichael, "What We Can Do," Apr. 30, 1998, fax, box 32, Carter Papers.

57. "Economy Training Evaluations 1996," box 32, Carter Papers.

58. "Economy Training Evaluations 1996."

59. Carter interview by Rose Norman; SONG Economics Training, Teresa Amott, March 6, 1996," p. 3, box 31, Carter Papers; SONG, "Report to Unitarian Universalist Veatch Program at Shelter Rock, for period Jan. 1–Oct. 30, 1996," box 32, Carter Papers.

60. "SONG Staff and Board Training of Trainers," p. 8, Aug. 4–5, 1998, Kannapolis, NC, box 1, SONG Papers; pamphlet for "Training of Trainers," n.d., box 31, Carter Papers.

61. "Undoing Racism" flyer, July 22, 1998, fax, box 32, Carter Papers.

62. For a few standout works in a field of vast scholarship, see Fields and Fields, *Racecraft*; Beckert, *Empire of Cotton*; Kendi, *Stamped from the Beginning*; Pikketty, *Capital in the Twenty-First Century*, chaps. 4 and 7–11; Klein, *No Is Not Enough*, 94; Horne, *Apocalypse of Settler Colonialism*; Dunbar-Ortiz, *Indigenous Peoples' History*; and Ortiz, *African American and Latinx History*.

63. "First Annual Leadership Summit. Arkansas Equality Network Anti-racism and Internalized Homophobia," presented with SONG, March 3–4, 2001, trainers: Kim Diehl and Pam McMichael, SONG; see also Judd Harbin, University of Arkansas Health Center, box 1, SONG Papers.

64. McMichael interview by Rose Norman. For more on the Kentucky Alliance, see http://www.kentuckyalliance.org/about.html (accessed Oct. 2, 2017).

65. O'Neal and McMichael, "Race," *Journal of Southerners on New Ground*, 3.

66. Pam McMichael, "Southern Stories," n.d., box 1, SONG Papers. On the effectiveness of the Cracker Barrel campaign, see Rane, "Twenty Years of Shareholder Proposals after Cracker Barrel: An Effective Tool for Implementing LGBT Employment Protections."

67. Deb, "Beyond the Black/White Paradigm," 9–11, 24–25. On stereotypes beyond the black-white dichotomy, see Moraga and Anzaldúa, eds., *This Bridge Called My Back*; S. Lee, *Unraveling the Model Minority Stereotype*; and Wu, *Color of Success*.

68. Morrison, "Slow Walk of Trees," 104.

69. SONG, "People of Color Leadership Retreat 1998," box 31, Carter Papers.

70. Similar workshop tools addressing economic and racial justice began to be developed in this period and through the 1990s by Project South, founded in 1986 by Jerome Scott and Walda Katz-Fishman in the wake of Jeff Sessions's prosecution of civil rights activists in west Alabama in the mid-1980s. Activists across the South largely saw Sessions's prosecution as an "attempt to intimidate black voters in the rural South and push back electoral gains made since the passage of the 1965 Voting Rights Act." Tullos, "Crackdown in the Black Belt." See also "About Project South," http://projectsouth.org/about/ (accessed July 27, 2017); and Horowitz et al., "Popular Education for Movement Building: A Project South Resource Guide."

71. Call to SONG Retreat, April 2001, box 82, Carter Papers.

72. "Women's Retreat Information Sheet," n.d. [2001], box 82, Carter Papers; Segrest, note to author, Sept. 9, 2017.

73. Offiah, "#OutSouth15."

74. SONG, "Report to Unitarian Universalist Veatch Program at Shelter Rock, for period Jan. 1–Oct. 30, 1996," box 32, Carter Papers.

75. Carter interview by Rose Norman.

76. Jones and Eubanks with Smith, *Ain't Gonna Let Nobody Turn Me Around*, 44.

77. Mandy Carter to Aida Rentas, "POC LGBT Skills Building Retreat," Feb. 10, 1998, fax, box 32, Carter Papers; Pam McMichael to Mandy Carter, Jan. 31, 1998, letter, box 32, Carter Papers; SONG Application to the Astraea Lesbian Foundation for Justice, Feb. 15, 2006, box 81, Carter Papers.

78. SONG codirector Kim Diehl noted that four sites had strong Bayard Rustin Project work established by 2000: Durham, Atlanta, Louisville, and New Orleans. Kim Diehl to Mandy Carter, Nov. 2, 2000, box 237, Carter Papers. On Rustin, see Rustin and Long, *I Must Resist*; D'Emilio, *Lost Prophet*; J. Anderson, *Bayard Rustin*; and Mumford, *Not Straight*.

79. Pat Hussain and Pam McMichael to "Friend," Mar. 19, 1997, box 32, Carter Papers.

80. SONG, "Report to Unitarian Universalist Veatch Program at Shelter Rock, for period Jan. 1–Oct. 30, 1996," p. 9, box 32, Carter Papers.

81. The "major work" included calling people into conversations and pushing them to act. This included "big" actions like a march but also smaller daily interactions. In May 1995, Pam McMichael moderated a discussion in Louisville sparked by six activists "whose experiences of class combined with race, ethnicity, gender and age does not always mirror the expected image." From "Queerly Classed," n.d. [1995?], box 32, Carter Papers. See also Wendi O'Neal and Pam McMichael, "Race," *Journal of Southerners on New Ground* 3, no. 1 (Summer 2000): 3.

CHAPTER THREE

1. Darris Young interview by the author. All quotes from Young in this chapter are from this interview.

2. Mandela, *Long Walk to Freedom*; Malcolm X, *The Autobiography of Malcolm X*; McCall, *Makes Me Wanna Holler*. Multiple scholars have written about Disney's race politics. For recent accounts, see Spurb, *Disney's Most Notorious Film*; Booker, *Disney, Pixar, and the Hidden Messages of Children's Film*; Giroux, *Mouse That Roared*; and Badger, "'Yeah, But Look How Far We've Come.'" On prisons as sites of liberation education in the 1960s and 1970s, see Berger, *Captive Nation*, chap. 4.

3. See for example milestone publications such as Gilmore, *Golden Gulag*; Darity and Myers, *Persistent Disparity*; Gottschalk, *Prison and the Gallows*; Alexander, *New Jim Crow*; H. Thompson, "Why Mass Incarceration Matters" and *Blood in the Water*; Bonilla-Silva, *Racism without Racists*; Berger, "Social Movements and Mass Incarceration"; and Forman, *Locking Up Our Own*.

4. On fines and fees, see W. Johnson, "Ferguson's Fortune 500 Company," and chapter 5. See as well Bannon, Nagrecha, and Diller, "Criminal Justice Debt"; and Semuels, "Fines and Fees."

5. Michelle Alexander, foreword to Burton and Lynn, *Becoming Ms. Burton*.

6. See for example Walsh, *Three Strikes Laws*; Provine, *Unequal under Law*; Alexander, *New Jim Crow*; Pfaff, *Locked In*; Wacquant, *Punishing the Poor*; and Gilmore, *Golden Gulag*.

7. Ella Baker Center, Facebook post, July 23, 2014; "Night Out for Safety and Liberation," Ella Baker Center for Human Rights, http://ellabakercenter.org/night-out-for-safety-and-liberation (July 12, 2016).

8. "Night Out for Safety and Liberation."

9. Honigblum, "Van Jones," 46.

10. Van Jones in Griffith, *Redefining Black Power*, Kindle location 1686; Strickland, "New Face of Environmentalism."

11. Van Jones in Griffith, *Redefining Black Power*, Kindle location 1686; Strickland, "New Face of Environmentalism." On Shirley Chisholm, see Chisholm, *Unbought and Unbossed*; Winslow, *Shirley Chisholm*; and Joshua Guild, "To Make That Someday Come: Shirley Chisholm's Radical Politics of Possibility," in Gore, Theoharis, and Woodard, *Want to Start a Revolution?*, 248–70.

12. Jones quoted in K. Johnson, "Grio's 100."

13. See E. Hinton, *From the War on Poverty to the War on Crime*. On unjust sentencing, see for example Murakawa, *First Civil Right*; and van Cleve, *Crook County*.

14. Honigblum, "Van Jones," 46; "Our Victories," Ella Baker Center for Human Rights, http://ellabakercenter.org/our-victories (accessed June 15, 2016).

15. Honigblum, "Van Jones," 46; "Our Victories."

16. Jones quoted in K. Johnson, "Grio's 100"; "Our History," Ella Baker Center for Human Rights, http://ellabakercenter.org/our-history (accessed Jan. 2, 2016); Strickland, "New Face of Environmentalism."

17. Strickland, "New Face of Environmentalism"; K. Johnson, "Grio's 100."

18. Sward, "S.F. Panel Fires Officer in Aaron Williams Case"; "Our History"; Van Jones interview by Kerry Kennedy Cuomo, *Speak Truth to Power*.

19. Macallair, "California Reforms Cause Youth Incarceration Rates to Plummet." See also the Youth Law Center's Juvenile Institutional Conditions website, updated regularly: http://www.ylc.org/our-work/action-litigation/juvenile-institutional-conditions-example/ (accessed June 13, 2016). On the school-to-prison pipeline, see Heitzeg, *School-to-Prison Pipeline*; Kim, Losen, and Hewitt, *School-to-Prison Pipeline*; Behena et al., *Disrupting the School-to-Prison Pipeline*; Nocella, Parmar, and Stovall, *From Education to Incarceration*; and M. Morris, *Pushout*.

20. The Soledad Brothers, George Jackson, John Clutchette, and Fleeta Drumgo were three Black men incarcerated in California's Soledad State Prison who became a cause célèbre in 1970 when they were charged with killing a white prison guard. Jones quoted in Griffith, *Redefining Black Power*, Kindle location 1698–1714. Cluchette quoted in Samuels, "Improvising on Reality," 27. On prison abolition, see for example A. Y. Davis et al., *If They Come in the Morning*; A. Y. Davis, *Abolition Democracy*; Prison Research Education Action Project, *Instead of Prisons*; and CR10 Publications Collective, *Abolition Now!* On incarceration as a strategy for managing poor black and brown people, see Gilmore, *Golden Gulag*; Alexander, *New Jim Crow*; Pfaff, *Locked In*; and Wacquant, *Punishing the Poor*.

21. Jones quoted in Griffith, *Redefining Black Power*, Kindle location 1698–1714.

22. On the profit incentives of the criminal justice system, see Thompson, "The Prison Industrial Complex"; Blumenson and Nilsen, "Policing for Profit"; Benson, *To Serve and Protect*; Bowman, Hakim, and Seidenstat, *Privatizing Correctional Institutions*; Brickner and Diaz, "Prisons for Profit," 13; Sudbury, "Celling Black Bodies"; Wood, "Globalization and Prison Privatization"; V. Jones, *Green Collar Economy*, 12, 14; and Jones quoted in Griffith, *Redefining Black Power*, Kindle location 1729.

23. V. Jones, *Green Collar Economy*, 100–102. On Silicon Valley's dominant environmental preoccupations, see Sustainable Silicon Valley, http://www.wp.sustainablesv.org/history/ (accessed Apr. 23, 2018); the Silicon Valley Leadership Group, http://svlg.org/policy-areas/environment/ (accessed Apr. 23, 2018); and McCarthy, "John Chambers." See also David Pellow's *Silicon Valley of Dreams* for some of these contradictions between the mainstream environmental movement and the environmental justice framework created by Black and brown organizers.

24. V. Jones, *Green Collar Economy*, 100.

25. V. Jones, 110. It was an echo of Bertolt Brecht's lament that "we knew only too well: Even the hatred of squalor makes the brow grow stern. Even anger against injustice makes the voice grow harsh. Alas, we who wished to lay the foundations of kindness could not ourselves be kind." Brecht, "To Posterity." Much work has been done on evolutions of similar kinds of process inside social movements in the twentieth century. For a few important examples of such work, see Payne, *I've Got the Light of Freedom*; Breines, *Trouble between Us* and *Great Refusal*; Kelley, *Hammer and Hoe*; and Goodwyn, *Populist Moment*.

26. V. Jones, *Green Collar*, 110. I examine SNCC's attempts to address these "old habits" in a chapter written with Robyn Spencer, "Telling Freedom Stories from the Inside Out." Carruthers, *Unapologetic*, Kindle Location 1201. Beth Richie's work, represented in part with her book *Arrested Justice*, started from her work with women on Riker's Island. "I felt like I was carrying Riker's Island women with me, looking for a political home," she recalled in 2017. When she found the abolitionist group Critical Resistance, "this was a space to talk about the violence, the way class played into the fact that [women of color] were in jail, not shelter. Not theoretically, but literally the places, and such a presence of people who were still caught under criminal legal system. [Critical Resistance] wasn't without problems, there were hard discussions there. Where women fit, where sexuality gets played out, how we will seriously talk about class. Women at Riker's can go home, but home is what led them there, so what then?" Richie, panel with Asha Ransby-Sporn and Mariame Kaba, "Prison Abolition, Mass Incarceration, and Black Feminism: What's the Connection? 20th Anniversary of Critical Resistance," National Women's Studies Association, Baltimore, MD, Nov. 18, 2017, notes in the author's possession.

27. The gist of this criticism has been consistent since the mid-1990s and is actually evident in Jones's interview by Rodney Carmichael, "In Midst of Racial Hatred," https://www.npr.org/sections/therecord/2017/08/16/543394845/in-midst-of-racial-hatred-van-jones-still-pushes-love (Dec. 20, 2018), where Jones takes credit in a way that could appear egotistical and not reflecting group-centered leadership: "I've got people in their 20s criticizing me and I've been doing this work, literally, their entire lives. I started as a serious activist in '89. Got out of law school in '93 and you can ask anybody that knows me, I've very rarely taken more than two days off in a row in two-plus decades. I've closed five prisons. I've stopped them from building the super-jail for youth in Oakland; I stopped that. I've gotten a police officer fired. I've reformed two police departments. So all this stuff that people are talking about that needs to happen, I've done." For more recent criticism, see Justin George, "Van Jones Answers His Critics," *The Marshall Project*, June 8, 2018, https://www.the

marshallproject.org/2018/06/18/van-jones-answers-his-critics (Dec. 20, 2018); and Natasha Alford, "Exclusive: CNN's Van Jones Addresses Criticism of Soft-Pedaling Jared Kushner," *The Grio*, Dec. 18, 2018, https://thegrio.com/2018/12/18/van-jones-criticism-jared-kushner-and-working-with-gop-on-criminal-justice-reform/.

28. See, for example, Hersh, "How Obama Got Rolled by Wall Street"; Taibi, "Why Isn't Wall Street in Jail?"; and "Obama Prosecuting Fewer Financial Crimes Than Either Reagan or Bush." See also D. Graham, "How a Small Team of Democrats Defeated Larry Summers and Obama."

29. Obama's decision to stifle the power of organized people—in this case, those at the grassroots who "Organized for America" in 2007–9—is one of the most important political stories of the early twenty-first century. No one has yet written a sustained treatment of this key juncture in American democratic life. For early treatments, see Tim Dickinson's "No We Can't," and Sifry, "The Obama Disconnect"; Berman, *Herding Donkeys* and "Jim Messina"; and Ganz, "How Obama Lost His Voice." "Well-intentioned deference" is from Purdy, "Normcore."

30. See for example David Kreutzer, "Impact of CO_2 Restrictions on Employment and Income: Green Jobs or Gone Jobs?," Heritage Foundation, Nov. 5, 2008, https://www.heritage.org/environment/report/impact-co2-restrictions-employment-and-income-green-jobs-or-gone-jobs; Ernest Istook, "Red Faces about 'Green' Jobs," Feb. 6, 2009, https://www.heritage.org/budget-and-spending/commentary/red-faces-about-green-jobs; Ben Lieberman, "Green Job Subsidies Will Destroy Far More Jobs Than They Will Create," Heritage Foundation, Oct. 2, 2009, https://www.heritage.org/environment/commentary/green-job-subsidies-will-destroy-far-more-jobs-they-create; Farley, "Glenn Beck Says Van Jones Is an Avowed Communist"; Van Jones quoted in Mark, "Conversation," 45–47.

31. It was not just a surrender of high ground. It was part of a broader Obama administration pattern to hew to the conventional politics of organized money instead of building power around "organized people." Thousands of local "Organizing for America" grassroots organizers learned this immediately after the November 2008 election when David Plouffe's team ruthlessly cut them out of the transition. This could also be seen in the way the Obama administration treated veteran civil rights agricultural expert Shirley Sherrod in 2010. Still, White House adviser David Axelrod denied the president had asked for Jones's resignation or forced him out. "This was Van Jones's own decision," Axelrod asserted, contrary to Jones's assertion. Axelrod quoted in "Obama Did Not Order Van Jones's Resignation, Adviser Says," CNN News, Sept. 6, 2009, http://www.cnn.com/2009/POLITICS/09/06/obama.adviser.resigns/index.html; Van Jones quoted in Mark, "Conversation," 45–47; Farley, "Glenn Beck Says Van Jones Is an Avowed Communist." See also Ganz, "How Obama Lost His Voice." On Shirley Sherrod, see Sherrod, July 11, 2016, Durham, NC, notes in the author's possession. Ella Baker's expression about prophetic leaders' "feet of clay" is from her speech, "Bigger Than a Hamburger."

32. Color of Change "is the nation's largest online racial justice organization. We help people respond effectively to injustice in the world around us. As a national online force driven by over one million members, we move decision-makers in corporations and government to create a more human and less hostile world for Black people in America" (www.colorofchange.org). Green for All "works to build

an inclusive green economy strong enough to lift people out of poverty. Our goal is to make sure people of color have a place and a voice in the climate movement. That our neighborhoods are strong, resilient, and healthy. That as the clean energy economy grows, it brings jobs and opportunity to our communities" (www.greenforall.org), and Rebuild the Dream (www.rebuildthedream.com) formed in 2011 to support a crowd-sourced economic agenda called the "Contract for the American Dream" to help underwater homeowners and students who had significant loans.

33. The Facebook site for the Ella Baker Center has archived thousands of such day-to-day and week-to-week initiatives. For a few representative samples, see the 2011 Ella Awards, Facebook, https://www.facebook.com/ellabakercenter/photos/a.10150317381478602.340713.39055178601/10150317463753602/?type=3&theater (accessed July 7, 2016); "Today We Won #JobsNotJails," Mar. 24, 2015, https://www.facebook.com/ellabakercenter/?fref=nf; and #JobsForFreedom video at the Alameda County Board of Supervisors, June 28, 2016, https://www.facebook.com/ellabakercenter/videos/10153758544508602/. For a similar strategy using Twitter, see "#SafetyIs" Twitter chat, Aug. 4, 2015, https://twitter.com/hashtag/safetyis?src=hash. On the end of youth solitary confinement in California, see Editorial Board, "End to Abusive Solitary Confinement." On #WhoPays, see *Who Pays: The True Cost of Incarceration on Families*, Ella Baker Center for Human Rights, Sept. 2015, http://ellabakercenter.org/sites/default/files/downloads/who-pays.pdf. See also Tutashinda, *It's Our Time*, 156. On green jobs, see Leslie Guevarra, "Governor Launches 'Green Corps' to Train At-Risk Youths for Green-Collar Jobs," Green Biz, Mar. 16, 2009, https://www.greenbiz.com/news/2009/03/16/california-governor-launches-green-corps-train-risk-youths-green-collar-jobs; and "Recovery Spotlight: Statewide Green Corps in California," #GreenForAll, n.d. [2009], http://www.greenforall.org/recovery_spotlight_statewide_green_corps_in_california (accessed Aug. 21, 2016).

34. Tutashinda, *It's Our Time*, 157.

35. Lanise Frazier interview by the author. All other quotes from Frazier in this chapter are from this interview.

36. On ALANA, see https://www.gordon.edu/alana (accessed Feb. 2, 2018). For the events, see the history of the group's Facebook page, https://www.facebook.com/pg/Gordon-College-ALANA-551049731652005/events/?ref=page_internal (accessed Feb. 2, 2018).

37. Frazier, who had participated in a range of organizing prior to coming to Oakland, convened a series of campus-wide conversations at Gordon College called "Real Talk." When students and administrators who were white asked why they had to be involved, she responded with clarity: "This is a *you* problem, not just a me problem. This race issue is not a *me* problem. It's your problem too. We're in this together; let's have this conversation." She recognized that underlying some white students' reluctance stemmed from the fact they were "afraid to say, 'Well I feel this way,' if their black friend is sitting right next to them." Frazier continually set up a new format: "Honestly this is the reason why we don't deal with our mess, is because we're a really **** up dysfunctional family. The human race? We're just one big, dysfunctional family. We don't talk about our issues." At the EBC, she discovered a different model for organizing that included training in how to facilitate healthier internal dynamics and how to effectively organize communities to promote policies that served them.

38. Nona Perry interview by the author. All other quotes from Perry in this chapter are from this interview.

39. On Boal, see Boal, *Theater of the Oppressed*, and his autobiography, *Hamlet and the Baker's Son*.

40. While there is an extensive literature on school inequality, some of the key work of the last decade includes Erickson, *Making the Unequal Metropolis*; McCaskell, *Race to Equity*; Perry et al., *Quality Education as a Civil Right*; Rebell, *Courts and Kids*; and Shedd, *Unequal City*. On John Dewey's vision for US schools as a training ground for democratic citizens, see his 1916 book, *Democracy and Education*; and Jenlink, *Dewey's Democracy*.

41. Perry's experience is reflected in the wider literature on schools in the twenty-first century. See for example Metzger, *Prison Called School*; and Goyal, *Schools on Trial*.

42. The innovative school's philosophy can be found online: http://oaklandstreetacademy.org/about// (accessed Jan. 8, 2015). The

> school recognizes the social realities which rule our society today. Despite the persistence of racism, sexism, classism, heterosexism, and other injustices, the Street Academy strives to help students reach their fullest potential. It is a school that has dedicated itself to developing effective solutions to many of the problems confronting youth today. By providing a meaningful and appropriate educational program which focuses on survival skills, educational achievement, promotion of strength of character through support, counseling and one on one teaching, the Street Academy succeeds in helping students take charge of their lives, and to become active members of their communities.

43. Susan Quinlan interview by the author.

44. Quinlan interview by the author.

45. Recent work on theater in this context includes von Kotze and Walters, *Forging Solidarity*; Harding and Rosenthal, *Restaging the Sixties*; Nicholson, *Theatre, Education and Performance*; and Kohr and Lin, *Good Practices*.

46. For recent research on youth recidivism, see Soyer, *Dream Denied*; and Lumba-Brown et al., "Mentoring Pediatric Victims."

47. Studies on the utility of early intervention began in earnest in the 1970s and took a decisive turn in the 1990s alongside a significant surge in overall brain research. See for example the brief history of early intervention in Lillas and Turnbull, *Infant/Child Mental Health*.

48. "Truth and Reinvestment," Ella Baker Center for Human Rights, http://ellabakercenter.org/about/about-us (accessed Dec. 1, 2016).

CHAPTER FOUR

1. See for instance the fascinating account by journalist Atossa Araxia Abrahamian, *The Cosmopolites*.

2. Warsan Shire, "Home," reprinted in Bausells and Shearlaw, "Poets Speak Out for Refugees."

3. For years people called these young activists "DREAMers," referring to

proposed federal legislation, the DREAM Act. That language has evolved and is contentious, as Laura Emiko Soltis points out, since not all young people qualify for it and the language around the legislation often demonizes their parents. Soltis, annotation to draft chapter, Sept. 8 2017, in author's possession.

4. Ronald Reagan famously went to Germany in June 1987. He stood and gave a speech at the Berlin Wall's Brandenburg Gate, asking Soviet leader Mikhail Gorbachev to "tear down this wall." Available on YouTube, https://www.youtube.com/watch?v=5MDFX-dNtsM (accessed June 20, 2018).

5. McFarland, "UN Report." For a recent history of white poverty, see Isenberg, *White Trash*. For an overview of the bipartisan consensus stymying immigration reform, see Daniel Denvir, "The Roots of Trump's Immigration Barbarity," *Jacobin*, June 20, 2018, https://www.jacobinmag.com/2018/06/trump-immigration-child-family-separation-policy (accessed Nov. 10, 2018).

6. "The "x" makes "Latino," a masculine identifier, gender-neutral. "Latinx" also reaches wider than terms like "Latino/a" or "Latin@"—which have been used to include both masculine and feminine identities—"to encompass genders outside of that limiting man-woman binary." Reichard, "Why We Say Latinx"; Kiefer, "Sheriff Joe Arpaio."

7. Arpaio once bragged that he participated in two hundred media events a month; the primary and secondary sources on him are vast. On Judge Snow's 2011 ruling, see *Melendres v. Arpaio*, available online (https://www.aclu.org/legal-document/ortega-melendres-et-al-v-arpaio-et-al-first-amended-complaint?redirect=immigrants-rights/ortega-melendres-et-al-v-arpaio-et-al-first-amended-complaint [accessed Aug. 28, 2017]); and R. Stern, "US District Judge G. Murray Snow." See also "Trump Should Reject Arpaio Pardon," Human Rights Watch, https://www.hrw.org/news/2017/08/23/us-trump-should-reject-arpaio-pardon (accessed Aug. 31, 2017). Many accounts of Arpaio's twenty-four years as Maricopa County sheriff are available in his own words, as well as in legal documents and journalistic accounts. See Arpaio with Sherman, *Joe's Law*; Attwood, *Hard Time*; Hagan, "Long Lawless Road of Joe Arpaio"; Lynch, "(Im)Migrating Penal Excess"; Sellers, "Economic Nomads"; and Ryan Gabrielson, "The Joe Arpaio I Knew," *Pro Publica*, Aug. 15, 2017, https://www.propublica.org/article/the-joe-arpaio-i-knew.

8. See González, "Illegal Migrants across U.S."; and Truax, *Dreamers*, 115.

9. The two young men were a Bolivian man, Benito, who lived in Indiana, and DreamActivist Mohammad Abdollahi, whose parents settled in Ann Arbor from Iran when he was a child. Both are briefly profiled in Truax, *Dreamers*. For more on Abdollahi, see "Gay Immigrant Seeks Asylum with Deportation to Iran Pending," ABC News, July 27, 2010, http://abcnews.go.com/Politics/immigration-gay-iranian-seeks-us-asylum-faces-deportation/story?id=10865471 (accessed Sept. 1, 2015); and "Dream Now Letters," *Citizen Orange*, July 19, 2010, http://www.citizenorange.com/orange/2010/07/dream-now-letters-mohammad-abd.html (accessed Sept. 1, 2015).

10. Truax, *Dreamers*, 119.

11. Douglass, "West India Emancipation."

12. Truax, *Dreamers*, 26.

13. The video the activists released the day of the protest is "Arrested in Phoenix, Undocumented! Unafraid! You Ready?," YouTube, Mar. 20, 2012, https://www

.youtube.com/watch?v=8rLaAyNFSCg. See also Van Le, "Six DREAMers Arrested in Arizona during Anti-Arpaio Protest," *America's Voice*, Mar. 21, 2012, http://americas voice.org/blog/six_dreamers_arrested_in_arizona_during_anti-arpaio_protest/; "Dreamers Arrested at 75th Ave. Phoenix," YouTube, Mar. 21, 2012, https://www .youtube.com/watch?v=rqjmPVua018; and Jackie Sanchez quoted in John Genovese, "Protestors in Custody after Arpaio Protest outside School," *AZCentral*, Mar. 20, 2012, http://www.azcentral.com/community/phoenix/articles/2012/03/20/20120320 arpaio-phoenix-student-protest-abrk.html#ixzz4JOYzpxap. For more on the Community Defense Committees, see "Community Defense Courses," Puente website, http://puenteaz.org/programs/community-defense-course/ (accessed Aug. 1, 2018).

14. Ali quoted in Corrunker, "Coming Out of the Shadows," 160.

15. Yasmin interview by the author. All further quotes from Yasmin in this chapter are from this interview.

16. Yasmin's story is singular but not unique. Thousands of oral histories, blogs, social media posts, articles, plays, books, songs, and exposés have emerged that mirror Yasmin's experience. See for example *Un Encuentro: Theater of and for the Borderlands/Teatro de la Frontera*, The Border Project, The Border Film Project, *The 800 Mile Wall* (2009), and John Burnett's NPR piece "Who is Smuggling Children Across the Border?" Just two of the hundreds of available books include Diaz's *Border Contraband* and Loustaunau and Sánchez-Bane, *Life, Death, and In-Between on the US-Mexico Border*.

17. Documentation of human rights abuses in the borderlands is massive. For representative work, see Staudt, Payan, and Kruszewski, *Human Rights along the US-Mexico Border*; and Lorentzen, *Hidden Lives*.

18. See Rubio-Goldsmith et al., *Migrant Deaths*; and Nevins, *Dying to Live*. See also Marco Williams's film *The Undocumented* and accompanying website, http://theundocumented.com; and *Radiolab's* podcast series on the border, "A Border Trilogy," March/April 2018, https://www.wnycstudios.org/story/border-trilogy-part-1.

19. Barriers prevent undocumented youth from achieving three major milestones of independence—acquiring a driver's license, submitting college applications, and working legally. The circumstances repeat again and again in the accounts of undocumented youth. Elioenai Santos recalled, "Living like that is a real problem. It's a real blow to your self-esteem, because you always feel like you are somehow less. It's awful to always feel like you're inferior. You see your friends driving around, traveling to other countries, while I don't have money to go to school." See Truax, *Dreamers*, 21, 111, 163, 174.

20. Institute for Policy Studies, the Poor People's Campaign, et al., *Souls of Poor Folk*, 29.

21. See Bruce Drake, "Unauthorized Immigrants: How Pew Research Counts Them and What We Know About Them," Pew Research Center, Apr. 17, 2013, http:// www.pewresearch.org/2013/04/17/unauthorized-immigrants-how-pew-research -counts-them-and-what-we-know-about-them/; and Truax, *Dreamers*, 1, 12. The Pew Research Center estimates that 55 million Americans are Latinx and now make up the largest minority group in the US, 17.4 percent. Jens Manuel Krogstad and Mark Hugo Lopez, "Hispanic Population Reaches Record 55 million, But Growth Cools," Pew Research Center, June 25, 2015, http://www.pewresearch.org/fact-tank

/2015/06/25/u-s-hispanic-population-growth-surge-cools/. Despite the fact that only 18 percent of the Latinx community is undocumented, many non-Latinx Americans refer to the entire community as made up of "illegals." Chuang and Roemer, "Beyond the Positive-Negative Paradigm," 1047; Gilberto Mendoza, "States Offering Driver's Licenses to Immigrants," National Conference of State Legislatures, Nov. 30, 2016, http://www.ncsl.org/research/immigration/states-offering-driver-s-licenses-to-immigrants.aspx; "Basic Facts about In-State Tuition," National Immigration Law Center, 1 June 2018, https://www.nilc.org/issues/education/basic-facts-instate/.

22. Chomsky, *Undocumented*, 9–10; Ngai, *Impossible Subjects*, 2–6. As scholar-activist Laura Emiko Soltis notes, the "bootstraps model" of the European immigration experience, where "economic success and assimilation is attributed to . . . work ethic alone," is fundamentally flawed, for it does not account for several key differences. European immigrants were, by and large, never subject to deeply ingrained discriminatory stereotypes of "race, criminality, and notions of inferior citizenship." For non-European immigrants, both the US legal system and American culture invented a range of bigoted labels such as "enslaved African non-citizens, incarcerated partial citizens, separate and unequal citizens, Asians racially ineligible for citizenship, rented Mexican braceros, temporary guest workers, undocumented non-citizens, or simply, 'illegals.'" Such labels always had two fundamental purposes: making immigrants of color "physically exploitable for cheap labor" and reducing them to a status from which they were "politically powerless to change things through voting and other institutionalized means" (Soltis, 21). As the recent Trump phenomenon has once again demonstrated, the charge of real or potential criminality is potent and insidious. It effectively assigns entire ethnic groups to a status of "economic exploitation and political exclusion." Soltis, "From Freedom Schools to Freedom University," 21. Scholarship on racialized immigration before 1965 includes everything from a government official writing a report to the US secretary of labor titled *The Racial Problems Involved in Immigration from Latin America and the West Indies to the United States* (Government Printing Office, 1925), through three or four generations of scholars since. See Shepherd and Penna, *Racism and the Underclass*; Bustamante, Reynolds, and Ojeda, *US–Mexico Relations*; Fitzpatrick, *Nationalism, Racism and the Rule of Law*; and Bebout, *Whiteness on the Border*.

23. Chomsky, *Undocumented*, 15–19.

24. Richard Gonzales, "ACLU Report: Detained Immigrant Children Subjected to Widespread Abuse by Officials," National Public Radio, May 23, 2018, https://www.npr.org/sections/thetwo-way/2018/05/23/613907893/aclu-report-detained-immigrant-children-subjected-to-widespread-abuse-by-officia%20Accessed%2025%20May%202018; "Neglect and Abuse of Unaccompanied Migrant Children by U.S. Customs and Border Enforcement," ACLU, May 2018, https://www.dropbox.com/s/lplnnufj bwcioxn/CBP%20Report%20ACLU_IHRC%205.23%20FINAL.pdf?dl=0 (accessed May 25, 2018).

25. On the sustained anti-immigrant movement, see Chomsky, *Undocumented*; Ngai, *Impossible Subjects*; Paik, *Rightlessness*; and Hernández, *Migra!*; as well as García, *Latino Generation*, 7–9; Iyer, *We Too Sing America*; and Camacho, *Migrant Imaginaries*, especially chaps. 1–5. Hundreds of scholars have examined the history

of anti-immigrant sentiment in the US; for a recent treatment with a list of sources, see Schrag, *Not Fit for Our Society*. Since the election of Donald Trump in 2016, see Vasquez, "New ICE Age"; Antar Davidson on *Democracy Now!*, June 18, 2018, https://www.democracynow.org/2018/6/18/whistleblower_i_quit_my_child_detention; and John Bowden, "North Carolina Governor Recalls National Guard from Border over Family Separation," *The Hill*, June 19, 2018, http://thehill.com/homenews/state-watch/393071-north-carolina-governor-recalls-national-guard-troops-from-border-over.

26. The DREAM Act, most commentators at the time from right to left concluded, failed to pass because the Republican base, mobilized by talk radio, revolted against a compromise bill put forward with bipartisan support. Thomas F. Schaller wrote in *Salon*, "The Wall Street wing of the GOP, which finances the party, wants to keep open the spigot of pliant and cheap Spanish-speaking labor. It finds itself opposed by much of the Main Street wing, which provides millions of crucial primary and general election votes and would like to build a fence along the Mexican border as high as Lou Dobbs' ratings or the pitch of Pat Buchanan's voice. And it's simply impossible for any political party to win if it has to choose between money and votes." See Schaller, "Is Rush Limbaugh Right?," *Salon*, May 23, 2007, http://www.salon.com/2007/05/23/immigration_20/. See also Rachel Weiner, "How Immigration Reform Failed, Over and Over," *Washington Post*, Jan. 30, 2013, https://www.washingtonpost.com/news/the-fix/wp/2013/01/30/how-immigration-reform-failed-over-and-over/; and "Immigration and Paris Hilton," Pew Research Center, Aug. 20, 2007, http://www.journalism.org/2007/08/20/immigration-and-paris-hilton/#1.

27. Elspeth Gould's bibliography on this topic is comprehensive in *Security and Migration in the 21st Century*; for a more recent list of scholarship, see Estavadeordal and Goodman, *21st Century Cooperation*, chaps. 6–8. See also Iyer, *We Too Sing America*; and Camacho, *Migrant Imaginaries*. Weber-Shirk, a recent Phi Beta Kappa graduate of Earlham College's peace and global studies program, adopted her article from her award-winning senior thesis. See "PAGS Student Work," http://www.earlham.edu/peace-and-global-studies/pags-student-work/ (Aug. 2, 2017).

28. Members of the G7 are the US, Great Britain, Japan, Germany, Canada, France, and Italy; for the widening gap, see reference to the OECD study in Anthony Reuben, "Gap between Rich and Poor Keeps Widening," BBC News, http://www.bbc.com/news/business-32824770 (accessed Aug. 23, 2017).

29. Weber-Shirk, "Deviant Citizenship," 593. Joseph Nevins used the term "global apartheid" in reference to the US-Mexico border in *Dying to Live*; the concept evolved in the late 1980s through the work of Titus Alexander, Vandana Shiva, and others and may have first been used by Gernot Kohler in a working paper for the World Order Models Project. Thabo Mbeki, at that time president of South Africa, brought it to a wider audience in 2001 when describing why FIFA awarded Germany the 2006 World Cup over South Africa. Yash Tandon, "What Is Global Apartheid and Why Do We Fight It?," South African Civil Society Information Service, Mar. 11, 2010, http://sacsis.org.za/site/article/442.1. Indigenous scholars have made interventions critiquing the liberal democratic citizen and state for well over a century. For a recent overview of colonial North America, see Woolford, Benvenuto, and Hinton, *Colonial Genocide*; and a case study that moves through the current era,

A. Simpson, *Mohawk Interruptus*. See also A. Simpson, "Consent's Revenge"; Spice, "Interrupting Industrial and Academic Extraction"; and john a. powell, "Opening to the Question of Belonging," *On Being*, May 10, 2018, https://onbeing.org/programs/john-a-powell-opening-to-the-question-of-belonging-may2018/. Marisol de la Cadena notes that the Latin American epistemologies where "the presence of earth-beings" like mountains, animals, plants, and landscapes that have sentience "in social protests invites us to slow down reasoning because it may evince an intriguing moment of epistemic rupture with this theory of politics. Their public emergence contends—to use Rancière's word—with both science and politics; it may house the capacity to upset the locus of enunciation of what 'politics' is about—who can be a politician or what can be considered a political issue, and thus reshuffle the hegemonic antagonisms that for more than 500 years organized the political field." Cadena, "Indigenous Cosmopolitics," 342.

30. Soltis also notes that a Freedom University student action on November 9, 2016, a day after Donald Trump's election, in front of the board of regents, forced the regents to allow students to attend two previously banned schools, Augusta and Georgia State. Soltis, annotation to draft chapter, Sept. 8, 2017, in author's possession; Soltis, "From Freedom Schools to Freedom University," 21. E4FC, an advocacy group for undocumented students, noted in 2016 that only fourteen states have

> passed laws that allow undocumented students to qualify for in-state tuition at the public colleges and universities in their state of residence: California, Connecticut, Illinois, Kansas, Maryland, Nebraska, New Mexico, New York, Oklahoma, Rhode Island, Texas, Utah, Washington, and Wisconsin. To receive the in-state tuition discount, undocumented students must reside in state, attend high school for a specified period (1–4 years) in state, and graduate or receive their GED in state. In addition to allowing students to qualify for in-state tuition, California, Illinois, New Mexico, and Texas provide undocumented students access to financial aid. Arizona, Colorado, Georgia and Indiana have banned undocumented students from receiving in-state tuition. South Carolina was the first state to ban undocumented students outright from attending public colleges and universities, followed by Alabama and Georgia. ("Fact Sheet," E4FC, n.d., http://www.e4fc.org/images/Fact_Sheet.pdf [accessed Aug. 9, 2016]. See also "Fact Sheet," https://jhfc.duke.edu/latinamericauncduke/files/2017/02/Fact-Sheet-for-College-Bound-Undocumented-Students.pdf (accessed May 11, 2019).

31. Soltis, "From Freedom Schools to Freedom University," 21. Soltis is the executive director of Freedom University. See "Faculty and Staff," available online at http://www.freedomuniversitygeorgia.com/faculty-and-staff.html (accessed Aug. 2, 2017). See Berman, "Man behind Trump's Voter-Fraud Obsession."

32. Zack de la Rocha, "Stop Arapaio March," Phoenix, AZ, Feb. 28, 2009, National Day Laborer Organizing Network, http://ndlon.org/en/arts-culture/our-videos/item/37-zack-2009; also available on You Tube, https://www.youtube.com/watch?v=KWF-5laiS8k.

33. Cristina Jimenez, panel, "How to Increase Voter Registration in the South," One Person, One Vote: Learning from the Past, Organizing for the Future conference, Duke University, Sept. 20, 2015, SNCC VRC 2015.

34. Jimenez, "How to Increase Voter Registration in the South."

35. Jimenez, "How to Increase Voter Registration in the South." Josh Bernstein, an SEIU organizer who co-drafted the original DREAM Act in 2001, noted the similarity to SNCC as well: "The only thing I can compare it to is SNCC. It's the same thing . . . young people being the ones to take the reins and be courageous on behalf of what's right, without being limited to a narrow vision of what they want to accomplish. The young people at SNCC changed the world. And I feel that these young people at United We Dream are in that category." Bernstein quoted in Altschuler, "Dreamers' Movement Comes of Age."

36. Jimenez, "How to Increase Voter Registration in the South."

37. Harding, *There Is a River*, 44–45, 67–68, 279; Ortiz, *African American and Latinx History*, 26–27; Isenberg, *White Trash*, chaps. 1–5. Recent scholarship on the Underground Railroad and family reunification includes LaRoche, *Free Black Communities*; Foner, *Gateway to Freedom*; and Frost and Tucker, *Fluid Frontier*.

38. Megan O'Neil, "Cristina Jimenez, Giving Dreamers a Voice," *Chronicle of Philanthropy*, Jan. 5, 2016, https://www.philanthropy.com/article/40-Under-40-Cristina-Jimenez/234730.

39. Cristina Jimenez and Bob Moses developed the idea of making "a little room in the circle" based on the song written by SNCC activist and music scholar Bernice Johnson Reagon, "Room in the Circle," during remarks during the afternoon break, One Person, One Vote: Learning From the Past, Organizing for the Future conference, Duke University, Sept. 20, 2015, SNCC VRC 2015.

40. Bernice Johnson Reagon, "Room in the Circle," *Give Your Hands to Struggle*, Smithsonian Folkways Recording, 1997.

41. Voss and Bloemraad, *Rallying for Immigrant Rights*, chaps. 1, 13; *manifestaciones* in Suro, "Out of the Shadows"; Milkman, Bloom, and Bloom, *LA Model*, esp. Kindle location 4833–84; Altschuler, "Dreamers' Movement Comes of Age." See also Latino Union of Chicago, https://www.latinounion.org/about- (accessed July 2, 2017); Puente Arizona, http://puenteaz.org/about-us/our-history/ (accessed July 2, 2017); NDLON, http://www.ndlon.org/en/about-us (accessed July 2, 2017); and HR 4437, the Sensenbrenner Bill, https://www.congress.gov/bill/109th-congress/house-bill/4437 (accessed Nov. 1, 2018).

42. On the transition to "Undocumented and Unafraid" see Dream Act Portal, "Lounge," https://dreamact.info/forum/forumdisplay.php?f=26 (accessed July 2, 2017), which serves as an online archive of undocumented youth discourse between 2006 and the present; and Anguiano and Chávez, "DREAMers' Discourse," 81–100. Soltis on the formation of Freedom U, annotation to draft chapter, Sept. 9, 2017, in author's possession.

43. On the transition to "undocumented and unafraid," see Wong et al., *Undocumented and Unafraid*. Cynthia quoted in Swerts, "Gaining a Voice," 351.

44. Swerts, 351.

45. *Testimonios*, a genre of oral history coming out of Latin American cultural and intellectual traditions, involves the collaboration of a scholar or journalist with the activist to create a text. It archives the reality of people who would otherwise go "undocumented" in the historical sense, providing a guidepost for listeners or reader both to reflect and potentially to act as well. *Testimonios* from

undocumented youth give them a political voice when they are excluded from formal citizenship or barred from the opportunities, resources, and networks that social movement participants have otherwise drawn on. On *testimonios*, see Latina Feminist Group, *Telling to Live*; and García, *Chicano Generation*. For a sociologist's take on the role of *testimonios* among the Dreamers, see De Genova, "Queer Politics of Migration"; and Swerts, "Gaining a Voice," especially 346–49. Swerts finds that the Immigrant Youth Justice League was the first DREAMer group to experiment with storytelling as a political strategy. See also Ortiz, *African American and Latinx History*, 187: "The oft-ignored role of the citizens of Mexico as carriers of traditions of social democracy to the U.S. needs to be better understood. Mexican migrants to the U.S. hail from a country that abolished slavery long before the U.S., fought off repeated imperial invasions from Europe, and promoted ideals of sharing the nation's wealth on a roughly equal basis."

46. On domestic workers and day laborers, see Fish, *Domestic Workers of the World Unite*; Poo, *Age of Dignity*; Milkman, Bloom, and Bloom, *LA Model*; and Nadasen, *Household Workers Unite* for recent scholarship. See also Grattan, *Populism's Power*, 179; and "National Come Out of the Shadows Day!," *Immigrant Youth Justice League*, posted Feb. 17, 2010. http://www.iyjl.org/national-coming-out-of-the-shadows-day/.

47. Marisa Franco interviewed by Ai-Jen Poo, Nov. 15, 2016, Lenny Letter, https://www.lennyletter.com/story/transforming-pain-into-power. Franco has eloquently and frequently spoken about the slogans of "coming out" as intersectional practice. See a recent example in "Movement Spaces Must Be Sanctuaries," YouTube, https://www.youtube.com/watch?v=OLuOohA5rOY (accessed Aug. 2, 2017). Coming out within the context of an LGBT identity has a long history as well. See D'Emilio and Freedman, *History of Sexuality in America*; Faderman, *Gay Revolution*; and Stein, *Rethinking the Gay and Lesbian Movement*; as well as the direct intersection examined in Pastrana, Battle, and Harris, *Examination of Latinx LGBT Populations*.

48. Soltis, "From Freedom Schools to Freedom University," 32; De Genova, "Queer Politics of Migration." Many other undocumented youth activists have used this photography exhibit strategy. For a recent example, see "I Define Myself: Undocumented and Unafraid Portrait Exhibit," *Immigrant Youth Justice League*, http://www.iyjl.org/i-define-myself-undocumented-unafraid-portrait-exhibit/ (accessed Aug. 14, 2016). Soltis, annotation to draft chapter, Sept. 8, 2017, in the author's possession. On Freedom University, see also Peña, "New Freedom Fights"; Voekel, "Organizing for Freedom"; and Muñoz and Espino, "Freedom to Learn."

49. Soltis, "From Freedom Schools to Freedom University," 32, 41; Grattan, *Populism's Power*, 179–80. The Combahee River Collective Statement, shared publicly first in 1977, emerged from a collective of women who had been in the National Black Feminist Organization. See Jones and Eubanks with Smith, *Ain't Gonna Let Nobody Turn Me Around*, 45–54, 268–88. Audre Lorde's organizing emerges most clearly in her "biomythography" *Zami* and in essays in *Sister Outsider*, as well as De Veaux's biography *Warrior Poet*. On Stonewall, see Duberman, *Stonewall*; and D. Carter, *Stonewall*. On organizing to support people with AIDS, see D. Gould, *Moving Emotions*; B. Roth, *Life and Death of ACT UP/LA*; France, *How to Survive a Plague*; and Carroll, *Mobilizing New York*.

50. Soltis, "From Freedom Schools to Freedom University," 41.

51. Building a grassroots group of youth leaders also held the promise of breaking the school-to-prison pipeline. Grow enough youth leaders, and they will advocate for themselves, demand educations that prepare them for living wage work and full development of their talents, and in the process rebuild the original purpose of John Dewey's public school system: a school-to-society pipeline. In the end, of course, the larger vision that people gathered around was to empower youth to help "bring about comprehensive federal immigration reform." Soltis, "From Freedom Schools to Freedom University," 32, 41. On the importance of such "free spaces," see Boyte and Evans, *Free Spaces*.

52. Paulina Helm-Hernández and Tania Unzueta quoted in Cindy Carcamo, "LGBT Immigrants Taking a More Forceful Stand as Reform Efforts Languish," *Los Angeles Times*, July 11, 2015, http://www.latimes.com/local/california/la-me-lgbt-immigrant-rights-20150711-story.html. For examples of different perspectives on LGBT inclusion, see "FIRM Calls for LGBT Inclusion in Immigration Reform," *Fair Immigration Reform Movement*, Mar. 2, 2010, https://fairimmigration.org/firm-calls-for-lgbt-inclusion-in-immigration-reform/; and Kris Kelkar, "The LGBT Provision: Too Much to Lose," Fair Immigration Reform Movement website, June 25, 2013, https://fairimmigration.org/the-lgbt-provision-too-much-to-lose/. As scholar Walter Nicholls observed in Carcamo's article, immigrants without legal status and members of the LGBT community "both operate in closets and both experience greater empowerment from coming out of the closet and sharing their stories with the public, gaining support."

53. Laura Emiko Soltis, annotations to draft chapter, Sept. 8, 2017, in the author's possession. Paulina Helm-Hernández and Tania Unzueta quoted in Carcamo, "LGBT Immigrants Taking a More Forceful Stand as Reform Efforts Languish." For examples of different perspectives on inclusion of LGBT, see "FIRM Calls for LGBT Inclusion in Immigration Reform"; and Kelkar, "LGBT Provision."

54. Voekel, "Organizing for Freedom," 69. On the Georgia Board of Regents, see Laura Diamond, "Plan Would Allow Some Georgia Colleges to Ban Illegal Immigrants," *Atlanta Journal-Constitution*, Sept. 22, 2010, http://www.ajc.com/news/news/local-govt-politics/plan-would-allow-some-georgia-colleges-to-ban-ille/nQkPY/; and "Georgia Policy," ULead Network, http://uleadnet.org/map/georgia-policy (accessed Aug. 14, 2016); Soltis, annotations to draft chapter, Sept. 9, 2017, in the author's possession; Soltis, "From Freedom Schools to Freedom University." Soltis noted that immigrant activists went out of their way to learn from American history: "They turned to the examples set forth by young people of SNCC: in particular, their establishment of Freedom Schools and their creative tactics of civil disobedience" (20). The 1964 SNCC Freedom School model provided a practical solution, Soltis explained, "a tangible example of how to build alternatives in the face of separate and unequal access to education, how to develop leaders from the grassroots, and how to practice being free in order to bring about the world they know is possible" (23).

55. On Freedom U, see Voekel, "Organizing for Freedom"; and Soltis, "From Freedom Schools to Freedom University," 22–26. Soltis notes that most students have been from Latin America, with one student from Ghana in 2015 and an Indian

student from Kenya in 2016, annotations to draft chapter, Sept. 8, 2017, in the author's possession. On Highlander, some important studies include Horton, *Highlander Folk School*; Adams with Horton, *Unearthing Seeds of Fire*; Schneider, *You Can't Padlock an Idea*; and Horton, Kohl, and Kohl, *Long Haul*. On Latin American popular education, see Freire, *Pedagogy of the Oppressed* and *Pedagogy of Hope*; Motta and Cole, *Education and Social Change in Latin America*; and Kane, *Popular Education*. See Horton and Freire, *We Make the Road By Walking*, for a comparative framework for these traditions.

56. Quoted in Truax, *Dreamers*, 30.

57. Abdollahi quoted in Truax, *Dreamers*, 29; Soltis, "Freedom Schools to Freedom University," 35.

58. Rev. James Lawson, "The DREAM Act Students Have Taught Me New Things about Strategy and Planning," remarks at the Fletcher Summer Institute, *Narco News Bulletin*, July 11, 2012, http://narconews.com/Issue67/article4610.html; Paulina Gonzalez, "The Strategy and Organizing behind the Successful DREAM Act Movement," *Narco News Bulletin*, July 10, 2012, http://narconews.com/print.php3?Article ID=4607&lang=en. On Lawson's central role in training SNCC workers in nonviolence, see Hogan, *Many Minds*, chap. 1. SNCC veterans Hollis Watkins, Courtland Cox, Charlie Cobb, and Bob Moses also attended youth immigrant right conferences in the 2010s, offering insights on nonviolent direct action and community organizing. See Altschuler, "Dreamers' Movement Comes of Age" on Watkins. Moses, Cox, and Cobb were working with me on the SNCC Digital Gateway at the time and so I heard about these conference trainings directly from them.

59. John Genovese, "Anti-Arpaio Protestors Won't Face Deportation," *AZCentral*, Mar. 21, 2016, http://www.azcentral.com/news/articles/2012/03/21/20120321phoenix-police-release-names-protestors-arrested-abrk.html#ixzz4JOegZq5Q. See also "In Mixed Ruling Supreme Court Overturns Part of SB1040, Upholds 'Show Me Your Papers,'" *Democracy Now!*, June 26, 2012, http://www.democracynow.org/2012/6/26/in_mixed_ruling_supreme_court_overturns.

60. Chuang and Roemer, "Beyond the Positive-Negative Paradigm," 1047.

61. Acuña, Woodson, and Pharr, "Race, the Election and Regenerating Our Democracy."

62. Weber-Shirk, "Deviant Citizenship," 583.

63. Mateo, "Fight to Keep Families Together."

64. Still, investors such as the Bill and Melinda Gates Foundation profit from investing in the GEO Group. Alex Altman, "Prison Hunger Strike Puts Spotlight on Immigration," *Time*, Mar. 17, 2014, http://time.com/27663/prison-hunger-strike-spotlights-on-immigration-detention/; Mike Carter, "Hunger Strike at Tacoma Immigration Detention Center Grows to 750," *Seattle Times*, Apr. 13, 2017, http://www.seattletimes.com/seattle-news/hunger-strike-at-tacoma-immigration-detention-center-growing-activist-says/; Aviva Shen, "Private Prisons Spent $45 Million on Lobbying, Rake in $5.1 Billion for Immigrant Detention Alone," *Think Progress*, Aug. 3, 2012, https://thinkprogress.org/private-prisons-spend-45-million-on-lobbying-rake-in-5-1-billion-for-immigrant-detention-alone-b9ef073758be/; Jomo, "Fighting Obama's Immigration Policies." For scholarship on privatization, see for example Farmar, *Delta Prisons*; D. Walker, *Penology for Profit*; Shichor, *Punishment for Profit*;

Michaels, *Constitutional Coup*; Brooke-Eisen, *Inside Private Prisons*; and Coyle, Campbell, and Neufeld, *Capitalist Punishment*.

65. Invocations of the collapse of the Roman Empire are so commonplace as to be cliché. Jeet Heer's 2018 article in the *New Republic* recaps some of the more visible ones from across the political spectrum: "Are We Witnessing the Fall of the American Empire?," *New Republic*, Mar. 7, 2018, https://newrepublic.com/article/147319/witnessing-fall-american-empire. The "New Jim Crow" is from Michelle Alexander's trailblazing 2010 book. On the literary dystopists, see Stuart McMillen, "Amusing Ourselves to Death: Huxley v. Orwell," *High Existence*, http://highexistence.com/amusing-ourselves-to-death-huxley-vs-orwell/ (accessed May 24, 2018); and Charles McGrath, "Which Dystopian Novel Got It Right?," *New York Times*, Feb. 13, 2017, https://www.nytimes.com/2017/02/13/books/review/which-dystopian-novel-got-it-right-orwells-1984-or-huxleys-brave-new-world.html%20Accessed%2024%20May%202018.

66. Voekel, "Organizing for Freedom," 71.

67. See for example Matuz, "Arizona Dreamers Five Years Later."

68. "Political Power," Movement for Black Lives, Aug. 1, 2016, https://policy.m4bl.org/political-power/. On the centuries-long pattern, see B. Wagner, *Disturbing the Peace*; Singh, *Race and America's Long War*; and Horne, *Apocalypse of Settler Colonialism*.

69. Ille the gal, "I Am a Sovereign Migrant," Dreamers Adrift website, Aug. 21, 2012, http://dreamersadrift.com/featured1/i-am-a-sovereign-migrant; and unknown author, "Words as Borders, Words as Actions, Actions as Processes," n.d., https://static1.squarespace.com/static/526fcfdae4b0cc2a07040984/t/52957764e4b0bef66fc9dc0e/1385527140165/Words+as+Borders%2C+Words+as+Actions%2C+Actions+as+Process.pdf (accessed Aug. 2, 2017). See also Wang's essay, "Against Innocence"; and Park, "Money, Mortgages and the Conquest of America."

70. Greg Bluestein, "Federal Government Asks Appeals Court to Stop Immigration Law," Associated Press via the *Gadsden (AL) Times*, Oct. 7, 2011, http://www.gadsdentimes.com/article/20111007/wire/111009806?p=1&tc=pg. Fernanda and Cesar quoted in Truax, *Dreamers*, 49–51. See also Richard Fausset, "13 Arrested in Protest against Alabama's Immigration Law," *Los Angeles Times*, Nov. 16, 2011, http://articles.latimes.com/2011/nov/16/nation/la-na-alabama-immigration-20111116.

71. Cullors and Franco quoted in Collier Meyerson, "Meet the New Social Change Coalition: The Majority," *The Nation*, Mar. 31, 2017, https://www.thenation.com/article/black-lives-matter-just-launched-a-major-campaign-for-the-age-of-trump/.

72. Rogers, "Obama Has Deported More Immigrants."

73. Jimenez, "How to Increase Voter Registration in the South."

74. Jimenez, "How to Increase Voter Registration in the South"; Vasquez, "How Anti-blackness Thrives in Latinx Communities."

75. Hermelinda Cortés, "Con Toda La Fuerza de Mijente," *Medium*, Dec. 14, 2015, https://medium.com/@hermelindacortes/con-toda-la-fuerza-de-mijente-fedc91e00365#.64or372wv. See also "Give Out Day" where Cortés summarizes SONG's more recent work, 2015, https://www.giveoutday.org/c/GO/a/southernersonnewground/p/Hermelinda/ (accessed July 2, 2016).

76. Cortés, "Con Toda La Fuerza de Mijente."

77. "Lánzate" on Mijente website, http://mijente.net/lanzate/ (accessed July 12, 2016).

78. Amanda Sakuma, "Deportation Crackdown Rounds Up 121 Immigrant Women and Children," MSNBC, Jan. 4, 2016, http://www.notonemoredeportation.com/2016/02/08/georgia-condemns-ice-raids/; "Georgia Condemns ICE Raids," #Not1More, Feb. 8, 2016. http://www.notonemoredeportation.com/2016/02/08/georgia-condemns-ice-raids/.

79. Voekel, "Organizing for Freedom," 75; Soltis, annotations to draft chapter, Sept. 8, 2017, in author's possession; press release, "Students Protest Georgia's Admissions Ban on Undocumented Students," *Freedom University Georgia*, http://www.freedomuniversitygeorgia.com/press.html (accessed Sept. 9, 2017); "SNCC Freedom Singers Join Freedom University Singers," YouTube, Feb. 1, 2016, https://youtube/P4ewuF3hh1A.

80. National Immigrant Youth Alliance, Facebook page, https://www.facebook.com/NationalImmigrantYouthAlliance/info?tab=page_info (accessed Jan. 11, 2016).

81. Rosario Lopez quoted in Jomo, "Fighting Obama's Immigration Policies."

82. Weber-Shirk, "Deviant Citizenship," 594; Rosario Lopez quoted in Jomo, "Fighting Obama's Immigration Policies."

83. Vasquez, "New ICE Age." Trump issued Executive Order 13767 on the fifth day of his presidency, calling for a border wall and swift deportation of undocumented people living in the US. "Executive Order: Border Security and Immigration Enforcement Improvements," WhiteHouse.gov, Jan. 25, 2017, https://www.whitehouse.gov/presidential-actions/executive-order-border-security-immigration-enforcement-improvements/. United We Dream's focus, for example, had four areas: (1) achieving policy protection for immigrations, (2) defending against deportation, (3) education access, and (4) justice and liberation for LGBTQ immigrants. Trump's marshalling of tools, financial resources, and rhetorical support for deportation meant that those in the immigrant rights movement had to by necessity devote more resources to defending against deportation. See "The United We Dream Way," United We Dream, https://unitedwedream.org/our-work/ (accessed June 2, 2018).

CHAPTER FIVE

1. To encompass the relative fluidity of identity, I use Gyan Pandey's eloquent phrase "identities we inherit and inhabit." It encapsulates the complex interplay between what we experience (internal identities) and what is imposed on us by others, as well as how these change over time. See Pandey, "Politics and Democracy in Our Time."

2. On Black citizens and police, hundreds of books have been published since the end of World War II. For a vital set of recent studies, see B. Wagner, *Disturbing the Peace*; J. Vargas, *Catching Hell*; Eterno and Silverman, *New York City Police Department*; E. Hinton, *From the War on Poverty to the War on Crime*; Vitale, *End of Policing*; Felkor-Kantor, "Liberal Law and Order"; Schrader, *Badges without Borders*; A. J. Davis, *Policing the Black Man*; and Ransby, *Making All Black Lives Matter*. See also Paul Hirschfeld, "Why Do American Cops Kill So Many Compared to

European Cops?," *The Conversation*, Nov. 25, 2015, http://theconversation.com/why-do-american-cops-kill-so-many-compared-to-european-cops-49696.

3. Young interview by the author. The history of police departments and their interactions with African American communities is vast; hundreds of studies, thousands of newspaper articles, and hundreds of thousands of affidavits document this history. In addition to the note above, see for example Jill Nelson, *Police Brutality*; Holmes and Smith, *Race and Police Brutality*; Sugrue, *Origins of the Urban Crisis*; Balko, *Rise of the Warrior Cop*; and Parenti, *Lockdown America*. Recently, Kimberlé Crenshaw and others have brought forward a policy brief on the experiences of black women with police brutality; see African American Policy Forum, "Say Her Name"; and Ritchie, *Invisible No More*. Scholarship on police training in the US includes Amnesty International USA, *Unmatched Power*; Morrison and Garner, "Latitude in Deadly Force Training"; American Civil Liberties Union, *War Comes Home*; M. Davis, "Fortress Los Angeles"; and Kraska, *Militarizing the American Criminal Justice System*.

4. Young interview by the author.

5. Tupac Shakur interview by Davey D, 1991, Davey D's Hip Hop Corner, http://www.daveyd.com/pacinterview.html (accessed Feb. 2, 2016). On policing cultures in other parts of the world, see for instance He and Das, *Policing in Finland*; Das, *Policing in Canada*; Palmiotto and Unnithan, *Policing and Society*; Nalla and Newman, *Community Policing*; and Klockars, Ivkovic, and Haberfeld, *Contours of Police Integrity*.

6. See for example Khan-Cullors and Bandele, *When They Call You a Terrorist*, 158–65, 170–72, 194–97. On misogynoir, see Moya Bailey, "They Aren't Talking About Me," Crunk Feminist Collective, Mar. 14, 2010, http://www.crunkfeministcollective.com/2010/03/14/they-arent-talking-about-me/; and Kesiena Boom, "4 Tired Tropes That Perfectly Explain What Misogynoir Is—and How You Can Stop It," Everyday Feminism, Aug. 3, 2015, https://everydayfeminism.com/2015/08/4-tired-tropes-misogynoir/.

7. "Yes, U.S. Locks Up at a Higher Rate Than Any Other Country," *Washington Post*, July 7, 2015, https://www.washingtonpost.com/news/fact-checker/wp/2015/07/07/yes-u-s-locks-people-up-at-a-higher-rate-than-any-other-country/?utm_term=.03b8d445c2ca. Recent scholarship on US rates of incarceration include not only the field-altering Michelle Alexander's *New Jim Crow* but also C. Graham, *Happiness for All?*; Murakawa, *First Civil Right*; Forman, *Locking Up Our Own*; and E. Hinton, *From the War on Poverty to the War on Crime*. See also "Ending Mass Incarceration: Charting a New Justice Reinvestment," The Sentencing Project, http://sentencingproject.org/wp-content/uploads/2015/12/Ending-Mass-Incarceration-Charting-a-New-Justice-Reinvestment.pdf (accessed May 4, 2018).

8. Veronica Toney, "Jesse Williams Gave One of the Most Memorable Speeches in Award Show History," *Washington Post*, June 27, 2016, https://www.washingtonpost.com/news/arts-and-entertainment/wp/2016/06/27/jesse-williams-gave-one-of-the-most-memorable-speeches-in-award-show-history-full-transcript/.

9. Melina Abdullah quoted in Aron, "These Savvy Women."

10. The transcript of George Zimmerman's 911 call can be found in multiple places, with and without annotation. For example, without annotation, https://www

.documentcloud.org/documents/326700-full-transcript-zimmerman.html (accessed Sept. 1, 2017); and with annotation, https://genius.com/1982070 (accessed Sept. 1, 2017).

11. James Baldwin, "A Letter to My Nephew," *The Progressive*, Dec. 1, 1962, https://progressive.org/magazine/letter-nephew/.

12. Audra D. S. Burch, Evan Benn, and David Ovalle, "George Zimmerman Not Guilty in Murder of Trayvon Martin," *Miami Herald*, July 13, 2017, http://www.miamiherald.com/news/state/florida/trayvon-martin/article1953237.html; Lizette Alvarez and Cara Buckley, "Zimmerman Is Acquitted in Trayvon Martin Killing," *New York Times*, July 13, 2013, http://www.nytimes.com/2013/07/14/us/george-zimmerman-verdict-trayvon-martin.html?mcubz=0.

13. Emanuella Grinberg, "Anger, Sadness, but Little 'Surprise' over Zimmerman Verdict," CNN, July 14, 2013, https://www.cnn.com/2013/07/13/justice/zimmerman-verdict-reax/index.html. On Emmett Till, see Tyson, *Blood of Emmett Till*. As BYP100 leader Charlene Carruthers noted, there is debate on whether the M4BL era started with the Jena Six, Troy Davis, Trayvon Martin, or Michael Brown in Ferguson. Carruthers, *Unapologetic*, Kindle location 474.

14. Political philosopher Jill Stauffer notes that moments like the stunning impact of the Zimmerman verdict can shift people's sense of self. Speaking of Susan Brinson, a woman raped and left for dead, Stauffer observed, "Extreme violence delivered a message to her: that her self's own sovereignty remains intact only as long as others observe its boundaries." Stauffer, *Ethical Loneliness*, 28. This was a conception of self different from the Western autonomous self. It was a recognition of the limits of sovereignty, that individual autonomy had to be under mutual agreement. This massive conceptual shift is hard to recognize as a reality within the Western jurisprudence model.

15. Bill Quigley and editorial staff, "Dream Defenders Continue to Take Over Florida State Capitol," *African Globe*, Aug. 11, 2013, http://www.africanglobe.net/headlines/dream-defenders-continue-florida-state-capitol/.

16. Bill Quigley and editorial staff, "Dream Defenders Continue to Take Over Florida State Capitol"; Brittany Jones interviewing Jamaya Peeples, ABC WTXL-TV, available on YouTube, https://www.youtube.com/watch?v=6aHolXJ5-s8 (accessed July 5, 2016).

17. Chabeli Herrera, "Who Are the Dream Defenders?," WUFT-FM, Oct. 13, 2013, https://www.wuft.org/news/2013/10/15/who-are-the-dream-defenders/. The name came from an unidentified woman on a conference call soon after the Zimmerman verdict. Herrera reported that Dream Defender Ahmad Abuznaid recalled of an early conference call that an unidentified woman piped up in the discussion about a name for the group: "She said, 'You all are defending the dream. You should call yourselves the dream defenders,' and we all really liked that."

18. Recent scholarship on the school-to-prison pipeline includes Okilwa, Khalifa, and Briscoe, *School to Prison Pipeline*; Heitzeg, *School-to-Prison Pipeline*; Annamma, *Pedagogy of Pathologization*; Love, *We Want to Do More Than Survive*; and Black, *Ending Zero Tolerance*. Supporters claimed "stand your ground" laws supported self-defense in one's own home—yet when women of color used weapons to defend themselves, they were continually denied its protections. See for example the

Marissa Alexander case, "Another Florida Case Puts Crosshairs on 'Stand Your Ground,'" NPR, Feb. 1, 2015, https://www.npr.org/2015/02/01/383121919/another-florida-case-puts-crosshairs-on-stand-your-ground.

19. Many Dream Defenders identify as African American, yet key members identify as mixed, Latinx, Arab American, and a host of other ethnic or racial identities. On incarceration rates for youth of color across the board, see Rios, *Punished*; Fader, *Falling Back*; Hattery and Smith, *Policing Black Bodies*; and Meiners and Winn, *Education and Incarceration*.

20. Bill Quigley and editorial staff, "Dream Defenders Continue to Take Over Florida State Capitol"; Herrera, "Who Are the Dream Defenders?"; Kathleen McGrory, "Dream Defenders: 'We Will Stay until Stand Your Ground Is Repealed,'" *Tampa Bay Times*, July 23, 2013, http://www.tampabay.com/news/politics/gubernatorial/dream-defenders-well-stay-in-florida-capitol-until-stand-your-ground-law/2132860.

21. McGrory, "Dream Defenders."

22. Lucky Thomas, n.d. [July 2013], YouTube, https://www.youtube.com/watch?v=2LiTOoWgQCY (accessed July 6, 2016). There are many other examples of young African American women leading out. Melanie Andrade and Ciara Thomas gave powerful testimony at a press conference during the first week of the sit-in that can be seen here: "Dream Defenders Call Special Session in Florida," YouTube, https://www.youtube.com/watch?v=7rGwo5TVwUk (accessed July 6, 2016).

23. Lucky Thomas, n.d. [July 2013], YouTube.

24. Bill Quigley and editorial staff, "Dream Defenders Continue to Take Over Florida State Capitol."

25. Kathleen McGrory, "Dream Defenders End Sit-In Protest at Capitol in Tallahassee," *Miami Herald*, Aug. 15, 2013, http://www.miamiherald.com/news/state/article1954155.html.

26. Phillip Agnew, speaking at Howard University, "Dream Defenders March on Washington," Aug. 28, 2013, available on YouTube, https://www.youtube.com/watch?v=newg8QAcG7U. This is the source of the quotes in three paragraphs. As scholar Keeanga-Yamahtta Taylor noted, "The Black political establishment, led by President Barack Obama, had shown over and over again that it was not capable of the most basic task: keeping Black children alive. The young people would have to do it themselves." Taylor, *From #BlackLivesMatter to Black Liberation*, Kindle location 3137–39.

27. Agnew changed his name to Umi Selah after a dream on the eve of his thirtieth birthday, June 22, 2015. He talked about the name change at the Center for Constitutional Rights, "Red Talks," Summer 2015, available on YouTube, https://www.youtube.com/watch?v=bu3odVpR5kA (accessed July 4, 2016). Subsequently, he returned to using Phillip Agnew.

28. For the video responses linked to #OurMarch, see the Dream Defenders YouTube playlist, available at https://www.youtube.com/playlist?list=PLSWpzHFvURMbTUfrw_eGCsCRVf6F3RGSA (accessed Jan. 19, 2015).

29. Garza, "HerStory of the #BlackLivesMatter Movement"; Aron, "These Savvy Women"; Khan-Cullors and Bandele, *When They Call You a Terrorist*, 179–80, 196–99.

30. Woodard Henderson, "Grassroots Organizing"; also available online at https://vimeo.com/270135809 (accessed Sept. 2, 2018). See also Khan-Cullors and Bandele, *When They Call You a Terrorist*, 167.

31. Garza, "HerStory of the #BlackLivesMatter Movement"; Alicia Garza, panel, "How to Increase Voter Registration in the South," SNCC VRC 2015; Khan-Cullors and Bandele, *When They Call You a Terrorist*, 180. Jason Buel's powerful scholarship on the way the Black Lives Matter hashtag works is cited here from chapter 2, "Black Lives Matter: Data Power and Evidentiary Flows," in his dissertation, "Whose Screen?"

32. Khan-Cullors lays out the larger "guiding principles" of their early work in her and Bandele's *When They Call You a Terrorist*, 199–203.

33. Kim TallBear, "Badass (Indigenous) Women Caretake Relations: #NoDAPL, #IdleNoMore, #BlackLivesMatter," Hot Spots, *Fieldsights*, Dec. 22, 2016, https://culanth.org/fieldsights/badass-indigenous-women-caretake-relations-no-dapl-idle-no-more-black-lives-matter.

34. Cullors quoted in Aron, "These Savvy Women"; Khan-Cullors and Bandele, *When They Call You a Terrorist*, 180–81.

35. Cullors quoted in Aron, "These Savvy Women." See also C. Anderson, "Politics of Respectability." Evelyn Brooks Higginbotham's 1993 book, *Righteous Discontent: The Women's Movement in the Black Church, 1880–1920*, popularized the concept of the "politics of respectability," and she updated and clarified the concept in the #BLM era in a conversation with For Harriet website's founder and editor in chief, Kimberly Foster, in 2015, http://www.forharriet.com/2015/10/wrestling-with-respectability-in-age-of.html#axzz4ohk14Tln (accessed Aug. 2, 2017). For recent scholarship on the politics of respectability, see Cooper, *Beyond Respectability*. See also Randall Kennedy, "Lifting as We Climb: A Progressive Defense of Respectability Politics," *Harper's*, Oct. 2015, https://harpers.org/archive/2015/10/lifting-as-we-climb/.

36. Khan-Cullors and Bandele, *When They Call You a Terrorist*, 199.

37. As journalist Hillel Aron observed, "In a nation where black women are still stuck at the bottom of the power structure, Black Lives Matter is the only major national protest movement to be led by them in modern times." Garza, "HerStory of the #BlackLivesMatter Movement"; Aron, "These Savvy Women." Ransby, *Making All Black Lives Matter*, Kindle location 80–84: "The movement is politically and ideologically grounded in the US-based Black feminist tradition, a tradition that embraces an intersectional analysis while insisting on the interlocking and interconnected nature of different systems of oppression; advocates the importance of women's group–centered leadership; supports LGBTQIA issues; and seeks to center the most marginalized and vulnerable members of the Black community in terms of the language and priorities of the movement."

38. Ransby traced it back to Sojourner Truth's "Ain't I a Woman" speech in 1851 to the Women's Convention in Akron, Ohio, and to Anna Julia Cooper's *A Voice from the South* (1892) and its 1990 republication, edited by Mary Helen Washington (Ransby, *Making All Black Lives Matter*, Kindle location 2593). The Combahee River Collective statement is likely the first use of "identity politics" in the current historical era. Combahee River Collective, *Combahee River Collective Statement*. See Jones

and Eubanks with Smith, *Ain't Gonna Let Nobody Turn Me Around*, especially chap. 3; and Moraga and Anzaldúa, *This Bridge Called My Back*. See Springer, *Living for the Revolution*, especially chaps. 1 and 2. On the impact of black feminist lesbian organizers in the 1970s through the 1990s, see Cathy Cohen, "Punks, Bulldaggers, and Welfare Queens Symposium." See also Taylor, *How We Get Free*; Crenshaw, "Mapping the Margins"; and Collins, *Black Feminist Thought*.

39. It took education and organizing work to train media people to see the work that Garza, Cullors, and Tometi did at the center. In the first year of the movement, "it [took] a long time for us to occur to most reporters in the mainstream," Khan-Cullors reflected. "Living in patriarchy means that the default inclination is to center men and their voices, not women and their work." Small wonder, then, as she noted, that the first time all three women told their story in a national publication, it was in *Essence* (Khan-Cullors and Bandele, *When They Call You a Terrorist*, 219–20). The *Essence* issue is Jan. 5, 2015, http://www.essence.com/2015/01/06/historic-essence-cover-and-path-forward. On using a queer black feminist lens, see also Carruthers, *Unapologetic*, Kindle location 321:

> As I define it, the Black queer feminist (BQF) lens is a political praxis (practice and theory) based in Black feminist and LGBTQ traditions and knowledge, through which people and groups see to bring their full selves into the process of dismantling all systems of oppression. By using this lens, we are aided in creating alternatives of self-governance and self-determination, and by using it we can more effectively prioritize problems and methods that center historically marginalized people in our communities. It is an aspiration and liberatory politic that Black folks must take up for the sake of our collective liberation and acts on the basic notion that none of us will be free unless all of us are free.

40. Mwende "FreeQuency" Katwiwa quoted in Bentley, "Unapologetically Black."
41. BLM uses the term "unapologetically Black" as one of ten founding principles. Information on the Black Youth Project can be found at http://blackyouthproject.com/about-us/history/ (accessed Jan. 19, 2016); See also Carruthers in Adrienne Samuels Gibbs, "Charlene Carruthers: The Leader of Unapologetically Black Activism," *Good.Is*, Mar. 15, 2016, https://www.good.is/features/issue-36-charlene-carruthers; Maria Varela, "Critical Oral History: Black Power Culture and Education," July 11, 2011, SNCC COH 2016. The critical oral history sessions conducted in July 2016 on the origins of black power included perspectives from many SNCC people present in the early years of black power in the organization. Carruthers, *Unapologetic*, Kindle location 148–50; Ransby, *Making All Black Lives Matter*, Kindle location 1562–90.
42. Garza, panel, "How to Increase Voter Registration in the South"; Povi-Tamu Bryant quoted in Aron, "These Savvy Women." See also Ciara Taylor: "Dream Defenders served as a platform for rebellion for many oppressed people. Different nationalities, different genders, different sexual orientations. Dream Defenders has allowed people to express their frustrations with the status quo, with society as it is, and enable us and empower us to insert our vision of the society that we want to see, that we want to live in." "The Womyn's Faction," Dream Defenders, http://www.dreamdefenders.org/womyns_faction (accessed July 3, 2016).

43. Clare Foran, "A Year of Black Lives Matter," *The Atlantic*, Dec. 31, 2015, https://www.theatlantic.com/politics/archive/2015/12/black-lives-matter/421839/; Elizabeth Day, "#BlackLivesMatter: The Birth of a New Civil Rights Movement," *The Guardian*, July 13, 2015, https://www.theguardian.com/world/2015/jul/19/blacklivesmatter-birth-civil-rights-movement; Janell Ross and Wesley Lowery, "Black Lives Matter Shifts from Protest to Policy under Trump," *Chicago Tribune*, May 4, 2017, http://www.chicagotribune.com/news/nationworld/ct-black-lives-matter-trump-20170504-story.html; Lowery, *They Can't Kill Us All*, 221–33.

44. On policing cultures in other parts of the world, see for instance Whitmore, *Harsh Justice*; He and Das, *Policing in Finland*; Das, *Policing in Canada*; and Palmiotto and Unnithan, *Policing and Society*.

45. Bynes quoted in Julie Bosman and Joseph Goldstein, "Timeline for a Body: 4 Hours in the Middle of a Ferguson Street," *New York Times*, Aug. 23, 2014, http://www.nytimes.com/2014/08/24/us/michael-brown-a-bodys-timeline-4-hours-on-a-ferguson-street.html?_r=0.

46. On Ferguson police as debt collectors, see W. Johnson, "Ferguson's Fortune 500 Company"; and Murch, "Paying for Punishment." On the connection to lynching images, see Hasan Kwame Jeffries, "Session IV," We Who Believe in Freedom symposium, Ohio State University, Columbus, June 2, 2018, notes in the author's possession; and Wells, "Lynch Law in America."

47. Frances Nobles, "As White Nationalists in Charlottesville Fired, Police 'Never Moved,'" *New York Times*, Aug. 25, 2017, https://www.nytimes.com/2017/08/25/us/charlottesville-protest-police.html; Ned Oliver and Graham Moomaw, "Charlottesville Review: Faulty Planning, Passive Police Led to 'Disastrous Results' at Aug. 12 Rally," *Richmond Times-Dispatch*, Dec. 1, 2017, https://www.richmond.com/news/virginia/charlottesville-review-faulty-planning-passive-police-led-to-disastrous-results/article_90234a84-9cc2-59f4-bb6f-9dfb158cf154.html. An independent report commissioned by the city of Charlottesville and carried out by Hunton and Williams is available online: http://www.charlottesville.org/home/showdocument?id=59615 (accessed Jan. 12, 2018). The state task force report is available online: https://pshs.virginia.gov/media/9737/task-force-on-public-safety-preparedness-and-response-to-civil-unrest-final-report.pdf (accessed Jan. 12, 2018). Both reports were released to the public in December 2017.

48. See also Johnetta (Netta) Elzie in Grant, *Stay Woke*. Elizabeth Hinton's recent history of the militarization of the police beginning with the Johnson administration details how such policies began and expanded. Hinton, *From the War on Poverty to the War on Crime*. On Birmingham, hundreds of accounts tell the tale. See McWhorter, *Carry Me Home*, 416–18. For Tulsa, see Ellsworth, *Death in a Promised Land*, 45–70. On New York, see M. Johnson, *Street Justice*, 60.

49. Many such critiques from within the movement have surfaced since Ferguson. For a brief overview, see Janet Mock, "Vested Interests: Why DeRay Mckesson Matters," *The Advocate*, Feb. 25, 2016, https://www.advocate.com/current-issue/2016/2/25/janet-mock-why-deray-mckesson-matters; Darren Sands, "The Success and Controversy of #CampaignZero," BuzzFeed, Sept. 13, 2015, https://www.buzzfeed.com/darrensands/the-success-and-controversy-of-campaignzero-and-its-successf?utm_term=.uf83PRpo5#.edMdxY1be; and Ransby, *Making All Black Lives Matter*, Kindle location 1645–47.

50. #EricGarner, the hashtag protesting the killing of the New York City father by the NYPD in July 2014, was appended to about 4.3 million tweets in the study period, while #ferguson showed up in 21.6 million tweets and #michaelbrown/#mikebrown in about 9.4 million. See Freelon, McIlwain, and Clark, "Beyond the Hashtags."

51. Khan-Cullors and Bandele, *When They Call You a Terrorist*, 214. See also Lowery, *They Can't Kill Us All*, chap. 1.

52. Eric Garner's death brought this to high visibility in July 2014, and then Michael Brown was shot less than a month later—by white officer Darren Wilson. Again, little was left to interpretation about the police officers' views of black men. Wilson, himself a muscular six-foot-four and 210 pounds, told the grand jury later that fall, "When I grabbed [Michael Brown] the only way I can describe it is I felt like a 5-year-old holding onto Hulk Hogan." Here it was again: the image of the Black brute, deeply inscribed in the psyche of millions of white Americans. Brown ran away when officer Wilson pulled the gun and started shooting. Hearing shots, Brown stopped and looked back. Wilson at that point shot the teenager dead. Why? Because Brown, in Wilson's memorable words, "had the most aggressive face. That's the only way I can describe it, it looks like a demon, that's how angry he looked." "It's the fear that's most striking," journalist Jamelle Bouie wrote after Wilson's testimony became public. "Wilson was trained, armed, and empowered with the force of law." Wilson was big, and he was strong. He could have de-escalated at almost any point by calling for backup, or at least removing himself from physical contact with Brown. Yet what he said was that he was "too gripped with terror to do anything but shoot." Jonathon Sizemore, "Eric Garner's Death: No Justice, No Peace," *City Land*, Mar. 16, 2017, http://www.citylandnyc.org/eric-garner-death-no-justice-no-peace/; Gene Denby, "What We See in the Eric Garner Video and What We Don't," *Code Switch*, NPR, July 29, 2014, http://www.npr.org/sections/codeswitch/2014/07/29/335847224/what-we-see-in-the-eric-garner-video-and-what-we-dont; Bennett Gershman and Joel Cohen, "This Case Cries Out for Disclosure," *Slate*, Dec. 8, 2014, http://www.slate.com/articles/news_and_politics/jurisprudence/2014/12/daniel_pantaleo_staten_island_grand_jury_why_did_it_refuse_to_indict_eric.html; Evan Horowitz, "An Interpretation of the Grand Jury's Decision on Eric Garner's Death," *Boston Globe*, Dec. 4, 2014, https://www.bostonglobe.com/metro/2014/12/04/understanding-eric-garner-death-and-grand-jury-decision/s9uQPMvcKPD2mAmFy2ln9J/story.html. Darren Wilson's testimony was posted by Zeke Miller on Scribd, https://www.scribd.com/document/248132491/Darren-Wilson-testimony (accessed July 2, 2016). Jamelle Bouie, "Michael Brown Wasn't a Superhero Demon," *Slate*, Nov. 26, 2014, http://www.slate.com/articles/news_and_politics/politics/2014/11/darren_wilson_s_racial_portrayal_of_michael_brown_as_a_superhuman_demon.html. Stanford psychologist Jennifer Eberhardt's recent work on implicit bias in law enforcement can be found here: http://web.stanford.edu/~eberhard/videos-presentations.html (accessed July 1, 2016). Here must be noted the long history of visual stereotypes of Black and brown men, women, and children. See for example Shah, "Between 'Oriental Depravity' and 'Natural Degenerates'"; Hawkins, "Savage Visions"; Campt, *Image Matters*; hooks, *Black Looks*; and Bederman, *Manliness and Civilization*.

53. Taylor, *From #BlackLivesMatter to Black Liberation*, Kindle location 2707–10, 3243.

54. Taylor, Kindle locations 2710, 3243.

55. Wesley Lowery's case was particularly instructive. See Lowery, *They Can't Kill Us All*. Even though reporters of color seemed singled out, reporters of all backgrounds, including those from outside the country, documented unprofessional treatment. See Abby Phillip, "Police Arrest and Threaten More Journalists," *Washington Post*, Aug. 14, 2014, https://www.washingtonpost.com/news/post-nation/wp/2014/08/18/police-in-ferguson-arrest-and-threaten-more-journalists/?utm_term=.117d73d9cd8e.

56. This is nearly identical to the dynamics of the Polish solidarity movement, where "the working class in Gdansk took to the streets in October [1956] in an undisciplined expression of emotion that had been too long bottled up. 'Out with the Russians' was a street song of release and splendor, but it scarcely substituted as a working-class program for liberation from the party-state." It would be another twenty-five years before the Poles created enough bottom-up organizations to topple the Soviet satellite state. Goodwyn, *Breaking the Barrier*, 104. The intersection between organizers in the Occupy Wall Street and BLM movements is a fascinating and important area for future research. See Taylor, *From #BlackLivesMatter to Black Liberation*, Kindle locations 3030–32, 3056: for her, the Occupy movement worked to "popularize economic and class inequality in the United States by demonstrating against corporate greed, fraud, and corruption throughout the finance industry," and "it also helped to make connections between those issues and racism."

57. Starsky Wilson, "Politics of Jesus."

58. Wilson, "Politics of Jesus"; W. Johnson, "Ferguson's Fortune 500 Company"; Murch, "Paying for Punishment." See also Taylor, *From #BlackLivesMatter to Black Liberation*, Kindle location 2641. Khan-Cullors and Bandele, *When They Call You a Terrorist*, 210.

59. Umi Selah (Phillip Agnew), Center for Constitutional Rights, "Red Talks"; Khan-Cullors and Bandele, *When They Call You a Terrorist*, 210.

60. Phillip Agnew (Umi Selah) interviewed by Audie Cornish, *All Things Considered*, Dec. 9, 2014, NPR, http://www.npr.org/2014/12/09/369667288/nationwide-protests-are-decentralized-but-coordinated. Selah later noted that Dream Defenders and BLM are distinct and have different priorities, SNCC VRC 2015.

61. Ransby, *Making All Black Lives Matter*, Kindle location 1637. See Grubbs, *Cry from the Cotton*; Kelley, *Hammer and Hoe*; and Honey, *Sharecroppers Troubadour*. On the Indian freedom movement, see Slate, *Colored Cosmopolitanism*; Chandra et al., *India's Struggle for Independence*; and Ghosh, *Gentlemanly Terrorists*. In Poland, "[Walesa] had learned over the years . . . that the key to solidarity was communications. Uncertainty and weakening resolve appeared when rumors appeared, and rumors came when people did not know what was happening." Goodwyn, *Breaking the Barrier*, 135, 160. On SNCC, see Payne, *I've Got the Light of Freedom*, chaps. 12, 13; Dittmer, *Local People*, chaps. 13, 14; and Hogan, *Many Minds*, chap. 11.

62. On SNCC communication, see Carson, *In Struggle*, chaps. 2, 6, 8, 10; Payne, *I've Got the Light of Freedom*, chaps. 3, 7, 8, 13; Hogan, *Many Minds*, chaps. 3, 4, 6, 10;

and Jeffries, *Bloody Lowndes*, chaps. 2, 4, 5, 7. On Poland, see Goodwyn, *Breaking the Barrier*, especially 115, 266, 277–91. On Zapatistas, see Marcos and Vincente, *¡Ya Basta!*; and Hayden, *Zapatista Reader*, particularly part 2. See chapter 6 in the present book for examples of internal communication within the Standing Rock encampment.

63. In certain situations, reliance on social media as a form of communication is a weakness. For example, in Turkey, Iran, Russia, and China, the central government has periodically cut off access to social media in times of social unrest and movement activity. This attempt to dampen the flow of information has increased over the last six years. See Freedom House's reports between 2011 and 2017, https://freedomhouse.org/sites/default/files/FOTN_2017_Final.pdf (accessed May 12, 2018).

64. Mark Anthony Neal, "Ferguson Syllabus," New Black Man in Exile, Sept. 1, 2014, http://www.newblackmaninexile.net/2014/12/mark-anthony-neal-black twitter-hashtag.html. See also Taylor, *From #BlackLivesMatter to Black Liberation*, Kindle location 3599.

65. Amandla Stenberg interviewed by Solange Knowles, "How Our February Cover Star Amandla Stenberg Learned to Love Her Blackness," *Teen Vogue*, Jan. 7, 2016, http://www.teenvogue.com/story/amandla-stenberg-interview-teen-vogue -february-2016. See also Mottahedeh, *#iranelection*.

66. Gerbaudo, *Tweets and the Streets*, examines the way social media functioned in similar ways in the Arab Spring and Occupy Wall Street movements.

67. Freelon, McIlwain, and Clark, "Beyond the Hashtags." See also Earl and Kimport, *Digitally Enabled Social Change*, 190, on how scholars might measure the size of mobilizations when people do not have to be physically present to participate. Left unsaid is how one might assess effectiveness with online mobilizations.

68. Michael Moore, *The Awful Truth*, on YouTube, https://www.youtube.com /watch?v=xeOaTpYl8mE (accessed Sept. 23, 2013).

69. See Freelon, McIlwain, and Clark. "Beyond the Hashtags." Tweet posted by skittlez @MidwestSkit [Candice Price], July 27, 2015, https://twitter.com/Midwest Skit/status/625832473188896768.

70. Charles Mills's "epistemology of ignorance" in *The Racial Contract* asserts that whites are unlikely to understand certain dynamics because their educations are decidedly incomplete. Alice Walker, Katie G. Cannon, Toni Morrison, and Patricia Hill Collins all write on the need to reclaim and focus on Black women's histories and stories as valid, important epistemologies. See Alice Walker's 1972 convocation presentation at Sarah Lawrence College on how racist ideologies have been sewn into the curriculum of universities simply by ignoring or not teaching marginalized people's history, literature, and work. Walker satirizes universities as sites of "superior knowledge": "That is why historians are generally enemies of women, certainly of blacks, and so are, all too often, the very people we must sit under in order to learn. Ignorance, arrogance, and racism have bloomed as Superior Knowledge in all too many universities." A. Walker, *In Search of Our Mothers' Gardens*, 36. See also DiAngelo, *White Fragility*.

71. Huggins, "Deforming Mirror of Truth," 25–29. On DeBlasio, see Erin Durkin, "Bill DeBlasio Details Talk with Biracial Son," *New York Daily News*, Dec. 8, 2014, http://www.nydailynews.com/news/politics/de-blasio-details-talk-son-dealing

-cops-article-1.2036870. On white privilege, see the now-iconic article by Macintosh, "White Privilege." See also Rachel L. Swarns, "'I Have a Black Son in Baltimore': Anxious New Parents and an Era of Unease," *New York Times*, Aug. 23, 2016, http://www.nytimes.com/2016/08/24/us/i-have-a-black-son-in-baltimore-anxious-new-parents-and-an-era-of-unease.html?smprod=nytcore-iphone&smid=nytcore-iphone-share&_r=0. Two recent useful works on racialized ignorance include Kendi, *Stamped from the Beginning*; and Wilder, *Ebony and Ivy*. See also Sullivan and Tuana, *Race and Epistemologies of Ignorance*; and Harper and Newman, "Surprise, Sensemaking and Success."

72. Woodard Henderson, "Grassroots Organizing."
73. Woodard Henderson, "Grassroots Organizing."
74. Summers, "Documenting Ferguson"; Ransby, "Ella Taught Me"; Umi Selah, panel, "How to Increase Voter Registration in the South," SNCC VRC 2015. On surveillance of BLM, see for example Darnell Moore, "Why Some Black Activists Feel Like They're Being Watched by the Government," mic.com, June 3, 2015, https://mic.com/articles/119792/why-some-black-activists-believe-they-re-being-watched-by-the-government#.H1iTkCz97 (accessed Aug. 2, 2016); Caitlin Dickson, "Why the NSA's Vietnam-Era Watch List Is Still Relevant," *Daily Beast*, Sept. 26, 2013, http://www.thedailybeast.com/articles/2013/09/26/why-the-nsa-s-vietnam-era-watch-list-is-still-relevant.html; and Clarence Lang, Q&A session following McKinney, "Teaching the Civil Rights Movement during a Time of Universal Deceit."
75. Summers, "Documenting Ferguson"; and Phil Agnew, SNCC VRC 2015 and SNCC COH 2018.
76. Woodard Henderson, "Grassroots Organizing"; adrienne maree brown, @adriennemaree, quoted on Twitter, Oct. 7, 2014, https://twitter.com/adriennemaree/status/519584348618506243. Brown cites Mervyn Marcano and #BlackLivesMatter; see Twitter, June 11, 2016; and brown, *Emergent Strategy*, 42. On hospitality, see Harding and Harding, "Radical Hospitality."
77. See Jones, *Green Collar Economy*, 110.
78. Charlene Carruthers, panel, "How to Increase Voter Registration in the South," SNCC VRC 2015; "Charlene A. Carruthers," BYP website bio, http://byp100.org/charlene-a-carruthers/ (accessed Nov. 11, 2015); Carruthers, *Unapologetic*, Kindle location 1318–65.
79. For comparison to descriptions of labor organizing, see for example Windham, *Knocking on Labor's Door*, 36, 162; on descriptions of civil rights activity, see Theoharis, *More Beautiful and Terrible History*, 4 and chaps. 7 and 8; for examples in the Movement for Black Lives, see Lowery, *They Can't Kill Us All*, 174–75, and Taylor, *From #BlackLivesMatter to Black Liberation*, Kindle location 424; and for descriptions of the same "spontaneity" in the movement of Polish Solidarity, see Goodwyn, *Breaking the Barrier*, 156.
80. Courtland Cox, "Critical Oral History: Black Power Culture and Education," July 11, 2016, SNCC COH 2016.
81. On Rogers and Themba, see for example Ransby, *Making All Black Lives Matter*, Kindle location 1316. There are others in the country who are acting Baker-style. However, listing them verges on the impossible. I have opted instead to put forward several representative women, but similar fundis have been vital to M4BL

work across the country. Cohen started the Black Youth Project, was a founding board member and former cochair of the board of the Audre Lorde Project in New York, was on the boards of Kitchen Table—Women of Color Press and the Center for Lesbian and Gay Studies at CUNY, and was a founding member of Black AIDS Mobilization (BAM!) and an active member in numerous organizations such as the Black Radical Congress, African American Women in Defense of Ourselves, and Ella's Daughters (a network of women working in Ella Baker's tradition). Ransby, who wrote a pioneering biography of Ella Baker, was initiator of the African American Women in Defense of Ourselves campaign in 1991, a co-convener of the Black Radical Congress in 1998, and a founder of Ella's Daughters. Much of her work can be seen in Jones and Eubanks with Smith, *Ain't Gonna Let Nobody Turn Me Around*, 21–22, 28–34, 52–59, 88–89, 156–65, 208–11.

82. Many SNCC conference proceedings are housed at the John Hope Franklin Research Collection at the David M. Rubenstein Rare Book and Manuscript Library, Duke University, including those from the SNCC Fortieth Anniversary, the SNCC Fiftieth Anniversary, the SNCC VRC 2015, and the SNCC Digital Gateway Launch of 2018. Also see the proceedings of the 2016 and 2018 Critical Oral Histories sessions held at Duke on Black Power (SNCC COH 2016) and the Mississippi Freedom Democratic Party (SNCC COH 2018). The SNCC Digital Gateway's "Today" section is online: https://snccdigital.org/today/ (accessed Jan. 12, 2018).

83. On Katrina and Jena Six, see Flaherty, *Floodlines*, chap. 10.

84. John Herbers, "Dr. King and 770 Others Seized in Alabama Protest," *New York Times*, February 2, 1965, 1.

85. Taylor, *From #BlackLivesMatter to Black Liberation*, Kindle locations 1637–39, 2193–94.

86. Forman, *Locking Up Our Own*, especially chap. 5. See also Taylor, *From #BlackLivesMatter to Black Liberation*, Kindle location 1568–98.

87. "About Us," Movement 4 Black Lives, https://policy.m4bl.org/about/ (accessed Dec. 3, 2017); Khan-Cullors and Bandele, *When They Call You a Terrorist*, 232. On Tamir Rice, see also Lowery, *They Can't Kill Us All*, chap. 2. See also Ransby, *Making All Black Lives Matter*, chap. 8 on "political quilters" such as Blackbird, BOLD, and the BlackOUT Collective.

88. Crenshaw et al., *Say Her Name*; Ritchie, *Invisible No More*; Carruthers, *Unapologetic*, Kindle location 1933–60.

89. Carruthers, *Unapologetic*, Kindle location 1933–60; Annie Sweeney, "Police Detective Dante Servin Resigns before Possible Firing over Fatal Shooting," *Chicago Tribune*, May 18, 2016, https://www.chicagotribune.com/news/local/breaking/ct-chicago-cop-dante-servin-resigns-met-20160518-story.html.

90. On the shooting and subsequent trial of Yanez, see Stacia Brown, "Philando, Prince and Futures Untold," Stacia L. Brown, July 19, 2016, https://stacialbrown.com/tag/philando-castile/; MPR News Staff, "What Happens Now," *74 Seconds* podcast, Aug. 14, 2017, https://www.mprnews.org/story/2017/08/14/74-seconds-podcast-episode-22-what-happens-now.

91. "FBI Report Blames Black Lives Matter, Media for Killings of Police Officers," *Telesur*, May 4, 2017, https://www.telesurtv.net/english/news/FBI-Report-Blames-Black-Lives-Matter-Media-for-Killings-of-Police-Officers.-Just-Dont-Expect-Actual

-Evidence.-20170504–0008.html; Paul Bedard, "Cops Feel Betrayed by Politicians," *Washington Examiner*, May 3, 2017, https://www.washingtonexaminer.com/report-cops-feel-betrayed-by-politicians-say-they-encourage-attacks. A few months later, the counterterrorism division of the FBI identified movement activists as "black identity extremists." See Shanelle Matthews and Malkia Cyril, "We Say Black Lives Matter, the FBI Says That Makes Us a Security Threat," *Washington Post*, Oct. 19, 2017, https://www.washingtonpost.com/news/posteverything/wp/2017/10/19/we-say-black-lives-matter-the-fbi-says-that-makes-us-a-security-threat/?noredirect=on&utm_term=.61991180dfe.

92. The "war on police" framing of BLM can be seen for example in Heather Mac Donald's writing in the wake of Ferguson, which led to her publication of *The War on Cops*; see Vitale's rebuttal, *End of Policing*. See also "Black Lives Kill," *Drudge Report*, July 8, 2016, http://www.drudgereportarchives.com/data/2016/07/08/20160708_052104.htm; "The Rush Limbaugh Show," July 8, 2016, https://www.rushlimbaugh.com/daily/2016/07/08/rush_s_stack_of_stuff-41/; Winter and Weinberger, "FBI's New Terrorist Threat."

93. "About Us," Movement 4 Black Lives. The push to develop M4BL came out of the Cleveland Black Lives Matter convening, July 24–26, 2015. See Kesi Foster quoted in Olivia Anderson, "Free College Tops Black Lives Reparations List," *Yes Magazine*, Sept. 2, 2016, http://www.yesmagazine.org/peace-justice/free-college-tops-black-lives-reparations-list-20160902. Campaign Zero's platform is available online: https://www.joincampaignzero.org/solutions/#brokenwindows (accessed June 11, 2018).

94. Khan-Cullors and Bandele, *When They Call You a Terrorist*, 167.

95. Khan-Cullors and Bandele, 249–50; Carruthers, *Unapologetic*, Kindle location 739; Kelley, "Forum: Black Study." For more on the centrality of healing practices to M4BL, see Black Emotional and Mental Health Collective, http://www.beam.community/healing-justice/ (accessed Dec. 12, 2018).

96. Carruthers, *Unapologetic*, Kindle location 1886; D'Atra Jackson, Dec. 1, 2018, SNCC Legacy Project Voting Rights Book Project Conference, 2018; "35 States Reform Criminal Justice Policies through Justice Reinvestment," Pew Charitable Trusts, July 2018, https://www.pewtrusts.org/-/media/assets/2018/07/pspp_reform_matrix.pdf; Kira Lerner, "Florida Overturns Jim Crow–Era Felon Disfranchisement Law," Think Progress, Nov. 6, 2018, https://thinkprogress.org/breaking-florida-overturns-jim-crow-era-felon-disenfranchisement-law-10d60be06cf4/.

CHAPTER SIX

1. "Oceti Sakowin Youth and Allies: Relay Run to Washington," *ReZpect Our Water*, July 18, 2016, available on YouTube, https://www.youtube.com/watch?v=Ei4nKWxiG-M.

2. Bobbi Jean Three Legs had a vision dream. In it, her daughter awoke one night, asking for water. Due to water pollution, she had none to give. Soon after, she and Joseph White Eyes decided to set up a relay run, five hundred miles to Omaha, and then two thousand miles to Washington, both times to deliver a letter to the Army Corps of Engineers, asking them to deny DAPL a permit. "Oceti Sakowin Youth and

Allies: Relay Run to Washington." See also Bobbi Jean Three Legs, "Water Is Life, Water Is Sacred," *Democracy Now!*, Jan. 25, 2017, https://www.democracynow.org/2017/1/25/water_is_life_water_is_sacred; and Matt Petronzio, "How Young Native Americans Used Social Media to Build Up the #NoDAPL Movement," *Mashable*, Dec. 7, 2016, http://mashable.com/2016/12/07/standing-rock-nodapl-youth/#CFpLqQj9dqqL.

3. Elbein, "The Youth Group That Launched a Movement at Standing Rock."

4. Elbein, "Youth Group That Launched a Movement at Standing Rock." On the relay run invoking older traditions, see Marshall, *Returning to the Lakota Way*.

5. Jasilyn Charger quoted in Elbein, "Youth Group That Launched a Movement at Standing Rock."

6. This was similar to one of the most important dynamics of SNCC, as Charles Cobb noted in *This Nonviolent Stuff'll Get You Killed*, 21. Lawrence Guyot challenged him to stay in Mississippi and fight. "All progress in my mind inside the black community flows out of the independent efforts that are the results of the challenges that black people make to one another," he later reflected. Cobb, "Critical Oral Histories Conference: The Emergence of Black Power," July 9–11, 2016, SNCC COH 2016.

7. Charger quoted in de Leon and Ritsher, *One Year at Standing Rock*."

8. Terrell Iron Shell quoted in E. Simon, "Seventh Generation"; see also comments in the same piece by Danny Grassrope and Lauren Howland.

9. Duane interview by Bill Prouty, Nov. 6, 2016, available at https://itunes.apple.com/us/podcast/voices-of-standing-rock-duane/id1173368814?i=1000377558276&mt=2. On infrastructure and manufacturing destroying communities of color in North America, see for example Bullard, *Dumping in Dixie*; Bullard, Johnson and Torres, *Highway Robbery*; Pietro, *Not in My Neighborhood*; Rothstein, *Color of Law*; and Lerner and Bullard, *Diamond*.

10. "Dispatches from Standing Rock with Desiree Kane," *Bi Any Means*, July 6, 2017, https://freethoughtblogs.com/bianymeans/2017/07/06/bi-any-means-podcast-106-dispatches-from-standing-rock-with-desiree-kane/.

11. Cannupa Hanska Luger quoted in Miranda, "Art, Celebrity"; Eryn Wise quoted in Zambelich and Alexandra, "In Their Own Words"; Ome Tlaloc quoted in Enzinna, "'I Didn't Come Here to Lose.'" See also the moment in the news story where Lauren Howland says, "The youth are gonna kill this black snake," in E. Simon, "Seventh Generation." Non-Indigenous witnesses repeatedly noted the power of the youth water protectors. See for example Cathy Rankin: "The Standing Rock youth gave me hope that their generation can save the planet. They united a world like no one ever has!" (https://twitter.com/Tabbatcat/status/889942068294012929 [July 25, 2017]). For more on the use of the term "Indigenous," see the definition published by the Independent Commission on International Humanitarian Issues and Zed Books in 1987, Icihi and Talal, *Indigenous Peoples*: "Indigenous populations are composed of the existing descendants of the peoples who inhabited the present territory of a country wholly or partially at the time when persons of a different culture or ethnic origin arrived there from other parts of the world, overcame them and, by Conquest, settlement or other means reduced them to a non-dominant or colonial situation," 1-2.

12. Josh Garrett-Davis, "Standing Rock: Art and Solidarity," KCET, May 16, 2017, https://www.kcet.org/shows/earth-focus/standing-rock-art-and-solidarity.

13. Shauneen Peet, "Idle No More: Radical Indigeneity in Teacher Education," in Pirbhai-Illich, Peet, and Martin, *Culturally Responsive Pedagogy*, 53. The women who started the movement are Sylvia McAdam, Nina Wilson, Jess Gordon, and Sheila McLean. #IdleNoMore's activities and their demand for fundamental change in Canada's accountability to Indigenous people and nations in the winters of 2012–13 can also be traced in Kino-nda-nimii Collective, *Winter We Danced*; and Manuel and Derrickson, *Unsettling Canada*. See also L. Simpson, "Aambe!"; Julian Brave NoiseCat, "Indigenous Sovereignty Is on the Rise; Can It Shape the Course of History?," *The Guardian*, May 30, 2017, https://www.theguardian.com/commentisfree/2017/may/30/indigenous-sovereignty-growth-history-australia; Coulthard, *Red Skin*; and Pablo Orellana Matute, "Meet Ecuador's Water Protectors," Waging Nonviolence, Nov. 15, 2016, https://wagingnonviolence.org/feature/ecuador-cuenca-water-mining-gold/.

14. David Uahikeaikaleiʻohu Maile, "On the Violence of the Thirty Meter Telescope and the Dakota Access Pipeline," Hot Spots, *Fieldsights*, Dec. 22, 2016, https://culanth.org/fieldsights/on-the-violence-of-the-thirty-meter-telescope-and-the-dakota-access-pipeline. On the ignoble story of criminalizing protest in recent US history, see Goluboff, *Vagrant Nation*; Luff, *Commonsense Anticommunism*; Melgaço and Monaghan, *Protests in the Information Age*; Chang, *Silencing Political Dissent*; and Welsh, *Flag Burning*.

15. "Voices of Mni Wiconi Call to Action: Call Obama to Stop the Dakota Access Pipeline," Wingspan Media, Oct. 12, 2016, available on YouTube at https://www.youtube.com/watch?v=b-wAIt7O9eQ; Nunpa quoted in Edward Valandra, "We Are Blood Relatives: No to the DAPL," Hot Spots, *Fieldsights*, Dec. 22, 2016, https://culanth.org/fieldsights/we-are-blood-relatives-no-to-the-dapl; Katherine Morris quoted in Tavis Smiley, "Protectors Not Protestors: The People of Standing Rock," PBS, aired Dec. 6, 2016, http://www.pbs.org/video/tavis-smiley-protection-not-protest-people-standing-rock/. Prolific the Rapper, "Stadium Pow Wow," https://m.facebook.com/RedWarriorCamp/posts/1750969815154971 (Aug. 2, 2017). For a parallel development in India, see "India Court Gives Sacred Ganges and Yamuna Rivers Human Status," *BBC News*, Mar. 21, 2017, http://www.bbc.com/news/world-asia-india-39336284?SThisFB. For more on the "ruptures" caused in Western theories of politics by Indigenous worldviews, see Marisol de la Cadena, who notes that the Latin American epistemologies where "the presence of earth-beings" like mountains, animals, plants, and landscapes that have sentience "in social protests invites us to slow down reasoning because it may evince an intriguing moment of epistemic rupture with this [Western] theory of politics. Their public emergence contends—to use Rancière's word—with both science and politics; it may house the capacity to upset the locus of enunciation of what 'politics' is about—who can be a politician or what can be considered a political issue, and thus reshuffle the hegemonic antagonisms that for more than 500 years organized the political field." Cadena, "Indigenous Cosmopolitics," 342, 350. For a recent survey on corporate personhood and its impact on US governance, see Lamoreaux and Novak, *Corporations and American Democracy*.

16. Bobbi Jean Three Legs, "Water Is Life, Water Is Sacred."

17. Angela Maxwell quoted in C. Walker, "Black Lives Matter 5280 Recaps Trip." Dakota Eagle quoted in Greg Archer, "Native American Student Sheds Light on the Power of Indigenous Youth in Upcoming Standing Rock Documentary," *Huffington Post*, July 17, 2017, http://www.huffingtonpost.com/entry/native-american-student-sheds-light-on-the-power-of_us_596ed24ee4b07f87578e6d1f.

18. Kyle Hill interview by Bill Prouty, Dec. 3, 2016, available at https://itunes.apple.com/us/podcast/voices-of-standing-rock-kyle/id1173368814?i=1000378543825&mt=2.

19. Eva Cardenas, training session, in "The Stakes: Revisiting Standing Rock," MTV podcasts, Apr. 28, 2017, http://www.mtv.com/news/podcasts/the-stakes/revisiting-standing-rock/.

20. Elbein, "Youth Group That Launched a Movement at Standing Rock."

21. Nahko Bear, concert for Water Protectors, Standing Rock, Sept. 8, 2016, available on YouTube at https://www.youtube.com/watch?v=dQ1r989oIrg.

22. Pierce, "Standing Rock Fire."

23. Hussey et al., "Rise of a New Global, Indigenous, Left."

24. Enzinna, "'I Didn't Come Here to Lose.'"

25. David Archambault II interview by Amy Goodman, *Democracy Now!*, Oct. 17, 2016, https://www.democracynow.org/2016/10/17/standing_rock_sioux_tribe_chair_we.

26. Liz Hampton, "Sunoco, behind Protested Dakota Pipeline, Tops U.S. Crude Spill Charts," Reuters, Sept. 23, 2016, http://www.reuters.com/article/us-usa-pipeline-nativeamericans-safety-i-idUSKCN11T1UW; Lauren Reid, "Oil and Water: ETP and Sunoco's History of Pipeline Spills," Greenpeace, Apr. 17, 2018, https://www.greenpeace.org/usa/oil-water-etp-sunocos-history-pipeline-spills/; Pipeline Operator Information 2006–2018, PHMSA, https://primis.phmsa.dot.gov/comm/reports/operator/Operatorlist.html?nocache=8864# (accessed Jan. 23, 2019).

27. Ostler and Estes trace the path by which a 1980 Supreme Court decision reaffirmed the 1851 treaty boundaries, yet since the federal government does not have the authority to return lands illegally taken, they offered monetary compensation, which the Sioux rejected. The Sioux demanded a return of the federal, not private, lands in the original treaty. Ostler and Estes, "'Supreme Law of the Land.'" On the long history of legal conflict between Indigenous and US governments, see for example Den Ouden and O'Brien, *Recognition*; L. Robinson, *Conquest by Law*; and Churchill, *Perversions of Justice*. See also Park, "Money, Mortgages and the Conquest of America."

28. Estes, "Fighting for Our Lives."

29. "Declaration of Continuing Independence," International Indigenous Treaty Council, June 1974, https://www.iitc.org/about-iitc/the-declaration-of-continuing-independence-june-1974/; Estes, "Fighting for Our Lives"; Dunbar-Ortiz, "How Indigenous Peoples Wound Up at the United Nations." For a broader legal examination of treaties in the context of the past half-millennium, see Anghie, *Imperialism*; Newcombe, *Pagans in the Promised Land*; Bhandar, *Colonial Lives of Property*; Park, "Money, Mortgages and the Conquest of America" and "Insuring Conquest"; and

Ford, *Settler Sovereignty*. The expansion and deepening of Indigenous frameworks appearing in scholarly publications over the last two decades has been one of the most important research frames in American studies and associated disciplines. For a good starting place for some of this rich work, see Hinton et al., *Colonial Genocide*; Coulthard, *Red Skin*; and Horne, *Apocalypse of Settler Colonialism*.

30. Dhillon and Estes, "Introduction."

31. Dhillon and Estes, "Introduction." One of the most useful archives documenting the recent US history of might-makes-right is the National Security Archive at George Washington University. More information is available at https://nsarchive.gwu.edu/about (accessed Aug. 12, 2018).

32. Indigenous Environmental Network, Facebook, Aug. 11, 2016, https://www.facebook.com/ienearth/photos/a.346330010641.150464.186264980641/10153879409930642/?type=3&theater; "Blocking the Dakota Access Pipeline," Facebook, Aug. 11, 2016, https://www.facebook.com/ienearth/videos/10153874073435642/; IEN, Facebook, Aug. 26, 2016, https://www.facebook.com/ienearth/videos/10153921577365642/; Elbein, "Youth Group That Launched a Movement at Standing Rock"; "Dispatches from Standing Rock with Desiree Kane"; Kane, "20 Photos."

33. Lauren Howland quoted in E. Simon, "Seventh Generation."

34. On Trump's tendency to use false equivalence, see James Hohmann, "The Daily 202: False Moral Equivalency Is Not a Bug of Trumpism. It's a Feature," *Washington Post*, Aug. 16, 2017, https://www.washingtonpost.com/news/powerpost/paloma/daily-202/2017/08/16/daily-202-false-moral-equivalency-is-not-a-bug-of-trumpism-it-s-a-feature/5993b25930fb0433811d6965/?utm_term=.6411737dc78f. On the tendency of the powerful to use this as a tool to minimize, see Scott, *Weapons of the Weak* and *Seeing Like a State*; James Fallows, "False Equivalence: The Master Class," *The Atlantic*, Feb. 26, 2013, https://www.theatlantic.com/politics/archive/2013/02/false-equivalence-the-master-class/273505/; and James Fallows, "'False Equivalence' Reaches Onionesque Heights, but in a Real Paper," *The Atlantic*, Oct. 15, 2011, https://www.theatlantic.com/politics/archive/2011/10/false-equivalence-reaches-onionesque-heights-but-in-a-real-paper/246754/.

35. Crow quoted in "Dakota Access Pipeline Company Attacks Native American Protesters with Dogs & Pepper Spray," Sept. 3, 2016, available on YouTube at https://www.youtube.com/watch?v=kuZcx2zEo4k.

36. Enzinna, "'I Didn't Come Here to Lose.'"

37. Grasshope quoted in E. Simon, "Seventh Generation."

38. Charger quoted in de Leon and Ritsher, *One Year at Standing Rock*.

39. Iron Shell quoted in E. Simon, "Seventh Generation"; Lauren Howland quoted in Women's Earth and Climate Action Network, "15 Indigenous Women."

40. Eryn Wise quoted in Elbein, "Youth Group That Launched a Movement at Standing Rock."

41. Avalos et al., "Standing with Standing Rock."

42. Lyla June Johnston and Jacquilyn Córdoba quoted in E. Simon, "Seventh Generation." See also Lyla June Johnston, Facebook post, https://www.facebook.com/pg/lylajune/videos/ (accessed Aug. 12, 2017).

43. Lyla June Johnston quoted in E. Simon, "Seventh Generation."

44. Terrell Iron Shell quoted in E. Simon, "Seventh Generation."

45. Catherine Flowers, Franklin Humanities Institute, Duke University, Jan. 30, 2017, notes in the author's possession.

46. Liz George quoted in "The Stakes: Revisiting Standing Rock."

47. Thomas Frazier quoted in *Dundon v. Kirchmeier*, 2017, "In the U.S. District Court for the District of North Dakota," https://www.courthousenews.com/wp-content/uploads/2017/02/No-preliminary-injunction-Dakota-Access.pdf (accessed Aug. 2, 2017).

48. Jacquilyn Córdoba and Lauren Howland quoted in E. Simon, "Seventh Generation."

49. Kalamaokaʻaina Niheu quoted in Hussey et al., "Rise of a New Global, Indigenous, Left."

50. One training for newcomers by Eva Cardenas of IP3 can be heard on "The Stakes: Revisiting Standing Rock"; Andrea Bowers and Susanna Battin quoted in Miranda, "Art, Celebrity." IP3 defined itself as "a nonviolent direct action training and support network advancing Indigenous communities' ability to exercise their inherent rights to environmental justice, cultural livelihood, and self-determination. Formed in 2004 as a project of the Ruckus Society, IP3 works across Turtle Island with communities that are most vulnerable to threats of ecological devastation and resource exploitation, and most poised to lead solution-oriented action." "Who We Are," IP3, https://ip3action.org/who-we-are/ (accessed Aug. 2, 2017).

51. Andrea Bowers quoted in Miranda, "Art, Celebrity."

52. Christopher quoted in William Yardley, "Waning Days of the Standing Rock Protest," *Los Angeles Times*, Feb. 11, 2017, http://www.latimes.com/nation/la-na-standing-rock-improvised-tribe-20170202-story.html. See also "A Note from Our Founders," Red Road Awareness, http://www.redroadawareness.org/about-us.html (accessed Aug. 23, 2017).

53. One training for newcomers by Eva Cardenas of IP3 can be heard on "The Stakes: Revisiting Standing Rock."

54. Emery-Brown and Maxwell quoted in C. Walker, "Black Lives Matter 5280 Recaps Trip."

55. Emery-Brown and Maxwell quoted in C. Walker, "Black Lives Matter 5280 Recaps Trip."

56. Eva Cardenas quoted in "The Stakes: Revisiting Standing Rock."

57. Two Bulls quoted in Hussey et al., "Rise of a New Global, Indigenous, Left"; Petronzio, "How Young Native Americans Used Social Media to Build Up the #NoDAPL Movement"; Tess Owen, "Who's At Standing Rock?," *Vice News*, Oct. 31, 2016, https://news.vice.com/en_us/article/j5venb/facebook-users-are-falsely-checking-in-at-standing-rock-to-confuse-police.

58. Wise quoted in Petronzio, "How Young Native Americans Used Social Media to Build Up the #NoDAPL Movement"; Hanna Kozlowska, "Dakota Pipeline Protestors Are Broadcasting Their Tense Standoff with the Police Using Facebook Live," *Quartz*, Oct. 29, 2016, https://qz.com/822731/dakota-pipeline-protesters-are-broadcasting-their-tense-standoff-with-police-using-facebook-live/. For an important recent study of how online architecture and bias distorts information, see Noble, *Algorithms of Oppression*.

59. Wise quoted in Petronzio, "How Young Native Americans Used Social Media to Build Up the #NoDAPL Movement."

60. Avalos et al., "Standing with Standing Rock."

61. Spice, "Interrupting Industrial and Academic Extraction." On Indigenous youth documentation, see Wapikoni, http://www.wapikoni.ca (accessed Oct. 2, 2018); and Myron Dewey's Digital Smoke Signals, http://www.digitalsmokesignals.com (accessed Oct. 2, 2018).

62. Miranda, "Art, Celebrity"; Ransby, *Making All Black Lives Matter*, Kindle location 991.

63. Nic Gabriel quoted in A Tribe Called Red, "Stadium Pow Wow," Facebook, https://m.facebook.com/RedWarriorCamp/posts/1750969815154971 (accessed Aug. 2, 2017). For more on Indigenous and European worldviews that challenge individualism, competition, and consumerism, see for example Todd, "Indigenous Feminist's Take"; Cadena, "Indigenous Cosmopolitics"; and Daniel Comacho, "Latin America: A Society in Motion," in Wignaraja, *New Social Movements*, 43. On European histories of the commons, see Linebaugh and Rediker, *Many-Headed Hydra*; and Linebaugh, *Stop, Thief!*

64. Marcella Ernest (Ojibwe) interview by Nancy Mithlo, "Standing Rock, Protest, Sound and Power," *Sounding Out! Podcast #60*, Mar. 30, 2017, https://soundstudiesblog.com/2017/03/30/sounding-out-podcast-60-standing-rock-protest-sound-and-power/; Nic Gabriel quoted in A Tribe Called Red, "Stadium Pow Wow," Facebook, https://m.facebook.com/RedWarriorCamp/posts/1750969815154971 (accessed Aug. 2, 2017); Sarain Fox quoted in Kara Weisenstein, "Sarain Fox, the Host of 'Rise' on VICELAND, Tells Creators Why Art Was Vital to the #NoDAPL Movement," *Creators*, Feb. 28, 2017, https://creators.vice.com/en_us/article/gv3pg3/how-art-immortalized-nodapl-protests-at-standing-rock. On Belcourt and Murdoch, see "Who We Are," Onaman Collective, http://onamancollective.com/who-we-are/ (accessed Aug. 5, 2017). Melanie Cervantes has collected an online archive of Standing Rock posters at https://www.facebook.com/melaniecervantes/media_set?set=a.10105656477191173.1073741884.1217286&type=3.

65. For some examples of recent scholarship on the structural barriers faced by Indigenous youth, see Dhillon, *Prairie Rising*; Ansloos, *Medicine of Peace*; Talaga, *Seven Fallen Feathers*; and Friedel, "Outdoor Education."

66. Jasilyn Charger quoted in Elbein, "Youth Group That Launched a Movement at Standing Rock."

67. Eryn Wise and Alexander Howland quoted in Zambelich and Alexandra, "In Their Own Words."

68. Candi Brings Plenty (Oglala Lakota Sioux), *natch'a* or lead person of the Two-Spirit Camp at Standing Rock, defined Two-Spirit as "a coined term that was created intentionally by a group of Indigenous LGBTQAI+ leaders in the early 1990s because they were being labeled in a derogative way." In response, they used "Two-Spirit as an umbrella term for indigenous people who identify as LGBTQAI+ from what we call Turtle Island, which encompasses North America, Central America, and South America." Before colonization, "there was a strong sacred presence of Two-Spirit people, who were revered as honored people. We were the folks who had the perception of both male and female, so we were counselors, we were the foster parents, we

were the people who did the naming ceremonies. Because we had this connection with our own feminine and masculine walks of life, we brought balance back to our communities. And because we didn't live in the gender binary, we held the medicine that bridges the gaps between genders." Brings Plenty quoted in Molly Larkey, "Meet the Leader of the Two-Spirit Camp at Standing Rock," *Go Mag*, Jan. 13, 2017, http://gomag.com/article/meet-the-leader-of-the-two-spirit-camp-at-standing-rock/.

69. Kelli Love, MC Preach, and Jordan Walker of One Tribe, "We Stand," available on Facebook at https://www.facebook.com/OneTribeMusic/videos/vb.594227117412550/676959292472665/?type=2&theater (accessed Aug. 11, 2018).

70. Allard quoted in Women's Earth and Climate Action Network, "15 Indigenous Women." See also Merlan, "Meet the Brave, Audacious, Astonishing Women."

71. "Vision and Mission" Facebook post, Nov. 11, 2016, https://www.facebook.com/StandingRockTwoSpiritNation/photos/a.1416211555075077.1073741829.1402505466445686/1434789913217241/?type=3&theater.

72. Zaysha Grinnell quoted in Dhillon, "'This Fight Has Become My Life.'"

73. Nagle quoted in Underhill, "Fighting for the Future."

74. Zaysha Grinnell quoted in Dhillon, "'This Fight Has Become My Life.'" On Rosa Parks and other Black women who furthered organizing within the civil rights movement in order to protect and defend Black women from white male sexual assault, see McGuire, *At the Dark End of the Street*.

75. Zaysha Grinnell quoted in Dhillon, "'This Fight Has Become My Life.'"

76. Isa Barajas de Benavidez and Hāwane Rios quoted in Hussey et al., "Rise of a New Global, Indigenous, Left"; Madonna Thunder Hawk, "Activist Women Within: Re-thinking Red, Yellow, Brown and Black Power through Oral History," Oral History Association Annual Conference, Long Beach, CA, Oct. 13, 2016, notes in the author's possession. "Our people traversed across the ocean for thousands of years, and connected with peoples wherever they went. We are connecting in the same way," says Hāwane Rios. "There's an old connection, an old memory that surfaces, and I think we're all remembering now how to bring people together, and not be divided by history, color or race. We're all made of the same thing. We're letting go of all things in society that are telling us that we're separate. . . . Everyone is on a search to connect and to find their creation stories, their grounding," she continues. "They're trying to find their mountains; trying to find their rivers. This is an opportunity for a widespread healing. We all have to recognize our privileges, and understand what society has done to us, but this is a chance to heal." For more on Women of All Red Nations, see https://equalityarchive.com/issues/women-of-all-red-nations/; and Castle, *Warrior Women*.

77. Raven Chacon quoted in Miranda, "Art, Celebrity."

78. Isa Barajas de Benavidez quoted in C. Walker, "Black Lives Matter 5280 Recaps Trip"; Jeanne Dorado quoted in Zambelich and Alexandra, "In Their Own Words"; Kane, "20 Photos."

79. Kyle, "Black Lives Matter Stands in Solidarity with Water Protectors at Standing Rock," n.d. [Aug./Sept. 2016], http://blacklivesmatter.com/solidarity-with-standing-rock/ (accessed June 2, 2017).

80. Emery-Brown quoted in C. Walker, "Black Lives Matter 5280 Recaps Trip." On the intertwined history of Indigenous and African peoples, see Horne, *Apocalypse of*

Settler Colonialism; Dunbar-Ortiz, *Indigenous People's History*; and the Smithsonian's recent exhibit "indiVisible: African-Native American Lives in the Americas," http://nmai.si.edu/exhibitions/indivisible/ (accessed Aug. 1, 2018).

81. Two Bulls quoted in Hussey et al., "Rise of a New Global, Indigenous, Left."

82. The Pipeline Fighters Fund is one outcome of the Standing Rock media work, telling the stories of people resisting the Keystone XL Pipeline in Nebraska, the SABAL Trail Pipeline in Florida, the Bayou Bridge Pipeline in Louisiana, the Pilgrim and AIM Pipelines in New York, and the Penn East Pipeline in Pennsylvania. Two Bulls quoted in Hussey et al., "Rise of a New Global, Indigenous, Left." One expert noted that Vietnamese activists have a lot of access to information through opendevelopmentmekong.net. Chanse Adams-Zavalla quoted in Enzinna, "'I Didn't Come Here to Lose.'" An overview of environmental Indigenous movements can be found in Grossman, *Unlikely Alliances*; and on Link TV, "Living Desert," episode 6 of *Tending the Wild*, produced by KCET Link Media Group and the Autry Museum, https://www.linktv.org/shows/tending-the-wild/episodes/living-desert (accessed July 27, 2017).

83. Garcia quoted in Miranda, "Art, Celebrity."

84. Avalos et al., "Standing with Standing Rock"; Two Bulls quoted in Hussey et al., "Rise of a New Global, Indigenous Left."

85. Kris Mayer and Alison Sider, "Clashes Halt Work on North Dakota Pipeline," *Wall Street Journal*, Aug. 18, 2016, https://www.wsj.com/articles/clashes-halt-work-on-north-dakota-pipeline-1471554332.

86. David Archambault II quoted in ICMN Staff, "Dakota Access: 6 Peaceful Images from the Water Protectors at Standing Rock," Indian Country Media Network, Aug. 23, 2016, https://indiancountrymedianetwork.com/news/native-news/dakota-access-6-peaceful-images-from-the-water-protectors-at-standing-rock/.

87. Sandy Tolan, "Journalist Faces Charges after Arrest while Covering Dakota Access Pipeline Protest," *Los Angeles Times*, Feb. 5, 2017, http://www.latimes.com/nation/la-na-standing-rock-journalist-arrest-20170205-story.html.

88. Paul Laney, "Protest on the Prairie," National Sheriffs Association, webinar, https://nsa.adobeconnect.com/p3z04qjvdyjr?proto=true (accessed July 27, 2017). For the Emergency Management Assistance Compact, see Horn, "This Natural Disaster Assistance Law."

89. Brown, Parrish, and Speri, "Leaked Documents Reveal Counter-terrorism Tactics." Dakota Access LLC is the umbrella company for the Pipeline. The Pipeline itself is owned by Dakota Access (75 percent) and Phillips 66 (25 percent), while access is owned by Energy Transfer Partners and Sunoco Logistics (51 percent) and Enbridge and Marathon Petroleum (49 percent). Timothy Cama, "Dakota Access Pipeline Now in Service," *The Hill*, June 1, 2017, http://thehill.com/policy/energy-environment/335898-dakota-access-pipeline-now-in-service. TigerSwan's founder, Jim Reese, retired after twenty-five years from Delta Force, an elite US Army force, in 2007 as a lieutenant colonel; the organization's other executives are veterans of the FBI, navy, and Special Forces (https://www.tigerswan.com/meet-our-team/ [accessed Nov. 2, 2018]).

90. Jasilyn Charger, "Real Talk with Zeb," Facebook, Sept. 16, 2016, https://www

.facebook.com/zebpitsfilm/videos/vb.122012087841623/1154548494587972/?type
=2&theater.

91. O'Hara, *Inventing the Pinkertons*; M. Miller, *Foundations of Modern Terrorism*, 128.

92. Tim Mathern quoted in Sandy Tolan, "Taxpayer Funded Horror at Standing Rock," *Daily Beast*, Feb. 22, 2017, http://www.thedailybeast.com/taxpayer-funded-horror-at-standing-rock. Mathern continued, "North Dakota's taxpayer-funded aggression, with enthusiastic backing from the Trump administration, is now at the center of a federal class-action civil rights lawsuit and a United Nations fact-finding tour to Standing Rock." On private security today, see Abrahamsen and Leander, *Routledge Handbook of Private Security Studies*, especially chaps. 10, 14, and 18; and Gabbiden, "Crime Prevention," 335–46.

93. Brown, Parrish, and Speri, "Leaked Documents Reveal Counter-Terrorism Tactics."

94. Tilsen quoted in "Standing Rock's Fight against Dakota Pipeline Continues while Tribe Plans for a Fossil-Fuel-Free Future," *Democracy Now!*, July 4, 2017, https://www.democracynow.org/2017/7/4/standing_rocks_fight_against_dakota_pipeline. On the COINTELPRO-style tactics today, see Brown, Parrish, and Speri, "Leaked Documents Reveal Counter-Terrorism Tactics."

95. The COINTELPRO hearings in 1975 revealed massive law enforcement violations of citizens' constitutional rights. See the fourteen published volumes of the Church Committee, http://www.aarclibrary.org/publib/church/reports/contents.htm (accessed May 18, 2018), as well as monographs by Brian Glick, Kenneth O'Reilly, Ward Churchill and Jim Vander Wall, Ernesto Vigil, and David Cunningham, all in the bibliography. On the Panthers, see Grady-Willis, "Black Panther Party"; Umoja, "Set Our Warriors Free"; Spencer, *Revolution Has Come*; and Bloom and Martin, *Black against Empire*. For more on the disruptions of COINTELPRO within solidarity movements, see J. Williams, *From the Bullet to the Ballot*; and Sonnie and Tracy, *Hillbilly Nationalists*.

96. The expansion of the number of Joint Terrorism Task Forces from thirty-five to over one hundred in the wake of 9/11 is particularly notable; President George W. Bush asked Congress to provide $300 million to the Department of Homeland Security to fund "fusion centers" to share anti-terrorism information between local, state, and federal law enforcement. There was no requirement in this funding bill to restrict the sharing of "anti-terrorism" information to those who had attacked the country on 9/11. Alleen Brown et al., "Standing Rock Documents Expose Inner Workings of 'Surveillance Industrial Complex,'" *The Intercept*, June 3, 2017, https://theintercept.com/2017/06/03/standing-rock-documents-expose-inner-workings-of-surveillance-industrial-complex/. Tilsen quoted in "Standing Rock's Fight against Dakota Pipeline Continues While Tribe Plans for a Fossil-Fuel-Free Future." On the increase in use of COINTELPRO tactics over the last few decades, see Kienscherf, *U.S. Domestic and International Regimes of Security*; Graff, *Threat Matrix*; Herman and Finkleman, *Terrorism, Government, and Law*; and McQuade, "Puzzle of Intelligence Expertise."

97. Tilsen quoted in "Standing Rock's Fight against Dakota Pipeline Continues while Tribe Plans for a Fossil-Fuel-Free Future."

98. Maile, "On the Violence of the Thirty Meter Telescope and the Dakota Access Pipeline," citing Alfred, *Wasáse*, 120.

99. On Smith-Kramer, see Rahima Nasa, "A Killing at Donkey Creek," *Pro-Publica*, Apr. 25, 2018, https://www.propublica.org/article/a-killing-at-donkey-creek; on Heyer see Vanessa Romo, "Charlottesville Jury Convicts 'Unite the Right' Protestor Who Killed Woman," NPR, Dec. 7, 2018, https://www.npr.org/2018/12/07/674672922/james-alex-fields-unite-the-right-protester-who-killed-heather-heyer-found-guilt. Local and national journalists have covered scores of examples of white motorists driving into Indigenous and black protesters. Other recent examples include "Pittsburgh Man Charged with Driving Car through Crowd of Antwon Rose Protestors," *Atlanta Journal Constitution*, June 29, 2018, https://www.ajc.com/news/national/pittsburgh-man-charged-with-driving-car-through-crowd-antwon-rose-protesters/r48aVoReZUGWHNajQzktBI/; and Sam Levin, "Video Shows Pickup Truck Plowing into Native American Rights Protestors," *The Guardian*, Oct. 11, 2016, https://www.theguardian.com/us-news/2016/oct/11/native-american-rights-protesters-hit-by-truck-nevada. On "slow violence" see Nixon, *Slow Violence*.

100. Stephanie Woodard, "The Police Killings No One Is Talking About," *In These Times*, Oct. 17, 2016, http://inthesetimes.com/features/native_american_police_killings_native_lives_matter.html; A. J. Vincens, "Native Americans Get Shot by Cops at an Astonishing Rate," *Mother Jones*, July 15, 2015, http://www.motherjones.com/politics/2015/07/native-americans-getting-shot-police/; Montoya, "Violence on the Ground"; Dhillon, *Prairie Rising*, chaps. 1, 5, and 6; see also Linda Black Elk in Tolan, "Taxpayer Funded Horror at Standing Rock."

101. David Archambault II quoted in Elbein, "Youth Group That Launched a Movement at Standing Rock."

102. Naomi Klein interview with Tokata Iron Eyes, available on Facebook at https://www.facebook.com/naomikleinofficial/videos/10154731788609919/ (accessed Aug. 7, 2017).

103. Charger quoted in Elbein, "Youth Group That Launched a Movement at Standing Rock." See also Jacquilyn Córdoba at https://www.youtube.com/watch?v=BSNqrTVtpwA (accessed Aug. 8, 2017).

104. Niheu quoted in Hussey et al., "Rise of a New Global, Indigenous, Left."

105. Adams-Zavalla quoted in Enzinna, "'I Didn't Come Here to Lose.'" For examples of how this work spread to other Indigenous homelands and urban communities, see Benny Polaca, "Wha-Zha-Zhi Youth Council Learns about Water Quality," *Osage News*, Mar. 6, 2017, http://www.osagenews.org/en/article/2017/03/06/wah-zha-zhi-youth-council-learns-about-water-quality/.

106. Montoya, "Violence on the Ground"; Pellow, *Resisting Global Toxics*; Coulthard, "For Our Nations to Live, Capitalism Must Die."

107. A. Simpson, "Consent's Revenge," 328–29.

108. One participant observer, Jaskiran Dhillon, advocated putting more resources into these frontline youth activists. She urged investing in the "wisdom and knowledge of Indigenous youth and their communities as they attempt to heal and protect our planet from the harm that comes in the wake of a never-ending demand for more energy, regardless of the cost." Similarly, documentary filmmakers Myron Dewey (Newe-Numah/Paiute-Shoshone) and James Spione started a Youth Indigenous Media

Fund to assist young Native American journalists and filmmakers with their current and future projects. Fifty percent of the proceeds from their film *Awake: A Dream from Standing Rock* (http://awakethefilm.org) will go toward this fund, which will be governed by an advisory board of filmmakers, as well as Indigenous elders Doug Good Feather and Floris White Bull. See also Myron Dewey quoted in James Archer, "Indigenous Journalist Myron Dewey Opens Up about His Upcoming Trial and Standing Rock," *HuffPost*, July 13, 2017, http://www.huffingtonpost.com/entry/indigenous-journalist-myron-dewey-opens-up-about-his_us_5962a381e4b0cf3c8e8d59c8; and Myron Dewey on podcast "Connect the Dots: Guest Myron Dewey and James Spione," May 24, 2017, https://player.fm/series/progressive-radio-network/connect-the-dots-guest-myron-dewey-james-spione-052417.

109. Spice, "Interrupting Industrial and Academic Extraction."

110. Jared Keller, "Oil and Gas Ties Run Deep in the Trump Administration," *Pacific Standard*, Jan. 5, 2018, https://psmag.com/environment/oil-and-gas-ties-run-deep-in-trump-administration; Steve Cohen, "Trump's Energy Dominance and the Future of Fossil Fuels," Phys.org, Feb. 20, 2018, https://phys.org/news/2018-02-trump-energy-dominance-future-fossil.html; Marianne Lavelle, "Trump's Executive Order: More Fossil Fuels, Regardless of Climate Change," *Inside Climate News*, Mar. 28, 2017, https://insideclimatenews.org/news/28032017/trump-executive-order-climate-change-paris-climate-agreement-clean-power-plan-pruitt.

111. President Donald Trump, speech in Cincinnati, OH, June 7, 2017, Real Clear Politics, https://www.realclearpolitics.com/video/2017/06/07/full_replay_president_trump_proposes_renewing_americas_rivers_runways_roads_and_railways.html. As of December 2018, a transcript of these remarks was not available on whitehouse.gov.

112. Nick Tilsen quoted in "Standing Rock's Fight against Dakota Pipeline Continues while Tribe Plans for a Fossil-Fuel-Free Future."

113. Morgan Brings Plenty quoted in Karen Savage, "Discrimination Motivates Young Activist to Protect Water for Future Generations," *Youth Today*, Nov. 17, 2016, http://youthtoday.org/2016/11/discrimination-motivates-young-activist-to-protect-water-for-future-generations/, Thomas Lopez quoted in E. Simon, "Seventh Generation."

114. Thomas Lopez quoted in E. Simon, "Seventh Generation."

CONCLUSION

1. Howard Zinn, quoted by Bernice Johnson Reagon, "Solidarity of Past, Present and Future," SNCC Fiftieth Anniversary; James Lawson quoted by Suzanne Pharr in Acuña et al., "Race, The Election and Regenerating Our Democracy"; Mindock, "UN Says Trump Separation of Migrant Children from Parents May Amount to Torture"; Saadi, "Detention Facilities Display"; Stewart, "Nationwide Protests." "Detention of children is punitive, severely hampers their development, and in some cases may amount to torture," the experts said. "Children are being used as a deterrent to irregular migration, which is unacceptable." UN Human Rights Office of the High Commissioner, "UN Experts to US."

2. Fernandez and Qiu, "Is the Border in Crisis?"; Joe Ward and Anjali Singhvi, "Trump Claims There's a Crisis at the Border. What's the Reality?," *New York Times*, Jan. 11, 2019, https://www.nytimes.com/interactive/2019/01/11/us/politics/trump-border-crisis-reality.html.

3. Tania Unzueta, Maru Mora Villalpando, and Angélica Cházaro, "We Fell in Love in a Hopeless Place: A Grassroots History from #Not1More to #AbolishICE," *Medium*, June 29, 2018, https://medium.com/@LaTania/we-fell-in-love-in-a-hopeless-place-a-grassroots-history-from-not1more-to-abolish-ice-23089cf21711.

4. National Congress of American Indians, "Official Statement"; Black Mamas Matter Alliance, "History Always Repeats Itself"; Hunter, "The Long History of Child Snatching."

5. Dream Defenders, "Notice: We're Coming for Geo Group."

6. Nse Ufot, Dec. 1, 2018, SNCC Legacy Project Voting Rights Book Project Conference, 2018, Rare Book, Manuscript and Special Collections Library, Duke University. For a clear portrait of what roadblocks stand in the way of the Dream Defenders, Ufot, and others who pursue democracy's idea of representative government, see MacLean, *Democracy in Chains*, especially 219–20.

7. SNCC in the 1960s created the Lowndes County Freedom Organization, or LCFO, with Black Alabamians. Their work has been described by scholar Hasan Jeffries as "freedom politics." It was a "new kind of political engagement," he notes, that "combined SNCC's egalitarian organizing methods with people's civil and human rights goals. Freedom politics was a substitute for the undemocratic traditions that defined American politics, which ranged from disenfranchising poor people to choosing candidates exclusively from the propertied and the privileged." As local African Americans created the LCFO, they "transformed local black political behavior. More importantly, they created a model for exporting freedom politics beyond the black community to democratize American politics." Jeffries, *Bloody Lowndes*, 5, 177–78, 243–45.

8. On the founders, see Holton, *Unruly Americans*, part 1; on Jefferson, see Gordon-Reed, *Thomas Jefferson and Sally Hemings* and *Hemingses of Monticello*. See also Rana, *Two Faces of American Freedom*. Nancy MacLean's work suggests there may be a need to further delineate the kinds of "elite politics" pursued between those that stay within the general constitutional framework and those envisioned by James Buchanan and Charles Koch, which would change the US Constitution in fundamental ways. See MacLean, *Democracy in Chains*, conclusion.

9. Martin Luther King popularized this aphorism, used by ministers, rabbis, and philosophers since at least the nineteenth century's Theodore Parker. Barack Obama used it as well, attributing it to King. See King, *Testament of Hope*, 141, 207, 230, 277.

10. For coverage of the Parkland shooting and the mass movement young people are building under groups like March for Our Lives and Never Again, see Charlotte Alter, "The School Shooting Generation Has Had Enough," *Time*, Mar. 22, 2018, http://time.com/longform/never-again-movement/; Emily Witt, "How the Survivors of Parkland Began the 'Never Again' Movement," *New Yorker*, Feb. 18, 2018, https://www.newyorker.com/news/news-desk/how-the-survivors-of-parkland-began-the-never-again-movement; and Ryan Bort, "The Parkland Students Are Embarking on

a Nationwide Summer Activism Tour," *Rolling Stone*, June 4, 2018, https://www.rollingstone.com/politics/news/march-for-our-lives-bus-tour-w521029.

11. "Racial capitalism" is a term coined by Cedric Robinson, who heard scholars of South Africa's apartheid regime using it and subsequently developed it as a term to illuminate the broader world system of modern capitalism "dependent on slavery, violence, imperialism, and genocide." Robinson, *Black Marxism*; and Kelley, "What Did Cedric Robinson Mean by Racial Capitalism?" It has been further developed, Walter Johnson notes, by "scholars such as Ruth Wilson Gilmore, Adam Green, Cheryl Harris, Peter Hudson, Robin D. G. Kelley, George Lipsitz, Lisa Lowe, Gary Okihiro, Nell Irvin Painter, David Roediger, Alexander Saxton, and Stephanie Smallwood. And no longer should the 'capitalism-slavery debate' proceed without a full and forthright acknowledgement of and engagement with the pioneering work and enduring insights of W. E. B. Du Bois, C. L. R. James, Eric Williams, Walter Rodney, Angela Davis, and Cedric Robinson." Johnson with Kelley, "To Remake the World."

12. Aja Monet, June 16, 2018, SNCC COH 2018.

13. Sunny Osment, June 16, 2018, SNCC COH 2018. On people organized around consumption, see W. Brown, *Undoing the Demos*; Duggan, *Twilight of Equality?*; and Cherniavsky, *Neocitizenship*. Also see Hong, *Death beyond Disavowal*.

14. Aja Monet and Sunny Osment, June 16, 2018, SNCC COH 2018; Kelley, "Forum: Black Study."

15. For some ways this notion is seeping into the broader culture, see "Circular," TED Talks, NPR, Dec. 6, 2018, available at https://itunes.apple.com/us/podcast/ted-radio-hour/id523121474?mt=2&i=1000425324590#; and Jason Hickel, "Why Growth Can't Be Green," Jason Hickel, Sept. 14, 2018, https://www.jasonhickel.org/blog/2018/9/14/why-growth-cant-be-green.

16. Phelps, *Shattered Voices*, 126.

17. This is as true of scholars as it is of politicians and everyday citizens. As urban scholar Michael Katz argued in 2010, scholars who chronicled failed public policy histories risked reinforcing a conservative agenda to privatize public goods. Katz, "Existential Problem" and "Narratives of Failure?"

18. See Goodwyn, *Breaking the Barrier*, 358–59. See also the essay at the end of this book, "Who's the Expert?"

19. Jefferson to Joel Barlow, May 3, 1802, in Boyd, ed., *Jefferson Papers*, 1:vii.

20. For particularly clear chronicles of this process, see Moses and Cobb, *Radical Equations*; and brown, *Emergent Strategy*.

21. The Dream Defenders have begun to pass on their knowledge, meeting with the March for Our Lives youth, and Climate Justice Now supported Thunberg's speech. Morrison, "Slow Walk of Trees"; Phil Agnew to author, June 15, 2018, notes in the author's possession. On Thunberg see John Sutter and Lawrence Davidson, "Teen Tells Climate Negotiators They Aren't Mature Enough," CNN.com, Dec. 17, 2018, https://www.cnn.com/2018/12/16/world/greta-thunberg-cop24/index.html; and Masha Gessen, "The 15-Year-Old Climate Activist Who Is Demanding a Different Kind of Politics," *New Yorker*, Oct. 2, 2018, https://www.newyorker.com/news/our-columnists/the-fifteen-year-old-climate-activist-who-is-demanding-a-new-kind-of-politics.

22. See for example the debate on "moderates" and "moderation" in Michael McBride et al., "Waiting for the Perfect Protest?," *New York Times*, Sept. 1, 2017, https://www.nytimes.com/2017/09/01/opinion/civil-rights-protest-resistance.html?_r=1. One can see this debate over "moderates" clearly in the 1960s as well, particularly focused on Dr. King. For example see his 1963 "Letter from a Birmingham Jail," King Institute, Stanford University, https://kinginstitute.stanford.edu/king-papers/documents/letter-birmingham-jail (accessed Nov. 3, 2018). And when white journalists asked Dr. Martin King, "Was the march worth the cost?" on *Meet the Press* following the 1965 Selma campaign, see his response, available on YouTube, https://www.youtube.com/watch?v=fAtsAwGreyE (accessed Sept. 3, 2017). See Bree Newsome on white moderates, https://twitter.com/BreeNewsome/status/903840679129907200 (accessed Sept. 3, 2017).

23. Goodwyn, *Breaking the Barrier*, 145.

24. Goodwyn, 86–87.

25. Payne, *I've Got the Light of Freedom*, chap. 13; Goodwyn, *Breaking the Barrier*, 145–57.

26. This on-the-ground lived democracy can and should be in wider conversation with those writing in more theoretical terms about the fate of democracy today. Robin D. G. Kelley is an example of someone pulling people together to do that work. See "Forum: Black Study." For other commentators on the fate of democracy in the current era, see Purdy, "Normcore"; Jason Brennan, *Against Democracy*, and Aziz Rana, "Goodbye Cold War"; and Rebecca Solnit, "Tyranny of the Minority," *Harper's*, March 2017, https://harpers.org/archive/2017/03/tyranny-of-the-minority/.

27. MacLean, *Democracy in Chains*, 219–28.

28. To reprise scholar Ponna Wignaraja: "There is little need to criticize the dangers of centralized power, repressive state structures and absolute power that corrupts." Worldwide, libraries are full of books cataloging these realities. What we are short on are models that work: "What needs to be elaborated is the concept of participatory democracy and the building of countervailing power, initially within the political spaces that are already available." Wignaraja, *New Social Movements*, 10. See Teaching for Change, an organization that provides one important counterbalance, making resources of popular democratic movements available to K–12 teachers; see http://www.teachingforchange.org. See also Daniel Comacho, "Latin America: A Society in Motion," in Wignaraja, *New Social Movements*, 38.

WHO'S THE EXPERT?
AN ESSAY ON EVIDENCE AND AUTHORITY

1. Thanks to Nishani Frazier for her feedback on this essay. For clear examples of this process, movement activists' memoirs are vital. See for example Moses and Cobb, *Radical Equations*; Segrest, *My Mama's Dead Squirrel*; V. Jones, *Green Collar Economy*; and Carruthers, *Unapologetic*.

2. Those who have critiqued this extractive method are growing. Some examples include Smith, *Decolonizing Methodologies*; and Shawn Wilson, *Research Is Ceremony*. Several larger trends pushed people toward a small-*d* democratic approach

within archival work in the last four decades, though these projects remained largely on the margins: participatory research in the 1970s; the Canadian "total archives" movement of the 1980s; the human rights community-driven archive creation in South Africa, Cambodia, Australia, Brazil, and elsewhere; and the possibilities for online archive-building provided by the internet in the 1990s. In 2017, the Annual Meeting of the Society of American Archivists devoted an entire day of the annual conference to "The Liberated Archive: A Forum for Envisioning and Implementing a Community-Based Approach." Bryan Giemza considers this as "a paradigm shift in archival science" (Giemza, "More Than Words," 36). Lisa Darms lays out some of the challenges radical archives face when trying to fit into archival workflows. Darms, "Radical Archives." See also the idea of community-accountable intellectuals, a term from Alexis Pauline Gumbs, interview by Talley. On organizers being accountable to the communities in which they work, see Carruthers, *Unapologetic*, Kindle location 1548–89.

3. A brief description of how this works is available online: https://genius.com/web-annotator (accessed May 18, 2018).

4. This builds on an idea developed in Polletta, *It Was Like a Fever*, 54, 107. Milkman, Bloom, and Bloom developed a similar framework in 2007–8 for *LA Model*; see their introduction.

5. For examples of people working to partner together to position the production of knowledge as a process of "co-creation" among scholars, students, knowledge seekers, and communities "working together through extended information commons," see Giemza, "More than Words," 34–36. See also Portelli, "Research as an Experiment in Equality"; Caswell, "What Is a Community-Based Archives Anyway?" and "Seeing Yourself in History"; K. Brown, "On the Participatory Archive"; Cook, "Evidence, Memory, Identity and Community"; and Gilliland and McKemmish, "Role of Participatory Archives." I am also very grateful to Sarah Loose and Isabell Moore for running a workshop on the intersection of community organizing and oral history at the 2018 Oral History Association conference.

6. "Who Is the Interviewer?," History Matters, http://historymatters.gmu.edu/mse/oral/question2.html (accessed Aug. 3, 2017).

7. I'm grateful for the guidance of scholars who have wrestled many of these issues to the ground and illuminated new paths forward, including Alpern et al., *Challenge of Feminist Biography*; Denetdale, *Reclaiming Diné History*; Blee, "Evidence, Empathy and Ethics"; Gumbs, "Seek the Roots"; Kumbier, "Inventing History"; Spencer, "Mad at History," 67–69; and Coles, *Doing Documentary Work*, Kindle location 398–99. Ashley Farmer's important recent piece, "In Search of the Black Women's History Archive," illuminates the challenges of a profoundly limited archive. Nishani Frazier's exploration of these power dynamics in the preface and introduction to *Harambee City* has been particularly instructive (x). For a very helpful overview of the tension between positivist approaches and the epistemological intersubjectivity questions inevitably drawn out of oral history practice, see Shopes, "Insights and Oversights."

8. Corbett and Miller, "Shared Inquiry," 15. Corbett and Miller trace reflective practice among historians back to Schön, *Reflective Practitioner*, and his critics, as

well as early twentieth-century professionals Frederick Jackson Turner, Charles Beard, and Carl Becker.

9. Virginia Eubanks and Alethia Jones, "Chronicling an Activist Life," in Jones and Eubanks with Smith, *Ain't Gonna Let Nobody Turn Me Around*, 4. See also Robert Coles's powerful meditation on "location ma[king] a huge difference, not only the location of a particular documentary project with respect to someone's analytic scheme of things (it is this, it is that, it should go under some other name, be described as something different) but the very location of the person doing the project." Coles, *Doing Documentary Work*, Kindle location 537–38.

10. Frazier, *Harambee City*, introduction. Multiple generations of scholars have challenged the possibility, to say nothing of the ethic, of objectivity. See for example Charlotte Linde: "Various studies show that the social production of medical, legal, and bureaucratic records is not a simple matter of recording facts; instead, it is the result of social processes, negotiations, and rules of thumb to be followed when standard procedures cannot be applied, as is often the case." Linde, *Life Stories*, 15. She cites Garfinkle and Bittner, "Good Organizational Reasons"; Meehan, "Record-Keeping Practices in the Policing of Juveniles"; and Zimmerman, "Record-Keeping and the Intake Process."

11. Lisa Randall, "Seeing Dark Matter as the Key to the Universe—and Human Empathy," *Boston Globe*, Oct. 26, 2015, https://www.bostonglobe.com/opinion/2015/10/25/seeing-dark-matter-key-universe-and-human-empathy/NXNMBXAa7WEWejN63fFCNL/story.html.

12. Hine, *Hine Sight*, 57. Sullivan and Tuana, *Race and Epistemologies of Ignorance*, gathers central pieces of the scholarship responding to Charles Mills's *The Racial Contract*. Bonilla-Silva's *Racism without Racists* and Zuberi and Bonilla-Silva's *White Logic* examine the ways language and social science continue to support white supremacist ideologies despite development of "color-blind" vocabulary. Linda Tuhiwai Smith's *Decolonizing Methodologies* opened up a huge and vital area of scholarship, shifting and expanding the conceptual terrain. Michael Roth's analysis of Michel Foucault's writing and impact on reflexivity in the humanities and social sciences is also useful. Roth, "Foucault's History of the Present."

13. The Tuskegee syphilis study and Milgram/Zimbardo experiments are only the most well known examples. Anne Spice's eloquent framing might be cited at length here:

> The so-called founding fathers of [anthropology] created and defended university positions in anthropology by writing about native peoples, while their native informants, students, and collaborators struggled to make a living in academia, their voices eclipsed by white anthropologists like John Wesley Powell, Frederic Ward Putnam, Lewis Henry Morgan, Franz Boas, and Alfred Kroeber. . . . Most of these early anthropological writers omitted Indigenous political resistance to colonial violence in their analysis. Instead, Indigenous peoples were often portrayed as static cultures on the verge of extinction, despite fervent and powerful efforts to resist erasure and assimilation. Then, as now, Indigenous communities were fighting for survival against a ruthless

structure of elimination (Wolfe 2006). Then, as now, Indigenous lives and cultural practices were made into ethnographic material to advance academic careers. And although native people have been key to the production of anthropological theory all along (Ely Parker, Francis La Flesche, George Hunt, Ella Deloria), today the discipline has a renewed opportunity to honor the contributions of Indigenous scholars by supporting our embedded analyses of Indigenous resistance. In a moment when Indigenous communities across the continent are threatened by state-supported extractive industry, anthropology must not mirror this with extractive scholarship. If Indigenous land defense and solidarity movements are timely, it is because it is time for us to act, not to ruminate. We need you to support our work as Indigenous activist scholars. This means centering and citing our research and writing, but also acknowledging that our commitments to land-defense movements extend beyond ethnographic description. We are working to help our nations survive, on the page and on the ground. I fervently believe in our collective right to refuse to let yet another river be contaminated, to let more land be stolen and destroyed. The fight against the DAPL is fundamentally about a refusal to disappear as Indigenous peoples (see Simpson 2014). The Oceti Sakowin are exercising a right long denied by colonial settler states—the right to say no. No to the Pipeline, no to the poison, no to the vacuous political theater of reconciliation (Coulthard 2014). No, perhaps, to anthropological study, to representations of the noble savage that still pervade environmentalist accounts of native activism. ("Interrupting Industrial and Academic Extraction")

On Tuskegee, see J. Jones, *Bad Blood*; and Reverby, *Tuskegee's Truths* and *Examining Tuskegee*. On iconic examples of scholarly ethics gone missing, see Zimbardo, *Lucifer Effect*; Milgram, *Obedience to Authority*; Adams and Balfour, *Unmasking Administrative Evil*; and Bowman, *Public Service Ethics*.

14. Harding, *Hope and History*; Harding and Harding, "Freedom's Sacred Dance"; Harding with Harding, "Hospitality, Haints, and Healing"; Zinn, *On History*; Lynd and Lynd, *Stepping Stones*; Lynd, *Accompanying*; Dunbar-Ortiz, *Indigenous People's History*; Cohen, *Democracy Remixed*; Ransby, *Ella Baker*. As Bob Moses told Robert Coles in April 1964,

> Don't you see, that's been our story—the black story: everyone calls us something! It's so hard for any single one of us to be seen by you folks [white people], even the kindest of you, even our friends [among you] as a person, nothing more. That's where we are; that's where we're coming from; that's our "place" in all this! You folks—can be yourselves! You can wander all over the map. You can be here and you can be there. You can go set up your tent wherever you think it'll do you good! That's great—for you! That's what it means to be white, and have a good education. You can look at things with a microscope or a telescope, scope, and from way up in the mountains and down near the seashore, and when it's sunny and when it's raining cats and dogs, and then, later, when you write or you publish your photographs—you're not a white writer, or a white photographer. You're free of the biggest label of them all, the

one that defines us every single minute of our lives! So, you can take all roads, and you can stop at any gas station or restaurant while on the way. Us—we're trying to get people to give us just a little break, to call us Mister or Missus, to let me go where I please without thinking I might get arrested, and even killed. So, it's location, man, location, for us: where we're at, and where you're at, and where we can go, and where you can go—that's why I favor stopping to look at one person, then the next, and not running all which ways to corral folks into someone's pen, some circle, with a fence around it. (quoted in Coles, *Doing Documentary Work*, Kindle location 450–59)

15. Virginia Eubanks, "Chronicling an Activist Life," in Jones and Eubanks with Smith, *Ain't Gonna Let Nobody Turn Me Around*, 10.

16. In this work, I was inspired by the reflective pedagogy practices developed within the Association for Contemplative Mind in Higher Education. For example, see Zajonc, "Contemplative Pedagogy"; and Parker Palmer's series of publications on reflection and the life of the mind, especially his coauthored piece, *The Heart of Higher Education*. Lynn Abram's survey of the theories of power and narrative within the practice of oral history are essential, in *Oral History Theory*, as are Trinh T. Minh-Ha's pathbreaking insights on questions and the structure of interviews in *Framer Framed*, 186, 192.

17. Evans, *Black Women in the Ivory Tower*; White, *Telling Histories*; Gutiérrez y Muhs et al., *Presumed Incompetent*. Thavolia Glymph's important work on the ways white women physically and emotionally abused Black women living as slaves and servants in their households, *Out of the House of Bondage*, invites reflection on how white women unconsciously or consciously continue/d to embody those patterns of abuse beyond emancipation, and particularly on how historians and popular culture lie/d and often portray/ed white women as victims comparable to the subjugation experienced by enslaved women and men. See also for example Srigley and Sutherland, "Decolonizing, Indigenizing, and Learning"; Denetdale, *Reclaiming Diné History*; and Hong, *Death before Disavowal*. See also Cite Black Women Collective, "Cite Black Women," on Facebook, https://www.facebook.com/citeblackwomen/, (accessed Dec. 3, 2018); and N. D. B. Connolly's useful call to examine scholarly circles and their often-segregated nature, "Notes on a Desegregated Method," especially 586–89.

18. Many generations of social science and humanities scholars who reside on the margins (self-chosen or not) write about similar learning through relationship. For a recent example see Srigley and Sutherland, "Decolonizing, Indigenizing, and Learning."

19. Portelli provides a powerful model of this way of knowledge-production in "Research as an Experiment in Equality," 29–33.

20. Kenneth Campbell and Wesley Hogan, "From the Inside Out," *The Oxford American*, http://www.oxfordamerican.org/item/1272-from-inside-out, (accessed July 20, 2017). See also the pathbreaking work of the filmmakers in the StoryShift Advisory Committee, "Principles & Praxis."

21. Ben-David and Amram, "Computational Methods for Web History," chap. 12.

22. Documenting the Now can be found at http://www.docnow.io/. See also Alexis

Pauline Gumbs's important article "Seek the Roots," 17–18. Gumbs describes how she and her partner Julia Wallace use "night schools, potlucks, podcasts, internet videos, a public access channel TV program, an internet TV station, ongoing interview process, traveling workshops, blogs and zine publications" to make sure that "previously undocumented [or out of print] Black feminist strategies, poems, essays, newsletters, and practices [are] accessible to a diverse community of parents, teachers, workers, organizers and writers." Two other vital pieces on the difficulties of reading primary sources on popular movements are Payne, "Bibliographic Essay: The Social Construction of History," in *I've Got the Light of Freedom*, 413–42; and Goodwyn, "Ways of Seeing: A Critical Essay on Authorities," in *Breaking the Barrier*, 442–59.

23. Frazier, Hyman and Greene, "African American Studies and Digital Humanities"; Ernst, *Digital Memory and the Archive*.

24. Michael Frisch's pathbreaking work on shared authority fostered two decades worth of conversation after the publication of his *A Shared Authority* and the entire issue of the *Oral History Review* 30, no. 1 (2003), which reviewed the concept, including Frisch's own "Commentary Sharing Authority and the Collaborative Process." Many have developed the framework since in powerful ways. See Adair, Filene, and Koloski, *Letting Go*; Wong, "Conversations for the Real World"; Barber, "Shared Authority in the Context of Tribal Sovereignty"; Kerr, "Allan Nevins Is Not My Grandfather"; and Frazier, *Harambee City*, introduction. Sherna Berger Gluck et al., "OHA Principles and Best Practices," includes an historical overview of these developments as well as current best practices from the Oral Historians Association, https://www.oralhistory.org/principles-and-best-practices-revised-2018/ (accessed Sept. 14, 2018).

25. The work we've done with the SNCC Legacy Project since 2013 has allowed us to carve out one set of institutional pathways to include activists in the knowledge creation, preservation, and dissemination processes. I wrote this essay as I worked on the collective piece with the SNCC Legacy Project, so there is a certain amount of overlap between the two. See Cox et al., "Building and Transferring Movement Informational Wealth." Yet much more work on these institutional pathways must be done along these lines, as different activist groups will require a range of approaches.

BIBLIOGRAPHY

ARCHIVES

Durham, NC
    David M. Rubenstein Rare Book and Manuscript Library, Duke University
        Bobbye Ortiz Papers
        Joseph Andrew Sinsheimer Papers, 1983–1986
        Judy Richardson Papers, 1963–2014
        Mab Segrest Papers, 1889–2014
        Mandy Carter Papers, 1970–2013
        SNCC Digital Gateway Launch Conference, Mar. 23–24, 2018
        SNCC Fiftieth Anniversary Conference, 2010
        SNCC Fortieth Anniversary Conference, 2000
        SNCC Legacy Project Critical Oral History Interviews, 2016
        SNCC Legacy Project Critical Oral History Interviews, 2018
        SNCC Legacy Project Voting Rights Book Project Conference, 2018
        SNCC Legacy Project Voting Rights Conference, 2015
        Southerners on New Ground Papers, 1993–2003
Madison, WI
    State Historical Society of Wisconsin
        Ella Baker Papers, 1959–1965
Washington, DC
    Manuscript Division, Library of Congress
        Joseph Rauh Papers, 1913–1994

INTERVIEWS BY THE AUTHOR

Chatfield, Jack. Jan. 6, 2001. Telephone. Transcript in the author's possession.
Frazier, Lanise. Dec. 30, 2014. Telephone. Transcript in the author's possession.
Moses, Bob. Jan. 28, 2018. Princeton, NJ. Notes in the author's possession.
Perry, Nona. Jan. 8, 2015. Oakland, CA. Transcript in the author's possession.
Quinlan, Susan. Jan. 8, 2015. Oakland, CA. Notes in the author's possession.
Sherrod, Shirley. July 11, 2016. Durham, NC. Notes in the author's possession.
Yasmin. Sept. 2, 2015. Durham, NC. Transcript in the author's possession.
Young, Darris. Jan. 7, 2015. Oakland, CA. Transcript in the author's possession.

ARCHIVAL INTERVIEWS DONE BY OTHERS

Adams, Victoria Gray. Interview by Joseph Sinsheimer. Petersburg, VA, Aug. 23, 1987. Joseph Andrew Sinsheimer Papers, 1983–1986, Rare Book, Manuscript and Special Collections Library, Duke University.

Allen, Emma. Interview by Joseph Sinsheimer. Greenwood, MS, May 5, 1986. Joseph Andrew Sinsheimer Papers, 1983–1986, Rare Book, Manuscript and Special Collections Library, Duke University.

Arpaio Joe with Len Sherman. *Joe's Law: America's Toughest Sheriff Takes on Illegal Immigration, Drugs, and Everything Else That Threatens America*. New York: Amacom, 2008.

Attwood, Shaun. *Hard Time: Life with Sheriff Joe Arpaio in America's Toughest Jail*. New York: Skyhorse Publishing, 2011.

Baker, Ella. "Ella Baker Interview, March 4, 1979." Interview by Lenore Hagan. Highlander Research and Education Center Archives, New Market, TN.

———. "Interview with Ella Baker: June 19, 1968." Interview by John Britton. Moorland-Spingarn Research Center, Howard University.

———. "Interview with Ella Baker, 1968." Interview by Emily Stoper. In *The Student Nonviolent Coordinating Committee: The Growth of Radicalism in a Civil Rights Organization*, edited by Emily Stoper, 265–72. New York: Carlson Publishing, 1989. Also available at http://www.crmvet.org/nars/bakere.htm.

———. "Oral History Interview with Ella Baker, September 4, 1974." Interview by Eugene Walker. Southern Oral History Program Collection (#4007). Documenting the American South. http://docsouth.unc.edu/sohp/G-0007/menu.html.

———. "Oral History Interview with Ella Baker, April 19, 1977." Interview by Casey Hayden and Sue Thrasher. Southern Oral History Program Collection (#4007). Documenting the American South. http://docsouth.unc.edu/sohp/G-0008/menu.html.

Block, Sam. Interview by Joseph Sinsheimer. Montgomery, AL, Dec. 12, 1986. Joseph Andrew Sinsheimer Papers, 1983–1986, Rare Book, Manuscript and Special Collections Library, Duke University.

Carter, Mandy. Interview by Rose Norman. Telephone. Mar. 26, 2013. Partial transcript. *Sinister Wisdom: A Multicultural Lesbian Literary and Art Journal*. http://www.sinisterwisdom.org/SW93Supplement/Carter.

Coles, Robert. Interview by Joseph Sinsheimer. Boston, MA, Nov. 19, 1983. Joseph Andrew Sinsheimer Papers, 1983–1986, Rare Book, Manuscript and Special Collections Library, Duke University.

Garner, Joan. Interview by Rose Norman. Telephone. Apr. 12, 2013. *Sinister Wisdom: A Multicultural Lesbian Literary and Art Journal*. http://www.sinisterwisdom.org/SW93Supplement/Garner.

Gumbs, Alexis Pauline. Interview by Heather Laine Talley. "Teaching Resources Brilliance Remastered." *Feminist Teacher* 2, no. 2 (2012): 165–67.

Hussain, Pat. Interview by Lorraine Fontana. Atlanta, GA, May 6, 2013. *Sinister Wisdom: A Multicultural Lesbian Literary and Art Journal*. http://www.sinisterwisdom.org/SW93Supplement/Hussain.

Johnson, June. Interview by Joseph Sinsheimer. Washington, DC, May 5, 1987.

Joseph Andrew Sinsheimer Papers, 1983–1986, Rare Book, Manuscript and Special Collections Library, Duke University.

Jones, Van. Interview by Kerry Kennedy Cuomo. *Speak Truth to Power*. PBS series. Initially broadcast Oct. 8. 2000. Partial transcript. PBS. http://www.pbs.org/speaktruthtopower/van.html.

McMichael, Pam. Interview by Rose Norman. Telephone. Apr. 23, 2013. *Sinister Wisdom: A Multicultural Lesbian Literary and Art Journal*. http://www.sinisterwisdom.org/SW93Supplement/McMichael.

Moses, Bob. Interview by John Dittmer. Cambridge, MA, Aug. 15, 1983. Joseph Andrew Sinsheimer Papers, 1983–1986, Rare Book, Manuscript and Special Collections Library, Duke University.

Palmer, Hazel. Interview by Joseph Sinsheimer. Jackson, MS, June 19, 1985. Joseph Andrew Sinsheimer Papers, 1983–1986, Rare Book, Manuscript and Special Collections Library, Duke University.

Palmer, Hazel, with Bob Moses. Group interview. Duke University, Durham, NC, Oct. 26–27, 1985. Joseph Andrew Sinsheimer Papers, 1983–1986, Rare Book, Manuscript and Special Collections Library, Duke University.

Pharr, Suzanne. Interview by Kelly Anderson. Video recording. June 28, 2005. Voices of Feminism Oral History Project, Sophia Smith Collection, Smith College, Northampton, MA. http://www.smith.edu/libraries/libs/ssc/vof/transcripts/Pharr.pdf .

———. Interview by Rose Norman. Telephone. Mar. 28, 2013. *Sinister Wisdom: A Multicultural Lesbian Literary and Art Journal*. http://www.sinisterwisdom.org/SW93Supplement/Pharr.

Roy, Arundhati. "Arundhati Roy on the Rising Hindu Right in India, the Gujarat Massacre and Her Love of Eduardo Galeano." *Democracy Now!*, June 26, 2017. https://www.democracynow.org/2017/6/26/arundhati_roy_on_the_rising_hindu.

Segrest, Mab. Interview by Rose Norman. Telephone. May 10, 2013. *Sinister Wisdom: A Multicultural Lesbian Literary and Art Journal*. http://www.sinisterwisdom.org/SW93Supplement/Segrest.

SECONDARY SOURCES

Aaron, Darian. "Queer, Trans Identities Centered in Black Lives Matter Atlanta Chapter." *Georgia Voice*, Dec. 18, 2015. http://thegavoice.com/queer-trans-identities-centered-in-black-lives-matter-atlanta-chapter/.

Abrahamian, Atossa Araxia. *The Cosmopolites: The Coming of the Global Citizen*. New York: Columbia Global Reports, 2015.

Abrahamsen, Rita, and Anna Leander. *Routledge Handbook of Private Security Studies*. New York: Routledge, 2016.

Abram, Lynn. *Oral History Theory*. New York: Routledge, 2010.

Acuña, Salem, Cathy Woodson, and Suzanne Pharr. "Race, the Election and Regenerating Our Democracy." Panel at Virginia Commonwealth University, Nov. 8, 2012. Available online: https://vimeo.com/53452625.

Adair, Bill, Benjamin Filene, and Laura Koloski, eds. *Letting Go: Sharing Historical Authority in a User-Generated World*. Walnut Creek, CA: Left Coast Press, 2011.

Adams, Frank, with Myles Horton. *Unearthing Seeds of Fire: The Idea of Highlander.* Winston-Salem, NC: John Blair, 1975.

Adams, Guy B., and Danny Balfour. *Unmasking Administrative Evil.* Armonk, NY: M. E. Sharpe, 2004.

African American Policy Forum. "Say Her Name: Resisting Police Brutality against Black Women." Center for Intersectionality and Social Policy Studies, May 2015. African American Policy Forum. http://www.aapf.org/sayhernamereport/.

Agnew, Phil, interviewed by Ben Wikler. *The Flaming Sword of Justice* podcast. Aug. 2, 2013. https://itunes.apple.com/us/podcast/18-dream-defenders-origins/id497260543?i=163562900&mt=2.

Agnew, Philip/Umi Selah. "Moments and Movements." Fall 2015. Fund for Democratic Communities. Greensboro, NC. https://www.youtube.com/watch?v=bu30dVpR5kA.

Alexander, Michelle. *The New Jim Crow: Mass Incarceration in the Age of Colorblindness.* New York: New Press, 2010.

Alfred, Taiaiake. *Wasáse: Indigenous Pathways of Action and Freedom.* Toronto: University of Toronto Press, 2005.

Allen, Chude Pam. "Confronting the -isms." *Against the Current* 133 (March–April 2008). Reprinted in *Solidarity* newsletter, http://www.solidarity-us.org/site/node/1398.

Allen, Danielle, and Jennifer S. Light. *From Voice to Influence: Understanding Citizenship in a Digital Age.* Chicago: University of Chicago Press, 2015.

Allen, Robert, and Pamela Allen. *Reluctant Reformers: Racism and Social Reform Movements in the United States.* Washington, DC: Howard University Press, 1974.

Alpern, Sara, Joyce Antler, Elisabeth Israels Perry, and Ingrid Winther Scobie, eds. *The Challenge of Feminist Biography: Writing the Lives of Modern American Women.* Champaign: University of Illinois Press, 1992.

Altschuler, Daniel. "The Dreamers' Movement Comes of Age." *Dissent*, May 16, 2011. https://www.dissentmagazine.org/online_articles/the-dreamers-movement-comes-of-age.

American Civil Liberties Union. *War Comes Home: The Excessive Militarization of American Policing.* ACLU, 2014. https://www.aclu.org/feature/war-comes-home.

American Immigration Council. "A Comparison of the DREAM Act and Other Proposals for Undocumented Youth." Immigration Policy Center, June 5, 2012. http://www.immigrationpolicy.org/sites/default/files/docs/dream_comparison_060112.pdf.

Amnesty International USA. *Unmatched Power, Unmet Principles: The Human Rights Dimension of U.S. Training of Foreign Military and Police Forces.* New York: Amnesty International Publications, 2002.

Anderson, Benedict. *Imagined Communities: Reflections on the Origin and Spread of Nationalism.* London: Verso Books, 2006.

Anderson, Carol. "The Politics of Respectability: The Devaluation of Black Lives and Erosion of American Democracy's Legitimacy." Paper presented at Emory University, Atlanta, GA, April 16, 2016.

———. *White Rage: The Unspoken Truth of Our Racial Divide.* New York: Bloomsbury, 2016.

Anderson, Jervis. *Bayard Rustin: Troubles I've Seen; A Biography*. New York: HarperCollins, 1997.

Anderson, Kiera James. "We Made the Change by Talking about It: Movement Narratives of Antiviolence Activism in the Radical Environmental Organization Cascadia Forest Defenders." *Frontiers: A Journal of Women Studies* 39, no. 2 (2018): 136–70.

Anghie, Anthony. *Imperialism, Sovereignty, and the Making of International Law*. Cambridge: Cambridge University Press, 2007.

Anguiano, Claudia A., and Karma R. Chávez. "DREAMers' Discourse: Young Latino/a Immigrants and the Naturalization of the American Dream." In *Latino/a Discourse in Vernacular Spaces: Somos de Una Voz?*, edited by Michelle A. Holling and Bernadette Calafell, 81–100. Lanham, MD: Lexington Books, 2011.

Annamma, Subini Ancy. *The Pedagogy of Pathologization: Dis/abled Girls of Color in the School-Prison Nexus*. New York: Routledge, 2018.

Ansloos, Jeffrey Paul. *The Medicine of Peace: Indigenous Youth Decolonizing Healing and Resisting Violence*. Nova Scotia: Fernwood, 2017.

Aparicio, Ana. "Reconstituting Political Genealogies: Reflections on Youth, Racial Justice, and the Uses of History." In *New Social Movements in the African Diaspora: Challenging Global Apartheid*, edited by Leith Mullins, 234–46. New York: St. Martin's Press, 2009.

Applebaum, Yoni. "Americans Aren't Practicing Democracy Anymore." *The Atlantic*, Oct. 2018. https://www.theatlantic.com/magazine/archive/2018/10/losing-the-democratic-habit/568336/.

Aron, Hillel. "These Savvy Women Have Made Black Lives Matter the Most Crucial Left Wing Movement Today." *LA Weekly*, Nov. 9, 2015. http://www.laweekly.com/news/these-savvy-women-have-made-black-lives-matter-the-most-crucial-left-wing-movement-today-6252489.

Arsenault, Raymond. *Freedom Riders: 1961 and the Struggle for Racial Justice*. Rev. ed. New York: Oxford University Press, 2011.

Avalos, Natalie, Sandy Grande, Jason Mancini, Rijuta Mehta, Michelle Neely, and Christopher Newell. "Standing with Standing Rock." Hot Spots, *Fieldsights*, Dec. 22, 2016. https://culanth.org/fieldsights/1024-standing-with-standing-rock.

Axelrod, David. *Believer: My Forty Years in Politics*. New York: Penguin, 2016.

Badger, William. "'Yeah, but Look How Far We've Come': Disney and the Depiction of Blackness in *The Princess and the Frog*." *Bright Lights Film Journal*, Mar. 11, 2016. http://brightlightsfilm.com/yeah-but-look-how-far-weve-come-disney-and-the-depiction-of-blackness-in-the-princess-and-the-frog/#.WVJ1gTO-LU0.

Bailey, Kristian Davis. "Dream Defenders, Black Lives Matter and Ferguson Reps Take Historic Trip to Palestine." *Ebony*, Jan. 9, 2015. http://www.ebony.com/news-views/dream-defenders-black-lives-matter-ferguson-reps-take-historic-trip-to-palestine#ixzz4DcnzlmWq.

Bakan, Abigail, and Daiva Stasiulis. *Not One of the Family: Foreign Domestic Workers in Canada*. Toronto: University of Toronto Press, 1997.

Baker, Ella. "Bigger Than a Hamburger." *Southern Patriot*, June 1960. Civil Rights Movement Veterans. http://www.crmvet.org/docs/sncc2.htm.

———. "Colloquium Session III: Ethics and Morality, Friday, Feb. 1, 1980." Program in African American Culture, Voices of the Civil Rights Movement (VCRM) conference, Jan. 30–Feb. 3, 1980. Disc 21. RTC408.5.23. Smithsonian Institution Archives, Washington, DC.

———. "Developing Community Leadership." In *Black Women in White America*, edited by Gerda Lerner, 345–51. New York: Vintage, 1973.

Baker, Ella, with Marvel Cooke. "The Bronx Slave Market." *Crisis*, Nov. 1935, 330–31.

Balko, Radley. *Rise of the Warrior Cop: The Militarization of America's Police Forces*. New York: Public Affairs, 2013.

Bambara, Toni Cade, ed. *The Black Woman: An Anthology*. Reprint. New York: Washington Square Press, 2005.

Bannon, Alicia, Mitali Nagrecha, Rebekah Diller. "Criminal Justice Debt: A Barrier to Reentry." The Brennan Center, 2010. http://www.brennancenter.org/sites/default/files/legacy/Fees%20and%20Fines%20FINAL.pdf.

Barber, Katrine. "Shared Authority in the Context of Tribal Sovereignty: Building Capacity for Partnerships with Indigenous Nations." *Public Historian* 35, no. 4 (2013): 20–39.

Bastian, Jeannette A. "The Records of Memory, the Archives of Identity: Celebrations, Texts and Archival Sensibilities." *Archival Science* 13, nos. 2–3 (2013): 121–31.

Bausells, Marta, and Maeve Shearlaw. "Poets Speak Out for Refugees." *The Guardian*, Sept. 16, 2015. https://www.theguardian.com/books/2015/sep/16/poets-speak-out-for-refugees-.

Bayat, Asef. *Life as Politics: How Ordinary People Change the Middle East*. 2nd ed. Stanford: Stanford University Press, 2013.

Bebout, Lee. *Whiteness on the Border: Mapping the U.S. Racial Imagination in Brown and White*. New York: New York University Press, 2017.

Beckert, Sven. *Empire of Cotton: A Global History*. New York: Vintage, 2015.

Bederman, Gail. *Manliness and Civilization: A Cultural History of Gender and Race in the U.S., 1880–1917*. Chicago: University of Chicago Press, 1995.

Behena, Sofía, North Cooc, Rachel Currie-Rubin, Paul Cuttner, and Monica Ng, eds. *Disrupting the School-to-Prison Pipeline*. Cambridge, MA: Harvard Education Review Reprints, 2012.

Ben-David, Anat, and Adam Amram. "Computational Methods for Web History." In *The SAGE Handbook of Web History*, edited by Niels Brügger and Ian Milligan, 153–67. London: SAGE, 2019.

Bennett, W. Lance. "Social Movements beyond Borders: Understanding Two Eras of Transnational Activism." In *Transnational Protest and Global Activism*, edited by Donatella della Porta and Sydney Tarrow, 203–26. Lanham, MD: Rowman and Littlefield, 2004.

Bennion, David. "In 2013, the Dream 30 Fought to Come Home. *Open Borders*, Dec. 30, 2013. http://openborders.info/blog/in-2013-the-dream-30-fought-to-come-home/.

Benson, Bruce L. *To Serve and Protect: Privatization and Community in Criminal Justice*. New York: New York University Press, 1998.

Bentley, Jules. "Unapologetically Black: Activism On (and Off) the Streets with

BYP100." *Antigravity*, March 2015. http://www.antigravitymagazine.com/2015/03/unapologetically-black-activism-on-and-off-the-streets-with-the-black-youth-project-100/.

Berger, Dan. *Captive Nation: Black Prison Organizing in the Civil Rights Era*. Chapel Hill: University of North Carolina Press, 2016.

———. "Social Movements and Mass Incarceration: What Is to Be Done?" *Souls* 15, nos. 1–2 (2013): 3–18.

———, ed. *The Hidden 1970s: Histories of Radicalism*. New Brunswick: Rutgers University Press, 2010.

Berger, Dan, Chesa Boudin, and Kenyon Farrow, eds. *Letters from Young Activists: Today's Rebels Speak Out*. New York: Nation Books, 2005.

Berman, Ari. *Give Us the Ballot: The Modern Struggle for Voting Rights in America*. New York: Macmillan, 2015.

———. *Herding Donkeys: The Fight to Rebuild the Democratic Party and Reshape American Politics*. New York: Farrar, Straus and Giroux, 2010.

———. "Jim Messina, Obama's Enforcer." *The Nation*, Mar. 30, 2011. https://www.thenation.com/article/jim-messina-obamas-enforcer/.

———. "The Man behind Trump's Voter-Fraud Obsession." *New York Times Magazine*, June 13, 2017. https://www.nytimes.com/2017/06/13/magazine/the-man-behind-trumps-voter-fraud-obsession.html.

Bermanzohn, Sally Avery. *Through Survivors' Eyes: From the Sixties to the Greensboro Massacre*. Nashville: Vanderbilt University Press, 2003.

Berry, Mary Frances. *History Teaches Us to Resist: How Progressive Movements Have Succeeded in Challenging Times*. Boston: Beacon, 2018.

Bhandar, Brenna. *Colonial Lives of Property: Land, Law, and Racial Regimes of Ownership*. Durham: Duke University Press, 2018.

Black, Derek W. *Ending Zero Tolerance: The Crisis of Absolute School Discipline*. New York: New York University Press, 2016.

Black Mamas Matter Alliance. "History Always Repeats Itself, Never Forget, #BlackMamasMatter." Instagram, June 21, 2018. https://www.instagram.com/p/BkSPGznlQvb/?taken-by=blackmamasmatter.

Blee, Kathleen. "Evidence, Empathy and Ethics: Lessons from Oral Histories of the Klan." In *The Oral History Reader*, edited by Robert Perks and Alistair Thomson, 424–33. 3rd ed. Oxford: Taylor and Francis, 2015.

Bloom, Joshua, and Waldo E. Martin. *Black against Empire: A History of the Black Panther Party*. Berkeley: University of California Press, 2013.

Blumenson, Eric D., and Eva S. Nilsen. "Policing for Profit: The Drug War's Hidden Agenda." *University of Chicago Law Review* 65 (1998): 35–114.

Boal, Augusto. *Hamlet and the Baker's Son: My Life in Theater and Politics*. New York: Routledge, 2001.

———. *Theater of the Oppressed*. Translated by Charles McBride. London: Theatre Communications Group, 1993.

Boggs, Grace Lee. *Living for Change: An Autobiography*. Minneapolis: University of Minnesota Press, 1998.

Bonilla-Silva, Eduardo. *Racism without Racists: Color-Blind Racism and the Persistence of Racial Inequality in America*. 4th ed. Lanham: Rowman and Littlefield, 2013.

Booker, M. Keith. *Disney, Pixar, and the Hidden Messages of Children's Film*. New York: Greenwood Press, 2010.

Borderlands Theater. *Un Encuentro: Theater of and for the Borderlands/Teatro de la Frontera*. Nov. 13, 2013. http://www.borderlandstheater.org/un-encuentro-theater-of-the-borderlandsteatro-de-la-frontera/.

"Boston Coding Camp and Demo Day. Hack/Reduce." Young People's Project. http://www.typp.org/ (accessed June 3, 2015).

Bowman, Gary W., Simon Hakim, and Paul Seidenstat, eds. *Privatizing Correctional Institutions*. Piscataway, NJ: Transaction Publishers, 1993.

Bowman, James. *Public Service Ethics: Individual and Institutional Responsibilities*. Thousand Oaks: SAGE, 2015.

Boyd, Julian P., ed. *Jefferson Papers*. Princeton: Princeton University Press, 1950.

Boyte, Harry, and Sara Evans. *Free Spaces: The Sources of Democratic Change in America*. Chicago: University of Chicago Press, 1992.

Braden, Anne. *The Fight against Racism: The Key to a New Society*. Pamphlet. Women's International League for Peace and Freedom, 1975.

Brah, Avtar, and Ann Phoenix. "Ain't I a Woman? Revisiting Intersectionality." *Journal of International Women's Studies* 5, no. 3 (2004): 75–86.

Branch, Taylor. *At Canaan's Edge: America in the King Years, 1965–68*. Reprint. New York: Simon and Schuster, 2007.

———. *Parting the Waters: America in the King Years, 1954–63*. Reprint ed. New York: Simon and Schuster, 1989.

———. *Pillar of Fire: America in the King Years, 1963–65*. New York: Simon and Schuster, 1999.

Brecht, Bertolt. "To Posterity" ["An Dei Nachgebornen," 1939]. Translated by H. R. Hays. Poem Hunter.com. http://www.poemhunter.com/best-poems/bertolt-brecht/to-posterity/ (accessed Aug. 2, 2016).

Breines, Winifred. *The Great Refusal: Community and Organization in the New Left, 1962–1968*. Reprint. Rutgers: Rutgers University Press, 1989.

———. *The Trouble between Us: An Uneasy History of White and Black Women in the Feminist Movement*. New York: Oxford University Press, 2006.

Breitbart, Joshua, and Ana Nogueira. "An Independent Media Center of One's Own: A Feminist Alternative to Corporate Media." In *The Fire This Time: Young Activists and the New Feminism*, edited by Vivien Labaton and Dawn Lundy Martin, 19–41. New York: Knopf, 2009.

Brennan, Jason. *Against Democracy*. Princeton: Princeton University Press, 2017.

Brickner, Michael, and Shakyra Diaz. "Prisons for Profit, Incarceration for Sale." *Human Rights* 38, no. 3 (2011): 13–16.

Brinson, Susan. *Aftermath: Violence and the Remaking of a Self*. Princeton: Princeton University Press, 2002.

Brooke-Eisen, Lauren. *Inside Private Prisons: An American Dilemma in the Age of Mass Incarceration*. New York: Columbia University Press, 2018.

brown, adrienne maree. *Emergent Strategy: Shaping Change, Changing Worlds*. Chico, CA: AK Press, 2017.

Brown, Alleen, Will Parrish, and Alice Speri. "Leaked Documents Reveal Counter-Terrorism Tactics Used at Standing Rock to 'Defeat Pipeline Insurgencies.'" *The

Intercept, May 27, 2017. https://theintercept.com/2017/05/27/leaked-documents-reveal-security-firms-counterterrorism-tactics-at-standing-rock-to-defeat-pipeline-insurgencies/.

Brown, Elsa Barkley. "Negotiating and Transforming the Public Sphere: African American Political Life in the Transition from Slavery to Freedom." In *The Black Public Sphere: A Public Culture Book*, edited by the Black Public Sphere Collective, 111–50. Chicago: University of Chicago Press, 1995.

Brown, Karida. "On the Participatory Archive: The Formation of the Eastern Kentucky African American Migration Project." *Southern Cultures* 22, no. 1 (2016): 113–127.

Brown, Wendy. *Undoing the Demos: Neoliberalism's Stealth Revolution*. Cambridge, MA: MIT Press, 2015.

Brown-Nagin, Tomiko. *Courage to Dissent: Atlanta and the Long History of the Civil Rights Movement*. New York: Oxford University Press, 2011.

Buel, Jason. "Whose Screen? Our Screen! Digital Documentary and Social Activism." PhD diss., North Carolina State University, 2017.

Bullard, Robert. *Dumping in Dixie: Race, Class and Environmental Quality*. 3rd ed. New York: Routledge, 2000.

Bullard, Robert, Glenn Johnson, and Angel Torres, eds. *Highway Robbery: Transportation Racism and New Routes to Equity*. Boston: South End Press, 2004.

Burgin, Sarah Nicole. "The Workshop as the Work: White Anti-racism Organizing in the 1960s 70s and 80s Social Movements." PhD diss., University of Leeds, 2013.

Burnett, John. "Who Is Smuggling Children across the Border?" NPR. July 15, 2014. http://www.npr.org/sections/parallels/2014/07/15/331477447/who-is-smuggling-immigrant-children-across-the-border.

Burrows, Nicole, Laura Helton, LaTasha Levy, and Deborah E. McDowell. "Freedom Summer and Its Legacies in the Classroom." *Southern Quarterly* 52, no. 1 (Fall 2014): 155–72.

Burton, Susan, and Cari Lynn. *Becoming Ms. Burton: From Prison to Recovery to Leading the Fight for Incarcerated Women*. New York: New Press, 2017.

Bustamante, Jorge A., Clark W. Reynolds, and Raúl A. Hinojosa Ojeda, eds. *U.S.–Mexico Relations: Labor Market Interdependence*. Palo Alto: Stanford University Press, 1992.

Cacho, Lisa Marie. *Social Death: Racialized Rightlessness and the Criminalization of the Unprotected*. New York: New York University Press, 2012.

Cadena, Marisol de la. "Indigenous Cosmopolitics in the Andes: Conceptual Reflections beyond 'Politics.'" *Cultural Anthropology* 25, no. 2 (2010): 334–70.

Camacho, Alicia Schmidt. *Migrant Imaginaries: Latino Cultural Politics in the US–Mexico Borderlands*. New York: New York University Press, 2008.

Camp, Jordan T., and Christina Heatherton, eds. *Policing the Planet: Why the Policing Crisis Led to Black Lives Matter*. New York: Verso Books, 2016.

Campt, Tina. *Image Matters: Archive, Photography, and the African Diaspora in Europe*. Durham: Duke University Press, 2012.

Carmichael, Stokely (Kwame Ture), with Ekwueme Michael Thelwell. *Ready for Revolution: The Life and Struggles of Stokely Carmichael*. New York: Scribner, 2003.

Carroll, Tamar W. *Mobilizing New York: AIDS, Antipoverty, and Feminist Activism.* Chapel Hill: University of North Carolina Press, 2015.

Carruthers, Charlene A. *Unapologetic: A Black, Queer, and Feminist Mandate for Radical Movements.* Boston: Beacon Press, 2018. Kindle.

Carson, Clayborne. *In Struggle: SNCC and the Black Awakening of the 1960s.* Cambridge, MA: Harvard University Press, 1981.

Carter, Dan. Review of *Conservative Bias: How Jesse Helms Pioneered the Rise of Right-Wing Media and Realigned the Republican Party,* by Bryan Hardin Thrift. *American Historical Review* 120, no. 2 (April 2015): 669–70.

Carter, David. *Stonewall: The Riots That Sparked the Gay Revolution.* New York: St. Martin's Press, 2004.

Carter, Mandy. "Justice or Just Us?" Keynote address, Feb. 8, 2011, Vanderbilt University. https://www.youtube.com/watch?v=nI5VRymRK6Q.

Castle, Elizabeth. "The Original Gangster: The Life and Times of Red Power Activist Madonna Thunder Hawk." In *The Hidden 1970s: Histories of Radicalism,* edited by Dan Berger, 267–83. New Brunswick: Rutgers University Press, 2010.

———. *Warrior Women: Native Women's Activism in the Red Power Movement.* Lincoln: University of Nebraska Press, forthcoming.

Caswell, Michele. "Seeing Yourself in History: Community Archives and the Fight against Symbolic Annihilation." *Public Historian* 36, no. 4 (2014). 26–37.

———. "What Is a Community-Based Archives Anyway?" *South Asian American Digital Archive,* Apr. 18, 2012. https://www.saada.org/tides/article/20120418-704.

Chafe, William. *Civilities and Civil Rights: Greensboro, North Carolina and the Black Struggle for Freedom.* New York: Oxford University Press, 1981.

Chandra, Bipan, Mridula Mukherjee, Aditya Mukherjee, Sucheta Mahadan, and K. N. Panikkar. *India's Struggle for Independence.* Reprint. New York: Viking, 2010.

Chang, Nancy. *Silencing Political Dissent: How Post–September 11 Anti terrorism Measures Threaten Our Civil Liberties.* New York: Seven Stories, 2002.

Charron, Katherine Mellen. *Freedom's Teacher: The Life of Septima Clark.* Chapel Hill: University of North Carolina Press, 2009.

Chen, Ching-in, Jail Dulani, and Leah Lakshmi Piepzna-Samarasinha. *The Revolution Starts at Home: Confronting Intimate Violence within Activist Communities.* Brooklyn: South End Press, 2011.

Cherniavsky, Eva. *Neocitizenship: Political Culture after Democracy.* New York: New York University Press, 2017.

Chisholm, Shirley. *Unbought and Unbossed: Expanded 40th Anniversary Edition.* Washington, DC: Take Root Media, 2010.

Chomsky, Aviva. *Undocumented: How Immigration Became Illegal.* Boston: Beacon, 2014.

Chuang, Angie, and Robin Chin Roemer. "Beyond the Positive-Negative Paradigm of Latino/Latina NewsMedia Representations: DREAM Act Exemplars, Stereotypical Selection, and American Otherness." *Journalism* 6, no. 8 (2015): 1045–61.

Chun, Wendy Hui Kyong. *Programmed Visions: Software and Memory.* Cambridge, MA: MIT Press, 2011.

Churchill, Ward. *Perversions of Justice: Indigenous Peoples and AngloAmerican Law.* San Francisco: City Lights, 2004.

Churchill, Ward, and Jim Vander Wall. *The COINTELPRO Papers: Documents from the FBI's Secret Wars against Dissent in the US.* Boston: South End Press, 1990.

Clark, Septima P.. *Ready from Within: Septima Clark and the Civil Rights Movement.* Edited by Cynthia Stokes Brown. Trenton: Africa World Press, 1990.

Clayton, Jace. *Uproot: Travels in 21st Century Music and Digital Culture.* New York: Farrar, Straus and Giroux, 2016.

Cobb, Charles. *This Nonviolent Stuff'll Get You Killed: How Guns Made the Civil Rights Movement Possible.* New York: Basic Books, 2014.

Cobble, Dorothy Sue, Linda Gordon, and Astrid Henry. *Feminism Unfinished: A Short Surprising History of American Women's Movements.* New York: Liverlight, 2014.

Codrington, Raymond. "New Forms: The Political Potential of Hip-Hop." In *New Social Movements in the African Diaspora: Challenging Global Apartheid*, edited by Leith Mullins, 247–62. New York: St. Martin's Press, 2009.

Cohen, Cathy J. *Democracy Remixed: Black Youth and the Future of American Politics.* New York: Oxford University Press, 2010.

——. "Punks, Bulldaggers, and Welfare Queens Symposium." Speech at the University of Maryland, Apr. 21, 2017. Available at https://twitter.com/BlackYouth Proj/status/855519845605146626.

Cohen, Robert, and David J. Snyder, eds. *Rebellion in Black and White: Southern Student Activism in the 1960s.* Baltimore: Johns Hopkins University Press, 2013.

Coleman, Willi. "Like Hot Lead to Pour on the Americans: Sarah Parker Remond from Salem, Mass. to the British Isles." In *Women's Rights and Transatlantic Slavery in the Era of Emancipation*, edited by Kathryn Kish Sklar and James Brewer Stewart, 173–88. New Haven: Yale University Press, 2007.

Coles, Robert. *Doing Documentary Work.* New York: New York Public Library, 1998. Kindle edition.

Collier-Thomas, Betty, and V. P. Franklin, eds. *Sisters in the Struggle: African American Women in the Civil Rights and Black Power Movements.* New York: New York University Press, 2001.

Collins, Patricia Hill. *Black Feminist Thought: Knowledge, Consciousness, and the Politics of Empowerment.* New York: Routledge, 1998.

——. *Fighting Words: Black Women and the Search for Justice.* Minneapolis: University of Minnesota Press, 1998.

Combahee River Collective. *The Combahee River Collective Statement: Black Feminist Organizing in the Seventies and Eighties.* Albany: Kitchen Table—Women of Color Press, 1986.

Conley, Dalton. *Being Black, Living in the Red: Race, Wealth and Social Policy in America.* Berkeley: University of California Press, 1999.

Connolly, N. D. B. "Notes on a Desegregated Method: Learning from Michael Katz and Others." *Journal of Urban History* 41, no. 4 (2015): 584–91.

Cook, Terry. "Evidence, Memory, Identity and Community: Four Shifting Archival Paradigms." *Archival Science* 13, nos. 2–3 (2013): 95–120.

Cooper, Brittney C. *Beyond Respectability: The Intellectual Thought of Race Women.* Urbana: University of Illinois Press, 2017.

Corbett, Katharine T., and Howard S. Miller. "A Shared Inquiry into Shared Inquiry." *Public Historian* 28, no. 1 (2006): 15–38.

Corrunker, Laura. "Coming Out of the Shadows: DREAM Act Activism in the Context of Global Anti-deportation Activism." *Indiana Journal of Global Legal Studies* 19, no. 1 (Winter 2012): 143–68.

Coulthard, Glen. "For Our Nations to Live, Capitalism Must Die." Unsettling America: Decolonization in Theory and Practice, Nov. 5, 2013. https://unsettlingamerica.wordpress.com/2013/11/05/for-our-nations-to-live-capitalism-must-die/.

———. *Red Skin, White Masks: Rejecting the Colonial Politics of Recognition.* Minneapolis: University of Minnesota Press, 2014.

Cox, Courtland, with Karlyn Forner, John Gartrell, Wesley Hogan, Jennifer Lawson, and Naomi Nelson. "Building and Transferring Movement Informational Wealth: The SNCC Digital Gateway." *Zapruder* 47 (Dec. 2018).

Coyle, Andrew, Allison Campbell, and Rodney Neufeld, eds. *Capitalist Punishment: Prison Privatization and Human Rights.* London: Zed Press, 2003.

CR10 Publications Collective. *Abolition Now! Ten Years of Strategy and Struggle against the Prison Industrial Complex.* Chico, CA: AK Press, 2008.

Crawford, Matthew. *The World beyond Your Head: On Becoming an Individual in the Age of Distraction.* New York: Farrar, Straus and Giroux, 2015.

Crenshaw, Kimberlé. Keynote address, Women of the World Festival. London, Mar. 14, 2016. You Tube. https://www.youtube.com/watch?v=-DW4HLgYPlA&index=40&list=PL_UmL9LyICNIKiSR4jwUGtkGgC4LAuBph.

———. "Mapping the Margins: Intersectionality, Identity Politics, and Violence against Women of Color." *Stanford Law Review* 43, no. 6 (1991): 1241–99.

Crenshaw, Kimberlé Williams, and Andrea J. Ritchie with Rachel Anspach, Rachel Gilmer, and Luke Harris. *Say Her Name: Resisting Police Brutality against Black Women.* African American Policy Forum and Center for Intersectionality and Policy Studies, July 2015. http://www.aapf.org/sayhernamereport/.

Crespino, Joseph. *In Search of Another Country: Mississippi and the Conservative Counterrevolution.* Princeton: Princeton University Press, 2007.

Critchley, Simon. "Occupy and the Arab Spring Will Continue to Revitalize Political Protest." *The Guardian*, Mar. 22, 2012. http://www.theguardian.com/commentisfree/2012/mar/22/occupy-arab-spring-political-protest.

Crosby, Emilye. *A Little Taste of Freedom: The Black Freedom Struggle in Claiborne County, Mississippi.* Chapel Hill: University of North Carolina Press, 2005.

———, ed. *Civil Rights History from the Ground Up: Local Struggles, a National Movement.* Athens: University of Georgia Press, 2011.

Cuádraz, Gloria Holguín, and Lynet Uttal. "Intersectionality and In-Depth Interviews: Methodological Strategies for Analyzing Race, Class, and Gender." *Race, Gender and Class* 6, no. 3 (1999): 156–86.

Cullen, David O'Donald, and Kyle G. Wilkison, eds. *The Texas Right: The Radical Roots of Lone Star Conservatism.* College Station: Texas A&M University Press, 2014.

Cunningham, David. *There's Something Happening Here: The New Left, the Klan, and FBI Counterintelligence*. Berkeley: University of California Press, 2004.

Curry, Constance. *Silver Rights*. Chapel Hill, NC: Algonquin Books, 1995.

Curry, Constance, et al. *Deep in Our Hearts: Nine White Women in the Freedom Movement*. Athens: University of Georgia Press, 2000.

Darity, William A., and Samuel L. Myers. *Persistent Disparity: Race and Economic Inequality since 1945*. Northampton, MA: Edward Elgar, 1998.

Darms, Lisa. "Radical Archives: Introduction." *Archive Journal*, Nov. 2015. http://www.archivejournal.net/essays/radical-archives/.

Das, Dilip K. *Policing in Canada, India, Germany, Australia, Finland and New Zealand: A Comparative Research Study*. Lewiston, NY: Edwin Mellen Press, 2005.

Davis, Angela J., ed. *Policing the Black Man: Arrest, Prosecution, Imprisonment*. New York: Pantheon, 2017.

Davis, Angela Y. *Abolition Democracy: Beyond Empire, Prisons, and Torture*. New York: Seven Stories Press, 2005.

Davis, Angela Y., et al., eds. *If They Come in the Morning: Voices of Resistance*. San Francisco: Third Press, 1971.

Davis, Mike. "Fortress Los Angeles. The Militarization of Urban Space." In *Variations on a Theme Park: The New American City and the End of Public Space*, edited by Michael Sorkin, 154–80. New York: Hill and Wang, 1992.

Davis, Peggy Cooper, Anderson François, and Colin Starger. "The Persistence of the Confederate Narrative." *Tennessee Law Review* 84, no. 301 (2017): 301–65.

Deb, Trishala. "Beyond the Black/White Paradigm." *Journal of Southerners on New Ground* 3, no. 1 (Summer 2000): 9–25.

De Genova, Nicholas. "The Queer Politics of Migration: Reflections on 'Illegality' and Incorrigibility." *Studies in Social Justice* 4, no. 2 (2010): 101–26.

De Guzman, Orlando, dir. *Ferguson: A Report from Occupied Territory*. Co-produced by Katina Parker. Reported/narrated by Tim Pool. Fusion, Mar. 30, 2015. https://www.youtube.com/watch?v=gq9pHONmaLc.

De Jong, Greta. *You Can't Eat Freedom: Southerners and Social Justice after the Civil Rights Movement*. Chapel Hill: University of North Carolina Press, 2018.

deLaure, Marilyn Bordwell. "Planting Seeds of Change: Ella Baker's Radical Rhetoric." *Women's Studies in Communication*, March 2008, 1–28. Highbeam Research, http://www.highbeam.com/doc/1G1-179934890.html.

de Leon, Rachel, and David Ritsher, dirs. *One Year at Standing Rock*. Reveal, Apr. 10, 2017, https://www.youtube.com/watch?v=Yb9HHtye1Tk.

D'Emilio, John. *Lost Prophet: The Life and Times of Bayard Rustin*. New York: Free Press, 2003.

D'Emilio, John, and Estelle Freedman. *A History of Sexuality in America*. 3rd ed. Chicago: University of Chicago Press, 2012.

Denby, Gene. "After Zimmerman Verdict, Activists Face a New Tougher Fight." *Code Switch*, July 25, 2013. http://www.npr.org/sections/codeswitch/2013/07/24/205119191/after-zimmerman-verdict-activists-face-a-new-tougher-fight.

———. "The Dream 9 Pushes the Envelope (and Their Allies' Buttons)." *Code Switch*,

Aug. 20, 2013. http://www.npr.org/sections/codeswitch/2013/08/20/213790881/the-dream-9-pushes-the-envelope-and-their-allies-buttons.

Denetdale, Jennifer Nez. *Reclaiming Diné History: The Legacies of Navajo Chief Manuelito and Juanita.* Tucson: University of Arizona Press, 2007.

Den Ouden, Amy E., and Jean M. O'Brien. *Recognition, Sovereignty Struggles, and Indigenous Rights in the US: A Sourcebook.* Chapel Hill: University of North Carolina Press, 2013.

DeSchweinitz, Rebecca. *If We Could Change the World: Young People and America's Long Struggle for Racial Equality.* Chapel Hill: University of North Carolina Press, 2009.

De Veaux, Alexis. *Warrior Poet: A Biography of Audre Lorde.* New York: Norton, 2004.

Dewey, John. *Democracy and Education: An Introduction to the Philosophy of Education.* New York: Macmillan, 1916.

Dhillon, Jaskiran. *Prairie Rising: Indigenous Youth, Decolonization, and the Politics of Intervention.* Toronto: University of Toronto Press, 2017.

——. "'This Fight Has Become My Life and It's Not Over': An Interview with Zaysha Grinnell." https://culanth.org/fieldsights/1017-this-fight-has-become-my-life-and-it-s-not-over-an-interview-with-zaysha-grinnell. (accessed Aug. 18, 2017).

Dhillon, Jaskiran, and Nick Estes. "Introduction: Standing Rock, #NoDAPL, and Mni Wiconi." Hot Spots, *Fieldsights*, Dec. 22, 2016. https://culanth.org/fieldsights/1007-introduction-standing-rock-nodapl-and-mni-wiconi .

"Diane Nash Remembers Activist Ella Baker." *USA Today*, Aug. 15, 2013. Video. http://www.usatoday.com/videos/news/2013/08/15/2663025/.

DiAngelo, Robin. *White Fragility: Why It's So Hard for White People to Talk about Racism.* Boston: Beacon, 2018.

Diaz, George T. *Border Contraband: A History of Smuggling across the Rio Grande.* Austin: University of Texas Press, 2015.

Dickinson, Tim. "No We Can't." *Rolling Stone*. Feb. 2, 2010. http://www.rollingstone.com/politics/news/no-we-cant-20100202.

Dittmer, John. *Local People: The Struggle for Civil Rights in Mississippi.* Urbana: University of Illinois Press, 1994.

Douglass, Frederick. "West India Emancipation." Speech delivered at Canadaigua, NY, Aug. 3, 1857. University of Rochester Frederick Douglass Project. http://rbscp.lib.rochester.edu/4398.

Dream Defenders. "Notice: We're Coming for Geo Group." Instagram, June 22, 2018. https://www.instagram.com/p/BkVWlRhBVzQ/?taken-by=thedreamdefenders.

"Dream Defenders March on Washington." YouTube, Aug. 28, 2013. https://www.youtube.com/watch?v=newg8QAcG7U.

Duberman, Martin. *Stonewall.* New York: Plume, 1994.

Du Bois, W. E. B. *The Souls of Black Folk.* Reprint. New York: Knopf, 1993.

Duggan, Lisa. *The Twilight of Equality? Neoliberalism, Cultural Politics, and the Attack on Democracy.* Boston: Beacon, 2003.

Dunbar-Ortiz, Roxanne. "How Indigenous Peoples Wound Up at the United Nations." In *The Hidden 1970s: Histories of Radicalism*, edited by Dan Berger, 115–34. New Brunswick: Rutgers University Press, 2010.

———. *An Indigenous Peoples' History of the United States.* Boston: Beacon, 2014.

Earl, Jennifer, and Katrina Kimport. *Digitally Enabled Social Change: Activism in the Internet Age.* Cambridge, MA: MIT Press, 2011.

Editorial Board. "The End to Abusive Solitary Confinement of Juveniles Is Finally in Sight." *Los Angeles Times*, Aug. 21, 2016. http://www.latimes.com/opinion/editorials/la-ed-juvenile-solitary-20160821-snap-story.html.

Elbein, Saul. "The Youth Group That Launched a Movement at Standing Rock." *New York Times.* Jan. 31, 2017, https://www.nytimes.com/2017/01/31/magazine/the-youth-group-that-launched-a-movement-at-standing-rock.html.

Elliott, Aprele. "Ella Baker: Free Agent in the Civil Rights Movement." *Journal of Black Studies* 26, no. 5 (May 1996): 593–603.

Ellsworth, Scott. *Death in a Promised Land: The Tulsa Race Riot of 1921.* Baton Rouge: Louisiana State University Press, 1982.

Enszer, Julie R. "Night Heron Press and Lesbian Print Culture in North Carolina, 1976–1983." *Southern Cultures* 21, no. 2 (Summer 2015). 43–56.

Enzinna, Wes. "'I Didn't Come Here to Lose': How a Movement Was Born at Standing Rock." *Mother Jones*, Jan.–Feb. 2017. http://www.motherjones.com/politics/2016/12/dakota-access-pipeline-standing-rock-oil-water-protest.

Erickson, Ansley. *Making the Unequal Metropolis: School Desegregation and Its Limits.* Chicago: University of Chicago Press, 2016.

Ernst, Wolfgang. *Digital Memory and the Archive.* Minneapolis: University of Minnesota Press, 2013.

Estavadeordal, Antoni, and Louis W. Goodman, eds. *21st Century Cooperation: Regional Public Goods, Global Governance, and Sustainable Development.* New York: Routledge, 2017.

Estes, Nick. "Fighting for Our Lives: #NoDAPL in Historical Context." *Red Nation*, Sept. 18, 2016. https://therednation.org/2016/09/18/fighting-for-our-lives-nodapl-in-context/.

Eterno, John, and Eli Silverman, eds. *The New York City Police Department: The Impact of Its Policies and Practices.* Boca Raton: CRC Press, 2014.

Evans, Stephanie. *Black Women in the Ivory Tower, 1850–1954: An Intellectual History.* Gainesville: University Press of Florida, 2007.

Fader, Jamie J. *Falling Back: Incarceration and Transitions to Adulthood among Urban Youth.* New Brunswick: Rutgers University Press, 2013.

Faderman, Lillian. *The Gay Revolution: The Story of Struggle.* New York: Simon and Schuster, 2015.

Fang, Lee. "RNC Adviser Alex Castellanos Admits That His Infamous Jesse Helms Ad Hurt Race Relations." *ThinkProgress*, Dec. 4, 2009. https://thinkprogress.org/rnc-adviser-alex-castellanos-admits-that-his-infamous-jesse-helms-ad-hurt-race-relations-cefca0bce7cb#.hb03014ns.

Farley, Robert. "Glenn Beck Says Van Jones Is an Avowed Communist." *Politifact*, Sept. 8, 2009. http://www.politifact.com/truth-o-meter/statements/2009/sep/08/glenn-beck/glenn-beck-says-van-jones-avowed-communist/.

Farmar, William J. *The Delta Prisons: Punishment for Profit.* Atlanta: Southern Regional Council, 1968.

Farmer, Ashley D. "In Search of the Black Women's History Archive." *Modern*

American History 1, no. 2 (July 2018). https://www.cambridge.org/core/journals/modern-american-history/article/in-search-of-the-black-womens-history-archive/B8A6EB0DDA9AD5F691B7BE867DE2B4FF.

———. *Remaking Black Power: How Black Women Transformed an Era*. Chapel Hill: University of North Carolina Press, 2017.

Felkor-Kantor, Max. "Liberal Law and Order: The Politics of Police Reform in Los Angeles." *Journal of Urban History*, April 2017, 1–25.

Fenton, Dominique. "HuffPost's Greatest Person of the Day: Omo Moses Who Sees Math as the Great Equalizer." *Huffington Post*, Nov. 5, 2010. https://www.huffingtonpost.com/2010/11/04/greatest-person-of-the-da_7_n_779272.html.

Fernandez, Manny, and Linda Qiu. "Is the Border in Crisis? 'We're Doing Fine, Quite Frankly,' a Border Mayor Says." *New York Times*, June 23, 2018. https://www.nytimes.com/2018/06/23/us/border-trump-immigration.html.

Field, Connie, and Marilyn Mulford, dirs. and prods. *Freedom on My Mind*. 110 min. California Newsreel, 1994. Videocassette.

Fields, Karen, and Barbara Fields. *Racecraft: The Soul of Inequality in American Life*. New York: Verso, 2012.

Fish, Jennifer. *Domestic Workers of the World Unite: A Global Movement for Dignity and Human Rights*. New York: New York University Press, 2017.

Fitzpatrick, Peter, ed. *Nationalism, Racism and the Rule of Law*. Hanover: Dartmouth College Press, 1995.

Flaherty, Jordan. *Floodlines: Community and Resistance from Katrina to the Jena Six*. Chicago: Haymarket Books, 2010.

Foner, Eric. *Gateway to Freedom: The Hidden History of the Underground Railroad*. New York: Norton, 2015.

Ford, Lisa. *Settler Sovereignty: Jurisdiction and Indigenous People in America and Australia, 1788–1836*. Cambridge, MA: Harvard University Press, 2010.

Forman, James, Jr. *Locking Up Our Own: Crime and Punishment in Black America*. New York: Farrar, Straus and Giroux, 2017.

Fosl, Catherine. *Subversive Southerner: Anne Braden and the Struggle for Racial Justice in the Cold War South*. Lexington: University Press of Kentucky, 2006.

France, David. *How to Survive a Plague: The Inside Story of How Citizens and Scientists Tamed AIDS*. New York: Vintage, 2016.

Franklin, H. Bruce. *Crash Course: From the Good War to the Forever War*. New Brunswick: Rutgers University Press, 2018.

Franklin, John Hope. "Talking, Not Shouting, about Race." *New York Times*, June 13, 1998. https://www.nytimes.com/books/99/08/15/specials/franklin-talking.html.

Frazier, Nishani. *Harambee City: The Congress of Racial Equality in Cleveland and the Rise of Black Power Populism*. Fayetteville: University of Arkansas Press, 2017.

Frazier, Nishani, Christy Hyman, and Hilary Greene. "African American Studies and Digital Humanities at the Crossroads: Recovery, Dissemination and Activist Intervention as an Intentional Model." Association for the Study of African American History and Life Annual Conference, Richmond, VA, Oct. 6, 2016.

Freelon, Deen, Charlton D. McIlwain, and Meredith D. Clark. "Beyond the Hashtags: #Ferguson, #BlackLivesMatter, and the Online Struggle for Offline

Justice." Center for Media and Social Impact, Feb. 2016. http://cmsimpact.org/wp-content/uploads/2016/03/beyond_the_hashtags_2016.pdf.

Freire, Paolo. *Pedagogy of Hope: Reliving Pedagogy of the Oppressed.* New York: Bloomsbury Academic, 1998.

———. *Pedagogy of the Oppressed, 50th Anniversary Edition.* Translated by Myra Bergman Ramos. New York: Bloomsbury Academic, 2018.

Frey, John Carlos, dir. *The 800 Mile Wall.* Los Angeles: Gatekeeper Productions, 2009. DVD.

Friedel, Tracy. "Outdoor Education as a Site of Epistemological Persistence: Unsettling an Understanding of Urban Indigenous Youth Resistance." In *Youth Resistance Research and Theories of Change*, edited by Eve Tuck and K. Wayne Yang. 195–208. New York: Routledge, 2014.

Friedersdorf, Conor. "Ferguson's Conspiracy against Black Citizens." *The Atlantic*, Mar. 5, 2015. https://www.theatlantic.com/national/archive/2015/03/ferguson-as-a-criminal-conspiracy-against-its-black-residents-michael-brown-department-of-justice-report/386887/.

Frisch, Michael. "Commentary Sharing Authority and the Collaborative Process." *Oral History Review* 30, no. 1 (2003): 111–13.

———. *A Shared Authority: Essays on the Craft and Meaning of Oral and Public History.* Albany: SUNY Press, 1990.

Frost, Karolyn Smardz, and Veta Smith Tucker, eds. *A Fluid Frontier: Slavery, Resistance and the Underground Railroad in the Detroit Borderland.* Detroit: Wayne State University Press, 2016.

Gabbiden, Shaun. "Crime Prevention in the African American Community: Lessons Learned from the Nation of Islam." In *Racializing Justice, Disenfranchising Lives: The Racism, Criminal Justice, and Law Reader*, edited by Manning Marable et al., 335–46. New York: Palgrave Macmillan, 2007.

Ganz, Marshall. "How Obama Lost His Voice, and How He Can Get It Back." *Los Angeles Times*, Nov. 3, 2010. http://articles.latimes.com/2010/nov/03/opinion/la-oe-1103-ganz-obama-20101103.

———. "Organizing Obama: Campaign, Organizing, Movement." American Sociological Association Annual Meeting, San Francisco, Aug. 2009. https://dash.harvard.edu/bitstream/handle/1/27306258/Organizing-Obama-Final.pdf?sequence=1.

———. *Why David Sometimes Wins: Leadership, Organization and Strategy in the California Farmworker Movement.* New York: Oxford University Press, 2010.

García, Mario T. *The Chicano Generation: Testimonios of the Movement.* Berkeley: University of California Press, 2015.

———. *The Latino Generation: Voices of the New America.* Chapel Hill: University of North Carolina Press, 2014.

Garfinkle, Harold, and E. Bittner. "Good Organizational Reasons for 'Bad' Clinical Records." In *Studies in Ethnomethodology*, edited by Harold Garfinkel, 186–207. Upper Saddle River, NJ: Prentice Hall, 1967.

Garrett, R. Kelly, and Paul N. Edwards. "Revolutionary Secrets: Technology's Role in the South African Anti-apartheid Movement." *Social Science Computer Review* 25 (2007): 202–24.

Garza, Alicia. "A HerStory of the #BlackLivesMatter Movement." #BlackLivesMatter website. http://blacklivesmatter.com/herstory/ (accessed July 1, 2016).

———. "What's Democracy Got to Do with It? How Black Power Aims to Transform Democracy." Personal Democracy Forum, New York University, June 10, 2016. YouTube. https://www.youtube.com/watch?v=vzsEh2A7J2w.

Gerbaudo, Paolo. *Tweets and the Streets: Social Media and Contemporary Activism*. London: Pluto Press, 2012.

Ghosh, Durba. *Gentlemanly Terrorists: Political Violence and the Colonial State in India, 1919–1947*. Cambridge: Cambridge University Press, 2017.

Giddings, Paula. *When and Where I Enter: The Impact of Black Women on Race and Sex in America*. New York: HarperCollins, 1984.

Giemza, Bryan. "More Than Words: Respectful Stewardship and the Balance of Community Archives." *Letonica* 36 (2017): 32–43.

Gilliland, Anne, and Sue McKemmish. "The Role of Participatory Archives in Furthering Human Rights, Reconciliation and Recovery." *Atlanti: Review for Modern Archival Theory and Practice* 24 (2014): 78–88.

Gilmore, Ruth Wilson. *Golden Gulag: Prisons, Surplus, Crisis and Opposition in Globalizing California*. Berkeley: University of California Press, 2007.

Giroux, Henry. *The Mouse That Roared: Disney and the End of Innocence*. Lanham, MD: Rowman and Littlefield, 2001.

Gitterman, Daniel, and Peter Coclanis, eds. *A Way Forward: Building a Globally Competitive South*. Chapel Hill: University of North Carolina Press, 2011.

Glenn, Evelyn Nakano. *Unequal Freedom: How Race and Gender Shaped American Citizenship and Labor*. Cambridge, MA: Harvard University Press, 2002.

Glick, Brian. *War at Home: Covert Action against U.S. Activists and What We Can Do about It*. Boston: South End Press, 1999.

Gluck, Sherna Berger, and Daphne Patai. *Women's Words: The Feminist Practice of Oral History*. New York: Routledge, 1991.

Glymph, Thavolia. *Out of the House of Bondage: The Transformation of the Plantation Household*. Cambridge: Cambridge University Press, 2008.

Godshalk, David Fort. *Veiled Visions: The 1906 Atlanta Race Riot and the Reshaping of American Race Relations*. Chapel Hill: University of North Carolina Press, 2005.

Goluboff, Risa. *Vagrant Nation: Police Power, Constitutional Change and the Making of the 1960s*. New York: Oxford University Press, 2016.

Gonzales, Roberto G., and Leo R. Chavez. "'Awakening to a Nightmare': Abjectivity and Illegality in the Lives of Undocumented 1.5-Generation Latino Immigrants in the United States." *Current Anthropology* 53, no. 3 (June 2012): 255–81.

González, Daniel. "Illegal Migrants across U.S. Taking Protests to a Defiant New Level." *Arizona Republic*, Sept. 20, 2012. http://archive.azcentral.com/arizonarepublic/news/articles/20120913illegal-migrants-us-protests-defiant-new-level.html.

Goode, Robin White. "Young People's Project Empowers Youth with Math Skills." *Black Enterprise*, Nov. 12, 2015. http://www.blackenterprise.com/education/young-peoples-project-empowers-youth-with-math-skills/.

Goodwin, Jeff, James Jasper, and Francesca Polletta, eds. *Passionate Politics: Emotions and Social Movements*. Chicago: University of Chicago Press, 2001.

Goodwyn, Lawrence. *Breaking the Barrier: The Rise of Solidarity in Poland.* New York: Oxford University Press, 1991.
———. *Democratic Promise: The Populist Moment in America.* New York: Oxford University Press, 1976.
Gordon-Reed, Annette. *The Hemingses of Monticello: An American Family.* New York: Norton, 2007.
———. *Thomas Jefferson and Sally Hemings: An American Controversy.* Updated ed. Charlottesville: University of Virginia Press, 1998.
Gordy, Lauriel, and Alice Pritchard. "Redirecting Our Voyage through History: A Content Analysis of Social Studies Textbooks." *Urban Education* 30, no. 2 (1995): 195–218.
Gore, Dayo, Jeanne Theoharis, and Komozi Woodard, eds. *Want to Start a Revolution? Radical Women in the Black Freedom Struggle.* New York: New York University Press, 2009.
Gottschalk, Marie. *The Prison and the Gallows: The Politics of Mass Incarceration in America.* Cambridge: Cambridge University Press, 2006.
Goudsouzian, Aram. *Down to the Crossroads: Civil Rights, Black Power, and the Meredith March against Fear.* New York: Farrar, Straus and Giroux, 2014.
Gould, Deborah B. *Moving Politics: Emotion and ACT UP's Fight against AIDS.* Chicago: University of Chicago Press, 2009.
Gould, Elspeth. *Security and Migration in the 21st Century.* Cambridge: Polity Press, 2009.
Goyal, Nikhil. *Schools on Trial: How Freedom and Creativity Can Fix Our Educational Malpractice.* New York: Anchor, 2016.
Grady-Willis, Winston. "The Black Panther Party: State Repression and Political Prisoners." In *The Black Panther Party Reconsidered*, edited by Charles E. Jones, 363–90. Baltimore: Black Classics Press, 1998.
Graeber, David. *Debt: The First 500 Years.* New York: Melville House, 2011.
———. "Occupy Wall Street's Anarchist Roots." *Al Jazeera English*, Nov. 30, 2011. http://www.aljazeera.com/indepth/opinion/2011/11/2011112872835904508.html.
Graff, Garrett. *The Threat Matrix: The FBI at War in the Age of Global Terror.* New York: Little, Brown, 2011.
Graham, Carol. *Happiness for All? Unequal Hopes and Lives in Pursuit of the American Dream.* Princeton: Princeton University Press, 2017.
Graham, David A. "How a Small Team of Democrats Defeated Larry Summers and Obama." *The Atlantic*, Sept. 15, 2013. https://www.theatlantic.com/politics/archive/2013/09/how-a-small-team-of-democrats-defeated-larry-summers-and-obama/279688/.
Grant, Joanne. *Ella Baker: Freedom Bound.* New York: Wiley, 1998.
———, dir. *Fundi: The Story of Ella Baker.* Brooklyn: First Run/Icarus Films, 2007. DVD. Originally released 1980.
———. "Godmother of the Student Movement: Civil Rights Organizer Ella Baker Worked with the NAACP and the SCLC, but Found Her Calling Helping SNCC Youth." *New Crisis* 108, no. 4 (July–August 2001): 38–41.
Grant, Laurens. Dir. *Stay Woke: The Black Lives Matter Movement.* BET original

documentary, May 26, 2016. http://www.bet.com/video/news/national/2016/stay-woke-behind-the-black-lives-matter-movement-full-show.html.

Grattan, Laura. *Populism's Power: Radical Grassroots Democracy in America*. New York: Oxford University Press, 2016.

Graves, William, and Heather A. Smith, eds. *Charlotte, NC: The Global Evolution of a New South City*. Athens: University of Georgia Press, 2012.

Greenberg, Cheryl Lynn, ed. *A Circle of Trust: Remembering SNCC*. New Brunswick: Rutgers University Press, 1998.

Greene, Christina. "'She Ain't No Rosa Parks': The Joan Little Rape-Murder Case and Jim Crow Justice in the Post–Civil Rights South." *Journal of African American History* 100, no. 3 (Summer 2015): 428–47.

Griffith, Joanne, ed. *Redefining Black Power: Reflections on the State of Black America*. San Francisco: City Lights, 2012. Kindle.

Grossman, Zoltán. *Unlikely Alliances: Native Nations and White Communities Join to Defend Rural Lands*. Seattle: University of Washington Press, 2017.

Grubbs, Donald. *Cry from the Cotton: The Southern Tenant Farmers' Union and the New Deal*. Chapel Hill: University of North Carolina Press, 1971.

Gumbs, Alexis Pauline. "Seek the Roots: An Immersive and Interactive Archive of Black Feminist Practice." *Feminist Collections: A Quarterly of Women's Studies Resources* 32, no. 1 (Mar. 2011): 17–20.

Gunkel, David J. *Of Remixology: Ethics and Aesthetics after Remix*. Cambridge, MA: MIT Press, 2016.

Gutiérrez y Muhs, Gabriella, Yolanda Flores Niemann, Carmen G. González, and Angela P. Harris, eds. *Presumed Incompetent: The Intersections of Race and Class for Women in Academia*. Logan: Utah State University Press, 2012.

Hagan, Joe. "The Long Lawless Road of Joe Arpaio." *Rolling Stone*, Aug. 2, 2012. https://www.rollingstone.com/culture/culture-news/the-long-lawless-ride-of-sheriff-joe-arpaio-231455/.

Halberstam, David. *The Children*. New York: Random House, 1998.

Halberstam, Judith. *The Queer Art of Failure*. Durham: Duke University Press, 2011.

Hampton, Henry, and Steve Fayer. *Voices of Freedom: An Oral History of the Civil Rights Movement from the 1950s through the 1980s*. New York: Bantam Books, 1990.

Harding, James Martin, and Cindy Rosenthal, eds. *Restaging the Sixties: Radical Theaters and Their Legacies*. Ann Arbor: University of Michigan Press, 2006.

Harding, Rosemarie, with Rachel Harding. "Hospitality, Haints, and Healing: A Southern African American Meaning of Religion." In *Deeper Shades of Purple: Womanism in Religion and Society*, edited by Stacey M. Floyd-Thomas, 98–114. New York: New York University Press, 2006.

———. "Radical Hospitality." *Sojourners* 32, no. 4 (July–August 2003): 42–46.

Harding, Vincent. *Hope and History: Why We Must Share the Story of the Movement*. Maryknoll, NY: Orbis Books, 1990.

———. *There Is a River: The Black Struggle for Freedom in America*. New York: Mariner Books, 1993.

Harding, Vincent, and Rosemarie Freeney Harding. "Freedom's Sacred Dance." *Yes*

Magazine, Oct. 27, 2000. https://www.yesmagazine.org/issues/a-new-culture-emerges/freedoms-sacred-dance.

Harfoush, Rahaf. *Yes We Did: An Inside Look at How Social Media Built the Obama Brand*. Berkeley: New Riders, 2009.

Harper, Shaun R., and Christopher B. Newman. "Surprise, Sensemaking and Success in the First College Year: Black Undergraduate Men's Academic Adjustment Experiences." *Teachers College Record* 118, no. 6 (Jan. 2016): 1–30.

Harris, Duchess. "From the Kennedy Commission to the Combahee Collective: Black Feminist Organizing, 1960–1980." In *Sisters in the Struggle: African American Women in the Civil Rights and Black Power Movements*, edited by Betty Collier-Thomas and V. P. Franklin, 280–305. New York: New York University Press, 2001.

Harris, Melanie L. *Gifts of Virtue, Alice Walker, and Womanist Ethics*. New York: Palgrave Macmillan, 2010.

Harris-Perry, Melissa V. *Sister Citizen: Shame, Stereotypes and Back Women in America*. New Haven: Yale University Press, 2011.

Harvey, David. *A Brief History of Neoliberalism*. New York: Oxford University Press, 2005.

Hass, Mary E. "An Analysis of the Social Studies and History Concepts in Elementary Social Studies Textbooks Grades 1–4." *Theory and Research in Social Education* 19, no. 2 (July 2012): 211–20.

Hattery, Angela J., and Earl Smith. *Policing Black Bodies: How Black Lives Are Surveilled and How to Work for Change*. New York: Rowman and Littlefield, 2018.

Hawkins, Stephanie. "Savage Visions: Ethnography, Photography, and Local-Color Fiction in National Geographic." *Arizona Quarterly: A Journal of American Literature, Culture, and Theory* 64, no. 2 (2008): 33–63.

Hayden, Tom, ed. *The Zapatista Reader*. New York: Nation Books, 2002.

He, Ni, and Dilip K. Das. *Policing in Finland: The Cultural Basis of Law Enforcement*. Lewiston, NY: Edwin Mellen Press, 2006.

Heilemann, John, and Mark Halperin. *Game Change: Obama and the Clintons, McCain and Palin, and the Race of a Lifetime*. New York: HarperCollins, 2010.

Heitzeg, Nancy. *The School-to-Prison Pipeline: Education, Discipline and Racialized Double Standards*. New York: Praeger, 2016.

Helms, Jesse. *Here's Where I Stand: A Memoir*. New York: Random House, 2005.

Herman, Susan, and Paul Finkleman. *Terrorism, Government, and Law: National Authority and Local Autonomy in the War on Terror*. Westport, CT: Praeger Security International, 2008.

Hernández, Kelly Lytle. *Migra! A History of the U.S. Border Patrol*. Berkeley: University of California Press, 2010.

Hersh, Michael. "How Obama Got Rolled by Wall Street." *Newsweek*, Aug. 29, 2010. http://www.newsweek.com/how-obama-got-rolled-wall-street-71733.

Hine, Darlene Clark. *Hine Sight: Black Women and the Reconstruction of American History*. Brooklyn: Carlson, 1994.

Hinojosa, Maria. "Driving Dreamers." *Latino USA*, June 6, 2014. http://www.npr.org/2014/06/06/319566500/driving-dreamers.

Hinton, Alexander Labon, et al. *Colonial Genocide in Indigenous North America.* Durham: Duke University Press, 2014.

Hinton, Elizabeth. *From the War on Poverty to the War on Crime: The Making of Mass Incarceration in America.* Cambridge, MA: Harvard University Press, 2016.

"History." The Young People's Project. http://www.typp.org/history (accessed July 12, 2017).

Hobbes, Michael. "Generation Screwed: FML." *HuffPost Highline*, Dec. 2017, https://highline.huffingtonpost.com/articles/en/poor-millennials-print/.

Hogan, Wesley. *Many Minds, One Heart: SNCC and the Dream for a New America.* Chapel Hill: University of North Carolina Press, 2007.

Holmes, Malcolm, and Brad Smith, eds. *Race and Police Brutality: Roots of an Urban Dilemma.* Albany: SUNY Press, 2008.

Holsaert, Faith, Martha Prescod Norman Noonan, Judy Richardson, Betty Garman Robinson, Jean Smith Young, and Dorothy M. Zellner, eds. *Hands on the Freedom Plow: Personal Accounts by Women in SNCC.* Urbana: University of Illinois Press, 2010.

Holton, Woody. *Unruly Americans and the Origins of the Constitution.* New York: Macmillan, 2007.

Honey, Michael K. *Sharecropper's Troubadour: John L. Handcox, the Southern Tenant Farmers' Union, and the African American Song Tradition.* New York: Palgrave Macmillan, 2013.

Hong, Grace Kyungwon. *Death beyond Disavowal: The Impossible Politics of Difference.* Minneapolis: University of Minnesota Press, 2015.

Honigblum, Shannon. "Van Jones: Finding Connections." *Lilipoh* 14: 55 (Spring 2009) 46.

Honwana, Alcinda. *Youth and Revolution in Tunisia.* London: Zed Books, 2013.

hooks, bell. *Ain't I a Woman? Black Women and Feminism.* Boston: South End Press, 1981.

———. *Black Looks: Race and Representation.* Boston: South End Press, 1992.

Horn, Steve. "This Natural Disaster Assistance Law Is Why Other States Are Policing Dakota Access Pipeline." *Desmog*, Oct. 26, 2016. https://www.desmogblog.com/2016/10/27/emergency-assistance-law-dakota-access-pipeline-out-state-cops.

Horne, Gerald. *The Apocalypse of Settler Colonialism: The Roots of Slavery, White Supremacy and Capitalism in 17th Century North America and the Caribbean.* New York: Monthly Review Press, 2018.

Horowitz, Dan, et al. "Popular Education for Movement Building: A Project South Resource Guide." Atlanta: Project South, 2001.

Horton, Aimee. *The Highlander Folk School: A History of Its Major Programs, 1932–1961.* New York: Carlson, 1989.

Horton, Myles, and Paolo Freire. *We Make the Road by Walking: Conversations on Education and Social Change.* Philadelphia: Temple University Press, 1990.

Horton, Myles, Judith Kohl, and Herbert Kohl. *The Long Haul: An Autobiography.* New York: Teachers College Press, 1998.

Houck, Davis W., and David E. Dixon, eds. *Women and the Civil Rights Movement, 1954–1965.* Jackson: University Press of Mississippi, 2009.

Hudson, Hosea. *The Narrative of Hosea Hudson: His Life as a Negro Communist.* Edited by Nell Irvin Painter. Cambridge, MA: Harvard University Press, 1979.

Huggins, Nathan. "The Deforming Mirror of Truth: Slavery and the Master Narrative of American History." *Radical History Review* 49 (1991): 25–48.

Hunter, Tera W. "The Long History of Child Snatching." *New York Times*, June 3, 2018. https://www.nytimes.com/2018/06/03/opinion/children-border.html.

Hussey, Ikaika, Will Caron, Joshua Cooper, and Ed Lane. "The Rise of a New Global, Indigenous, Left." *The Summit*, May 10, 2017. http://www.summitzine.com/posts/the-rise-of-a-new-global-indigenous-left/.

Icihi, Sadruddin Aga Khan, and Hassan Bin Talal. *Indigenous Peoples: A Global Quest for Justice.* London: Zed Books, 1987.

Institute for Policy Studies, the Poor People's Campaign, et al. *The Souls of Poor Folk.* April 2018. Available online: http://www.ips-dc.org/wp-content/uploads/2018/04/PPC-Audit-Full-410835a.pdf.

Isenberg, Nancy. *White Trash: The 400-Year Untold History of Class in America.* New York: Penguin, 2017.

Iyengar, Michelle M. "Not Mere Abstractions: Language Policies and Language Ideologies in U.S. Settler Colonialism." *Decolonization: Indigeneity, Education, and Society* 3, no. 2 (2014): 33–59.

Iyer, Deepa. *We Too Sing America: South Asian, Arab, Muslim, and Sikh Immigrants Shape Our Multiracial Future.* New York: New Press, 2015.

Jackson, Phil. *More Than a Game.* New York: Seven Stories Press, 2001.

Jackson, Phil, with Hugh Delehanty. *Eleven Rings: The Soul of Success.* New York: Penguin, 2013.

James, Joy. "Ella Baker, 'Black Women's Work,' and Activist Intellectuals." *Black Scholar* 24, no. 2 (1994): 8–15.

———. "Protofeminists and Liberation Limbos." In *Shadowboxing: Representations of Black Feminist Politics*, 41–71. New York: St. Martin's Press, 1999.

Jeffries, Hasan Kwame. *Bloody Lowndes: Civil Rights and Black Power in Alabama's Black Belt.* New York: New York University Press, 2010.

Jenlink, Patrick M., ed. *Dewey's Democracy and Education Revisited: Contemporary Discourses for Democratic Leadership and Education.* Lanham, MD: Rowman and Littlefield, 2009.

Johnson, Gaye Theresa. *Spaces of Conflict, Sounds of Solidarity: Music, Race and Spatial Entitlement in Los Angeles.* Berkeley: University of California Press, 2013.

Johnson, Keosha. "The Grio's 100: Van Jones, Social Entrepreneur among the Most Influential in the World." The Grio.com. Jan. 31, 2012. http://thegrio.com/2012/01/31/2012-van-jones/.

Johnson, Marilynn S. *Street Justice: A History of Police Violence in New York City.* Boston: Beacon, 2003.

Johnson, Walter. "Ferguson's Fortune 500 Company." *The Atlantic*, Apr. 26, 2015. https://www.npr.org/2015/02/01/383121919/another-florida-case-puts-crosshairs-on-stand-your-ground.

Johnson, Walter, with Robin D. G. Kelley. "To Remake the World: Slavery, Racial

Capitalism, and Justice." *Boston Review,* Feb. 20, 2018. http://bostonreview.net/forum/walter-johnson-to-remake-the-world.

Jomo. "Fighting Obama's Immigration Policies without Papers and without Fear." *The Nation,* Apr. 14, 2014. http://www.thenation.com/article/fighting-obamas-deportation-policies-without-papers-and-without-fear/.

Jones, Alethia, and Virginia Eubanks, eds., with Barbara Smith. *Ain't Gonna Let Nobody Turn Me Around: Forty Years of Movement Building with Barbara Smith.* New York: SUNY Press, 2014.

Jones, Angela, ed. *A Critical Inquiry into Queer Utopias.* New York: Palgrave Macmillan, 2013.

Jones, Catherine. "The Work Is Not the Workshop: Talking and Doing, Visibility and Accountability in the White Anti-racist Community." Colors of Resistance Archive. N.d. www.coloursofresistance.org/?s=the+work+is+not+the+workshop (accessed Dec. 9, 2015).

Jones, Daniel Stedman, ed. *Masters of the Universe: Hayek, Friedman and the Birth of Neoliberal Politics.* Princeton: Princeton University Press, 2014.

Jones, James H. *Bad Blood: The Tuskegee Syphilis Experiment.* New York: Basic Books, 1994.

Jones, Van. *The Green Collar Economy: How One Solution Can Fix Our Two Biggest Problems.* New York: HarperCollins, 2008.

Jovanović, Spoma. *Democracy, Dialogue and Community Action: Truth and Reconciliation in Greensboro.* Fayetteville: University of Arkansas Press, 2012.

Juris, Jeffrey. *Networking Futures: The Movements against Corporate Globalization.* Durham: Duke University Press, 2008.

Kane, Desiree. "20 Photos: My Seven Months Living at Standing Rock." *Yes Magazine,* Dec. 28, 2016. http://www.yesmagazine.org/planet/20-photos-my-seven-months-of-living-at-standing-rock-20161228.

Kane, Liam. *Popular Education and Social Change in Latin America.* London: Latin American Bureau, 2001.

Karp, Mitchell. "The Challenge of Symbolism." *Review of Law and Social Change* 14 (1986): 943–47.

Katz, Michael B. "The Existential Problem of Urban Studies." *Dissent* 57, no. 4 (Fall 2010): 66–67.

———. "Narratives of Failure? Historical Interpretations of Federal Urban Policy." *City and Community* 9, no. 1 (March 2010): 13–22.

Katznelson, Ira. *When Affirmative Action Was White: An Untold History of Inequality in Twentieth-Century America.* New York: Norton, 2006.

Kelen, Leslie, ed. *This Light of Ours: Activist Photographers of the Civil Rights Movement.* Oxford: University Press of Mississippi, 2011.

Kelley, Robin D. G. "Forum: Black Study, Black Struggle." *Boston Review,* Mar. 7, 2016. http://bostonreview.net/forum/robin-d-g-kelley-black-study-black-struggle.

———. *Freedom Dreams: The Black Radical Imagination.* Boston: Beacon, 2002.

———. *Hammer and Hoe: Alabama Communists during the Great Depression.* Chapel Hill: University of North Carolina Press, 1990.

———. "What Did Cedric Robinson Mean by Racial Capitalism?" *Boston Review,*

Jan. 12, 2017. http://bostonreview.net/race/robin-d-g-kelley-what-did-cedric-robinson-mean-racial-capitalism.

Kelly, Michael. "The 1992 Campaign." *New York Times*, Oct. 31, 1992. https://www.nytimes.com/1992/10/31/us/1992-campaign-democrats-clinton-bush-compete-be-champion-change-democrat-fights.html.

Kendi, Ibram X. *Stamped from the Beginning: The Definitive History of Racist Ideas in America*. New York: Nation Books, 2016.

Kerber, Linda. *No Constitutional Right to Be Ladies: Women and the Obligations of Citizenship*. New York: Farrar, Straus and Giroux, 1999.

Kerr, Dan. "Allan Nevins Is Not My Grandfather: The Roots of Radical Oral History Practice in the US." *Oral History Review* 43, no. 2 (2016): 367–91.

Khan, Janaya. "Black Lives Matter Toronto Co-founder Responds to Pride Action Criticism." *Now*, July 6, 2016. https://nowtoronto.com/news/pride-2016/exclusive-black-lives-matter-pride-action-criticism/.

Khan-Cullors, Patrisse, and Asha Bandele. *When They Call You a Terrorist: A Black Lives Matter Memoir*. New York: St. Martin's Press, 2017.

Kiefer, Michael. "Sheriff Joe Arpaio Has Always Done It His Way." *AZ Republic*, Sept. 11, 2015. http://www.azcentral.com/story/news/arizona/investigations/2015/09/11/sheriff-joe-arpaio-legacy/71888720/.

Kienscherf, Markus. *U.S. Domestic and International Regimes of Security: Pacifying the Globe, Securing the Homeland*. New York: Routledge, 2013.

Kim, Catherine Y., Daniel Losen, and Damon T. Hewitt. *The School-to-Prison Pipeline: Structuring Legal Reform*. New York: New York University Press, 2010.

Kinchen, Shirletta J. *Black Power in the Bluff City: African American Youth and Student Activism in Memphis, 1965–75*. Knoxville: University of Tennessee Press, 2016.

King, Martin Luther, Jr.. *A Testament of Hope: The Essential Writings and Speeches*. New York: Harper One, 2003.

King, Thomas. *The Truth about Stories: A Native Narrative*. Minneapolis: University of Minnesota Press, 2008.

Kino-nda-nimii Collective. *The Winter We Danced: Voices from the Past, Voices from the Future, and the Idle No More Movement*. Winnipeg: Arbeiter Ring Press, 2014.

Klein, Naomi. *No Is Not Enough: Resisting Trump's Shock Politics and Winning the World We Need*. Chicago: Haymarket Books, 2017.

Klockars, Carl B., Sanja Kutjnak Ivkovic, and M. R. Haberfeld, eds. *The Contours of Police Integrity*. London: SAGE, 2004.

Kohr, Martin, and Lim Li Lin, eds. *Good Practices and Innovative Experiences in the South, Volume 3: Citizen Initiatives in Social Services, Popular Education, and Human Rights*. London: Zed Books, 2001.

Kotlowski, Dean. *Nixon's Civil Rights: Politics, Principle, and Policy*. Cambridge, MA: Harvard University Press, 2001.

Kraig, Beth. "The Activism of 'Little Interactions': A Historical Case Study." *Peace and Change* 37, no. 1 (2012): 37–63.

Kraska, Peter B. *Militarizing the American Criminal Justice System: The Changing Roles of the Armed Forces and the Police*. Boston: Northeastern University Press, 2001.

Krishnakumar, Priya. "Since Sandy Hook." *Los Angeles Times*, Oct. 1, 2015. http://www.latimes.com/projects/la-na-school-shootings-since-newtown.

Kruse, Kevin. "The Politics of Race and Public Space: Desegregation, Privitization, and the Tax Revolt in Atlanta." *Journal of Urban History* 31, no. 5 (July 2005): 610–33.

———. *White Flight: Atlanta and the Making of Modern Conservatism*. Princeton: Princeton University Press, 2005.

Kudva, Sowjanya, dir. and prod. *Marry the Movement*. SONG Vimeo channel, uploaded June 25, 2013. https://vimeo.com/69103461.

Kumbier, Alana. "Inventing History: The Watermelon Woman and Archive Activism." In *Make Your Own History: Documenting Feminist and Queer Activism in the 21st Century*, edited by Lyz Bly and Kelly Wooten, 89–104. Los Angeles: Litwin Books, 2012.

Lal, Prerna. "How Queer Undocumented Youth Built the Immigrant Rights Movement." *HuffPost Gay Voices*, Mar. 28, 2013. http://www.huffingtonpost.com/prerna-lal/how-queer-undocumented_b_2973670.html.

Lamoreaux, Naomi R., and William J. Novak, eds. *Corporations and American Democracy*. Cambridge, MA: Harvard University Press, 2017.

Landa, Nancy. "Dear Mr. President." *Mundo Citizen* (blog), June 17, 2012. http://mundocitizen.com/2012/10/08/dear-mr-president/.

Landesburg, Brian K. *Free at Last to Vote: The Alabama Origins of the 1965 Voting Rights Act*. Lawrence: University Press of Kansas, 2007.

LaRoche, Cheryl. *Free Black Communities and the Underground Railroad: The Geographies of Resistance*. Champaign: University of Illinois Press, 2014.

Lassiter, Matthew D. *The Silent Majority: Suburban Politics in the Sunbelt South*. Princeton: Princeton University Press, 2006.

Latina Feminist Group. *Telling to Live: Latina Feminist Testimonios*. Durham: Duke University Press, 2001.

Law, Victoria. *Resistance behind Bars: The Struggles of Incarcerated Women*. Oakland: PM Press, 2009.

Lawson, Steven. *Black Ballots: Voting Rights in the South, 1944–1969*. 2nd ed. Lanham: Lexington Books, 1999.

Lebron, Christopher. "Janelle Monáe for President." *Boston Review*, May 21, 2018. http://bostonreview.net/race-literature-culture/chris-lebron-janelle-monae-president.

Lee, Jesse. "Van Jones to CEQ." White House.gov, Mar. 10, 2009. https://www.whitehouse.gov/blog/2009/03/10/van-jones-ceq.

Lee, Stacey J. *Unraveling the Model Minority Stereotype: Listening to Asian American Youth*. 2nd ed. New York: Teachers College Press, 2009.

Leitner, Helga, and Christopher Strunk. "Spaces of Immigrant Advocacy and Liberal Democratic Citizenship." *Annals of the Association of American Geographers* 104 (2014): 348–56.

Lerner, Steve, and Robert Bullard. *Diamond: A Struggle for Environmental Justice in Louisiana's Chemical Corridor*. Cambridge, MA: MIT Press, 2006.

Levine, Peter. *The Future of Democracy: Developing the Next Generation of American Citizens*. Hanover, NH: University Press of New England, 2007.

Lewis, Abram. "'Within the Ashes of Our Survival': Lesbian and Gay Antiracist Organizing in New York City, 1980–1984." UCLA Center for the Study of Women, 2010. http://escholarship.org/uc/item/4zr1v4bq.

Lewis, John, with Michael D'orso. *Walking with the Wind: A Memoir of the Movement*. New York: Simon & Schuster, 1998.

Lillas, Connie, and Janice Turnbull. *Infant/Child Mental Health, Early Intervention, and Relationship-Based Therapies*. New York: Norton, 2009.

Linde, Charlotte. *Life Stories: The Creation of Coherence*. Oxford: Oxford University Press, 1993.

Lindert, Peter, and Jeffrey Williamson. *Unequal Gains: American Growth and Inequality since 1700*. Princeton: Princeton University Press, 2016.

Lindsay, Keisha. "Beyond 'Model Minority,' 'Superwoman,' and 'Endangered Species': Theorizing Intersectional Coalitions among Black Immigrants, African American Women, and African American Men." *Journal of African American Studies* 19, no. 1 (March 2015): 18–35.

Linebaugh, Peter. *Stop, Thief! The Commons, Enclosures and Resistance*. San Francisco: PM Press, 2013.

Linebaugh, Peter, and Marcus Rediker. *The Many-Headed Hydra: Sailors, Slaves, Commoners, and the Hidden History of the Revolutionary Atlantic*. Boston: Beacon, 2013.

Link, William. *Righteous Warrior: Jesse Helms and the Rise of Modern Conservatism*. New York: St. Martin's Press, 2008.

Long, Judy. *Telling Women's Lives: Subject, Narrator, Reader, Text*. New York: New York University Press, 1999.

Lorde, Audre. *Sister Outsider: Essays and Speeches*. New York: Crossing Press, 1984.

———. *Zami: A New Spelling of My Name, a Biomythography*. New York: Crossing Press, 1982.

Lorentzen, Lois Ann, ed. *Hidden Lives and Human Rights in the US: Understanding the Controversies and Tragedies of Undocumented Immigration*. New York: Praeger, 2014.

Loustaunau, Martha Oehmke, and Mary Sánchez-Bane, eds. *Life, Death, and In-Between on the US–Mexico Border: Asi es la Vida*. New York: Praeger, 1999.

Love, Bettina, dir. *Ella Baker and the Fifth Element of Hip Hop*. YouTube. Nov. 22, 2013. https://www.youtube.com/watch?v=AYXzPCE6kxU.

———. *We Want to Do More Than Survive: Abolitionist Teaching and the Pursuit of Educational Freedom*. Boston: Beacon, 2019.

Lowery, Wesley. *They Can't Kill Us All: Ferguson, Baltimore, and a New Era in America's Racial Justice Movement*. New York: Little, Brown, 2016.

Luff, Jennifer. *Commonsense Anticommunism: Labor and Civil Liberties between the World Wars*. Chapel Hill: University of North Carolina Press, 2012.

Lumba-Brown, Angela, et al. "Mentoring Pediatric Victims of Interpersonal Violence Reduces Recidivism." *Journal of Interpersonal Violence*, June 16, 2017. SAGE Journals. http://journals.sagepub.com/doi/abs/10.1177/0886260517705662.

Lutz, Helma, Maria Teresa Herrera Vivar, and Linda Supik. *Framing Intersectionality: Debates on a Multi-faceted Concept in Gender Studies*. London: Ashgate, 2011.

Lye, Colleen. "US Ethnic Studies and Third Worldism, 40 Years Later." *Inter-Asia Cultural Studies* 11, no. 2 (2010): 188–93.
Lynch, Mona. "(Im)Migrating Penal Excess: Sheriff Joe Arpaio and the Case of Maricopa County, Arizona." In *Extreme Punishment: Comparative Studies in Detention, Incarceration and Solitary Confinement,* edited by Keramet Reiter and Alexa Koenig, 68–90. New York: Palgrave Macmillan, 2015.
Lynd, Alice, and Staughton Lynd. *Moral Injury and Nonviolent Resistance: Breaking the Cycle of Violence in the Military and behind Bars.* Oakland: PM Press, 2017.
———. *Stepping Stones: Memoir of a Life Together.* Lanham, MD: Lexington Books, 2009.
Lynd, Staughton. *Accompanying: Pathways to Social Change.* San Francisco: PM Press, 2012.
———. *Doing History from the Bottom Up.* Chicago: Haymarket Books, 2014.
Macallair, Daniel. "California Reforms Cause Youth Incarceration Rates to Plummet." *JJIE News,* Mar. 16, 2016. http://www.socialjusticesolutions.org/2016/03/29/california-reforms-cause-youth-incarceration-rates-plummet/.
Mac Donald, Heather. *The War on Cops: How the New Attack on Law and Order Makes Everyone Less Safe.* New York: Encounter Books, 2017.
Macintosh, Peggy. "White Privilege: Unpacking the Invisible Knapsack." The National SEED Project, 1989. https://nationalseedproject.org/about-us/white-privilege.
MacLean, Nancy. *Democracy in Chains: The Deep History of the Radical Right's Stealth Plan for America.* New York: Penguin, 2017.
Malcolm X with Alex Haley. *The Autobiography of Malcolm X.* New York: Grove Press, 1965.
Mandela, Nelson. *Long Walk to Freedom: The Autobiography of Nelson Mandela.* New York: Back Bay Books, 1995.
Manuel, Arthur, and Grand Chief Ronald M. Derrickson. *Unsettling Canada: A National Wake Up Call.* Toronto: Between the Lines Press, 2015.
Marcos, Subcomandante Insurgente, and Rafael Guillen Vincente. *¡Ya Basta! Ten Years of the Zapatista Uprising.* Chico, CA: AK Press, 2004.
Mark, Jason. "Conversation: Van Jones." *Earth Island Journal* 28, no. 2 (Summer 2013): 45–47.
Marks, Gary, and Doug McAdam. "Social Movements and the Changing Structure of Political Opportunity in the European Union." *West European Politics* 19, no. 2 (1996): 249–78.
Marshall, Joseph. *Returning to the Lakota Way: Old Values to Save a Modern World.* Carlsbad, CA: Hay House, 2014.
Martin, Michael. "Does 'Marching' Digitally Send a Message?" *Tell Me More,* Aug. 29, 2013. http://www.npr.org/templates/story/story.php?storyId=216835808.
———, interviewing Van Jones. "What Progressives Like Van Jones Want in Next Term." *Tell Me More,* Dec. 12, 2012. http://www.npr.org/2012/11/12/164962537/what-progressives-like-van-jones-want-in-next-term.
Martinez, Elizabeth Betita, Matt Meyer, and Mandy Carter, eds. *We Have Not Been Moved: Resisting Racism and Militarism in 21st Century America.* Oakland: PM Press, 2012.

Mateo, Lizbeth. "The Fight to Keep Families Together Does Not End at Deportation." *HuffPost Latino Voices*, July 22, 2013. http://www.huffingtonpost.com/lizbeth-mateo/the-fight-to-keep-familie_b_3634915.html?utm_hp_ref=latino-voice.

Matuz, Dulce. "Arizona Dreamers Five Years Later." Interview on NPR's *Latino USA*. Aug. 28, 2015. http://www.npr.org/2015/08/28/435573960/arizona-dreamers-five-years-later.

May, Gary. *Bending toward Justice: The Voting Rights Act and the Transformation of American Democracy*. New York: Basic Books, 2013.

Mayer, Jane. *Dark Money: The Hidden History of the Billionaires behind the Rise of the Radical Right*. New York: Random House, 2016.

McCall, Nathan. *Makes Me Wanna Holler: A Young Black Man in America*. New York: Random House, 1994.

McCarthy, Megan. "John Chambers, Cisco CEO, Environmentalist." *Wired*, Feb. 20, 2008. https://www.wired.com/2008/02/john-chambers-c/.

McCarthy, Timothy, and John Stauffer, eds. *Prophets of Protest: Reconsidering the History of Abolitionism*. New York: New Press, 2006.

McCaskell, Tim. *Race to Equity: Disrupting Educational Inequality*. Toronto: Between the Lines Press, 2005.

McFarland, Susan. "UN Report: With 40M in Poverty, U.S. Most Unequal Developed Nation." *UPI*, June 22, 2018. https://www.upi.com/Top_News/US/2018/06/22/UN-report-With-40M-in-poverty-US-most-unequal-developed-nation/8671529664548/.

McGuire, Danielle. *At the Dark End of the Street: Black Women, Rape and Resistance—A New History of the Civil Rights Movement from Rosa Parks to the Rise of Black Power*. New York: Vintage, 2010.

———. "Joan Little and the Triumph of Testimony." In *Freedom Rights: New Perspectives on the Civil Rights Movement*, edited by Danielle McGuire and John Dittmer, 191–222. Lexington: University Press of Kentucky, 2011.

McKenzie, Mia, ed. *The Solidarity Struggle: How People of Color Succeed and Fail at Showing Up for Each Other in the Fight for Freedom*. Oakland: BGD Press, 2016.

McKinney, Charles. *Greater Freedom: The Evolution of the Civil Rights Struggle in Wilson, North Carolina*. Lanham, MD: University Press of America, 2010.

———. "Teaching the Civil Rights Movement during a Time of Universal Deceit." We Who Believe in Freedom Symposium, Ohio State University, June 1, 2018. Notes in the author's possession.

McNeil, Genna Rae. "'Joanne Is You, Joanne Is Me': A Consideration of African-American Women and the 'Free Joan Little' Campaign." In *Sisters in the Struggle: African American Women in the Civil Rights and Black Power Movements*, edited by Betty Collier-Thomas and V. P. Franklin, 259–79. New York: New York University Press, 2001.

McQuade, Brendan. "The Puzzle of Intelligence Expertise: Spaces of Intelligence Analysis and the Production of 'Political' Knowledge." *Qualitative Sociology* 39, no. 3 (2016): 247–65.

McSpadden, Lezley M. *Tell the Truth and Shame the Devil: The Life, Legacy and Love of My Son Michael Brown*. New York: Regan Arts, 2016.

McWhorter, Diane. *Carry Me Home: Birmingham, Alabama, the Climactic Battle of the Civil Rights Movement.* New York: Simon and Schuster, 2001.

Meehan, Albert J. "Record-Keeping Practices in the Policing of Juveniles." *Urban Life* 15 (1986): 70–102.

Meiners, Erica R., and Maisha T. Winn, eds. *Education and Incarceration.* New York: Routledge, 2012.

Melgaço, Lucas, and Jeffrey Monaghan, eds. *Protests in the Information Age: Social Movements, Digital Practices, and Surveillance.* New York: Routledge, 2018.

Merlan, Anna. "Meet the Brave, Audacious, Astonishing Women Who Built the Standing Rock Movement." *Jezebel*, Dec. 8, 2016. https://jezebel.com/meet-the-brave-audacious-astonishing-women-who-built-1789756669.

Metzger, Maure Ann. *A Prison Called School: Creating Effective Schools for All Learners.* Lanham, MD: Rowman and Littlefield, 2015.

Miceli, Melinda. *Standing Out, Standing Together: The Social and Political Impact of Gay-Straight Alliances.* New York: Routledge, 2005.

Michaels, Jon D. *Constitutional Coup: Privatization's Threat to the American Republic.* Cambridge, MA: Harvard University Press, 2017.

Milgram, Stanley. *Obedience to Authority.* New York: Harper Perennial, 2009.

Milkman, Ruth, Joshua Bloom, and Victor Bloom, eds. *The LA Model of Organizing and Advocacy.* Ithaca: Cornell University Press, 2010. Kindle.

Miller, Edward H. *Nut Country: Right-Wing Dallas and the Birth of the Southern Strategy.* Chicago: University of Chicago Press, 2015.

Miller, Martin. *The Foundations of Modern Terrorism: State, Society, and the Dynamics of Political Violence.* Cambridge: Cambridge University Press, 2013.

Mindock, Clark. "UN Says Trump Separation of Migrant Children from Parents May Amount to Torture." *The Independent*, June 22, 2018. https://www.independent.co.uk/news/world/americas/us-politics/un-trump-children-family-torture-separation-border-mexico-border-ice-detention-a8411676.html.

Minh-ha, Trinh T. *Framer Framed.* New York: Routledge, 1992.

Miranda, Carolina A. "Art, Celebrity, and How Standing Rock Will Shape Protest in the Trump Years." *Los Angeles Times*, Jan. 7, 2017. http://www.latimes.com/entertainment/la-et-hollywood-values-updates-art-celebrity-and-how-standing-rock-1483650229-htmlstory.html.

Mitchell, Michele. "Turns of the Kaleidoscope: 'Race,' Ethnicity and Analytical Patterns in American Women's and Gender History." *Journal of Women's History* 25, no. 4 (Winter 2013): 46–73.

Mixon, Gregory. *The Atlanta Riot: Race, Class and Violence in a New South City.* Gainesville: University of Florida Press, 2005.

Mogul, Joey L., Andrea J. Ritchie, and Kay Whitlock. *Queer (In)Justice: The Criminalization of LGBT People in the United States.* Boston: Beacon Press, 2011.

Mohanty, Chandra Talpade. *Feminism without Borders: Decolonizing Theory, Practicing Solidarity.* Durham: Duke University Press, 2003.

Mokoena, Tshepo. "Janelle Monáe Leads Protest against Police Brutality in North Philadelphia." *The Guardian*, Aug. 13, 2015. https://www.theguardian.com/music/2015/aug/13/janelle-monae-leads-protest-against-police-brutality-philadelphia.

Monáe, Janelle, and Wondaland. "Hell You Talmbout." Union Transfer, Philadelphia,

PA, Aug. 12, 2015. YouTube. https://www.youtube.com/watch?v=SttWb9mDp3Q. (12 Jan. 2016).

Monet, Aja. *My Mother Was a Freedom Fighter.* Chicago: Haymarket Books, 2017.

Monteith, Sharon. *SNCC Stories: Narrative Culture and the African American Freedom Struggle in the Civil Rights South.* Athens: University of Georgia Press, forthcoming.

Montoya, Teresa. "Violence on the Ground, Violence below the Ground." Hot Spots, *Fieldsights.* Dec. 22, 2016. https://culanth.org/fieldsights/violence-on-the-ground-violence-below-the-ground.

Moraga Cherrie, and Gloria Anzaldúa, eds. *This Bridge Called My Back: Writings by Radical Women of Color.* Latham, NY: Kitchen Table—Women of Color Press, 1983.

Morris, Aldon. "Reflections on Social Movement Theory: Criticisms and Proposals." *Contemporary Sociology* 29, no. 3 (2000): 445–54.

Morris, Monique. *Pushout: The Criminalization of Black Girls in Schools.* New York: New Press, 2016.

Morris, Tiyi M. *Womanpower Unlimited and the Black Freedom Struggle in Mississippi.* Athens: University of Georgia Press, 2015.

Morrison, Gregory B., and Timothy K. Garner. "Latitude in Deadly Force Training: Progress or Problem?" *Police Practice and Research* 12, no. 4 (Aug. 2011): 341–61.

Morrison, Toni. "Site of Memory." In *Inventing the Truth: The Art and Craft of Memoir,* edited by William Zinsser and Russell Baker, 183–200. Boston: Houghton Mifflin, 1987.

———. "A Slow Walk of Trees." *New York Times,* July 4, 1976, 104.

Moses, Bob. "Address at 75th Birthday Celebration for Ella Jo Baker." Carnegie International Center, New York, Dec. 9, 1978. Transcription by Clayborne Carson. Folder 1, box 10, Joseph Andrew Sinsheimer Papers, 1983–1986, David M. Rubenstein Rare Book & Manuscript Library, Duke University.

Moses, Robert P., and Charles E. Cobb Jr. *Radical Equations: Math Literacy and Civil Rights.* Boston: Beacon Press, 2001.

Motta, Sara C., and Mike Cole. *Education and Social Change in Latin America.* New York: Palgrave, 2013.

Mottahedeh, Negar. *#iranelection: Hashtag Solidarity and the Transformation of Online Life.* Palo Alto: Stanford University Press, 2015.

Moye, J. Todd. *Let the People Decide: Black Freedom and White Resistance Movements in Sunflower County, Mississippi, 1945–1986.* Chapel Hill: University of North Carolina Press, 2004.

Mueller, Carol. "Ella Baker and the Origins of 'Participatory Democracy.'" In *The Black Studies Reader,* edited by Jacqueline Bobo, Cynthia Hudley, and Claudein Michel, 79–90. New York: Routledge, 2004.

Mullings, Leith, ed. *New Social Movements in the African Diaspora: Challenging Global Apartheid.* New York: St. Martin's Press, 2009.

Mumford, Kevin J. *Not Straight, Not White: Black Gay Men from the March on Washington to the AIDS Crisis.* Chapel Hill: University of North Carolina Press, 2016.

Muñoz, Susana M., and Michelle M. Espino. "The Freedom to Learn: Experiences of

Students without Legal Status Attending Freedom University." *Review of Higher Education* 40, no. 4 (2017): 533–55.

Murakawa, Naomi. *The First Civil Right: How Liberals Built Prisons in America.* New York: Oxford University Press, 2014.

———. "The Origins of the Carceral Crisis: Racial Order as 'Law and Order' in Postwar American Politics." In *Race and American Political Development*, edited by Joseph Lowndes, Julie Novkov, and Dorian T. Warren, 234–55. New York: Routledge, 2008.

Murch, Donna. "Paying for Punishment: The New Debtors Prison." *Boston Review*, Aug. 1, 2016. http://bostonreview.net/editors-picks-us/donna-murch-paying-punishment.

Nadasen, Premilla. "Citizenship Rights, Domestic Work, and the Fair Labor Standards Act." *Journal of Policy History* 24, no. 1 (2012): 74–94.

———. *Household Workers Unite: The Untold Story of African American Women Who Built a Movement*. Boston: Beacon Press, 2015.

———. *Rethinking the Welfare Rights Movement*. New York: Routledge, 2012.

———. "Sista' Friends and Other Allies: Domestic Workers United and Coalition Politics." In *New Social Movements in the African Diaspora: Challenging Global Apartheid*, edited by Leith Mullings, 285–98. New York: St. Martin's Press, 2009.

Nair, Rukmini Bhaya. *Lying on the Postcolonial Couch: The Idea of Indifference*. Minneapolis: University of Minnesota Press, 2002.

Nalla, Mahesh K., and Graeme R. Newman. *Community Policing in Indigenous Communities*. Boca Raton: CRC Press, 2013.

Nash, Jennifer C. "Rethinking Intersectionality." *Feminist Review* 89 (2008): 1–15.

National Congress of American Indians. "Official Statement of NCAI President Jefferson Keel on the Forced Separation of Immigrant Families." National Congress of American Indians, June 19, 2018. http://www.ncai.org/news/articles/2018/06/19/official-statement-of-ncai-president-jefferson-keel-on-the-forced-separation-of-immigrant-families.

Neal, Mark Anthony. "My Mother Gave Me This Big-Ass Name: A Black Scholar in the Mix." Trinity Distinguished Lecture, Duke University, May 4, 2017. YouTube. https://www.youtube.com/watch?v=52adeDvvB_0.

Nelson, Jennifer. *Women of Color and the Reproductive Rights Movement*. New York: New York University Press, 2003.

Nelson, Jill, ed. *Police Brutality: An Anthology*. New York: Norton, 2001.

Nevins, Joseph. *Dying to Live: A Story of U.S. Immigration in an Age of Global Apartheid*. San Francisco: City Lights, 2008.

Newcombe, Steven. *Pagans in the Promised Land: Decoding the Doctrine of Christian Discovery*. Golden, CO: Fulcrum, 2008.

Ngai, Mae M. *Impossible Subjects: Illegal Aliens and the Making of Modern America*. Princeton: Princeton University Press, 2005.

Nicholls, Walter J. *The DREAMers: How the Undocumented Youth Movement Transformed the Immigrant Rights Debate*. Palo Alto: Stanford University Press, 2013.

Nicholson, Helen. *Theatre, Education and Performance: The Map and the Story*. New York: Palgrave Macmillan, 2011.

Nigam, Aditya. "The Arab Upsurge and the 'Viral' Revolutions of Our Times." *Interface: A Journal for and about Social Movements* 4, no. 1 (May 2012): 165–77. http://www.interfacejournal.net/wordpress/wp-content/uploads/2012/05/Interface-4-1-Nigam.pdf.

Nixon, Rob. *Slow Violence and the Environmentalism of the Poor.* Cambridge, MA: Harvard University Press, 2013.

Noble, Safiya. *Algorithms of Oppression: How Search Engines Reinforce Racism.* New York: New York University Press, 2018.

Nocella, Anthony, Priya Parmar, and David Stovall, eds. *From Education to Incarceration: Dismantling the School-to-Prison Pipeline.* Rev. ed. New York: Peter Lang, 2014.

"NPi Speaks with the Young People's Project." The New Prosperity Initiative. YouTube, uploaded Aug. 6, 2009. https://www.youtube.com/watch?v=_JKm1U2fejc.

Obama, Barack. "Why Organize? Problems and Promise in the Inner City." *Illinois Issues*, Sept. 1988. https://www.lib.niu.edu/1988/ii880840.html.

"Obama Prosecuting Fewer Financial Crimes Than Either Reagan or Bush." *Washington's Blog*, Nov. 16, 2011. http://www.washingtonsblog.com/2011/11/obama-prosecuting-fewer-financial-crimes-than-under-either-bush-presidency.html.

Offiah, Natt. "#OutSouth15." Mississippi Safe Schools Coalition. http://www.mssafeschools.org/2015/12/outsouth15/ (accessed Jan. 7, 2016).

O'Hara, S. Paul. *Inventing the Pinkertons: Spies, Sleuths, Mercenaries and Thugs.* Baltimore: Johns Hopkins University Press, 2016.

Okilwa, Nathern, Muhammad Khalifa, and Felecia Briscoe, eds. *The School to Prison Pipeline: The Role of Culture and Discipline in Schools.* West Yorkshire, UK: Emerald, 2017.

Oliver, Pamela E., Jorge Cadena-Roa, and Kelley D. Strawn. "Emerging Trends in the Study of Protest and Social Movements." In *Research in Political Sociology*, vol. 11, edited by Betty A. Dobratz, Lisa K. Waldner, and Timothy Buzzell. Bingley, UK: Emerald Publishing Limited, 2003.

Olson, Lynne. *Freedom's Daughters: The Unsung Heroines of the Civil Rights Movement from 1830–1970.* New York: Scribner's, 2001.

O'Neal, Wendi, and Pam McMichael. "Race." *Journal of Southerners on New Ground* 3, no. 1 (Summer 2000): 3.

Ong, Aiwah. *Neoliberalism as Exception: Mutations in Citizenship and Sovereignty.* Durham: Duke University Press, 2006.

O'Reilly, Kenneth. *Racial Matters: The FBI's Secret File on Black America, 1960–1972.* New York: Free Press, 1991.

Ortiz, Paul. *An African American and Latinx History of the United States.* Boston: Beacon Press, 2018.

Ostler, Jeffrey, and Nick Estes. "'The Supreme Law of the Land': Standing Rock and the Dakota Access Pipeline." *Indian Country Today*, Jan. 16, 2017. https://indiancountrymedianetwork.com/news/opinions/supreme-law-land-standing-rock-dakota-access-pipeline/.

"Out South Wrap Up." SONG Vimeo channel. https://vimeo.com/114395805 (accessed June 24, 2015).

Paik, Naomi. *Rightlessness: Testimony and Redress in U.S. Prison Camps since World War II*. Chapel Hill: University of North Carolina Press, 2016.
Pallard, Shyrlee. *Ella Baker: A Leader behind the Scenes*. Englewood Cliffs, NJ: Burdett Press, 1990.
Palmer, Parker, Arthur Zajonc, and Megan Scribner. *The Heart of Higher Education: A Call to Renewal*. Hoboken, NJ: Jossey-Bass, 2010.
Palmer, Phyllis. *Living as Equals: How Three White Communities Struggled to Make Interracial Connections during the Civil Rights Era*. Nashville: Vanderbilt University Press, 2008.
Palmiotto, Michael J., and N. Prabha Unnithan, eds. *Policing and Society: A Global Approach*. Boston: Cengage Learning, 2011.
Pandey, Gyanendra. "Politics and Democracy in Our Time: Terms of Analysis." *Economic and Political Weekly* 1, no. 20 (May 2015): 58–67.
Parenti, Christian. *Lockdown America: Police and Prisons in the Age of Crisis*. New York: Verso, 1999.
Park, K-Sue. "Insuring Conquest: U.S. Expansion and the Indian Depredation Claims System, 1796–1920." *History of the Present* 8, no. 1 (Apr. 2018): 57–87.
———. "Money, Mortgages and the Conquest of America." *Law and Social Inquiry* 41, no. 4 (2016): 1006–35.
———. "Shadow Nations: Tribal Sovereignty and the Limits of Legal Pluralism." *Law and Society Review* 48, no. 3 (2014): 692–94.
Pastrana, Antonio, Jr., Juan Battle, and Angelique Harris. *An Examination of Latinx LGBT Populations across the U.S.* New York: Palgrave, 2017.
Payne, Charles M. "Ella Baker and Models of Social Change." *Signs* 14, no. 4 (Summer 1989): 885–99. http://www.jstor.org/stable/3174689.
———. *I've Got the Light of Freedom: The Organizing Tradition and the Mississippi Freedom Struggle*. Berkeley: University of California Press, 1996.
Pellow, David. *Resisting Global Toxics: Transnational Movements for Environmental Justice*. Cambridge, MA: MIT Press, 2007.
———. *The Silicon Valley of Dreams: Environmental Justice, Immigrant Workers, and the High-Tech Global Economy*. New York: New York University Press, 2002.
Peña, Lorgia García. "New Freedom Fights: The Creation of Freedom University Georgia." *Latino Studies* 10, no. 1 (2012): 246–50.
Perry, Melissa Harris. *Sister Citizen: Shame, Stereotypes, and Black Women in America*. New Haven: Yale University Press, 2011.
Perry, Theresa, Robert Moses, Joan T. Wynne, Ernesto Cortes Jr., and Lisa Delpit, eds. *Quality Education as a Civil Right: Creating a Grassroots Movement to Transform Public Schools*. Boston: Beacon, 2010.
Pfaff, John. *Locked In: The True Causes of Mass Incarceration and How to Achieve Real Reform*. New York: Basic Books, 2017.
Pharr, Suzanne. "The Gift of Grace." Suzanne Pharr: Political Handywoman, Feb. 12, 2009. http://suzannepharr.org/2009/02/12/the-gift-of-grace/.
———. *Homophobia: A Weapon of Sexism*. Inverness, CA: Chardon Press, 1988.
———. *In the Time of the Right: Reflections on Liberation*. Inverness, CA: Chardon Press, 1996.
Phelan, Sarah, Sally Roesch Wagner, Barbara Lau, and María José Bolaña Caballero.

"Safe Containers and Dangerous Memories." *Public Historian* 37, no. 2 (May 2015): 61–72.

Phelps, Teresa Godwin. *Shattered Voices: Language, Violence, and the Work of Truth Commissions*. Philadelphia: University of Pennsylvania Press, 2011.

Phillips, Kevin P. *The Emerging Republican Majority*. New York: Arlington House, 1969.

Pierce, Charles. "The Standing Rock Fire Is Visible All Over the US." *Esquire*, Feb. 23, 2017. http://www.esquire.com/news-politics/politics/news/a53394/standing-rock-fire/.

Pietro, Antero. *Not in My Neighborhood: How Bigotry Shaped a Great American City*. Chicago: Ivan R. Dee, 2010.

Pikketty, Thomas. *Capital in the Twenty-First Century*. Cambridge, MA: Harvard University Press, 2014.

Pirbhai-Illich, Fatima, Shauneen Peet, and Fran Martin, eds. *Culturally Responsive Pedagogy: Working towards Decolonization, Indigeneity, and Interculturalism*. New York: Palgrave, 2017.

Pleasant, Liz. "Black Lives Matter." *Yes Magazine*, Summer 2015, 33–34.

Plouffe, David. *The Audacity to Win*. New York: Penguin, 2010.

Polletta, Francesca. *Freedom Is an Endless Meeting: Democracy in American Social Movements*. Chicago: University of Chicago Press, 2002.

———. *It Was Like a Fever: Storytelling in Protest and Politics*. Chicago: University of Chicago Press, 2006.

———. "Participatory Democracy in the New Millennium." *Contemporary Sociology* 42, no. 1 (2013): 40–49.

Poo, Ai-Jen. *The Age of Dignity: Preparing for the Elder Boom*. New York: New Press, 2015.

Portelli, Alessandro. "Research as an Experiment in Equality." In *The Death of Luigi Trastulli and Other Stories: Form and Meaning in Oral History*, 29–44. Albany: SUNY Press, 1991.

Powell, Tamara. "Look What Happened Here: North Carolina's Feminary Collective." *North Carolina Literary Review* 9 (2000): 91–102.

Prison Research Education Action Project. *Instead of Prisons: A Handbook for Abolitionists*. Oakland, CA: Critical Resistance, 2005.

Provine, Doris Marie. *Unequal under Law: Race and the War on Drugs*. Chicago: University of Chicago Press, 2007.

Purdy, Jed. "Normcore." *Dissent*, Summer 2018. https://www.dissentmagazine.org/article/normcore-trump-resistance-books-crisis-of-democracy.

Qacquant, Loic. *Punishing the Poor: The Neoliberal Government of Social Insecurity*. Durham: Duke University Press, 2009.

Radu, Ioana. "Blurred Boundaries, Feminisms, and Indigenisms: Cocreating an Indigenous Oral History for Decolonization." *Oral History Review* 41, no. 1 (2018): 29–47.

Rana, Aziz. "Goodbye Cold War." *n + 1* 30 (Winter 2018). https://nplusonemag.com/issue-30/politics/goodbye-cold-war/.

———. *The Two Faces of American Freedom*. Cambridge, MA: Harvard University Press, 2011.

Rancière, Jacques. *Hatred of Democracy*. Translated by Steve Corcoran. London: Verso, 2006.

Rands, Kat, Jess McDonald, and Lauren Clapp. "Landscaping Classrooms toward Queer Utopias." In *A Critical Inquiry into Queer Utopias*, edited by Angela Jones, 149–72. New York: Palgrave Macmillan, 2013.

Rane, Neel. "Twenty Years of Shareholder Proposals after Cracker Barrel: An Effective Tool for Implementing LGBT Employment Protections." *University of Pennsylvania Law Review* 162, no. 4 (Mar. 2014): 929–77.

Ransby, Barbara. *Ella Baker and the Black Freedom Movement: A Radical Democratic Vision*. Chapel Hill: University of North Carolina Press, 2003. Kindle.

——. "Ella Taught Me: Shattering the Myth of the Leaderless Movement." *Colorlines*, June 12, 2015. https://www.colorlines.com/articles/ella-taught-me-shattering-myth-leaderless-movement.

——. *Making All Black Lives Matter: Reimagining Freedom in the Twenty-First Century*. Oakland: University of California Press, 2018. Kindle.

Reagon, Bernice Johnson. "Coalition Politics: Turning the Century." In *Home Girls: A Black Feminist Anthology*, edited by Barbara Smith, 356–68. New York: Kitchen Table—Women of Color Press, 1983.

——. "Room in the Circle." *Give Your Hands to Struggle*. Smithsonian Folkways Recording, 1997.

——. "Solidarity of Past, Present and Future." SNCC Fiftieth Anniversary Conference, 2010, David M. Rubenstein Rare Book & Manuscript Library, Duke University.

Reagon, Bernice Johnson, and Sweet Honey in the Rock. *We Who Believe in Freedom: Sweet Honey in the Rock . . . Still on the Journey*. New York: Anchor, 1993.

Rebell, Michael. *Courts and Kids: Pursuing Educational Equity through the State Courts*. Chicago: University of Chicago Press, 2009.

Reddy, Chandon. *Freedom with Violence: Race, Sexuality and the U.S. State*. Durham: Duke University Press, 2011.

Reichard, Raquel. "Is Mijente the Start of the Social Justice Movement Latinxs Have Been Waiting For?" *Latina*, Dec. 16, 2015. http://www.latina.com/lifestyle/our-issues/mijente-social-justice-movement.

——. "Why We Say Latinx: Trans and Gender Nonconforming People Explain." *Latina*, Aug. 29, 2015. http://www.latina.com/lifestyle/our-issues/why-we-say-latinx-trans-gender-non-conforming-people-explain.

Reverby, Susan, ed. *Examining Tuskegee: The Infamous Syphilis Study and Its Legacy*. Chapel Hill: University of North Carolina Press, 2009.

——. *Tuskegee's Truths: Rethinking the Tuskegee Syphilis Study*. Chapel Hill: University of North Carolina Press, 2000.

Richie, Beth E. *Arrested Justice: Black Women, Violence, and America's Prison Nation*. New York: New York University Press, 2012.

Rios, Victor M. *Punished: Policing the Lives of Black and Latino Boys*. New York: New York University Press, 2011.

Ritchie, Andrea. *Invisible No More: Police Violence against Black Women and Women of Color*. Boston: Beacon Press, 2017.

Rivas, Jorge. "Meet Jennicet, One Month after She Interrupted President Obama."

Fusion, Aug. 3, 2015. http://fusion.net/story/175990/jennicet-gutierrez-interrupted-president-obama/.

Roberts, Dorothy, and Sujatha Jesudason. "Movement Intersectionality: The Case of Race, Gender, Disability, and Genetic Technologies." *Du Bois Review* 10, no. 2 (Fall 2013): 313–28.

Robinson, Cedric. *Black Marxism: The Making of the Black Radical Tradition*. 2nd ed. Chapel Hill: University of North Carolina Press, 2000.

Robinson, Lindsay G. *Conquest by Law: How the Discovery of America Dispossessed Indigenous Peoples of Their Lands*. New York: Oxford University Press, 2005.

Rogers, Tim. "Obama Has Deported More Immigrants Than Any Other President. Now He's Running Up the Score." *Fusion*, Jan. 7, 2016. http://fusion.net/story/252637/obama-has-deported-more-immigrants-than-any-other-president-now-hes-running-up-the-score/.

Romo, David Dorado. *Ringside Seat to a Revolution: An Underground Cultural History of Ciudad Juarez and El Paso*. El Paso: Cinco Puntos Press, 2005.

Rosas, Gilberto. *Barrio Libre: Criminalizing States and Delinquent Refusals of the New Frontier*. Durham: Duke University Press, 2012.

Ross, Catherine. *Lessons in Censorship: How Schools and Courts Subvert Students' First Amendment Rights*. Cambridge, MA: Harvard University Press, 2015.

Ross, Rosetta E. *Witnessing and Testifying: Black Women, Religion and Civil Rights*. Minneapolis: Fortress Press, 2003.

Roth, Benita. *The Life and Death of ACT UP/LA: Anti-AIDS Activism in Los Angeles from the 1980s to the 2000s*. New York: Cambridge University Press, 2017.

——. *Separate Roads to Feminism: Black, Chicana, and White Feminist Movements in America's Second Wave*. New York: Cambridge University Press, 2004.

Roth, Michael. "Foucault's History of the Present." *History and Theory* 20, no. 1 (1981): 32–46.

Rothstein, Richard. *The Color of Law: A Forgotten History of How Our Government Segregated America*. New York: Liveright, 2017.

Rubio-Goldsmith, Raquel, Celestino Fernández, Jessie K. Finch, and Araceli Masterson-Algar, eds. *Migrant Deaths in the Arizona Desert: La Vida no Vale Nada*. Tucson: University of Arizona Press, 2016.

Rukeyser, Muriel. "The Speed of Darkness." In *The Speed of Darkness*, 111. New York: Random House, 1968.

Russell, Tory. "Free Josh." *Ebony*, Jan. 2, 2015. http://www.ebony.com/news-views/free-josh-053#ixzz3O6wyywbg.

Rustin, Bayard, and Michael Long. *I Must Resist: Bayard Rustin's Life in Letters*. San Francisco: City Lights, 2012.

Saadi, Altaf. "Detention Facilities Display." Physicians for Human Rights, June 20, 2018. http://physiciansforhumanrights.org/blog/detention-facilities-display.html.

Samuels, Liz. "Improvising on Reality: The Roots of Prison Abolition." In *The Hidden 1970s: Histories of Radicalism*, edited by Dan Berger, 21–38. New Brunswick: Rutgers University Press, 2010.

Schneider, Stephen. *You Can't Padlock an Idea: Rhetorical Education at the Highlander Folk School, 1932–1961*. Columbia: University of South Carolina Press, 2014.

Schön, Donald. *The Reflective Practitioner: How Professionals Think in Action*. New York: Basic Books, 1984.

Schrader, Stuart. *Badges without Borders: How Global Counterinsurgency Transformed American Policing*. Berkeley: University of California Press, forthcoming.

Schrag, Peter. *Not Fit for Our Society: Immigration and Nativism in America*. Berkeley: University of California Press, 2010.

Schutz, Aaron, and Mike Miller, eds. *People Power: The Community Organizing Tradition of Saul Alinsky*. Nashville: Vanderbilt University Press, 2015.

Scott, James. *Seeing Like a State: How Certain Schemes to Improve the Human Condition Have Failed*. New Haven: Yale University Press, 1999.

———. *Weapons of the Weak: Everyday Forms of Peasant Resistance*. New Haven: Yale University Press, 1987.

Segrest, Mab. *Memoir of a Race Traitor*. Boston: South End Press, 1999.

———. *My Mama's Dead Squirrel: Lesbian Essays on Southern Culture*. Ann Arbor: Firebrand Books, 1985.

Sellers, Brian G. "Economic Nomads: A Theoretical Deconstruction of the Immigration Debacle." *Journal of Theoretical and Philosophical Criminology* 8, no. 1 (2016): 37–56.

Semuels, Alana. "The Fines and Fees That Keep Former Prisoners Poor." *The Atlantic*, July 5, 2016. http://www.theatlantic.com/business/archive/2016/07/the-cost-of-monetary-sanctions-for-prisoners/489026/.

Sengupta, Shuddhabrata. "I/Me/Mine—Intersectional Identities as Negotiated Minefields." *Signs* 31, no. 3 (Spring 2006): 629–39.

Shah, Nayan. "Between 'Oriental Depravity' and 'Natural Degenerates': Spatial Borderlands and the Making of Ordinary Americans." *American Quarterly* 57, no. 3 (2005): 703–25.

Shaw, Stephanie. *What a Woman Ought to Do and Be: Black Professional Workers during the Jim Crow Era*. Chicago: Chicago University Press, 1996.

Shedd, Carla. *Unequal City: Race, Schools, and Perceptions of Injustice*. New York: Russell Sage Foundation, 2015.

Shepherd, George W., Jr., and David Penna, eds. *Racism and the Underclass: State Policy and Discrimination against Minorities*. Westport, CT: Greenwood Press, 1991.

Shichor, David. *Punishment for Profit: Private Prisons/Public Concerns*. London: SAGE, 1995.

Shopes, Linda. "Insights and Oversights: Reflections on the Documentary Tradition and the Theoretical Turn in Oral History." *Oral History Review* 41, no. 2 (2014): 257–68.

Sifry, Micah. "The Obama Disconnect." TechPresident.com. Dec. 31, 2009. http://techpresident.com/blog-entry/the-obama-disconnect.

Simon, Evan. "The Seventh Generation: Youth at the Heart of the Standing Rock Protests." ABC News. Aired Feb. 25, 2017. YouTube. https://www.youtube.com/watch?v=1Rz_TkpysKk.

Simon, John J. "Ella Baker, Who Would Not Rest for Freedom." *Monthly Review* 50, no. 6 (November 1998): 45–51.

Simpson, Audra. "Consent's Revenge." *Cultural Anthropology* 31, no. 3 (2016): 326–33.

———. *Mohawk Interruptus: Political Life across the Borders of Settler States.* Durham: Duke University Press, 2014.
Simpson, Leanne. "Aambe! Maajaadaa! (What #IdleNoMore Means to Me)." Decolonization, Dec. 21, 2012. https://decolonization.wordpress.com/2012/12/21/aambe-maajaadaa-what-idlenomore-means-to-me/.
Singh, Nikhil. *Race and America's Long War.* Berkeley: University of California Press, 2017.
Slate, Nico. *Colored Cosmopolitanism: The Shared Struggle for Freedom in the United States and India.* Cambridge, MA: Harvard University Press, 2017.
Smith, Linda Tuhiwai. *Decolonizing Methodologies: Research and Indigenous Peoples.* London: Zed Books, 1999.
Smucker, Jonathan Matthew. *Hegemony How-To: A Roadmap for Radicals.* Chico, CA: AK Press, 2017.
"SNCC, Women and Stokely: An Email Dialog, 2013–14." Civil Rights Movement Veterans website.. http://www.crmvet.org/disc/women2.htm (accessed Feb. 12, 2015).
Solnit, Rebecca. Interview by Krista Tippett. "Falling Together." *On Being* podcast, May 26, 2016. http://www.onbeing.org/program/rebecca-solnit-falling-together/transcript/8695.
———. "The Loneliness of Donald Trump." *Literary Hub*, May 17, 2017. https://lithub.com/rebecca-solnit-the-loneliness-of-donald-trump/.
Solomon, Akiba. "Get On the Bus: Inside the Black Life Matters Freedom Ride to Ferguson." *ColorLines*, Sept. 5, 2014. http://www.colorlines.com/articles/get-bus-inside-black-life-matters-freedom-ride-ferguson.
Soltis, Laura Emiko. "From Freedom Schools to Freedom University: Liberatory Education, Interracial and Intergenerational Dialogue, and the Undocumented Student Movement in the U.S. South," *Souls: A Critical Journal of Black Politics, Culture and Society* 17, nos. 1–2 (2015): 20–53.
Sonnie, Amy, and James Tracy. *Hillbilly Nationalists, Urban Race Rebels, and Black Power: Community Organizing in Radical Times.* New York: Melville House, 2011.
Soyer, Michaela. *A Dream Denied: Incarceration, Recidivism, and Young Minority Men in America.* Berkeley: University of California Press, 2016.
Spencer, Robyn C. "Mad at History." *Radical Teacher* 85 (2009): 67–69.
———. *The Revolution Has Come: Black Power, Gender, and the Black Panther Party in Oakland.* Durham: Duke University Press, 2016.
Spencer, Robyn C., and Wesley C. Hogan. "Telling Freedom Stories from the Inside Out: Internal Politics and Movement Cultures in SNCC and the Black Panther Party." In *Civil Rights History from the Ground Up: Local Studies, a National Movement*, edited by Emilye Crosby, 330–65. Athens: University of Georgia Press, 2011.
Spice, Anne. "Interrupting Industrial and Academic Extraction on Native Land." Hot Spots, *Fieldsights*, Dec. 22, 2016. https://culanth.org/fieldsights/1021-interrupting-industrial-and-academic-extraction-on-native-land%20Accessed%2027%20July%202017.
Spivak, Gayatri Chakravorty. "Subaltern Studies: Deconstructing Historiography."

In *Selected Subaltern Studies*, edited by Ranjit Guha and Gayatri Chakravorty Spivak, 3–34. New York: Oxford University Press, 1988.

Springer, Kimberly. *Living for the Revolution: Black Feminist Organizations, 1968–1980*. Durham: Duke University Press, 2005.

Spurb, Jason. *Disney's Most Notorious Film: Race, Convergence, and the Hidden Histories of "Song of the South."* Austin: University of Texas Press, 2012.

Srigley, Katrina, and Lorraine Sutherland. "Decolonizing, Indigenizing, and Learning Biskaaybiiyang in the Field: Our Oral History Journey." *Oral History Review* 45, no. 1 (2018): 7–28.

Staudt, Kathleen, Tony Payan, and Z. Anthony Kruszewski, eds. *Human Rights along the US–Mexico Border: Gendered Violence and Insecurity*. Tucson: University of Arizona Press, 2009.

Stauffer, Jill. *Ethical Loneliness: The Injustice of Not Being Heard*. New York: Columbia University Press, 2015.

Steele, Sarah M. "Performing Utopia: Queer Counterpublics and Southerners on New Ground." In *A Critical Inquiry into Queer Utopias*, edited by Angela Jones, 131–47. New York: Palgrave Macmillan, 2013.

Stein, Marc. *Rethinking the Gay and Lesbian Movement*. New York: Routledge, 2012.

Stekelenburg, Jacquelien van, Conny Roggeband, and Bert Klandermans, eds. *The Future of Social Movement Research: Dynamics, Mechanisms, and Processes*. Minneapolis: University of Minnesota Press, 2013.

Stern, Alexandra Minna. "Buildings, Boundaries, and Blood: Medicalization and Nation-Building on the U.S.–Mexico Border, 1910–1930." *Hispanic American Historical Review* 79, no. 1 (1999): 41–81.

Stern, Ray. "US District Judge G. Murray Snow Sets Up Arpaio for Knock-Out in Racial Profiling Case." *Phoenix New Times*, Dec. 23, 2011. http://www.phoenixnewtimes.com/news/us-district-judge-g-murray-snow-sets-up-sheriff-arpaio-for-knockout-in-racial-profiling-case-ruling-describes-deputies-dirty-tricks-6664009.

Stewart, Brian. "Nationwide Protests against Family Separation Announced." MoveOn.org, June 18, 2018. https://front.moveon.org/breaking-nationwide-protests-against-family-separation-announced/.

StoryShift Advisory Committee. "Principles & Praxis." Working Films. http://www.workingfilms.org/storyshift-principles-praxis/ (accessed Aug. 12, 2018).

Strickland, Eliza. "The New Face of Environmentalism." *East Bay Express*, Nov. 2, 2005. http://www.eastbayexpress.com/oakland/the-new-face-of-environmentalism/Content?oid=1079539&showFullText=true.

Sturkey, William, and Jon N. Hale. *To Write in the Light of Freedom: The Newspapers of the 1964 Mississippi Freedom Schools*. Jackson: University Press of Mississippi, 2015.

Sudbury, Julia. "Celling Black Bodies: Black Women in the Global Industrial Prison Complex." *Feminist Review* 70, no. 1 (2002): 57–74.

———. "Rethinking Global Justice: Black Women Resist the Transnational Prison-Industrial Complex." In *New Social Movements in the African Diaspora: Challenging Global Apartheid*, edited by Leith Mullins, 213–31. New York: St. Martin's Press, 2009.

Sugrue, Thomas J. *The Origins of the Urban Crisis: Race and Inequality in Postwar Detroit*. Princeton: Princeton University Press, 2005.

Sullivan, Shannon, and Nancy Tuana, eds. *Race and Epistemologies of Ignorance*. Albany: SUNY Press, 2007.

Summers, Nailah. "Documenting Ferguson: Oral History, Virtual Technologies, and the Making of a Movement." Remarks to the Oral History Association, Tampa, FL, Oct. 17, 2015. Notes in the author's possession.

Suro, Roberto. "Out of the Shadows, into the Light: Questions Raised by the Spring of 2006." In *Rallying for Immigrant Rights: The Fight for Inclusion in 21st Century America*, edited by Kim Voss and Irene Bloemraad. 250–58. Berkeley: University of California Press, 2011.

Sward, Susan. "S.F. Panel Fires Officer in Aaron Williams Case." *SF Gate*, June 28, 1997. http://www.sfgate.com/news/article/S-F-Panel-Fires-Officer-In-Aaron-Williams-Case-2834167.php.

Sweeney, Kate, and Dana Goldman. "StoryCorps: Pat Hussain and Pam McMichael." WABE, Feb. 26, 2013. http://news.wabe.org/post/storycorps-pat-hussain-pam-mcmichael.

Sweet Honey in the Rock. "Ella's Song." *We All . . . Everyone of Us*. Flying Fish Records 317. 1983.

Swerts, Thomas. "Gaining a Voice: Storytelling and Undocumented Youth Activism in Chicago." *Mobilization: The International Quarterly Review of Social Movement Research* 20, no. 3 (Sept. 2015): 345–60.

Talaga, Tanya. *Seven Fallen Feathers: Racism, Death and Hard Truths in a Northern City*. Toronto: House of Anansi Press, 2017.

Taibi, Matt. "Why Isn't Wall Street in Jail?" *Rolling Stone*, Feb. 16, 2011. http://www.rollingstone.com/politics/news/why-isnt-wall-street-in-jail-20110216.

Taylor, Keeanga-Yamahtta. *From #BlackLivesMatter to Black Liberation*. Chicago: Haymarket Books, 2016. Kindle.

———, ed. *How We Get Free: Black Feminism and the Combahee River Collective*. Chicago: Haymarket Books, 2017.

Terry, Robert W. *For Whites Only*. Rev. ed. Grand Rapids, MI: Eerdmans, 1975.

Thahabu. "Unapologetically Black: An Interview with BYP100's Sana Bell." *Rookie*, May 25, 2016. http://www.rookiemag.com/2016/05/unapologetically-black-an-interview-with-sana-bell/.

Theoharis, Jeanne. *A More Beautiful and Terrible History: The Uses and Misuses of Civil Rights History*. Boston: Beacon, 2018.

"This Is Just the Beginning Baby." SONG Vimeo channel. https://vimeo.com/79810975 (accessed June 24, 2015).

Thompson, Becky. *A Promise and a Way of Life: White Antiracist Activism*. Minneapolis: University of Minnesota Press, 2001.

Thompson, Heather Ann. *Blood in the Water: The Attica Uprising of 1971 and Its Legacy*. New York: Vintage, 2017.

———. "The Prison Industrial Complex: A Growth Industry in a Shrinking Economy." *New Labor Forum* (Aug. 2012): 38–47.

———. "Why Mass Incarceration Matters: Rethinking Crisis, Decline, and

Transformation in Postwar American History." *Journal of American History* 97, no. 3 (2012): 703–34.

Thompson, Lisa, and Chris Tapscott, eds. *Citizenship and Social Movements: Perspectives from the Global South*. London: Zed Books, 2010.

Thrift, Bryan Hardin. *Conservative Bias: How Jesse Helms Pioneered the Rise of Right-Wing Media and Realigned the Republican Party*. Gainesville: University Press of Florida, 2014.

Tilly, Charles. "Contentious Repertoires in Great Britain." In *Repertoires and Cycles of Collective Action*, edited by Mark Traugott, 15–42. Durham: Duke University Press, 1995.

———. "Repertoires of Contention in America and Britain, 1750–1830." In *The Dynamics of Social Movements: Resource Mobilization, Social Control, and Tactics*, edited by Mayer N. Zald and John D. McCarthy, 126–55. Cambridge, MA: Winthrop, 1979.

———. "Social Movements and (All Sorts of) Other Political Interactions—Local, National and International—Including Identities." *Theory and Society* 27 (1998): 453–80.

Todd, Zoe. "An Indigenous Feminist's Take on the Ontological Turn: 'Ontology' Is Just Another Word for Colonialism." *Journal of Historical Sociology* 29, no. 1 (2016): 4–22.

Townes, Emilie M. "The Womanist Dancing Mind: Speaking to the Expansiveness of Womanist Discourse." In *Deeper Shades of Purple: Womanism in Religion and Society*, edited by Stacey Floyd-Thomas, 236–49. New York: New York University Press, 2006.

———. *Womanist Ethics and the Cultural Production of Evil*. New York: Palgrave Macmillan, 2006.

Truax, Eileen. *Dreamers: An Immigrant Generation's Fight for Their American Dream*. Boston: Beacon, 2015.

Tufekci, Zeynep, *Twitter and Tear Gas: The Power and Fragility of Networked Protest*. New Haven: Yale University Press, 2017.

Tullos, Allen. "Crackdown in the Black Belt." *Southern Changes* 7, no. 1 (1985): 1–5.

Tutashinda, K. *It's Our Time: Ella Baker, Participatory Democracy, and Oakland, California*. Berkeley: K. Tutashinda/Imhotep Publishing, 2008.

Tyson, Timothy. *The Blood of Emmett Till*. New York: Simon and Schuster, 2017.

———. "The Children of Emmett Till." *Oxford American*, Apr. 13, 2017. https://www.oxfordamerican.org/item/1169-the-children-of-emmett-till.

———. *Radio Free Dixie: Robert F. Williams and the Roots of Black Power*. Chapel Hill: University of North Carolina Press, 2001.

Umoja, Akinyele Omowale. "Set Our Warriors Free: The Legacy of the Black Panther Party and Political Prisoners." In *The Black Panther Party Reconsidered*, edited by Charles E. Jones, 417–41. Baltimore: Black Classics Press, 1998.

Underhill, Vivian. "Fighting for the Future: The Indigenous Water Protectors Leading Standing Rock's Movement Aren't Backing Down." *Bitch Media*, Sept. 14, 2016. https://www.bitchmedia.org/article/standing-rock-dakota-access-pipeline-protest-hearken-feminist.

UN Human Rights Office of the High Commissioner. "UN Experts to US: 'Release

Migrant Children.'" *United Nations Office of the High Commissioner, Human Rights.* June 22, 2018. https://www.ohchr.org/en/NewsEvents/Pages/DisplayNews.aspx?NewsID=23245&LangID=E.

Vaid, Urvashi. "The Politics of Intersection: Moving the Movements Together." *Off Our Backs,* June 1999, 9–11.

Vaillant, Gabriela Gonzalez, Juhi Tyagi, Idil Afife Akin, Fernanda Page Poma, Michael Schwartz, and Arnout van de Rijt. "A Field Experimental Study of Emergent Mobilization in Online Collective Action." *Mobilization: The International Quarterly Review of Social Movement Research* 20, no. 3 (Sept. 2015): 281–305.

van Cleve, Nicole Gonzalez. *Crook County: Racism and Injustice in America's Largest Criminal Court.* Palo Alto: Stanford University Press, 2016.

Vargas, João Costa. *Catching Hell in the City of Angels.* Minneapolis: University of Minnesota Press, 2006.

Vargas, Jose Antonio. "Define American: An Interview with Jose Antonio Vargas." *Journal of International Affairs* 68, no. 2 (2015): 267.

———. *Documented.* Netflix. New York: CNN Films with Apo Anak Productions, 2013.

———. "My Life as an Undocumented Immigrant." *New York Times Magazine,* June 22, 2011. http://www.nytimes.com/2011/06/26/magazine/my-life-as-an-undocumented-immigrant.html?_r=0.

Vasquez, Tina. "How Anti-blackness Thrives in Latinx Communities (and What to Do about It)." *Everyday Feminism,* Aug. 12, 2015. http://everydayfeminism.com/2015/08/anti-blackness-latinx-communities/.

———. "The New ICE Age: An Agency Unleashed." *New York Review of Books,* May 2, 2018. http://www.nybooks.com/daily/2018/05/02/the-new-ice-age-an-agency-unleashed/.

Vigil, Ernesto. *The Crusade for Justice: Chicano Militancy and the Government's War on Dissent.* Madison: University of Wisconsin Press, 1999.

Vitale, Alex. *The End of Policing.* New York: Verso, 2017.

Voekel, Pamela. "Organizing for Freedom." *NACLA Report on the Americas* 48, no. 1 (2016): 68–78.

von Kotze, Astrid, and Shirley Walters, eds. *Forging Solidarity: Popular Education at Work.* Boston: Sense Publishers, 2017.

Voss, Kim, and Irene Bloemraad, eds. *Rallying for Immigrant Rights: The Fight for Inclusion in 21st Century America.* Berkeley: University of California Press, 2011.

Wacquant, Loïc. *Punishing the Poor: The Neoliberal Government of Social Insecurity.* Durham: Duke University Press, 2009.

Wade, Rahima C., and Susan Everett. "Civic Participation in Third Grade Social Studies Textbooks." *Social Education* 58, no. 5 (1994): 308–11.

Wagner, Bryan. *Disturbing the Peace: Black Culture and the Police Power after Slavery.* Cambridge, MA: Harvard University Press, 2009.

Wagner, David. *What's Love Got to Do with It? A Critical Look at American Charity.* New York: New Press, 2000.

Walker, Alice. *In Search of Our Mothers' Gardens: Womanist Prose.* New York: Harcourt, 1983.

———. *Meridian.* New York: Harcourt, 1976.

Walker, Chris. "Black Lives Matter 5280 Recaps Trip to Standing Rock to Oppose Oil Pipeline." *Westword*, Nov. 23, 2016. http://www.westword.com/news/black-lives-matter-5280-recaps-trip-to-standing-rock-to-oppose-oil-pipeline-8526506.

Walker, Donald R. *Penology for Profit: A History of the Texas Prison System, 1867–1912*. College Station: Texas A&M University Press, 1988.

Waller, Signe. *Love and Revolution: A Political Memoir; People's History of the Greensboro Massacre, Its Setting and Aftermath*. Lanham, MD: Rowman and Littlefield, 2002.

Walsh, Jennifer. *Three Strikes Laws*. New York: Greenwood, 2007.

Wang, Jackie. "Against Innocence: Race, Gender, and the Politics of Safety." *LIES*, vol. 1. http://www.liesjournal.net/volume1-10-againstinnocence.html (accessed Oct. 13, 2018).

Watkins, Hollis, with C. Liegh McInnis. *Brother Hollis: The Sankofa of a Movement Man*. Clinton, MS: Sankofa Southern Publishing, 2015.

Weber-Shirk, Joaquina. "Deviant Citizenship: DREAMer Activism in the United States and Transnational Belonging." *Social Sciences* 4 (2015): 582–97.

Wells, Ida B. "Lynch Law in America." Chicago, IL, January 1900. *Civil Rights and Conflict in the United States: Selected Speeches*. Lit2Go. http://etc.usf.edu/lit2go/185/civil-rights-and-conflict-in-the-united-states-selected-speeches/ (accessed June 10, 2018).

Welsh, Michael. *Flag Burning: Moral Panic and the Criminalization of Protest*. Piscataway, NJ: Aldine de Gruyter, 2000.

White, Deborah Gray. *Too Heavy a Load: Black Women in Defense of Themselves, 1894–1994*. New York: Norton, 1999.

———, ed. *Telling Histories: Black Women Historians in the Ivory Tower*. Chapel Hill: University of North Carolina Press, 2008.

Whitman, James Q. *Hitler's American Model: The United States and the Making of Nazi Race Law*. Princeton: Princeton University Press, 2017.

Whitmore, James Q. *Harsh Justice: Criminal Punishment and the Widening Divide between America and Europe*. New York: Oxford University Press, 2003.

Wignaraja, Ponna. *New Social Movements in the South: Empowering the People*. New Delhi: Vistaar Publications, 1993.

Wilder, Craig. *Ebony and Ivy: Slavery and the Troubled History of America's Universities*. New York: Bloomsbury, 2013.

Wilentz, Sean. *No Property in Man: Slavery and Antislavery at the Nation's Founding*. Cambridge, MA: Harvard University Press, 2018.

Williams, Delores. "A Womanist Perspective on Sin." In *A Troubling in My Soul: Womanist Perspectives on Evil and Suffering*, edited by Emilie M. Townes, 130–49. Maryknoll, NY: Orbis, 1993.

Williams, Jakobi. *From the Bullet to the Ballot: The Illinois Chapter of the Black Panther Party*. Chapel Hill: University of North Carolina Press, 2013.

Williams, Marco, dir. *The Undocumented*. New York: Filmmakers' Library, 2013. DVD.

Williams, Patricia J. *The Alchemy of Race and Rights: Diary of a Law Professor*. Cambridge, MA: Harvard University Press, 1991.

Williams, Rhonda Y. *Concrete Demands: The Search for Black Power in the Twentieth Century*. New York: Routledge, 2015.
———. *The Politics of Public Housing: Black Women's Struggles against Urban Inequality*. New York: Oxford University Press, 2004.
Wilson, Shawn. *Research Is Ceremony: Indigenous Research Methods*. Halifax, Nova Scotia:: Fernwood, 2008.
Wilson, Starsky. "The Politics of Jesus." St. John's United Church of Christ, Ferguson, MO, Aug. 31, 2014. YouTube. https://www.youtube.com/watch?v=r_R_ezwhSlo.
Windham, Lane. *Knocking on Labor's Door: Union Organizing in the 1970s and the Roots of a New Economic Divide*. Chapel Hill: University of North Carolina Press, 2017.
Winslow, Barbara. *Shirley Chisholm: Catalyst for Change*. Boulder, CO: Westview, 2014.
Winter, Jana, and Sharon Weinberger. "The FBI's New Terrorist Threat: 'Black Identity Extremists.'" *Foreign Policy*, Oct. 6, 2017. https://foreignpolicy.com/2017/10/06/the-fbi-has-identified-a-new-domestic-terrorist-threat-and-its-black-identity-extremists/.
"Women and Men in the Freedom Movement: A Discussion." Civil Rights Movement Veterans. June, Aug., Sept. 2004. http://www.crmvet.org/disc/women1.htm.
Women's Earth and Climate Action Network. "15 Indigenous Women on the Frontlines of the Dakota Access Pipeline Resistance." *EcoWatch*. https://www.ecowatch.com/indigenous-women-dakota-access-pipeline-2069613663.html (accessed Aug. 1, 2017).
Wong, Alan. "Conversations for the Real World: Shared Authority, Self-Reflexivity, and Process in the Oral History Interview." *Journal of Canadian Studies* 43, no. 1 (2009): 239–58.
Wong, Kent, and Matias Ramos. "Undocumented and Unafraid: Tam Tran and Cinthya Felix." *Boom* 1, no. 1 (Spring 2011). http://www.boomcalifornia.com/2011/03/undocumented-and-unafraid-tam-tran-and-cinthya-felix/.
Wong, Kent, Janna Shadduck-Hernández, Fabiola Inzunza, Julie Monroe, Victor Narro, and Abel Valenzuela Jr. *Undocumented and Unafraid: Tam Tran, Cinthya Felix, and the Immigrant Youth Movement*. Los Angeles: UCLA Center for Labor Research and Education, 2012.
Wong, Tom K., and Carolina Valdivia. "In Their Own Words: A Nationwide Survey of Undocumented Millennials." Wix Media Platform, May 20, 2014. http://media.wix.com/ugd/bfd9f2_4ac79f01ab9f4247b580aeb3afd3da95.pdf.
Wood, Phillip J. "Globalization and Prison Privatization: Why Are Most of the World's For-Profit Adult Prisons to Be Found in the American South?" *International Political Sociology* 1, no. 3 (Sept. 2007): 222–39.
Woodard Henderson, Ash-Lee. "Grassroots Organizing." SNCC Digital Gateway Closing Conference, North Carolina Central University, Mar. 24, 2018, minutes 44–51. The John Hope Franklin Research Collection, Duke University Libraries. Also https://vimeo.com/270135809 (accessed May 18, 2018).

Woolford, Andrew, Jeff Benvenuto, and Alexander Laban Hinton, eds. *Colonial Genocide in Indigenous North America*. Durham: Duke University Press, 2014.

Wu, Ellen D. *The Color of Success: Asian Americans and the Origins of the Model Minority*. Princeton: Princeton University Press, 2014.

"The Young People's Project Inc., YPP Results—Internal and External Assessments 1997–2014." The Young People's Project. http://www.typp.org/ (accessed June 3, 2015).

"The Young People's Project—Michigan 2010." YouTube. https://www.youtube.com/watch?v=mldkkOs27HA (accessed Nov. 8, 2015).

"YPP Teen STEAM Day." The Young People's Project. http://www.typp.org/ (accessed June 3, 2015).

Zajonc, Arthur. "Contemplative Pedagogy: A Quiet Revolution in Higher Education." *New Directions for Teaching and Learning* 134 (2013): 83–94.

Zambelich, Ariel, and Cassi Alexandra. "In Their Own Words." NPR, Dec. 11, 2016. https://www.npr.org/2016/12/11/505147166/in-their-own-words-the-water-protectors-of-standing-rock.

Zellner, Bob. *The Wrong Side of Murder Creek: A White Southerner in the Freedom Movement*. Montgomery, AL: New South Books, 2008.

Zimbardo, Phillip. *The Lucifer Effect: How Good People Turn Evil*. London: Rider, 2007.

Zimmerman, Donald. "Record-Keeping and the Intake Process in a Public Welfare Agency." In *On Record: Files and Dossiers in American Life*, edited by Stanton Wheeler, 319–54. New York: Russell Sage Foundation, 1969.

Zinn, Howard. *Howard Zinn: On History*. New York: Seven Stories Press, 2011.

———. "Secrecy, Archives and the Public Interest." *Midwestern Archivist* 2, no. 2 (1977): 14–26.

Zuberi, Tufuku, and Eduardo Bonilla-Silva. *White Logic, White Methods: Racism and Methodology*. Lanham, MD: Rowman and Littlefield, 2008.

INDEX

Abdollahi, Mohammad, 110
Abdullah, Melina, 124
#AbolishICE, 198, 209
abolitionist organizations, 72, 74, 86–88, 146, 244n20. *See also* California Prison Focus; California Coalition for Women Prisoners; Critical Resistance; Ella Baker Center; Mothers Reclaiming Our Children; Prison Activist Resource Center
abortion, 45
Abu Ghraib, 3
abuse of power, 35, 73, 74, 76, 121, 122, 139–43, 148, 149, 164–66, 176, 181, 187–92, 199
accountability of lawmakers to ordinary people, 24–25, 51–55, 117, 128–29, 147, 149, 155, 164, 198, 199, 224; accountability of police, 73, 116, 122–25, 139–41; community-accountable institutions, 151, 214, 217, 220, 286n2; failure of accountability, 76, 122, 139–41, 149, 164–66, 185–92, 199, 202, 217, 221, 246n31. *See also* abuse of power; Constitution; people power
acting "as if," 14, 18, 111. *See also* living "as if"
acting democratically, 9, 23, 86–88, 118, 205
Acuña, Salem, 111
Adams, Victoria Gray, 25, 29–30, 234n18
Adams-Zavilla, Chanse, 184, 193
adultism, 83, 210. *See also* media condescension; Perry, Nona

affirmative action, 55
Agnew, Philip (Umi Selah), 129–30, 138, 140
Agricultural Stabilization Boards, 24
Ahwireng, Afua (Asibey), 219
Alexander, Michelle, 68, 74
Algebra Project, 221, 230n6
algebra I, 6
Ali, 93
Ali, Muhammad, 14
Alinsky, Saul, 39. *See also* Industrial Areas Foundation
Allard, LaDonna, 25, 181, 194, 207
Altar, Mexico, 94–95
alternative genealogies, 12
American Civil Liberties Union (ACLU), 90
American Friends Service Committee, 96–97
American Indian Movement (AIM), 2, 154, 165, 183, 184, 189, 230n3
Amnesty International, 90
anger, mislabeling youth as angry, 10
anti-blackness, 8, 116, 122, 131, 132, 146; feeding police violence, 139
anti-immigrant, 116, 132
antiracist organizing, 43, 44, 47, 55–58, 240n51
anti-southern bias, 42
anti-WTO movement, 219
apathy, mislabeling youth as apathetic, 10
Arab Spring, 166
Archambault, David II, 163, 186, 193

archive building, 212–24
Arpaio, Joe, 90–93, 120, 249n7
Art Action Camp, 178
arts organizing. *See* organizing
Asian American Justice Center, 105, 198
Asian-Pacific Islander organizers, 57–58, 194
Atlanta, Ga., 35–36, 236n1
Atlanta race riot, 187
Atlantic slave trade, 8
Audre Lorde Project, 48
Augusto, Geri, 221
authoritarianism, 202, 208–11; authoritarian habits, 155, 208; corporate authoritarianism, 53, 167, 210; government authoritarianism, 210. *See also* accountability of lawmakers to ordinary people: failure of accountability
Avery, Annie Pearl, 31
Awful Truth, The (Moore), 142

Baby Boomers, 112
backlash, 211
bait-and-switch, 42–44, 51, 76–77, 80, 90, 100–101, 108, 112–13, 128, 140, 151, 159, 161–65, 197, 198. *See also* divide and conquer tactic; freedom tools; solidarity
Baker, Ella, 9, 18–33, 83, 138, 160, 181, 207; invisible work of, 27, 76, 206; legacy, 31, 48–49, 129, 147, 200, 203. *See also* fundi; intergenerational organizing
Bakken Region, 157, 182
Baldwin, James, 121, 125
Baltimore, Md., 148–49, 210
Bank of North Dakota, 188
Barrientos, Walter, 101–2
Barry, Marion, 27
Battin, Susanna, 174
Bayard Rustin Project, 61–62
Bayard Rustin Receptions, 62
Bay Peace—Better Alternatives for Youth, 82–85

Beaman, Tyra, 118
Bear, Nahko, 163, 177
Beck, Glenn, 76
Belcourt, Christi, 178
Bell, Sean, 14, 148
Bellanger, Pat, 2
belonging, 13, 44, 50, 100–103, 106, 112, 116, 119, 120, 204. *See also* citizenship; hospitality; organizing; relationship building
"beloved community," 27, 235n23
Benavidez, Isa Barajas de, 183
Benito, 91
Berg, Mniluzahe, 186
Berlin truck attack, 188
Berlin Wall, 65, 90
Bethel Baptist Church, 17
Bin Laden, Osama, 189
Birmingham, Ala., 17, 137, 167
Bismarck, S.D., 159, 163
Black Arts movement, 38
Black feminism, 13, 43, 133, 147, 154, 263n37
Black freedom church, 134
"Black Hate Groups," 189
Black Hills Act of 1877, 165
"Black Identity Extremists," 151
Black Lives Matter, 10, 115, 116, 162, 168, 174, 183, 207, 208; hashtag, 131–32, 140, 142; origins, 131; transformed how people understood their Blackness, 131. *See also* Movement for Black Lives
Black Panther Party, 189
Black Power, 189
Black women's studies, 38
Black Youth Project 100. *See* BYP100
Bland, Sandra, 14, 124
Boal, Augusto, 82, 83
body cameras, 121
Bonilla-Silva, Eduardo, 220
Bonner Scholarship, 96
Books Not Bars, 73–4
borders, 89–90, 94–95, 100, 104, 109, 115, 118, 120, 250n17, 259n83

bottom-up history, 7, 118, 213, 222. *See also* evidence; inside-out history
bottom-up politics, 68, 77, 213. *See also* accountability of lawmakers to ordinary people
Bowers, Andrea, 174
boycotts. *See* economic boycott tactic
Boyd, Rekia, 124, 150
Boynton, Amelia, 147
Boyte, Harry, 208
Braden, Anne, 21, 30, 51, 234n10
Brahmaputra River, 184
Brave New World (Huxley), 112
Brown v. Board of Education, 211
Breakwater Bridge, 171
Brings Plenty, Morgan, 196
#BringThemHome, 119
brown, adrienne maree, 145, 146
Brown, Michael, 135–41
Brown, Michael, Jr., 13
Brown Power movement, 154
Bryant, Povi-Tamu, 134
Buffalo Federal Detention Center, 102
burnout, 79
Burton, Susan, 68
Burwell, Dollie, 3, 230n3
Bush, George W., 68, 90, 115, 211, 280n96
Butler, Octavia, 38
Bynes, Patricia, 135
BYP100, 76, 134, 145, 146, 153, 154, 155

California Coalition for Women Prisoners, 72
California Green Corps, 78
California Green Stimulus Coalition, 78
California Prison Focus, 72
California State–Los Angeles, 124
Campaign Zero, 153
Campbell, Kenneth, 222
Cannonball, N.D., 158
Cannon Ball River, 181
capitalism, 43, 51–55, 56, 117, 161, 200, 203, 240n62. *See also* neoliberalism
#CaravanForJustice, 78
Cardenas, Eva, 174, 175

Carmichael, Stokely (Kwame Turé), 62
Carruthers, Charlene, 76, 138, 145, 146, 150, 154
Carter, Mandy, 37, 40, 41, 55, 61, 133
Cass County, N.D., 186
Castile, Philando, 150, 176
Center for Democratic Renewal, 48, 63
Center for Documentary Studies, Duke University, 222
ceremony, 162, 166, 169–75, 177–80, 185–86, 189–91, 210
Cesar, 114
Chacon, Raven, 183
Charger, Jasilyn, 158, 178, 188, 193
Charlottesville, Va., 136, 166, 188, 191, 265n47
Chatfield, Jack, 18, 233n2
Chavez, Cesar, 117
Chenault, Reese, 219
Chicano high school student walkout of 1968, 2, 214
Chief Joseph, 187
Chisholm, Shirley, 71, 244n11
Chomsky, Aviva, 98
Church Committee hearings, 189
citizenship, 3, 5, 9, 11, 14, 23, 24, 36, 37, 41, 43, 48, 68, 73, 82, 89–90, 93, 98–103, 100, 111–12, 114, 116, 122, 125, 128, 133–37, 148, 149, 155, 161, 172, 173, 187, 188, 189, 194, 197, 199, 202, 207, 209, 211, 222; active citizenship, 83–85, 105, 119, 153, 189; Enlightenment ideal, 100, 120, 157–59, 161, 202; resistance citizenship, 101–7, 142, 204–12. *See also* self-worth as key to active citizenship
"citizens of a world not yet built," 5, 120, 212
Citizens' Oversight Commissions, 121
civil disobedience. *See* nonviolent direct action
Clark, Septima, 48
class-based organizing, 42, 51–55, 103, 140–41, 204, 245n26, 249n5, 267n56
Cleveland, Miss., 26

Cleveland, Ohio, 149
Clinton, Bill, 51, 68, 200, 211
Clinton, Hillary, 157
Clutchette, John, 74
coalition, 115; coalition building, 74–76;
Cobb, Charlie, 130, 147, 221, 272n6
Cohen, Cathy, 25, 147, 220
COINTELPRO, 189, 280n95
Cold War, 45, 46, 65
Coles, Robert, 218, 288n14
collective memory, 121, 142, 201, 214
collective ownership, 151
Collins, Patricia Hill, 38
colonialism, 118, 174, 252n29, 272n11
Color of Change, 77
Columbus, Christopher, 43, 114, 182
Combahee River Collective Statement, 38, 39, 43, 52, 107, 133, 255n49
Community for the Advancement of Native Studies, 161
Community Defense Committees, 92
condescension of the received culture, 10, 215, 222
conflict. *See* internal movement conflict
Congress, U.S., 101, 108, 115, 120, 173, 185
Congress of Racial Equality (CORE), 102, 155
Connor, Eugene "Bull," 137
consciousness-raising, 132
consensus-building, 25–27, 74–76, 149
Constitution, 8, 89, 120, 188, 189, 200
consumerism, 19, 203–5
Contract with America, 53, 65
Cooper, Anna Julia, 133, 153
Copeland, Rev. Brant, 128
Córdoba, Jacquilyn, 170, 173
corporate power, 52–55, 100, 116, 120, 133, 141, 153, 157, 160, 161, 163, 165, 167, 181, 187–92, 197, 267n56. *See also* accountability of lawmakers to ordinary people; deregulation; law enforcement: collusion with corporate surveillance; surveillance
Cortés, Hermalinda, 117
cosmopolite privilege, 89, 90, 100

Cox, Courtland, 130, 147, 221
Cracker Barrel, 57
crawl spaces for democracy, 37, 83, 208
creating knowledge, 212–24. *See also* epistemologies
Crenshaw, Kimberlé, 38, 150, 183
criminalization, 67, 113–14, 115–17, 136, 151, 266n52; of activists, 151, 161, 191; challenging Black criminalization, 126, 130, 136–41, 151
criminalizing activists, 151, 161, 191, 273n14
critical ethnography, 219
critical pedagogy. *See* popular education
critical race theory, 218
Critical Resistance, 72, 245n26
Crow, Raina, 167
Cruz, Daniela, 92
Cullors, Patrisse (Patrice Khan-Cullors), 115, 130–33, 138, 140, 142, 150, 154
cultural appropriation, 12
curriculum. *See* education
Custer, George, 165
#cut50, 77
Cynthia, 105–6

Dakota Access pipeline (DAPL), 132, 158, 159, 161, 162, 164, 167, 187, 188, 189, 191, 196, 279n89
Dalrymple, Jack, 185
Davidson, Antar, 99
Davis, Miles, 10
Davis, Troy, 148
Deb, Trishala, 57
De Blasio, Bill, 143
De Blasio, Dante, 143
Declaration of Independence, 7, 18, 154, 210
Declaration on the Rights of Indigenous Peoples, 165
deference to power, 153
Deferred Action for Childhood Arrivals (DACA), 111
De la Rocha, Zack, 101
Delgado, Amber, 222

Delta Force, 189
democracy, 5, 6–7, 13, 20, 86–88, 100, 129, 153, 161, 167, 188, 233n7; as aspirational, 8, 12; economic, 23, 25, 204; as an ethereal mist, 7, 9; as experiment, 13, 100, 135, 147, 167, 204–11, 214; Latin American cultural traditions of, 106, 118, 255n45; liberal, 161, 188, 202; lived, 118, 147, 205, 209; participatory, 20, 27, 77, 82–86, 145–47, 155, 205; SNCC agenda broadening democracy for all, 21, 118, 254n35; U.S. myths about its democracy, 18, 19, 21, 122, 291; youth as innovators in, 12, 82–86, 205–6, 213–15. *See also* accountability of lawmakers to ordinary people; acting democratically; listening
democratic education, 82–84, 141–47, 167, 214, 243n2, 248n40, 256n51
democratic forms, 84, 120, 155, 197, 209
democratic institutions, 100
democratic leadership, 29, 82–86, 167
Democratic Party, 155
democratic social relations as basis for political life, 28, 167, 203–11
Dennis, Dave, 6, 221
deportation, 90–93, 96–97, 110, 120, 139
deregulation, 53, 211
desegregation, 23, 109
detention centers, 102, 111, 113, 116, 198
Detroit race riot, 187
Dewey, John, 82, 248n40, 256n51
Diallo, Amadou, 14, 142, 148
DiCaprio, Leonardo, 176
dilemma actions, 110, 111. *See also* nonviolent direct action; role-play tactic
Disney cartoons, 67, 243n2
divide-and-conquer tactic, 36–37, 39, 43, 45–47, 52–53, 56–58, 61–64, 107–8, 113, 200, 239n35; role of assumptions in, 62, 107–8
documentary record, 212–24, 287n10; digital tools of, 222–23
Documenting the Now, 223
Domestic Workers United, 106

Dominguez, Maria, 81
Donaldson, Ivanhoe, 221
Dorado, Jeanne, 183
Dorsey, L. C., 7
Douglass, Frederick, 18, 92, 200, 211
DREAM Act, 99, 101, 105, 111, 114, 115, 118, 119, 201, 252n26, 254n35
DreamActivist, 109, 110
Dream Defenders, 102, 116, 126–30, 134, 144, 153, 155, 199, 201, 203; bringing direct action back, 154; social media blackout, 144–45
DREAMers, 248. *See* immigrant youth movement
Dream 9, 119
Dream 30, 110
drivers' license, 96, 97, 110, 201
Drudge Report, 151
dual labor market, 98
Du Bois, W. E. B., 220
Duke, David, 3
Duke University, 220
Dunbar-Ortiz, Roxanne, 220
Durham, N.C., 37, 41, 102

Eagle, Dakota, 162
Eastern Shore, Md., 24
economic boycott tactic, 21
economic democracy. *See* democracy: economic
economic deregulation. *See* neoliberalism
economic justice, 21, 39, 40, 42–43, 46, 51–55, 67, 113, 140, 148. *See also* capitalism; class-based organizing; fines and fees; inequality; Jim Crow; racial capitalism; slavery
Edmund Pettis Bridge, 7
education, 5–6, 82–86, 93, 96, 98, 248n40, 256n51, 268n70
educational malpractice, 214. *See also* racial ignorance
electoral politics. *See* voting rights
elite control of public life, 76–77, 92, 159, 163, 164, 197–203, 213

Ella Baker Center for Human Rights (EBC), 11, 65–88, 122, 153, 154, 155, 201, 208, 210
Emergency Management Assistance Compact, 187
Emery-Brown, Jumoke, 174, 184
Emiliano Zapata Street Academy, 83
Enbridge, Inc., 167
#EndYouthSolitary, 77
Energy Transfer Partners, 163–64, 187
Enlightenment framework for democracy, 100, 194, 202, 252n29
environmentalism, 75, 117, 154, 159, 182, 194, 245n23; environmental activism, 183, 194
environmental justice, 3, 75, 117, 157–96, 171, 245n23
environmental racism, 51, 159, 245n23
epistemologies, 165, 194, 212–24, 230n7, 268n70, 273n15, 277n63, 286n7; activist, 212–24; Indigenous, 161–63, 180, 194, 277n63; Latin American, 162, 253n29; Western, 162, 165, 194
Ernst, Wolfgang, 223
Esperanza House, 48
Estes, Nick, 165
Evans, Sara, 208
Evers, Medgar, 26
evidence, 212–24, 230n6
experiential knowledge, 27, 82, 128
extractive infrastructure, 151, 161, 164, 181, 184, 188, 193, 194, 201, 272n9, 288n13
extractive scholarship, 176, 214, 220, 221, 275n29, 285n2, 287n13
extractive wars, 187, 188, 201

failure, 18, 29, 36–39, 50, 68, 76, 79, 83, 100, 128, 140, 205, 207, 246n31
Fairbanks, Frances, 2
false equivalence, 167, 275n34
family separation, 91, 98, 99, 102, 104, 108, 120, 197–200, 210. *See also* immigrant youth movement; Underground Railroad
fascism, 19

fear-based investment, 78, 92, 98, 101, 106, 112–13, 151, 196. *See also* criminalization; public investment (as alternative)
Federal Bureau of Investigation (FBI), 187, 188
Federal Bureau of Prisons, 112
Federal Energy Regulatory Commission, 164
Feminary, 42
feminist theory, 218
Ferguson, Mo., 135–41, 148, 168, 177, 186, 187, 191, 210
Fernanda, 114
fines and fees, 67, 136, 140, 148, 243n4; way to keep people tagged, 67
First Seminole War, 187
Flores, Cristian Osvaldo, 107
Florida A&M University, 127
Florida Department of Law Enforcement, 128
Flowers, Catherine, 171
Forgiveness March, 170–71
Forman, James Jr., 149
Fort Berthold, 181
Fort Laramie treaties of 1851 and 1868, 164, 194, 274n27, 274n29
founding fathers, 8
Fox, Sarain, 178
Franco, Marisa, 106, 115
Franklin, John Hope, 220
Frappier, Diana, 72
Frazier, Dionne, 80
Frazier, Lanise, 79–81, 86, 88
Frazier, Nishani, 219, 223
Frazier, Thomas, 172
freedom movement, 4, 13, 22, 44, 87, 103, 108, 199, 214, 220; impact on wider culture, 47, 118, 155, 200–211, 214, 223
freedom politics, 9, 58, 76, 91–93, 101, 200–211, 231n11, 283n7. *See also* bait-and-switch; divide and conquer tactic; organizing
Freedom Rides, 17, 41, 116
Freedom Schools, 106, 109, 256n54
"Freedomside," 129

Freedom Singers, 14, 118
freedom songs, 13, 48, 103–4, 118, 170, 232n22
freedom struggle, 11, 12, 132, 134, 146, 149, 200
freedom tools, 12, 59, 61, 69–70, 75, 78, 82–87, 91–93, 101, 105, 107, 116, 118, 125, 147, 150, 154, 155, 157–59, 204–7, 214, 285n28
Freedom University, 106, 108–9, 113, 118
Free Southern Theater, 84
Freire, Paolo, 31, 48, 87, 203. *See also* popular education
Fund for Southern Communities, 47, 48
Fundi, 33, 68, 130, 269n81. *See also* intergenerational organizing
fund-raising, 28

Gabriel, Nic, 178
Gantt, Harvey, 46–47
Garcia, Joel, 184
Garner, Eric, 124
Garner, Joan, 5, 37, 47, 51
Garza, Alicia, 130–33
Gaventa, John, 48
Gay and Lesbian Alliance Against Defamation (GLAAD), 40
gay-baiting, 46. *See also* divide and conquer
Gaye, Marvin, 14
Gay Pride. *See* Pride march
gay-straight alliances, 3, 230n3
Genius annotation software, 215, 216
genocide, 114, 191
GEO Group, 112, 198–200
George, Liz, 172
Georgia Board of Regents, 108, 118, 253n30
Georgia Institute of Technology, 118
Georgia Latino Alliance for Human Rights, 198
Georgia State University, 118
GI Bill, 19, 233n6
Gig, The, 82
global apartheid, 100, 252n29

Goodwyn, Lawrence, 208
Gordon College, 80
Gramsci, Antonio, 31
Grant, Joanne, 27
Grassrope, Danny, 158, 169
Gray, Freddie, 14, 148
Greene, Hilary, 223
Green Feather Movement, 2, 229n3
Green for All, 77
green jobs campaign, 74–77, 78, 86, 146, 154
Greensboro, N.C., 59
Greensboro Four, 3, 20, 118, 214
Greensboro Massacre, 42, 63, 238n23
Gregory, Dick, 207
Grimké, Angelina, 153
Grinnell, Zaysha, 181, 182
group-centered leadership, 18, 23–25, 85–86, 154, 174, 254n17
Guilford College, 96
Gumbs, Alexis Pauline, 286n2, 298n22
Gustafson, John, 137
Gutiérrez, Jennicet, 89

Hamer, Fannie Lou, 31, 129
Hamlin, Susan, 218
Hammond House, 107
Handcox, John, 48
Hands Up United, 13
Harding, Rosemarie, 220
Harding, Vincent, 103, 220
Harris, Emory, 118. *See also* Freedom Singers
Harris, Rutha, 118. *See also* Freedom Singers
Harris-Perry, Melissa, 5
Hartford, Bruce, 221
Hasan, Rahi, 222
Hattiesburg, Miss., 25
Hayden, Casey, 221
HB 56, 114
healing justice practices, 85, 106, 151, 154, 178–81
"Hell You Talmbout" (freedom song), 13–14
Helm-Hernández, Paulina, 107, 117

Helms, Jesse, 38, 41, 42, 46–47, 52, 56
Helton, Angela, 150
Hennegler, Jessica, 219
Heriberto, 96
Heritage Foundation, 76
Hernandez, Viridiana, 92
Herring, Jeffrey, 219
Heyer, Heather, 191
higher education, 106. *See also* tuition equity
Highlander Folk School, 48, 109, 144, 257n55
Hill, Anita, 65
Hill, Kyle, 162
Hine, Darlene Clark, 220
hip-hop, 13–4, 101, 123
Historically Black Colleges and Universities (HBCU) 2, 47, 219; as movement incubators, 2, 19, 22
homophobia, 36, 43
Hooks, Mary, 117
Hopkins, Cheryl, 59
Horton, Myles, 48, 87, 203
hospitality, 28, 44, 49, 57, 68, 145, 193. *See also* belonging; listening as key to democratic relationship; relationship-building; spadework
Howard University, 47, 129
Howland, Alex, 170, 180
Howland, Lauren, 158, 166, 169, 173
how to grow ordinary people into full citizenship, 5–6, 9, 83, 214
Huerta, Delores, 117
Huggins, Nathan, 143
Human Rights Campaign, 44
Human Rights Watch, 90
hunger strikes, 105, 112. *See also* freedom tools
Hunt, Dorian, 124
Hunt, Jim, 46
Hurricane Katrina, 3, 148, 214
Hussain, Pat, 37, 40–42, 48, 154, 175, 209, 236–37n7
Huxley, Aldous, 112
Hyman, Christy, 223

identity, identity politics. *See* intersectionality
#IdleNoMore, 132, 161, 167, 273n13
#IfIDieInPoliceCustody, 116
Ille the gal, 114
immigrant as legal category, 98
Immigrant Workers Freedom Ride, 55
Immigrant Youth Justice League, 106
immigrant youth movement, 11, 39, 64, 86, 91–93, 102, 106, 201, 208, 210. *See also* undocumented youth
Immigration Act of 1924, 98
Immigration and Customs Enforcement (ICE), 91, 101, 110, 111, 115, 117, 120, 198, 208
Immigration and Naturalization Act (1965), 97
Immigration Enforcement Review Board (Ga.), 108
immigration reform, 115, 116; in practice, 119
implicit bias, 139, 266n52
incarceration, 67, 73, 78, 84–85, 116, 121, 123, 149, 151, 154, 161, 191, 201, 202, 243n3; for profit, 74, 112, 244n22, 257n64. *See also* Immigration and Customs Enforcement; law enforcement; school-to-prison pipeline; slow violence; trauma
Indian Appropriations Act of 1876, 165
Indigenous Environmental Network, 166
Indigenous homeland, 95, 114, 163, 184, 198
Indigenous People's Power Project (IP3), 174–75, 185
Indigenous resistance, 13, 114, 132, 141, 161, 182, 194
Indigenous scholarship, 218, 252n29
Indigenous traditions, 14, 180, 184, 272n11
Indigenous youth, 113, 157–96, 198
Industrial Areas Foundation (IAF), 37, 38, 39, 106, 237n15

inequality, 52, 74, 78, 90, 100, 140–41, 202, 220. *See also* class-based organizing
informational wealth, 221–24
information-sharing as organizing tactic, 29, 51–8, 63, 82, 105–7, 112, 116, 130, 132, 141–46, 150, 163, 174–76, 182, 203, 206, 214–17, 221. *See also* consciousness-raising; power: to define and name
innovations of youth organizers, 11, 12, 82–85, 91–93, 102–7, 166–85, 205–11
inside-out history, 222
Intercept, The, 187–92
interdependence, 100, 106, 261n14. *See also* belonging; ordinary people having a say in their own lives
intergenerational organizing, 22–26, 81, 87, 105, 130, 144, 147, 169, 181–83, 207. *See also* slow walk of the trees
internal movement conflict, 4, 28, 36, 75–76, 113–15, 141–46, 169, 223, 245n25, 245n26. *See also* information-sharing as organizing tactic; social media
International Indian Treaty Council, 165
International Indigenous Youth Council (IIYC), 11, 117, 166–95, 201, 207
intersectionality, 4, 38, 219, 236n4, 259n1
intersectional organizing, 4, 37–39, 52–55, 117, 132–33, 154, 183, 184, 210, 263n37
Iron Eyes, Tokata, 193, 202
Iron Shell, Terrell, 159, 169, 171

Jackson, Maynard, 47
Jackson, Phil, 10
Jefferson, Thomas, 153, 200, 206, 211
Jena Six, 1, 148, 214, 229n2
Jenkins, Tim, 27
Jim Crow, 17, 20, 21, 110, 111, 118, 121, 130, 143, 167; new Jim Crow, 112, 130, 136, 191
Jimenez, Cristina, 101–5, 116, 118
Johns, Barbara, 2, 229n3
Johnson, Andrew, 187

Johnson, Jewel Princess, 219
Johnson, Marsha P., 107
Johnston, Lyla June, 170, 177
Jones, Aiyana, 124
Jones, Anki, 219
Jones, Charles, 27
Jones, Van, 71–77, 86, 88, 146
Jones, Willie, 71
Jules, Bergis, 223
Juntos, 198
justice, 66, 127, 200
#JusticeForMikeBrown, 116
Justice League, 88

K-12, 3, 5–6, 82–84, 97, 101, 214
Kānaka Maoli, 161
Kane, Desiree, 159
Katwiwa, Mwende, 134
Kelley, Robin D. G., 203
Kennedy, John (JFK), 71
Kennedy, Robert (RFK), 71
Kennesaw State University, 108
Kentucky Alliance Against Racist and Political Repression, 57
Kentucky Fairness Alliance, 50
Khan-Cullors, Patrice. *See* Cullors, Patrisse
King, Rev. Dr. Martin Luther, Jr., 18, 38, 40, 61, 71, 82, 111, 148
King, Rodney, 72, 142, 148. *See also* Los Angeles uprising, 1992
King, Thomas, 14
Kinte, Kunte, 14
Kirchmeier, Kyle, 185, 186, 191
Knoxville, Tenn., 41
Krispy Kreme, 40
Ku Klux Klan (KKK), 41, 42, 43
Kyles, Termain, 35–36

Ladner, Joyce, 25, 234n17
Lafayette Square, 158
Land, Wilson, 222
Lang, Clarence, 145
Lake Oahe, 163
Latino Union of Chicago, 105

Latinx, 11, 63, 72, 90, 116–17, 154, 159, 249n6
law enforcement, 35–36, 65–66, 72, 73, 92–93, 95–97, 110–11, 115, 121–24, 135–41, 142, 143, 167, 170, 184, 210, 259n2, 260n3, 266n52; collusion with corporate surveillance, 172, 185–92, 210; as fee collectors, 136; resistance from within, 97, 99, 171, 185
Lawson, James, 110, 197, 212, 257n58
Lawson, Jennifer, 147, 221
Lawyers Committee for Civil Rights, 72
leadership, 23–25, 29–33
legal systems outdated, 100
Lemlich, Clara, 2
Lewis and Clark, 164
LGBTQ organizing, 36–63, 106–8, 133–34, 154, 255n47, 256n52
Limbaugh, Rush, 151
Lincoln Memorial, 129
listening as key to democratic relationship, 23, 24, 49, 69, 78, 85, 174, 209, 240n41
Little, Joan (Joanne), 42, 238n23
Little Big Horn, 165
Little Rock school integration crisis, 21
living "as if," 9, 14, 18, 28, 81, 111, 159, 171, 194, 199–212; living free, 119, 124
London truck attack, 188
Long Range Acoustic Devices, 168
Lopez, Rosario, 119
Lopez, Thomas, 196
Lorde, Audre, 38, 52, 107, 133, 255n49
Los Angeles uprising, 1992, 72
Louima, Abner, 142
Louisiana Purchase, 165
Lowndes County Freedom Organization (LCFO), 207, 283n7
Luger, Cannupa Hanska, 160, 177
lynching, 122, 136
Lynd, Alice, 220
Lynd, Staughton, 220

Machiavelli, Niccolò, 187
Macune, Charles, 153
Madison, James, 8, 200
Maidu homeland, 184
Maile, David Uahikeaikalei'ohu, 191
Majority, The, 115
Malcolm X, 38, 66, 82
Mandela, Nelson, 65, 66
March on Washington, 61, 129
Maricopa County, Ariz., 90
Marjory Stoneman Douglas High School, 201
maroon communities, 142
Martin, Trayvon, 11, 116, 124–28, 134, 148; as national agony, 130
mass incarceration. See incarceration
Massive Resistance, 211. See also backlash
Mateo, Lizbeth, 112
Mathern, Tim, 188
Mauna a Wākea, 161, 183
Mauna Kea, 184
Maxwell, Angela, 175
McCall, Nathan, 66
McConnell, Mitch, 200
McDew, Charles (Chuck), 27
McGill, Lillian, 147
McGuire, Danielle, 4
McHarris, Thenjiwe, 150
Mckesson, DeRay, 137–38
McKibben, Bill, 176, 194
McKinney, Charles, 11
McMichael, Pam, 37, 48, 51–53, 56
McNeill, Ambria, 222
media condescension, 127, 141–46, 148, 150, 174, 176, 209–10, 218, 264m39; mislabeling movements as spontaneous and impulsive, 146, 210, 215
Mekong Delta, 184
mental health, 106. See also healing justice practices; trauma
mentoring, 6
Mercano, Mervyn, 150
metrics of movement success, 23, 33, 57, 77, 115–20, 205–8. See also victories
M4BL Policy Table, 150–55, 209
microaggression, 80–81

micro-archives, 223
Mijente, 115, 117, 198
Miles, Nelson, 187
militarization of daily life in Black communities, 136–37, 265n48
millennials, 145, 207
Mills, Charles, 142, 220
Mirror Casket (2014 art piece), 177
misogynoir, 123, 260n6
misogyny, 43
missing youth histories, 7, 10, 82, 206, 214
Mississippi Delta, 23
Mississippi Freedom Democratic Party (MFDP), 155, 207, 234n15, 234n22
Missouri River, 165, 181, 201
Mitchell, Maurice, 150
mixtape, 4, 12
Mní wičoni, 157–96
Modern Day Warriors, 182
Monáe, Janelle, 13–14
Monet, Aja, 203
Montgomery, Ala., 114
Montgomery bus boycott, 21
Moore, Amzie, 26, 147, 234n19
Moore, Michael, 142
morality as foundation for politics as alternative to power-over, 191, 201, 221
Moral Majority, 37
Moral Monday movement, 102
Morales, Victor, 118
Morgan, Kacey, 219
Morrison, Toni, 32, 58, 207
Morton County, N.D., 170, 173, 185, 186, 187
Moses, Bob, 6, 26, 32–33, 103–7, 147, 207, 221, 288n14
Mothers Reclaiming Our Children, 72
Mother Teresa, 82
Mountaintop Festival, 50
Mount Olive pickle boycott, 55
movement building, 29, 76
movement culture, 12, 57, 62, 64, 80, 85, 103, 116–17, 142, 148, 160, 174, 178, 180–81, 194, 223. *See also* belonging; freedom songs; freedom tools; organizing; people power; remix culture
Movement for Black Lives (M4BL), 11, 14, 39, 67, 76, 102, 113, 124, 149–55, 170, 201, 209; healing as central, 76; platform 151–55
movement networks, 27, 29
movement success. *See* metrics of movement success
multinational corporations. *See* corporate power
Murdoch, Isaac, 178
music: as analysis for survival, 13; as freedom tool, 13–14, 48, 59, 64, 142, 170, 177
Myitsome Dam, 184
myths about movements, 145

Nagle, Mary Kathryn, 181
Nash, Diane, 2, 17, 23, 27, 28, 230n3, 233n1
National Action Network, 125
National Association for the Advancement of Colored People (NAACP), 20, 25, 40
National Black Feminist Organization, 38, 133, 255n49
National Coming Out of the Shadows Day, 106, 108, 255n47
National Day Laborer Organizing Network (NDLON), 105, 198
National Gay and Lesbian Task Force (NGLTF), 41–44
national governments unable to function, 100, 109
National Guard, 169, 185
National Immigrant Youth Alliance, 119
nationalism, 90–93, 100, 103, 251n25
national myths, 7, 62, 65, 100, 145
National Sheriffs Association, 186
National Women of Color in the Workplace, 48
nativism. *See* nationalism
Neal, Mark Anthony, 142

neoliberalism, 42, 45, 51–52, 74, 240n50; neoliberal citizenship, 203
Netflix, 204
New Deal, 153
New Georgia Project, 199
New Negro politics, 2
New Orleans, La., 134
New Orleans Congress of Day Laborers, 198
New York City's Tenderloin Riot, 137
Nice truck attack, 188
Night Out for Safety and Liberation, 69
Niheu, Dr. Kalamoaoka'aina, 173, 193
Nimi'ipuu (Nez Perce), 187
1984 (Orwell), 112
Nixon, Richard, 45, 46
#NoDAPL, 158, 166, 182, 184, 187, 191
nonbinary, 4, 278n68
nonviolent direct action, 41, 91–93, 105, 109, 110, 113, 114, 116, 118, 125, 130, 136, 154, 157, 161, 163, 177; discipline of, 166, 173
North American Free Trade Agreement (NAFTA), 42, 43, 45. *See also* neoliberalism
North Carolinians Against Racist and Religious Violence, 42, 43
North Charleston, S.C., 148
Northwest Detention Center, 112
Northwest Detention Center Resistance, 198
#Not1More, 115, 117, 198
Nunpa, Phil Wanbli, 161

Obama, Barack, 68, 76, 77, 115, 118, 173, 211, 246n31; shuts out bottom-up organizers, 76, 246n29
Occupy Wall Street movement, 52, 127, 141, 166
Oceti Sakowin, 158–59, 162, 163, 166, 175, 181, 183, 288n13
Offiah, Natt, 59
"Oh, Freedom," 118
Okri, Ben, 14
One Tribe, 181

oral history, 218, 221, 223, 289n16
ordinary people having a say in their own lives, 9, 13–14, 29–32, 46, 62, 67–68, 85–86, 155, 204, 211
Organized Community Against Deportation, 198
organized people, 13, 22, 81; see also organizing
organizing, 13, 37–39, 67–68, 81–82, 92, 88, 91–93, 101–7, 111, 115–20, 141–46, 148, 155, 203–11; arts-based organizing, 48–9, 58–63, 82–6, 177–80; models for organizing, 37–39, 74–76, 79–80, 91–93, 101, 124, 131–32, 141–47, 155, 167, 255n45; storytelling within, 27, 39, 49, 57, 72, 86, 91–93, 101–7, 110, 111, 116, 120, 123, 126–27, 129, 144, 159, 176, 181, 202, 255n45. *See also* freedom songs; freedom tools; information-sharing as organizing tactic; internal movement conflict; metrics of movement success; people power; political education; recruitment; relationship-building; social media; victories
organizing tradition, 10, 12, 44, 79, 147, 155, 160, 203
original political possibilities; *See* democracy as experiment; freedom tools
Ortiz, Paul, 103
Orwell, George, 112
Osment, Sunny, 203

Pachamama, 162
Paine, Thomas, 153
Pargett, Steven, 127
Parkland, FL, 201, 207
Parks, Rosa, 82, 182
participatory democracy. *See* democracy
Patterson, Eva Jefferson, 72
Payne, Charles, 10, 44
Peeples, Jamaya, 126
people power, 39, 55, 70, 74–77, 113, 116, 120, 155, 166, 182, 187, 195, 198, 200–211, 246n29, 246n31

People's Hearings, 125
Perry, Nona, 82–86, 88
personal politics, the personal is political, 32
Pete, Shauneen, 161
Petersburg, Va., 5
Pharr, Suzanne, 37, 42, 45–46, 48, 52
Phelps, Teresa, 204
Phillips, Kevin, 46. *See also* Southern Strategy
Phoenix, Ariz., 91–93, 110, 210
Pierce, Charles, 163
Pine Ridge homeland, 165, 189
Pinkerton Agency, 188
Plains Pipeline, 184
Plyer v. Doe, 101
police. *See* law enforcement
police abuse. *See* law enforcement
political education, 48, 82–85, 141–47, 167
politics of representation, 23, 101, 117, 135, 139, 142, 161, 195, 198, 204, 220
politics of respectability, 62, 65–66, 110, 132–35, 263n35
Poor People's Campaign, 40
popular education, 13, 82–85, 109, 257n55
postcolonial studies, 218
power, 209, 221; to define and name, 14–15, 48, 49, 107, 113–14, 119–20, 134, 161–62, 165, 201, 208; hierarchical power and elite control, 68, 77, 100, 195, 200, 209, 211. *See also* authoritarianism; democracy; freedom politics; freedom tools; law enforcement; people power
Pratt, Minnie Bruce, 57
prayer. *See* ceremony
Price, Candice (@MidwestSkit), 143
Pride march, 35–36, 41, 59
prison. *See* incarceration
prison abolition. *See* abolitionist organizations
Prison Activist Resource Center, 72
professionalism, 215

progress, 122; as ideology, 140; as lived reality; as narrative of history, 6, 122; as political abstraction, 140
Prolific the Rapper, 162
public investment, 78, 100–101, 112–13, 148, 151, 209
Puente, Ariz., 105, 198
Puerto Rican independence movement, 189
punishment economy, 72, 83, 186–92, 197. *See also* incarceration; school-to-prison pipeline

queer theory, 218
Quinlan, Susan, 83–84

race, history of, 36, 42, 43, 45, 61–62, 66, 118, 121–23, 134, 136, 137, 140, 143, 187, 200, 211, 218, 219, 220, 242n62, 268n70, 268n71. *See also* Jim Crow; racial capitalism; slavery
racial capitalism, 134, 201, 203, 242n62, 284n11. *See also* capitalism; slavery
racial ignorance, 80, 117, 136–41, 142–44, 178, 220, 268n70
racial justice, 11, 14, 21, 23, 36, 38, 40, 42, 55–58, 61, 113, 116, 122, 126–28, 133–34, 146, 154, 191, 194, 210–12
racism, structural, 35, 36, 44, 46–47, 55–58, 66, 77, 90–93, 98, 117, 118, 121–24, 130–41, 242n62, 243n2, 251n22; expressed through racial profiling, 125–28, 143; insufficient to explain, 149; invisible to whites, 122, 136, 178, 268n70
radical politics, 30, 33, 74
Raines, Dolly, 147
Randall, Lisa, 219
Randolph, A. Philip, 61
Ransby, Barbara, 25, 133, 134, 141, 145, 147, 220
Reagan, Ronald, 52, 90
Reagon, Bernice Johnson, 13, 28, 103–4, 232n22
Rebuild the Dream, 77

recruitment, 4, 21–23, 49–50, 65–87, 145, 159, 166–68, 182, 203, 205, 206–7, 210
Rector, Ricky Ray, 51
red-baiting, 77
Red Power movement, 165
Red Road Awareness, 174
Regional Council of Negro Leadership, 26
relationship building, 23–33, 48–50, 68–69, 75–76, 85–86, 106–8, 138–39, 154, 221. *See also* consensus-building; group-centered leadership; listening as key to democratic relationship; spadework
remix culture, 12–14, 49, 84, 107, 129, 207
Remond, Sarah Parker, 2, 229n3
repair harm, 151
representational government. *See* accountability of lawmakers to ordinary people; democracy
reproductive justice, 117, 183, 211
resignation, 7
resilience, 29, 80, 102, 134, 147, 194, 221
resistance. *See* ordinary people having a say in their own lives; organizing; people power; nonviolent direct action; self-determination
responsive representational government. *See* accountability of lawmakers to ordinary people
restorative justice, 67–70, 86–87
retreat format, 58–63, 141
Reuther, Walter, 62
Reynolds, Diamond, 150, 176
Rhythmfest, 48
Rice, Tamir, 14, 124, 149
Richardson, Judy, 24, 130, 147, 221, 234n16
Richie, Beth, 76
Richmond, Calif., 122
right-wing organizing, 45
Rios, Hāwane, 183
Ritchie, Andrea, 150
Rivas-Triana, Melissa, 118
Rivera, Sylvia, 107

Robinson, Betty Garman, 147
Robinson, Ruby Doris Smith, 31
Rodeo Drive, 133
Rodney, Walter, 203
Rogers, Jamala, 147
role-play tactic, 91–93, 110. *See also* freedom tools
Roman Empire, decline of, 112, 258n65
"Room in the Circle" (Reagon), 103
"Rosa Parks" frame, 4
Russell, Tory, 13
Russia, 202
Rustin, Bayard, 61–63

Sabal Trail Pipeline, 184
Sacred Stone Camp, 180
San Carlos Apache, 184
Sanchez, Hugo, 92
Sanchez, Jackie, 92, 111
Sanchez, Rocio, 92, 111
Sanchez, Stephanie, 92
Sand Creek Massacre, 182
Sanford, Fla., 124
Saudi Arabia, 202
#SayHerName, 14, 116, 149–50
SB1010, 77
scapegoating. *See* bait-and-switch; divide and conquer tactic
school-to-prison pipeline, 69, 72–74, 82–85, 98, 113, 126, 148, 201, 244n19, 248n40, 256n51. *See also* adultism; democratic education; healing justice practices
Schuyler, George, 10
Scott, Rick, 128
Scott, Walter, 14, 148
Second Reconstruction, 153
segregation. *See* Jim Crow
Segrest, Mab, 37, 38, 42, 48, 57, 59
self-determination, 114, 151, 165, 183, 201, 264n39. *See also* ordinary people having a say in their own lives; organizing
Self-Help Graphics, 184
self-worth as key to active citizenship, 5–6, 28, 83–86, 118, 119, 127, 138, 178, 193, 214

Selina, 117
Selma, Ala., 148, 171, 173
Sensenbrenner Bill, 105
Servin, Dante, 149, 150
settler colonists, 114; settler colonialism, 161, 165, 174, 194; settler-colonial capitalism, 191
sexism in the freedom movement, 31, 149, 235n38
sexual assault, 4, 32, 181–82
Shakur, Assata, 129
Shakur, Tupac, 123
shared authority, 223, 290n24. See also oral history
Sharpton, Al, 125
Shaw University, 22
Sherrod, Charles, 27
Shire, Warsan, 89
Shuttlesworth, Fred, 17
Shuttlesworth, Ruby, 17
Sicangu Lakota Treaty Council, 161
Silent Majority, 45. See also Southern Strategy
Simmons, Zoharah, 130, 147
Simpson, Audra, 193
single-identity politics, 43. See also intersectional organizing
Sioux nation, 164
sit-down strikers, 153
sit-ins, 2, 3, 18–22, 40, 91–93, 105, 109, 110, 126–28, 148, 159, 201
Slager, Michael, 148
slavery, 2, 14, 56, 143, 161, 191, 198, 200, 211, 218, 254n45, 284n11. See also capitalism; racial capitalism
slow violence, 191
slow walk of the trees, 32–33, 58, 207. See also intergenerational organizing
Smith, Barbara, 39, 61, 133
Smith, Linda Tuhiwai, 285n2
Smith-Kramer, Jimmy, 191
SNCC Digital Gateway, 148, 217, 222
Snow, G. Murray, 90
socialism, 43
social media, 69, 116, 123, 127, 131–32, 137, 139, 141–46, 150, 158, 163, 167, 178,
182, 197, 220, 268n63; documenting of, 222–23; law enforcement interference, 172; polarity of, 144; providing protection, 176; social media stardom as problem, 144. See also information-sharing as organizing tactic
Social Security number, 97
Soledad Brothers, 74, 244n20
solidarity, 46, 57–58, 97, 109–10, 114, 138–41, 183–84; between different groups, 74–75, 87, 114, 116, 183–84; central to organizing, 87, 109, 116, 141–46; international, 144, 176, 183. See also relationship-building
Solnit, Rebecca, 233n24
Soltis, Laura Emiko, 108, 109
Souljah, Sister, 51
sound bites, 7
Southern Christian Leadership Conference (SCLC), 20, 48, 155
Southerners for Economic Justice, 42, 43
Southerners on New Ground (SONG), 11, 37–64, 107, 108, 111, 117, 134, 153, 154, 155, 175, 208, 210, 223; formation, 34–44; journal, 63. See also retreat format; workshop format
Southern Negro Youth Congress, 2
Southern Strategy, 46, 239n35. See also Silent Majority
Southern Tenant Farmers Union, 48
Southwest Key Programs, 99
sovereignty, 100, 114, 165, 183–84, 194, 234n7, 258n69, 261n14, 273n13, 275n29
spadework, 25, 68, 86, 105, 106, 145
spectacles of violence and disorder, 10, 123
Spelman College, 118
Spice, Anne, 194, 287n13
Standing Rock, 12, 141, 159–96, 210
Standpoint theory, 218, 220
Steez, Fresco (Angie Rollins), 134. See unapologetically Black
Stenberg, Amandla, 142
Steptoe, E. W., 147
Sterling, Alton, 150

stigmatization, 98
Stonewall uprising, 107, 255n49
stories as potential energy, 15, 18, 82, 91, 106, 110, 148, 149, 159, 176, 180, 212
strategic thinking, 4
Student Action with Farmworkers, 96
Student Nonviolent Coordinating Committee (SNCC), 11, 17–33, 39, 43, 45, 76, 77, 130, 141, 155, 170, 171, 175, 201, 223; as opening wedge, 111; legacy, 84, 102, 130, 210, 214–15, 219, 220
students in U.S. politics, 1, 10
success metrics, 205–6
Summers, Nailah, 144
Sunoco Logistics, 163, 164
surveillance, 144, 151, 176; corporate surveillance, 166, 187–92; government surveillance, 144, 145, 151
Swarthmore College, 24
Sweet Honey in the Rock, 49
Swerts, Thomas, 105

Tallahassee, Fla., 126–27, 210
TallBear, Kim, 132
Taylor, Keeanga-Yamahtta, 46, 139, 149
Taylor, Recy, 182
teaching. *See* education
Teaching for Change, 232n19
technocratic logic, 188, 201
temporary worker, 98. *See also* immigrant as legal category
testimonios, 14, 106, 107, 116, 254–55n45
textbooks, 230n7, 232n19
Theater of the Oppressed, 82, 83
theft of Indigenous lands, 56
Themba, Makani, 147
Thirteenth Amendment, 161
Thirty Meter Telescope, 161
This Bridge Called My Back (anthology), 133
Thomas, Lucky, 127
Three Legs, Bobbi Jean, 158, 162, 200, 271n2
Thunberg, Greta, 208
Thunder Hawk, Madonna, 25, 183

Thunder Valley Community Development Corporation, 189
TigerSwan, 187–92
Till, Emmett, 14, 125
Tilsen, Nick, 189–91, 195
Tinker siblings, 2, 230n3
Tlaloc, Ome, 160
Tohono O'odham, 184
Tolan, Sandy, 191
Tometi, Opal, 130–33
Torres, Carmelita, 2
trans and queer liberation, 117, 264n39
Trans-Pecos Pipeline, 184
trauma, 80, 84, 106, 198
Trayvon's Law, 126
Trevor Browne High School, 92
Triangle Shirtwaist Company, 2
Tribe Called Red, A, 157
trickle-down economics, 52
Truax, Eileen, 114
Trump, Donald, 90, 115, 120, 157, 167, 171, 173, 184, 185, 194–96, 197–99
trust-building, 24, 27, 49–50, 69, 145
Truth, Sojourner, 37
Tubman, Harriet, 68, 129, 153
tuition equity, 97, 101, 108–9, 118, 253n30
Tulsa Race Riot, 137, 187
Tutashinda, Kwesi, 79
Two Bulls, Krystal, 176, 184, 185
Two-Spirit, 180–82, 277n68

Ufot, Nse, 199
unacknowledged legislators, activists as, 14, 232n23
unapologetic, 106
unapologetically Black, 134, 154. *See* politics of respectability
Underground Railroad, 102
#UndocumentedUnafraid, 93, 105, 106, 111, 113, 114, 254n42
undocumented youth, 89–120, 170, 201, 207, 250n16, 250n19. *See also* immigrant youth movement
United Farm Workers, 106
United Nations, 165

United We Dream, 102, 109, 116, 117, 198, 201, 254n35
universities as sites of "fugitive study," 155, 203
University of the District of Columbia, 47
University of Georgia, 109, 113, 118
University of Tennessee–Martin, 71
UN Sustainable Development Agenda, 171
Unzueta, Tania, 108
U.S. Army Corps of Engineers, 158, 163, 164, 165, 193, 196
use of force policies, 121, 122
U.S. Justice Department, 114
U.S. Supreme Court, 164

Valandra, Edward, 161, 162
Varela, Maria, 232n23
Vasquez, Tina, 116
Veracraz, Mexico, 93
victories, 18, 27, 32, 45, 77, 79, 101–2, 107, 115–20, 135, 155, 163, 192–96, 200, 205–8, 211. *See also* metrics of movement success
Virginia State University (VSU), 1, 6, 213, 219, 220
Voekel, Pamela, 108, 113
Voice from the South (Cooper), 133
Von Hoffman, Nicholas, 37
voting rights, 21, 23–27, 101–3, 132, 194, 211; voting and movement building, 26, 53, 93, 116, 234n15, 234n22; intersection of freedom movement and voting, 23–27, 93, 102–7, 148, 194, 199
Voting Rights Act of 1965, 26, 148, 173

Walesa, Lech, 141
Walsh, Joe, 151
Warner, Sylvia Ashton, 48
War Resisters' League, 61
Washington, Craig, 35–36
water cannon, 167, 172
Weatherford, Will, 128
Weber-Shirk, Joaquina, 111

well-being, 112, 151, 182, 184, 187, 202–12
Wells, Ida B., 136
Wells Fargo Bank, 112
"We Shall Overcome," 27
#WeStand, 14
We the People, 18, 58, 89, 120, 198, 200, 202, 204. *See also* Constitution; people power
"What Side Are You On?," 129
white citizenship, 53, 90, 98, 103, 120, 140, 194, 211
White Eyes, Joseph, 158
white identity politics
white nationalists, 136, 144, 211
white privilege, 44, 55–58, 80–81, 143, 175, 219, 220, 269n71. *See also* racial ignorance
white supremacy, 21, 25, 36, 38, 42–43, 80–81, 98, 134, 136, 142, 143, 167, 191, 208, 287n12
#WhoPays, 78
Wiley, John, 219
Williams, Chantel, 219
Williams, Jesse, 123
Willis, Ardelia, 32
Wilson, Darren, 142, 266n52
Wilson, Nikki, 219
Wilson, Starsky, 140
Wise, Eryn, 160, 170, 176, 180, 194
Wóakiktunže, 171
Woman's Place (Louisville, Ky.), 57
Women of All Red Nations (WARN), 183
women of color, 4–5, 39, 154–55, 221
Women's College of Georgia, 45
women's movement, 154
Womonwrites, 57
Woodard Henderson, Ash-Lee, 131, 144, 146
Woodley, Shailene, 176
workshop format, 51–58, 85–87, 141, 240n51, 242n70; as a movement lighthouse, 57. *See also* retreat format
World War II, 19
Wounded Knee, 165, 187

WRAL television station, 46
Wright, Richard, 80

Yale Law School, 71
Yanez, Jeronimo, 150, 176
Yasmin, 93–97, 118
Young, Darris, 65–69, 77, 81, 87–88, 122
Young, David, 219
Young, Ivy, 41
Young Negroes Cooperative League, 10
Young People's Project, 6, 230n6
youth absent from history, 7, 145, 210, 222. *See also* education
youth leadership, 6, 22, 29–30, 66–68, 76–79, 85–88, 106–11, 117, 133, 145, 146, 154, 159, 169, 210–22, 256n51, 262n26
youth water protectors, 157–96, 208; use of hashtags, 175

Zapatista movement, 141
Zimmerman, George, 11, 124, 125, 130, 134, 138
Zinn, Howard, 197, 220
Zuberi, Tufuku, 220